Reforming Juvenile Justice

Josine Junger-Tas · Frieder Dünkel
Editors

Reforming Juvenile Justice

 Springer

Editors
Josine Junger-Tas
Willem Pompe Institute
University of Utrecht
Utrecht
The Netherlands

Frieder Dünkel
Rechts-und Staatswissenschaftliche Fakultät
Universität Greifswald
Greifswald
Germany

ISBN: 978-0-387-89294-8   e-ISBN: 978-0-387-89295-5
DOI: 10.1007/978-0-387-89295-5
Springer Dordrecht Heidelberg London New York

Library of Congress Control Number: 2009928237

Printed on acid-free paper

Springer is part of Springer Science+Business Media (www.springer.com)

Foreword

Juvenile justice has experienced major transformations during the last decades worldwide, particularly in Europe. There are many reasons for this, one of the most prominent being the evolution of human rights in the context of juvenile justice and welfare as formulated by United Nations and Council of Europe standards since about 20 years. After the opening of borders and the fall of the Soviet empire, almost all of the Central and Eastern countries have reformed their criminal and juvenile laws since the early 1990s. In this context, international standards have played an important role.

Juvenile justice has experienced pressures from different sides. On the one hand, international instruments clearly claim for maintaining and further developing constructive and educational answers to juvenile delinquency such as restorative measures or training courses. On the other hand, specific serious events have created public or media demands for tougher reactions and a "responsibilization" of young offenders. The present volume tries to describe different approaches in order to reform juvenile justice systems. There is no unique and noncontradictory path for such reforms when looking at the various countries referred to in this volume. This has already been demonstrated by the national reports in the *International Handbook of Juvenile Justice* (see Junger-Tas and Decker, 2006). The present book is a follow-up to this handbook and tries to be more analytic and comparative when describing different aspects and problems of reforms.

We start with a state of the art of juvenile delinquency in Europe.

Chapter 1, considering all available data sources, concludes that despite contradictions between police figures and other sources such as victimization surveys, juvenile offence, including violence, has fallen since in the last 10 years. This development is in stark contrast with the tendency in many societies to intervene sooner and harsher in the lives of young people than has been the case since long.

In that respect, Chaps. 2 and 3 deal with the issue of juveniles' rights. Chapter 2 considers the UN Convention of the Rights on the Child (CRC) taking the form of a flyer addressed directly to the juvenile and explaining him his rights when arrested and confronted with the police, the prosecutor, the court, and eventually with incarceration. Chapter 3 examines the role of the Council of Europe, in particular with respect to the Recommendation "New ways of dealing with Juvenile Delinquency and the role of Juvenile Justice" of 2003 and the recent "Rules for juvenile offenders subject to sanctions and measures" of 2008. Both chapters (re)emphasize that juveniles should not have fewer legal rights and safeguards than adult offenders. The authors claim that authorities should provide for specialized training of institutional staff as well as for sufficient financial resources and adequate working conditions as essential conditions for the respect of juveniles' rights.

Chapter 4 examines the important and much controversial subject of the lower age of criminal responsibility of juveniles. To be precise, the state can intervene at any age, but below the age of criminal responsibility this intervention takes place under civil law, although this does not exclude punitive measures, such as the British *Child Safety Order* or the Dutch *Stop measure*. Moreover, the age of criminal responsibility may be conditional according to the *doli incapax* principle. Even if the age of criminal responsibility is fixed, rules exist in a number of countries for transferring juveniles to adult court in the case of a serious crime. The authors then discuss the scientific evidence on the development of the brain in adolescents as compared to adults, with respect to their cognitive, intellectual, and neurological functioning. They conclude that developmental shortcomings impair adolescents' decision-making capacities and psycho-social abilities, resulting in many impulsive acts without much thought about possible consequences. Chapter 5 then goes on to discuss the issue of parental responsibility for the behaviour of their children. Of course, everywhere parents are considered responsible for raising their children in respect of the law and in accordance with society's norms and values. However, the question is whether parents can be considered responsible for offenses committed by their 16-year-old son or daughter. The author debates the issue and concludes that, although parents' role in preventing offence is crucial, sanctioning parents by statutory and short-time interventions is ineffective, and does not take into account to what extent the fact of being raised in a family plagued by poverty, debts, mental and physical illness, alcohol, and drugs has an impact on offending.

The following two chapters deal with the transfer of juveniles under the age of criminal majority to adult court, both in the US and in two European countries, Belgium and the Netherlands. In the US transfer is frequently applied, but its application varies by state. American evaluation research shows that, in terms of criminal behavior, transferred juveniles are more likely to reoffend and to commit more serious offenses than juveniles detained in youth institutions. In Belgium and the Netherlands, transfer is only an option for those aged 16–18. Although transfer is rare in both countries, most transferred offenders have committed nonserious offences.

Chapter 8 deals with the prevention of delinquent behavior. It examines risk factors in the child and unfavorable conditions for a healthy upbringing in the family as well as in the environment. The main conclusion is that if important and evidence-based measures are taken by local authorities in terms of neighborhood safety, health and welfare services, and the education system, much delinquency as well as other adverse outcomes may be prevented.

The following four chapters consider some essential sanctions and measures. Chapter 9 compares diversionary practices in different European countries with respect to UN and Council of Europe's standards and comes to the conclusion that diversion is a meaningful and effective juvenile justice strategy with regard to the principle of minimum intervention and preventing reoffending. Opponents to these measures refer to insufficient evidence for demonstrating that such alternatives do a better job than incarceration in reducing recidivism. However, despite this skepticism, some very sound reasons to prefer them to custody are presented in Chap. 9.

Chapter 10 presents restorative justice, or – as others call it – victim–offender mediation or reconciliation, such as it is integrated in the juvenile justice system in Northern Ireland. The authors argue that this integration is important since it guarantees juveniles' rights and due process, while at the same time providing for alternative justice proceedings, particularly in cases of conflicts and disputes. Importantly, research shows high victim attendance as well as high satisfaction of victims and offenders alike.

Chapter 11 deals with alternatives to custody which may take the form of diversion – in particular in Germany (see Chap. 9) – or more general of community sanctions. The authors show that a large variety of alternative sanctions have been introduced into juvenile justice systems that are also widely accepted by the juvenile courts. As a result, juvenile imprisonment in most countries has really become a sanction of last resort. In most countries considered, there are no indications that the sanctioning practice has become more severe in last decades. By contrast, the developments in Eastern European countries show a decline in using youth imprisonment.

Chapter 12 demonstrates that custodial establishments for juveniles vary considerably. Particularly problematic seem to be large custodial settings within the penitentiary system (sometimes mixing adults and juveniles in the same institution), whereas new forms of (secure) training and treatment in France or Sweden outside the penitentiary system look more promising as they are smaller and much better staffed.

Finally, Chap. 13 gives an overview of the issues examined in the book and presents a sketch of the reforms we recommend to the relevant authorities and to policy makers as well as the necessary conditions for such reforms.

Reforming juvenile justice systems is a difficult and sometimes frustrating task, particularly when politicians follow populist and ad hoc strategies in order to survive in the political arena. We prefer and emphasize long-term policies for reforming juvenile justice systems. Successful juvenile law reforms often have been prepared cautiously by introducing model projects (such as mediation or community service schemes in Finland, Germany, the Netherlands, and the UK), and then extending them nationwide when being evaluated or estimated successful. The juvenile justice reform in Switzerland has been discussed for more than 20 years before the new law was enacted in 2007. We strongly recommend that juvenile justice policy does not follow an ad hoc and short-term approach as a reaction to specific – and often exceptional – events, but is developed and guided by theory and – in the words of the Council of Europe's Recommendation on "New ways of dealing with juvenile delinquency..." of 2003 – be "evidence-based." Viewed in that perspective, juvenile criminology is of growing importance both for increasing our knowledge of effective interventions as well as for improving juvenile justice policies.

The Editors

Biographical Notes

Josine Junger-Tas studied Sociology at the Free University of Brussels (Belgium). In 1972 she obtained her Ph.D. degree in the Netherlands at the University of Groningen with a study on "Characteristics and Social Integration of Juvenile Delinquents," which was the start of her involvement in criminology. She worked in a research centre in Brussels in the field of juvenile crime, but returned to her home country in 1975 where she was employed by the Dutch Ministry of Justice in its Research Institute. In 1979 she was appointed as Special Adviser and Director of the Research Unit on Juvenile Crime. In 1989 she was appointed as Director of the Institute. Josine Junger-Tas was active in the Council of Europe. From 1984 to 1989 she chaired an Expert Committee on Juvenile Delinquency which produced two reports with recommendations for member states, the first report treating "Social reactions to juvenile crime" and the second "Reactions to delinquent behaviour of young people belonging to an ethnic minority". She wrote several basic documents for the Council of Europe and in 1992 was appointed member of its Scientific Council. She was also active in the United Nations, where she also did preparatory work for the UN Criminology congresses, and served as an expert on juvenile delinquency for Central European and Middle Eastern states. In 1989 she received the *Sellin–Glueck Award* from the American Society of Criminology for her "Contributions to Criminology." She wrote a great number of articles and books, as well as reports for the Minister of Justice. In 1994 she was appointed professor of Youth Criminology at the University of Lausanne in Switzerland. She taught self-report methodology at the University of Cambridge for 3 years and since 2002 she is a visiting professor at the University of Utrecht. She is a member of the Council for the Administration of Criminal Law and the Protection of Juveniles, an independent consultant body for the Minister of Justice, which serves as an appeal court regarding decisions taken by the complaint committees of the institutions. In 2000 the University of Lausanne awarded her an honorary doctorate. In the same year, she took the initiative – with several close colleagues – to launch the *European Society of Criminology.* Together with Prof. Killias, she organized the first ESC conference in Lausanne and at that occasion she was elected the first ESC President. In November 2007 she received the *Distinguished International Scholar Award* from the American Society of Criminology.

Frieder Dünkel, born 1950 in Karlsruhe (Germany), studied law at the universities of Heidelberg and Freiburg (Germany). His Ph.D. in 1979 dealt with empirical research on the effectiveness of therapeutic treatment in prisons. From 1979 until 1992 he worked as a researcher at the Max-Plank-Institute of Foreign and International Penal Law, Criminological Unit, in Freiburg (with Prof. Günther Kaiser). The subject of his "Habilitation" in 1989 was "Juvenile imprisonment and other forms of deprivation of liberty in an international comparison". Since 1992 he teaches criminology, penology, juvenile justice, criminal procedure, and criminal law at the University of Greifswald in the north-east of Germany. Since 2006 he is organizing a postgraduate master program of "Criminology and Criminal Justice (LL.M.Crim)" at the Department of Criminology at Greifswald. The research program at the Department of Criminology covers a wide range of empirical studies in juvenile criminology, penology, prisons and community sanctions, alcohol and drunk driving, human rights, etc. (see http://jura.uni-greifswald. de/duenkel). He conducted several empirical research projects funded by the Deutsche Forschungsgemeinschaft (German Research Association), Volkswagen-Foundation, Federal Ministry of Justice, Bonn, Ministry of Culture and Education, Mecklenburg Western-Pomerania, etc. Since 2004 he conducted several empirical international comparative projects on men's prisons in the states of the Baltic Sea, on women's imprisonment in Europe, on long-term imprisonment in ten European countries, and on youth violence in the states of the Baltic Sea, two of them funded by the European AGIS-scheme. He has widely published in these areas (until 1 March 2009 29 books and 385 articles 1 October 2008: 28 books and 374 articles in journals and books, publications in German, English, French, Hungarian, Spanish, Catalonian, Portuguese, Polish, Russian, Czech, and Japanese language). He is the co-editor of the journal *Neue Kriminalpolitik* since 1989, and of the *European Journal of Criminology* since 2003. He has been a member of the Criminological Scientific Council of the Council of Europe 1998–2004, since 2001 as its president. Since 1994 he has coordinated several Tempus projects funded by the European Union. The subject of these projects was the reorganization of law education in Siberian law faculties (Krasnojarsk, Irkutsk, Barnaul, Omsk, Tomsk, organized together with the University of Tilburg, the Netherlands); furthermore, he coordinates Socrates exchange programs with about 35 universities in Western and Eastern Europe and teaches courses in German, English, and French as guest professor in several European universities (Nottingham, UK; Pau, Bayonne, and Agen, France; Bern, Switzerland; Krasnojarsk, Russia).

Contents

Contributors

Rob Allen
International Centre for Prison Studies, King's College, London, UK

Raymond Arthur
School of Social Sciences and Law, University of Teesside, Middlesbrough, Tees Valley, UK

Donna M. Bishop
College of Criminal Justice, Northeastern University, Boston, MA, USA

Jenneke Christiaens
Section Penal Law and Criminology, University of Gent, Gent, Belgium

Jonathan Doak
Nottingham Law School, Nottingham, UK

Jaap Doek
UN Committee of the Rights of the Child, Lisse, The Netherlands

Frieder Dünkel
Rechts- und Staatswissenschaftliche Fakultät, Universität Greifswald, Greifswald, Germany

Thomas Grisso
Medical School, University of Massachusetts, Boston, MA, USA

Josine Junger-Tas
Willem Pompe Institute, University of Utrecht, Utrecht, The Netherlands

An Nuytiens
Department of Criminology, Free University of Brussels, Brussels, Belgium

David O'Mahony
Department of Law, Durham University, Durham, UK

Ineke Pruin
Rechts- und Staatswissenschaftliche Fakultät, Universität Greifswald,
Greifswald, Germany

Alex Stevens
European Institute of Social Services, School of Social Policy, Sociology and
Social Research, Keynes College – University of Kent, Canterbury,
UK

Ido Weijers
Faculty of Social Sciences – Pedagogic, University of Utrecht, Utrecht,
The Netherlands

Chapter 1
Trends in Youth Offending in Europe

Alex Stevens

The issue of youth offending, and in particular whether young people are becoming more violent, is hotly debated in many European countries. It is very difficult to establish trends in juvenile delinquency and violence with certainty from statistical sources. This chapter will present the available evidence in order to inform debate on what has really happened to youth offending in Europe. It will focus on the period after 1990. Before this, officially recorded crime rose rapidly in the post-war years in Western Europe, before stabilising in the later part of the twentieth century. This levelling off was not seen in officially recorded violence, although there is some scepticism as to whether recent rises in the official records reflect actual increases or an increased sensitivity to violence (Pfeiffer 1998; Westfelt and Estrada 2005). It will use various sources to examine trends in offending – and particularly the offending of people who are under the age where they are treated as adults in the criminal justice system – in the countries of the European Union. The chapter will begin by discussing the important problems that affect attempts to compare the available data across countries and time. It will then explore the picture of increasing violent offending that is given in official statistics and use data from victimisation surveys to question whether this increase reflects real increases in the occurrence of juvenile crime in Europe.

Problems in Analysing the Trend of Youth Offending in Europe

Great care should be taken in interpreting the data that are available. They are subject to numerous caveats, of which the most important are as follows:

1. Youth offending incorporates different acts, which may change at different rates.
2. Trends in youth offending are uneven across geographic areas and groups of young people.

A. Stevens (✉)
European Institute of Social Services, School of Social Policy, Sociology and Social Research, Keynes College – University of Kent, Canterbury, UK

J. Junger-Tas and F. Dünkel (eds.), *Reforming Juvenile Justice*,
DOI: 10.1007/978-0-387-89295-5_1, © Springer Science + Business Media, LLC 2009

3. Recorded statistics may not accurately reflect the level of offending that is actually occurring.
4. Perceptions of the problem of youth offending may have grown independently from any change in its actual level.

First, the concept of offending incorporates different acts, which may change at different rates. And reporting and recording practices may change differently from each other. The discussion below focuses particularly on acts of violence, aggression and threats as they are captured by surveys and official records. This therefore includes acts as diverse as murder, assault, robbery, rape and other sexual offences.

Second, changes in crime are uneven across groups and areas. Given what is already known about the factors in the lives of individuals that put them at greater risk of becoming involved in offending (Wikström and Sampson 2006), it is unsurprising to find that certain groups and certain areas have been affected more than others. For example, national average increases in offending may be sharply inflated by highly localised problems; but, at the same time, national figures may downplay the extent of the problem at regional or local levels.

The third main set of caveats concerns the accuracy with which the recorded statistics reflect the problem of crime in the lives of ordinary citizens. Leaving aside the perennial problem of the divergence between the number of actual incidents and the numbers that get reported to the authorities, many sources (including Pfeiffer 1998) suggest that totals may have been inflated in recent years by a number of factors, including

- changes in what is included in the figures as a result, for example, of lowering the age of criminal responsibility or the transfer of responsibility for juvenile crime between agencies.
- pressure on the relevant agencies to keep more comprehensive records.
- an increasing formalisation of interventions in the problem (which may itself further have been encouraged by the increased availability of constructive, non-custodial sanctions).

Finally, perceptions of juvenile crime as a problem have also grown to some degree *independently of* any underlying rise. These perceptions have been driven by an interaction between media coverage, public opinion, and a heightened political focus on the problem (Estrada 2001, 2004; Wacquant 1999) and this may have contributed directly to the inflationary factors listed above.

The Use of Data to Establish Trends in Juvenile Crime

Estrada (1999) has written that the ideal description of trends in youth violence would

- use all available statistics (official records, as well as self-report and victimisation studies).
- use those statistics that "lie 'closer' to the crime" (e.g. crimes reported to police rather than convictions) (Estrada 1999: 27).

- use statistics on identified (suspected) offenders.
- present trends for different categories of crime.

We have attempted to follow these recommendations in the data that are presented below. We use data from both official records and from self-reported victimisation surveys in order to give an indication of the reliability of the trends that emerge from both types of data. We present data for different categories of violence. We include data at different "distances" from the offence (i.e. self-report, report to police, suspected offenders, convictions). We present and compare trends across groups of countries, rather than comparing the absolute recorded rates between countries, as also recommended by Westfelt and Estrada (2005). The trends are more likely to be valid, because they will be less affected by differences in recording practices between countries, and in individual countries across time.

Official Statistics

The sources for the official statistics presented here are the three editions of the *European Sourcebook of Crime and Criminal Justice Statistics* (Council of Europe 1999, 2003, 2006). These provide data from 1990 to 1995, from 1994 to 2000 and from 2000 to 2003. Here, the later editions have been used for data in the overlapping periods. The authors of the *Sourcebook* provide details of the processes for collating these statistics, and the necessary caution that should be applied to their interpretation. Despite these warnings, we believe that the data do provide an interesting picture of official statistics on recorded crime.

Previous research has looked at offending rates in individual countries (Barclay et al. 2001; Lamon 2002). To provide data for the whole of the European Union, this chapter uses the data provided in the *Sourcebook* to calculate rates per 100,000 population of convictions and recorded offences for various crimes separately in the 15 old and the 12 new EU member states.[1] It includes theft (which incorporates vehicle theft and burglary) and four of the five categories of violent crimes that are included in the *Sourcebook* (the data on armed robbery is only available for a few countries, and so is excluded). The results of these calculations are presented in the tables and charts below.

Information is separately presented for the 15 countries who were members of the EU on April 30, 2004, and for the 12 countries that have since joined. This is because the 15 older members share a more common, liberal democratic background than those more recent entrants who were members of the Eastern bloc until the tumultuous events of 1989. Their economies and criminal justice systems have undergone rapid change in the period covered by this chapter, and this is reflected in their patterns of recorded offending (Table 1.1).

---

[1] Special caution needs to be used in interpreting figures from the new member states, as several of them experienced big changes in their criminal justice systems in the transition from communism during the 1990s.

Table 1.1 Mean convictions per 100,000 population

		1990	1995	2000	2003
Theft	EU 15	203.7	162.5	166.3	158.7
	New member states	67.7	170.0	168.7	169.0
Homicide	EU 15	1.2	1.4	1.4	1.6
	New member states	1.4	2.6	2.4	1.9
Rape	EU 15	1.2	1.5	2.0	1.8
	New member states	2.1	2.5	2.2	2.6
Robbery	EU 15	9.1	11.3	11.7	11.5
	New member states	9.0	13.3	18.0	20.9
Assault	EU 15	53.8	47.3	65.4	73.4
	New member states	12.9	23.0	36.8	35.3

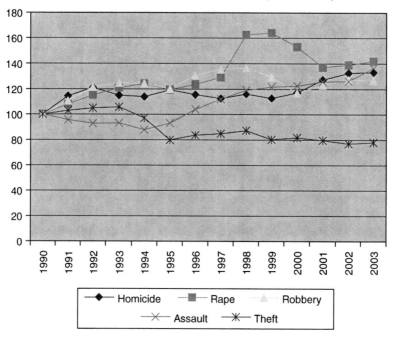

	1990	1992	1994	1996	1998	2000	2002	2003
Homicide	100	121	114	116	116	117	133	133
Rape	100	115	124	124	163	153	139	142
Robbery	100	122	124	131	137	117	127	127
Assault	100	93	88	104	119	123	126	137
Theft	100	105	97	84	87	82	77	78

Fig. 1.1 Conviction rates in the old 15 EU states, 1990–2003

Although not too much weight should be given to absolute differences between the groups of countries, it is interesting to note that in both groups there are many more convictions for theft than for violent crimes. Theft convictions tended to increase in the new member states from a relatively low level towards the level reported by the EU15. Assault accounts for the highest rates of convictions for violent offences. Again, assault convictions tended to rise towards EU15 levels in the new member states during the 1990s, but levels in the EU15 have also increased for assault and other violent offences.

The graphs below show the evolution of these conviction rates over the decade. They show the rates of conviction for various offences, indexed to 1990 in order to allow comparison of the increase or decrease of these rates (Fig. 1.1).

These graphs show that in the EU15, convictions for all violent offences increased across the 1990s, with bigger increases for rape, robbery and assault than for homicide. The figures on rape should be treated with caution; rape convictions are particularly vulnerable to changes in policy and recording practice. The large increase between 1997 and 1998 reflects a steep increase that year in the rate of convictions for rape in Germany (Figs. 1.2–1.4).

New EU members indices of conviction rates (base = 1990)

	1990	1992	1994	1996	1998	2000	2002	2003
Homicide	100	145	198	208	198	189	194	201
Rape	100	126	106	109	105	84	91	101
Robbery	100	161	175	216	226	259	282	303
Assault	100	156	189	363	369	368	387	402
Theft	100	169	197	265	275	249	249	249

Fig. 1.2 Conviction rates of the 12 new EU members states, 1990–2003

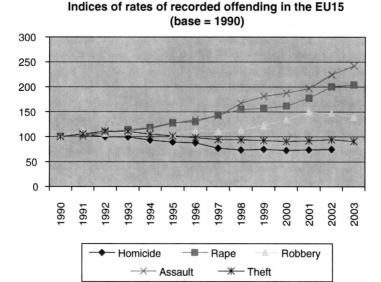

Indices of rates of recorded offending in the EU15 (base = 1990)

	1990	1992	1994	1996	1998	2000	2002	2003
Homicide	100	100	93	88	74	72	75	----
Rape	100	108	118	130	155	162	200	204
Robbery	100	107	114	112	114	134	147	140
Assault	100	109	117	134	168	188	224	242
Theft	100	111	105	98	94	90	94	91

Fig. 1.3 Recorded offending rates in the old 15 EU member states, 1990–2003

An increase in convictions for violent crime was also recorded in the new EU member states. Although rape convictions were steadier over the period, the rates of convictions for other offence categories rose more rapidly (especially for assault and robbery). Theft convictions declined in the EU15, while they rose in the new member states.

Conviction statistics measure the judicial response to violence, which increased in the European Union in the 1990s for all categories of violent crime, whereas theft fell in the EU15. However, conviction statistics relate to only a small proportion of crimes that are committed (Matthews and Pitts 2000). A larger proportion is reflected in official reports of recorded offending (Table 1.2).

Again, the figures suggest that theft is the most commonly recorded offence and that assault is the most commonly recorded violent offence in both the EU15 and the new member states. As the graphs below show, a slightly different pattern of violent offences emerges than from the conviction statistics (Table 1.3).

In the EU15, recorded instances of homicide (which is the most reliably recorded offence) and theft have fallen since 1990, while recorded assault, rape and robbery have all increased. The rates of recorded violence rose higher than did convictions (except for homicide) (Table 1.4).

Indices of rates of recorded offences in the new EU member states (base = 1990)

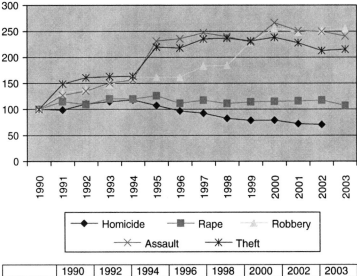

	1990	1992	1994	1996	1998	2000	2002	2003
Homicide	100	110	118	97	83	79	71	----
Rape	100	109	120	112	111	115	117	107
Robbery	100	139	162	161	185	256	251	255
Assault	100	135	156	236	239	266	249	241
Theft	100	161	164	218	237	238	213	215

Fig. 1.4   Recorded offending rates in the 12 new EU member states, 1990–2003

Table 1.2   Mean offending rates: Offences per 100,000 population

		1990	1995	2000	2003
Homicide	EU 15	1.31	1.22	0.98	0.98
	New member states	3.99	4.70	3.13	2.82
Rape	EU 15	6.27	7.39	9.86	12.57
	New member states	4.98	5.97	5.67	5.83
Robbery	EU 15	100.83	114.47	123.39	148.04
	New member states	27.09	43.99	61.91	67.92
Assault	EU 15	191.84	223.51	347.48	430.13
	New member states	27.59	43.14	63.16	68.81
Theft	EU 15	3978.98	4187.85	3669.27	3744.31
	New member states	627.34	1026.84	1450.34	1334.65

The new EU member states also saw a fall in the recorded instances of homicide since 1990, despite a rise in the first four years of the 1990s. Recorded rape was relatively stable, while there were large increases in rates of recorded robbery and assault in that decade, which seem to have stabilised more recently. In contrast to the EU15, the rates of convictions for assault and rape exceeded the increases in the recorded

Table 1.3 Percentage of minors among suspected offenders in EU member states, 1995–2003 (weighted means)

		1995	2000	2003
Homicide	EU 15	5.27	6.13	5.61
	New member states	5.63	5.36	4.11
Rape	EU 15	8.31	11.37	12.05
	New member states	12.88	11.35	10.13
Robbery	EU 15	27.18	31.19	29.21
	New member states	24.49	24.88	24.98
Assault	EU 15	12.72	13.94	13.68
	New member states	11.02	11.79	12.10
Theft	EU 15	25.02	25.51	23.47
	New member states	25.71	21.33	18.88

Table 1.4 ICVS/EUICS: Victimisation prevalence in 2004 (%) in some EU member states

	Robbery	Sexual incidents	Assaults and threats	Theft	Burglary
Austria	0.6	2.2	2.1	3.3	0.9
Belgium	1.2	0.9	3.5	3.5	1.8
Denmark	1.0	1.9	3.4	3.5	2.8
Finland	0.3	1.4	2.2	2.3	0.8
France	0.8	0.4	2.1	3.3	1.6
Italy	0.3	0.7	0.8	2.4	2.1
Netherlands	0.5	1.9	4.3	3.7	1.4
Poland[a]	1.8	0.5	2.8	5.3	2.0
Portugal	1.0	0.5	0.9	1.6	1.4
Spain	1.3	0.3	1.5	2.1	0.8
Sweden	1.1	3.3	3.5	2.4	0.7
United Kingdom	1.3	1.9	5.4	5.7	3.3

[a]Poland was missing from the 2004 survey. The rates included here are from 1999

instances of these offences and recorded rates of theft rose in the 1990s. It should be noted that the increase in the rates of theft and assault between 1994 and 1995 reflects large increases in Poland, which includes the effect of changes in recording practices.

The three editions of the *European Sourcebook* also give data (for 1995, 1999 and 2003) on the proportion of minors among suspected offenders,[2] although these data are available for fewer countries.[3] The table below presents the means for each group of countries, weighted by the estimated populations of the countries at the year of observation. This weighting ensures that the means will more accurately reflect the situation over the combined population of the countries involved, rather than allowing the means of small countries to distort the means for the group of countries (Table 1.3; Figs. 1.5 and 1.6).

[2]These figures come from police statistics. The definition of a "suspected offender" varies between countries, ranging from being recorded when the police themselves are convinced who the offender is, to being recorded only when a prosecutor starts proceedings against a suspect.

[3]In the EU15, the figures are not available for Belgium, Denmark, Portugal, Northern Ireland and Scotland. In the new EU members, the figures are not available for Cyprus, Lithuania and Malta.

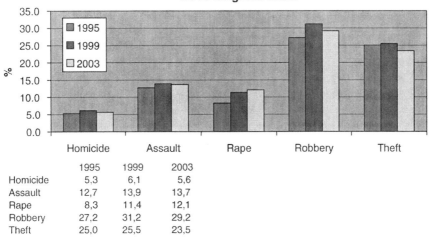

Fig. 1.5 Percentage of minors among suspected offenders in the 15 old EU member states, 1995–2003

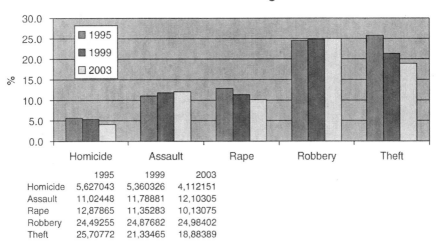

Fig. 1.6 Percentage of minors among suspected offenders in the 12 new EU member states, 1995–2003

A similar pattern emerges from both groups of countries. People under 18 comprise a much higher proportion of the suspects for robbery and theft than for homicide. Both groups saw reductions between 1995 and 2003 in the proportion of theft suspects who were under 18. This reduction was more rapid in the new member states. These reductions occurred while officially recorded theft was falling in the EU15, but rising in the new member states. In the EU15, there were slight increases in the proportions of minors among suspects for violent offences in the second half of the 1990s, with some reduction between 1999 and 2003 (except for rape). It should be remembered that these increases have taken place in a period in which the officially recorded prevalence of violent offences and convictions have also been rising.

The picture that emerges from these various statistics is that official records suggest that there have been increases in the rate of violent offending. Violent offending, according to these records, has risen faster than all criminal offending in both the EU15 and new member states from 1995 to 2000. Combining these figures with the proportion of minors among suspected offenders would suggest that there has been an increase in violent offending by young people, both in terms of their absolute rate of offending, but also as a proportion of the offences that are being committed. The picture for theft is rather different. Official figures suggest that it has risen since 1990 in the new member states, but fallen in the EU15. In both groups, the proportion of minors suspected of this category of offending has fallen.

The proportion of minors amongst suspected offenders is probably the statistic that is most likely to be affected by changes in police practices, as the police will catch a larger proportion of children if they focus their attention on this group, even if offending by children does not change. Wacquant (1999) argues that there has not been a major increase in the proportion of violent offenders who are young, and suggests that increases in the numbers of young people coming to the attention of the authorities are an artifact of increased political and police attention on the young. Not much data are available to check the trends in rates of offending by young people. However, we can check the reliability of the apparent increase in officially recorded offending by comparing official data with those from surveys of self-reported victimisation.

Data from Victimisation Surveys

Comparable data are available from the *International Criminal Victimisation Survey* (ICVS) (van Kesteren et al. 2000) and its successor, the *European Crime and Safety Survey* (EUICS) (van Dijk et al. 2005). These collected information from national victimisation surveys in five years: 1988, 1991, 1995, 1999 and 2004. We have used data from those countries for which data were available in at least two of these years in order to provide information on trends in these countries, which can be compared with official data from the *European Sourcebook*.[4] These countries are Austria, Belgium, Denmark, Finland, France, Italy, the Netherlands, Poland, Portugal, Spain, Sweden and the United Kingdom. Mean rates were calculated that were weighted by the populations of these countries for use in the graphs below.

---

[4]Data for missing years for individual countries has been imputed by using the average of the previous and subsequent years, or the previous or subsequent year for years at the end or beginning of the series.

These surveys give figures on the proportion of the respondents who reported being a victim of each type of crime. Such prevalence figures are considered to be more reliable than reported incidence (i.e. the number of times that people being victimized in any one year) (Westfelt and Estrada 2005). However, there are still limitations in using data from these surveys. The sample sizes are relatively small and differences over time and between countries may reflect differences in sensitivity to crime, as well as changes in the actual level of offending. They include only crimes against private individuals, and not crimes against businesses (e.g. shoplifting and fraud). And the offence categories used by these victimisation surveys are not directly comparable to those in the *European Sourcebook*. Their categories for "sexual incidents" and "assaults and threats" are much wider than the *Sourcebook*'s "rape" and "assault" categories (Table 1.4).

Rates of self-reported victimisation are much higher than those recorded for the equivalent categories in official statistics. This may be partly explained by the broader definitions of sexual incidents and assault. But the weighted mean of the available rates of self-reported robbery for the 12 countries in 2004 was 0.84% – nearly six times as high as the 2003 rate of recorded offences for the EU15.

National rates of victimisation are not consistent across categories of offence. Only the UK has relatively high rates of all five categories of offence. The other countries tend to show a mixed pattern of self-reported victimisation, but there is some correlation between reported rates of offence types. Those countries that had higher reported rates of assault and threats also tended to have higher rates of sexual incidents (Spearman's rho = 0.588, $p < 0.05$) and theft (0.737, $p < 0.01$). Countries with high reported rates of theft in 2004 also tended to report high rates of burglary (0.646, $p < 0.05$).

To enable comparison of trends, the weighted mean rates of victimisation were indexed for presentation in the graph below, using the 1988 rates as the base (Fig. 1.7).

According to the available data on self-reported victimisation, only assault was higher in 2004 than it was in 1988, and there was an apparent reduction in all offence types between 1999 and 2004. The greatest decreases since 1988 have been in reports of sexual incidents, but self-reported victimisation by theft, burglary and robbery also reduced by at least 20%.

Comparison of Official to Victimisation Data

Official records provide different information compared to victimisation studies. For example, Schwind (2001), using longitudinal victimisation studies, showed that a 128% rise in police recorded violence in the German city of Bochum between 1975 and 1998 probably reflected an actual rise of only 24%, with much of the difference accounted for by increased reporting to the police. Bol (1998) reported similar findings in the Netherlands, where Wittebrood and Nieuwbeerta (2006) have also found that an increase over 25 years in police-recorded crime was not matched by an increase reported to victimisation surveys. Westfelt and Estrada (2005) found

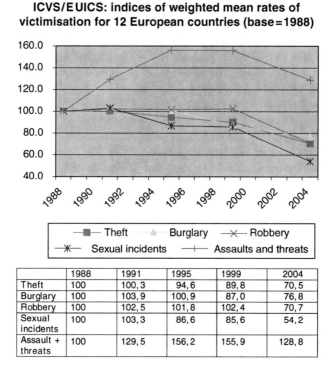

ICVS/EUICS: indices of weighted mean rates of victimisation for 12 European countries (base=1988)

	1988	1991	1995	1999	2004
Theft	100	100,3	94,6	89,8	70,5
Burglary	100	103,9	100,9	87,0	76,8
Robbery	100	102,5	101,8	102,4	70,7
Sexual incidents	100	103,3	86,6	85,6	54,2
Assault + threats	100	129,5	156,2	155,9	128,8

Fig. 1.7 Weighted mean victimisation rates for some EU member states, 1988–2004

that other types of data, including hospital admission statistics, often suggest different trends in offending from those seen in police records. It has been shown that there is a correlation between European police-recorded and victim-reported levels of crime at the level of the country (Gruszczyñska and Gruszczyñski 2005), but this finding covered only the 1995 and 1999 sweeps of the ICVS, and there were large changes in the reported levels between the 1999 and 2004 surveys.

Direct comparison of police records and reported crime victimisations is problematic, because of differences in offence definitions, and the different populations that tend to be covered by the two types of data (police records tend to overrepresent poor people and prisoners, while they are underrepresented in victimisation surveys, which also miss out crime against businesses and children) (Lamon 2002). Nevertheless, it is possible to compare the suggestions from both types of data on the direction of change in crime in the European countries where victimisation surveys have been done. Here, this comparison is presented in the form of a graph for each of five types of offence, comparing the indices of the population-weighted means from police-recorded and victimisation surveys for the 12 countries that were included above in the analysis of ICVS/EUICS data. It should be remembered that the categories of crimes used by the ICVS/EUICS and the *Sourcebook* are not identical, but do overlap. The *Sourcebook* category includes burglary within the category of theft, while the ICVS/EUICS presents data separately for these two categories. The year 1991 is used as the base for these indices as it is the earliest year in which data are available from both sources (Figs. 1.8–1.11).

These graphs suggest some congruence between police records and reported victimisations for property offences, such as theft and burglary. However, there is a striking divergence between these two sources of data for violent offences, especially since the mid-1990s. As police-recorded violent offences climbed steeply, rates of victimisation tended to reduce. This suggests that the increases seen in official records of convictions and offences recorded by the police may not reflect the underlying reality of the crimes experienced by private individuals. This suggestion

Indices of police-recorded theft and self-reported theft and burglary for 12 countries (base=1991)

	Police recorded theft	Victim reported theft	Victim reported burglary
1988		99,67	96,23
1989	--	--	--
1990	92,95	--	--
1991	100,00	100,00	100,00
1992	101,51	--	--
1993	99,40	--	--
1994	95,79	--	--
1995	94,04	94,24	97,14
1996	90,91	--	--
1997	87,87	--	--
1998	89,41	--	--
1999	89,63	89,53	83,73
2000	89,25	--	--
2001	90,82	--	--
2002	92,30	--	--
2003	88,70	--	--
2004	--	70,31	73,86

Fig. 1.8 Police-recorded and victim-reported theft and burglary in some EU member states, 1988–2004

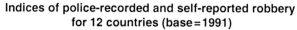

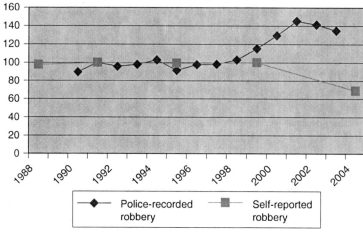

	Police recorded robbery	Victim reported robbery
1988		97,57
1989		
1990	89,37	
1991	100,00	100,00
1992	96,66	
1993	97,89	
1994	102,96	
1995	91,29	99,34
1996	97,57	
1997	98,04	
1998	102,78	
1999	115,10	99,96
2000	129,39	
2001	145,18	
2002	141,40	
2003	134,69	
2004		68,99

Fig. 1.9 Police-recorded and victim-reported robbery in some EU member states, 1988–2004

is supported by the downward trend in homicide. Homicide obviously does not feature in victimisation surveys (the victims not being able to report), but it is one of the most reliably recorded offences. One would expect homicide to be influenced by levels of other types of violence and a correlation has been found between homicide

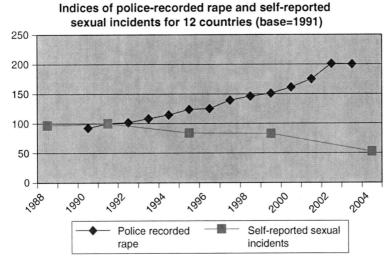

Indices of police-recorded rape and self-reported sexual incidents for 12 countries (base=1991)

	Police reported rape	Victim reported sexual incidents
1988		96,82
1989		
1990	92,57	
1991	100,00	100,00
1992	101,67	
1993	108,07	
1994	114,65	
1995	123,59	83,89
1996	125,01	
1997	139,24	
1998	146	
1999	151,18	82,91
2000	161,36	
2001	175,42	
2002	200,91	
2003	200,31	
2004		52,46

Fig. 1.10 Police-recorded and victim-reported sexual offenses in some EU member states, 1988–2004

and levels of victimisation by other types of violence (Eisner 2002). The reduction in homicide in Europe since 1990 supports the idea that real levels of violence have fallen, while official records present an increase.

This is a finding that requires explanation. It is even more puzzling in the light of the report from the EUICS that there have not been major changes over time in the rate at which offences are reported to the police (van Dijk et al. 2005). If the divergence between police records and victimisations is not caused by changes in the propensity of victims to report crimes to the police, then something else must be causing it. One possibility is that there is an increasing likelihood for the police to

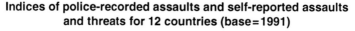

**Indices of police-recorded assaults and self-reported assaults
and threats for 12 countries (base = 1991)**

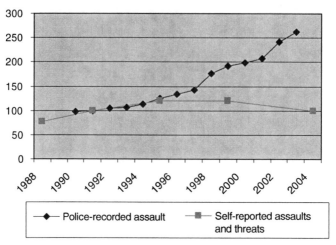

	Police recorded assault	Victim reported assault and threats
1988		77,25
1989		
1990	97,08	
1991	100,00	100,00
1992	104,93	
1993	106,85	
1994	113,37	
1995	125,43	120,69
1996	133,16	
1997	141,72	
1998	175,86	
1999	191,67	120,43
2000	198,61	
2001	207,73	
2002	241,96	
2003	262,89	
2004		99,53

Fig. 1.11 Police-recorded and victim-reported assaults and threats in some EU member states, 1988–2004

record the offences that are reported to them. There are no internationally comparable figures on the rate at which police record offences reported to them, but one British study, using data from official records and the British Crime Survey (a large-scale household victimisation survey), estimated that 46% of offences that were reported to the police were not recorded by them (Barclay and Tavares 1999). It is likely that the level of such attrition is variable between countries and over time. Such changes may reflect the level of political and managerial attention that is devoted to certain categories of crime. This suggests that the divergence between reported victimisations of violence and police-recorded violence may be caused by increasing attention by politicians and criminal justice systems to violent offences.

This hypothesis awaits confirmation by further empirical research. It is also possible that some disparities arise because of the different categories used by the *Sourcebook* and the ICVS/EUICS. For example, it is possible that rape has increased while other types of sexual incident that are included in the ICVS/EUICS category (such as offensive sexual touching) have declined. People may have become less sensitive to threats (and so less likely to remember and report them to researchers) while actual cases of assault have risen. These possibilities would suggest that it is the ICVS/EUICS data that are presenting a misleading picture of European trends in violent offending. For this chapter, it is suggested that we place more credence in sources that lie closer to the crime, so we are led towards the conclusion that the falls in violence presented in the ICVS/EUICS are more likely to reflect reality than the increases reported in the *Sourcebook*.

Conclusion

Overall these figures suggest that property offences, such as theft and burglary have tended to fall in Europe since the early 1990s. The picture for violent offences is more complicated. Records of convictions suggest increases of all the types of violent offending included in these analyses. Police records suggest increases for all types except homicide. But victimisation surveys suggest that violent offending has actually fallen. This supports the idea, suggested elsewhere (Westfelt and Estrada 2005), that the rise in officially recorded offences does not reflect an underlying increase in the level of violent offending.

As for the level of offences that are committed by juveniles, the available data are limited. There is a pattern in official records of the proportion of suspected offenders who are minors to have increased for violent offences and decreased for property offences. However, as suggested above, official records of violent offences seem highly susceptible to changes in police recording practices. It can be assumed that the proportion of suspected offenders who are children is even more likely to change according to the operational priority that the police give to arresting young people. So, little reliance can be placed on such figures. Nevertheless, there are consistent reports from the research literature that the mid to late teenage years are the peak ages for both the prevalence and frequency of the types of offending that are discussed in this chapter (Piquero et al. 2007). If this is the case, then it is very likely that changes in the overall rates of offending are reflective of changes in offending by young people. Given the data from the victimisation surveys presented above, it seems likely that the rate of offending by young people in Europe has fallen for both property and violent offences. This may not be true for all cities and countries, but it is suggested by the aggregated data presented in this chapter. While youth offending seems to have been falling, the attention paid by the criminal justice system to their violent offending in particular has risen.

Chapter 2
The UN Convention on the Rights of the Child

Jaap Doek

Introduction

The UN Convention on the Rights of the Child (hereafter the CRC) is a human rights treaty that covers many different areas such as civil rights and freedoms, family environment, health and welfare, education and child protection.[1] But none of these areas have been so much elaborated in international guidelines and standards as Juvenile Justice.[2]

The core provisions of the CRC directly relevant for children in conflict with the (penal) law are the articles 40 and 37. A rather detailed elaboration of these provisions as well as additional rules can be found in the following:

- United Nations Standard Minimum Rules for the Administration of Juvenile Justice, also known as the Beijing Rules[3]
- The United Nations Rules for the Protection of Juveniles Deprived of their Liberty, also known as the Havana rules[4]

---

[1] There are also two Optional Protocols to the CRC, one on the Involvement of Children in Armed Conflict and one on the Sale of Children, Child Prostitution. Each of these protocols has been ratified by more than 110 states; see, for the latest update, http://www.ohchr.org under 'CRC Committee'.

[2] In some documents and other publications "juvenile justice" is used in a rather broad sense; that is, it covers all provisions and actions meant to do justice to children and by that also covers child protection issues. But the more common meaning of the term "juvenile justice" is all legal provisions and practices (including social and other measures) relevant for treating children in conflict with the law, or in the wording of art. 40(1) CRC, "children alleged as, accused of, or recognized as having infringed the penal law".

[3] The Standard Minimum Rules were adopted by the General Assembly of the UN in Resolution 40/33 of 29 November 1985 and named after the city where the drafting of the Rules was completed.

[4] These Rules were adopted by the General Assembly of the UN in Resolution 45/113 of December 1990 and named after the city where the drafting was completed.

J. Doek (✉)
UN Committee of the Rights of the Child, Lisse, The Netherlands

J. Junger-Tas and F. Dünkel (eds.), *Reforming Juvenile Justice*,
DOI: 10.1007/978-0-387-89295-5_2, © Springer Science+Business Media, LLC 2009

In addition to the Havana Rules other international standards are also relevant for children deprived of their liberty such as the Standard Minimum rules for the Treatment of Prisoners.[5]

There are many more international rules and standards implicitly relevant for the field of juvenile justice.[6] But it is not my intention to give a full detailed presentation of all these provisions. The focus of this chapter will be on young people's rights in Juvenile Justice, meaning a presentation of the rights of children in conflict with the law in a very concrete manner. In this context young people/children are persons who are under the age of 18 years at the time of (alleged) commission of an offence.

The UN Committee on the Rights of the Child (hereafter the Committee) in charge of monitoring the implementation of the CRC[7] has issued in January 2007 General Comment No. 10 on Children's Rights in Juvenile Justice.[8]

The overall objective of this document is to provide the 193 states that ratified the CRC, with guidance and recommendations for their efforts to establish an administration of juvenile justice in compliance with the CRC.

These efforts should aim at the development and implementation of a comprehensive juvenile justice policy with special attention for the prevention of juvenile delinquency,[9] the introduction of alternative measures (diversion) and full observance of the rule that deprivation of liberty must be a measure of last resort for the shortest appropriate period of time. I will use this document in presenting young people's rights in juvenile justice. I will first deal with the objectives and principles of juvenile justice and the minimum age for criminal responsibility and some other age issues.

---

[5] These Rules were approved by the Economic and Social Council (ECOSOC) of the UN in its Resolutions 663C (XXIV) of 31 July 1957 and 2076 (LX11) of 13 May 1977.

[6] See Human Rights and Prisons. A compilation of International Human Rights Instruments concerning the Administration of Justice. Professional Training Series No. 11 Add.1; United Nations/ Office of the High Commissioner on Human Rights, New York and Geneva 2005.

[7] It goes beyond the scope of this contribution to elaborate on this monitoring task of the Committee. See for more information, e.g., Jutta Gras, Monitoring the Convention on the Rights of the Child. The Erik Castrén Institute of International Law and Human Rights, Research Reports 8/2001; Helsinki 2001.

[8] General Comments of the Committee are documents providing States Parties to the CRC with guidance for the implementation of children's rights via recommendations and interpretations. So far 10 General Comments have been issued, e.g., on HIV/AIDS and the rights of the child (No. 3), Adolescent Health and Development in the context of the CRC (No. 4), treatment of Unaccompanied and Separated Children outside of their country of origin (No. 6) and The Rights of Children with disabilities (No. 9). See, for the text of the General Comments, http://www.ohchr. org/english/bodies/crc/comments.htm

[9] In this chapter I will not cover the various aspects of the prevention of juvenile delinquency. I refer to General Comment No. 10, par. 5–9 and the United Nations Guidelines for the Prevention of Juvenile Delinquency, also known as the Riyadh Guidelines, adopted by the General Assembly of the UN in Resolution 45/112 of 14 December 1990.

The main part of this chapter will be a presentation of young people's rights following a young person on his journey through the juvenile justice system (the why of this approach will be explained). I will conclude with some observations on possible future developments.

Young People's Rights in Juvenile Justice: Objectives, Principles and Ages

Objectives and Principles

In States Parties to the CRC policy makers and politicians who call for a tougher, more punitive approach of juvenile delinquency are no exceptions. This call is often "inspired" by an incidence of serious crimes committed by juveniles, widely published in the media and described with a lot of concerns. It is therefore necessary to remind the 193 governments of these states (repeatedly) that they have committed themselves to a treatment of children in conflict with the law (also known as juvenile delinquents) in accordance with article 40(1) CRC. This means

- a treatment that is consistent with the child's sense of dignity and worth. All human beings are equal in dignity (art. 1. Universal Declaration of Human Rights) and the CRC requires that this dignity must be respected throughout the entire process of juvenile justice and govern the attitudes and measures of all professionals (police, prosecutors, judges, probation officers, staff of institutions/detention centres) and volunteers involved in the administration of juvenile justice.
- a treatment that reinforces the child's respect for human rights and freedom of others. This requirement is also in line with article 29, under b CRC stating among others that the education of the child shall be directed to the development of respect for human rights and fundamental freedoms. It means that all professionals and volunteers must fully respect and implement the rules set in the CRC and other international instruments (e.g. the Beijing Rules) such as the guarantees for a fair trial (art. 40(2) CRC).

As the Committee observes in General Comment No. 10 (par. 4e): "If the key actors in juvenile justice (…) do not fully respect and protect these guarantees, how can they expect that, with such poor examples, the child will respect human rights and the freedoms of others?"

- A treatment that takes into account the child's age and promotes the child's reintegration and the child's assuming a constructive role in society. This objective of the treatment of children in conflict with the law can be seen as an implementation of the rule of article 3 CRC that the best interest of the child shall be a primary consideration in all actions concerning children. It means that the traditional objectives of criminal justice (repression/retribution) must give way to rehabilitation and restorative justice objectives in dealing with children in conflict with the law and this can be done in concert with adequate attention to effective public safety.

Finally – not explicitly mentioned in art. 40 CRC, but in line with art. 37(a) CRC – respect for the dignity of the child means that all forms of violence in the treatment of the child are prohibited and must be prevented. In that regard I refer to the report of the independent expert, Paulo Sergio Pinheiro, for the United Nations Study on Violence against Children submitted to the General Assembly of the UN in October 2006.[10] It contains various recommendations for actions to be taken by states such as the establishment of effective and independent complaints, investigation and enforcement mechanisms to deal with cases of violence in the justice system, and of effective independent monitoring bodies empowered to conduct unannounced visits, conduct interviews with children in private and investigate allegations of violence.[11]

Another important provision of the CRC is article 2 containing the right to non-discrimination or in the wording of this article: "States Parties shall respect and ensure the rights set forth in the present Convention to each child within their jurisdiction (…)." All necessary measures must be taken to ensure that all children in conflict with the law are treated equally. According to the CRC Committee (General Comment No. 10, par. 4a), special attention must be paid to de facto discrimination and disparities which may be the result of a lack of a consistent policy and involve vulnerable groups of children such as street children, children belonging to minorities, children with disabilities and children who are recidivists.

Within the context of this same article 2 the CRC Committee recommends States Parties to abolish all provisions that criminalize behavioural problems of children such as truancy, running away from home or an institution, vagrancy and begging, also known as status offences.

From the perspective of nondiscrimination par. 56 of the Riyadh Guidelines for the prevention of juvenile delinquency states: "(…) Legislation should be enacted to ensure that any conduct not considered an offence or not penalized if committed by an adult is not considered an offence and not penalized if committed by a young person." These kinds of activities should be dealt with through the implementation of child protective measures, including effective support for parents and/or other caregivers and measures which address the root causes of this behaviour.

---

[10] UN Document A/61/299, 29 August 2006; see also the accompanying book: *World Report on Violence against Children*, Paulo Sérgio Pinheiro, published by the United Nations 2006. The book can be consulted and downloaded on http:///www.violencestudy.org; idem ohchr.org, unicef.org and who.int

[11] See par. 112 of the Report and par. 62 with the following information: "Children in detention are frequently subjected to violence by staff, including as a form of control or punishment for minor infractions. In at least 77 countries corporal and other violent punishments are accepted as legal disciplinary measures in penal institutions (…)."

The Minimum Age of Criminal Responsibility and Other Age-Matters

Article 40(3) CRC requires that States Parties shall establish a minimum age for criminal responsibility.[12] But it does not specify which minimum age is acceptable and the Beijing Rules limit its guidance to the recommendation to set this minimum age not at a too low level. But again, what is "too low"?

The reports States Parties to the CRC submit to the Committee[13] show that the minimum age of criminal responsibility (MACR) range from a very low level of age 7 or 8 to a commendable high level of age 14 or 16. In the Concluding Observations[14] the Committee has consistently recommended states to increase the minimum age to an internationally acceptable one and this was in particular done for states with a minimum age for criminal responsibility below age 12.

In other words: the Committee is of the opinion that the minimum age for criminal responsibility should be set at least at age 12 as an absolute minimum while it will encourage states to set it at a higher level.

It means that children at or above this MACR at the time of the commission of an offence can be formally charged and subject to penal law procedures. But the Committee has also (see General Comment No. 10, par. 11–13) emphasized the obligation of States Parties to promote measures for dealing with children in conflict with the law *without* resorting to judicial proceedings (art. 40, 3 under b CRC). These measures should not be limited to children who commit minor offences or are first offenders and they should be an integral part of the juvenile justice provisions.[15]

Concerning the upper age limit: the Committee is of the opinion that the special rules of juvenile justice should apply to all children at or above the MACR but not yet 18 years old at the time of the commission of the offence. The Committee therefore recommends all States Parties to the CRC to abolish the legal provisions which allow treating children under the age of 18 (at the time of the crime) as adults in order to achieve a nondiscriminatory full implementation of the special rules of juvenile justice.

---

[12] This is the Committee's interpretation of a text that is not clear: "the establishment of a minimum age below which children shall be presumed not to have the capacity to infringe the law". This presumption may apply to very young children, but the reality shows that children as young as 6 or 7 do in fact have the capacity to infringe the penal law. This does give reason to the Committee to explain what the MACR should mean (General Comment No. 10, par. 16).

[13] See about the reporting obligations of States Parties article 44 CRC.

[14] After a discussion with a delegation of a State Party about the report it submitted on the implementation of the CRC, the Committee presents a document to the State in which it acknowledges progress made, expresses concerns and makes recommendations for further actions. This document is known as the Concluding Observations (issued for each State Party).

[15] The Committee elaborates on the full respect for human rights and legal safeguards in cases of dealing with a child in conflict with the law without resorting to legal proceedings, a practice also known as Diversion; see General Comment No. 10, par. 13 (I will come back to this in the next paragraph). See also the Beijing Rules 11.1–11.4 on Diversion.

So if we discuss the young people/children's rights in juvenile justice we are covering an age group from 12 (at least) or higher till age 18. Children below the age of 12 can of course commit an offence.[16] But they should not be dealt with in the context of the rules of juvenile justice. It does not mean that the commission of the offence should not be given an appropriate response. Very important in that regard is the involvement of parents in responses by the child, such as writing a letter of apology or provide some symbolic compensation (17).

In many countries particularly in the developing part of the world the determination of the age of a child is a serious problem because of the lack of proper birth registration. The CRC Committee regularly urges States Parties to ensure that every child born on their territories is immediately registered after birth (as required by art. 7 CRC). International organisations, in particular UNICEF and PLAN International, undertake awareness raising campaigns and very concrete measures (e.g. use of mobile registration units) to improve birth registration. Lack of such registration makes a child very vulnerable to abuses, not only in juvenile justice.

If there is no proof of age the child is entitled to a reliable medical or social investigation that may establish her or his age. In case of conflicting outcome or inconclusive evidence, the child should be given the benefit of the doubt, meaning: if it cannot be proven that the child is at or above the MACR he or she should not be held criminally responsible.[17] The same applies for the age of 18: if it cannot be established that the child was 18 or older at the time of the commission of the offence, that child should be treated under the special rules of juvenile justice.[18]

The Young People's Rights in Juvenile Justice: What Are They?

Introduction to a Flyer

After having presented the overall objectives and principles of juvenile law and having defined the group (in principle) covered by the rules of juvenile justice, I would like to answer as concretely as possible the question: what are the rights of young people in juvenile justice. I will do that in the form of draft flyer/brochure addressed to young people (and their parents or other care givers). I will not try to cover all details/variations of the young people's rights but focus on the most crucial ones.

---

[16] See Self-reported delinquency research among children including those below age 12 in: P. H. van der Laan et al. 1997 "Jeugdcriminaliteit en Jeugdbescherming. Ontwikkelingen in de periode 1980–1994", Den Haag WODC (Juvenile Delinquency and Youth Protection, 1980–1994, The Hague, Research Centre of the Ministry of Justice).

[17] An example of a special set of rules and possible responses can be found in the Netherlands: the so-called Stop-reaction for children below age 12 (the mimimum age of criminal responsibility in the Netherlands is 12) who have committed an infraction of the law. Special Guidelines have been issued by the Prosecutor-General (Aanwijzing Stop-reactie 1999).

[18] See General Comment No. 10, par. 19 and 22.

From my experiences as the chairman of the UN Committee on the Rights of the Child (from May 2001 till March 2007) and the many country visits I made in that capacity, one of the most striking – and in my opinion very troublesome – facts is the lack of information for juveniles and parents when they get in contact with the juvenile justice system. Despite all the wonderful guarantees and good intentions, the child in conflict with the law has hardly a clue (if any) of what may happen to her or him and what her or his rights are. It is a reality in almost all States Parties, highly industrialised and very poor alike. The machinery of the juvenile justice system is of course supposed to act in full compliance with the CRC and other international standards. But for a child it is a powerful and often intimidating machinery, a feeling exacerbated by the lack of information. If we really want the child to be an active – and understanding – participant in the process of juvenile justice as required under article 12 CRC,[19] we should provide the child in conflict with the law with all the relevant information.

I am aware of the fact that a flyer does not fly very far in countries where a lot of children are illiterate because they had not received any education (currently about 100 million globally). It is clear that for those children the information should be given orally but the person in charge of the task can use the flyer. In this regard, it is very important that this oral information is given as early as possible and by an independent person. This is particularly necessary if the police decide to keep the child in custody (see also the next paragraph).

Finally I am also aware of the fact that in many countries the rights mentioned cannot be exercised because of the lack of adequate legislative provisions or the lack of necessary services (e.g. no probation service, no or very few alternative measures, etc.). It means that the flyer can also be considered as an agenda for action in these countries aiming at the establishment of a juvenile justice system in compliance with the CRC as elaborated in General Comment No. 10.

The (draft) flyer will be based on this General Comment with references where appropriate.

The Rights of Young People in Conflict with the Law

You have been taken to the police station, most likely because the police assume that you have committed an offence. What will happen to you depends, among other things, on your age, the seriousness of the offence you allegedly committed and whether this is your first contact with the police as a suspect of having committed an offence. In this flyer you will find information about the various actions that can be taken and your rights in that regard.

---

[19] See in this regard the Recommendations of the CRC Committee adopted after the Day of General Discussion 2006 on The Right of the Child to be heard (29 September 2006). For the text of these recommendations and others issued after Days of General Discussion, see http://www.ohchr.org/english/bodies/crc/discussion.htm.

In the first place you have the right to express your views and opinions freely and that applies to the whole process you are about to get involved in. This right includes your right to actively participate in the decisions the authorities, such as the police, the prosecutor and the judge, may make.

As far as the process is concerned the following information may help you to understand what is happening.

The police: Its role is to investigate the case against you which means collecting information that may prove that you committed the offence you are accused of.

Depending on the rules and regulations that exist in your country the police may give you a warning, refer the case to a service (e.g. probation) in order to carry out a community service or other alternative measures. If the case does not allow for this kind of action, it will be reported – with the available evidence – to the public prosecutor.

The public prosecutor is usually the authority with the power to bring the case before the court/juvenile judge for trial. But the prosecutor may also have the power to propose that you carry out a community service or participate in other alternative measures.

The court/juvenile judge is the authority that, based on the evidence presented by the prosecutor, will decide whether you are guilty (whether it is proven that you did commit the offence(s) you are accused of), and if so what kind of measure or sanction should be imposed on you.

We will now explain to you what your rights are when you are in contact with the authorities mentioned before.

Police: You have the right to be informed promptly and directly of the charges held against you.[20] Ask the police officer to tell you immediately what offence you are accused of and to explain it to you if you did not understand the information. Also ask him to inform your parents or guardians as soon as possible.

If you are interrogated by the police, do not hesitate to ask for explanations if necessary. You have the right not to answer the questions. The police are not allowed to put pressure on you or threaten or intimidate you, trying to force you to give a testimony or confess that you committed the offence the police accuse you of.[21] After you have been heard by the police you may be sent home with a warning. But it is also possible, as said before, that the police decide to divert the case. This usually means that you are told to undertake some community service or to repair the damages you have caused. There may be other actions you are told to undertake. The purpose of this decision is to avoid that your case is dealt with before a judge and therefore also known as diversion or as an alternative measure.

In this case you have the right to receive information about the nature, the content and the duration of this alternative measure and about the consequences if you do not want to cooperate or if you fail to carry out and complete the measure.[22] This is important because the alternative measure will only be taken if you consent with it in writing.

---

[20] Article 40, par. 2 Under b (ii) CRC.

[21] Article 40, par. 2 Under b (iv) CRC.

[22] See General Comment No. 10, par. 13.

Before you take your decision you have the right to talk to a lawyer or another qualified person about the pros and cons of carrying out the proposed alternative measure and ask her or him for further information if needed. Be aware of the fact that you are under no obligation to consent, especially not when in your opinion you did not commit the offence the police accuse you of. It is an important principle that you are innocent as long as it is not proven (beyond reasonable doubt) by the authorities that you did commit the alleged offence(s) and that you should be treated as such.

If you do consent and after you have completed the diversion measure, the case is closed. There will be no criminal record although the police may keep some registration of the case, e.g., in order to be able to note it when you recommit an offence.

Finally, it is possible that the police do keep you in custody in the police station or in another place for pretrial detention.

If this happens you have the right to be immediately provided with legal and other appropriate assistance.[23]

Within 24 h after the police decided to keep you in custody your case will be brought before a judge or another competent and independent authority. This person has to check whether the decision is in compliance with the rules for pretrial detention and whether it is really necessary to keep you in custody. This is an opportunity allowing you, with the assistance of the lawyer or any other qualified person, to argue in favour of your release and if desirable under certain conditions, e.g., that you will come to the police station for further interviews.

If you are not released, your pretrial detention will be reviewed every 2 weeks, which is another opportunity to plea for release from custody. If the authorities keep you in pretrial detention, the prosecutor must present the case with the formal charges against you before the court/judge within 30 days after the beginning of your pretrial detention.[24] Let your lawyer or other assistant ensure that this happens.

Prosecutor: If the police report the case to the prosecutor he or she will decide whether you will be formally charged in court or not. Discuss with your lawyer or any other assisting person what the possibilities are to avoid being brought before the court or judge. Let him or her talk to the prosecutor to find out whether and under which conditions he or she is willing to propose an alternative measure (diversion). If the prosecutor does offer the possibility to carry out an alternative measure the same rules apply mentioned before: full information about the nature, content and duration of the measure and your written consent.

If diversion is not possible (the prosecutor does not want it or you do not consent), your case will be presented in court.

Trial in court: You have the right to a fair trial and there are various rules to guarantee this.[25]

---

[23] See article 37 under d CRC.

[24] See General Comment No. 10, par. 28b.

[25] See article 40, par. 2 CRC.

First, you should receive well before the day of the hearing in court a document in which the prosecutor informs you about the offences you are accused of (the formal charges). This document is usually not easy to fully understand. But you have the right to legal or other appropriate assistance when you have to appear in court. This assistance must be given to you free of charge.

It is very important to meet with the lawyer or other assistant to prepare the presentation of your defence in court. He or she can explain to you what the accusations are and inform you about the procedure in court. You should provide your lawyer or assistant with all the information relevant to the accusations, in particular when in your opinion some or all of the accusations are false.

In court your privacy must be fully respected. This means that you should demand, if necessary, that the procedure in court is conducted behind closed doors (no public). This right to full respect of your privacy applies also for actions of the police and the prosecutor, e.g., no press releases in which your name is mentioned or information made public by which you can easily be identified as the accused person.[26] You are not obliged to give testimony in court. But you and/or your lawyer or assistant can raise questions to the witnesses brought to the court by the prosecutor. If useful (consult with your lawyer or assistant) you can bring your own witnesses to the court to support your defence.[27] As a rule your parents or guardian are present at the court hearing. But they can be excluded from (part of) the hearing if that is in your best interest. The court decides but you can ask for it (again consult with your lawyer or assistant).[28]

If you cannot understand or speak the language used in court you have the right to free assistance of an interpreter. So do not hesitate to ask for it.[29]

If, at the end of the trial, you are found guilty by the court or judge of some or all the offences you are charged with, you will be sentenced.

Sentences or dispositions: The law contains the sanctions or measures that can be imposed on a person like you that is a person less than 18 years old at the time of the commission of the offence. These provisions are also applicable if you have turned 18 at the time the sentence is issued by the court or judge.

The traditional sanctions are a fine, supervision or another noncustodial measures, or detention, imprisonment or placement in an institution for treatment (custodial measures). Let your lawyer brief you on this and in particular ask him to find out whether the court can impose on you alternative measures such as community service or compensation for the victim instead of custody. One of the important rules of the CRC is that custodial measures – meaning deprivation of your liberty – should only be imposed on you if no other sanctions are possible and that this sanction should

---

[26] See General Comment No. 10, par. 23l and article 14, par. 1 International Covenant on Civil and Political Rights.

[27] See General Comment No. 10, par. 23l.

[28] See General Comment No. 10, par. 23g.

[29] See General Comment No. 10, par. 23k.

not last longer than strictly necessary given your personal circumstances and the (serious) nature of your offence.[30]

It means that your lawyer must strongly argue (as much as possible) in favour of a noncustodial measure, including for example the possibility of a suspended detention or imprisonment with a probation period of, e.g., 2 years. This means that if you do not commit another offence in that period of 2 years you will not be detained or imprisoned. A nice bonus for 2 years of good behaviour. But do not start again with committing offences after these 2 years. Persons who do recommit offences are usually hit with rather severe sanctions.

When the court has decided which sanction will be imposed ask your lawyer what it means more concretely and in particular what is expected from you with regard to the execution of the sanction.

The death penalty and imprisonment for life without the possibility of release are absolutely prohibited. The CRC Committee is of the opinion that imprisonment for life should not be imposed at all, not even with the possibility of release.[31]

You have the right to appeal from the decision of the court.[32] You may want to do that because you are of the opinion that you did not get a fair trial (e.g., you were not given a lawyer or other assistant) or because you do not agree with the sentence of the court (if, for example, you were found guilty of offences you did not commit or the sanction is too severe). But you should consult with your lawyer; he knows what is needed to make an appeal and what the specific rules applicable are.

After the Trial or Deprivation of Liberty

With the decision of the court, and if you do not appeal, the case is closed. But there is one sanction that, if imposed, needs special attention: deprivation of liberty. This deprivation may be imposed under different names such as detention, imprisonment or placement in a juvenile justice institution (training school, etc.). Whatever the name, the deprivation means that you will be placed in an institution from which you are *not* permitted to leave at will. If such a sanction is imposed on you the following aspects need your special attention.

In court your lawyer should urge the court, if there are indications that a deprivation of liberty is the only option left, that the period of deprivation is as short as possible and that you are placed in a facility as close as possible to your parental home and family. You have the right to maintain personal relations and direct contact with your parents on a regular basis. In addition, you have the right to maintain contact with your family (not only parents but also your brothers/sisters/uncles/aunts) via correspondence and visits.[33] Visits by your parents or other family members in

---

[30] See article 37, under a CRC and General Comment No. 10, par. 28a.

[31] See article 37, under a CRC and General Comment No. 10, par. 26 and 27.

[32] See General Comment No. 10, par. 23j.

[33] See article 9, par. 3 and article 37 under c CRC.

particular will be very unlikely if you are placed in a facility far away from home. The institution can set rules for these visits in terms of frequency (every week, 2 weeks, and month) and duration (1, 3 or more hours of visits). Correspondence and telephone calls with family, other persons (including your lawyer) should be allowed at least twice a week (Havana Rules 60, 61, 62). Your right to privacy should be fully respected, meaning for example that visits may be watched but not overheard by staff, no opening of correspondence and no overhearing of phone calls. Exceptions to these rules are allowed in situations clearly described in the rules of the institution. Ask for a copy of the rules of the institution you are placed in.

You have to be kept separate from adults, which means that placement in a prison for adults is not allowed unless it is in a separate wing of that prison specially reserved for children, which must be completely separated from the parts where adults are kept.[34]

Establish an ongoing contact with your lawyer; ask him to agree that you can stay in touch with him, for example every 3 months (by letter or phone call) and at any other time when your rights are violated.

There is a document of the United Nations that contains rules for the protection of juveniles deprived of their liberty (also known as Havana Rules). Ask your lawyer to give you a copy and let him explain the rights you have when in the institution according to these rules. Just some examples:[35]

- You have the right to participate in sports, physical exercise, the arts and leisure time activities.
- You have the right to education, including, when appropriate, vocational training. You can ask for special permission to go to a school outside the institution.[36]
- You have the right to be examined by a doctor when you arrive in the institution and you are entitled to regular medical care during your stay.
- Disciplinary measures are possible but the institution must have written rules and procedures for these measures (ask for a copy of these). Physical punishment, placement in a dark cell and closed or solitary confinement are forbidden.
- If you behave in a manner that poses a direct threat of injury for yourself or others, the staff can use restraint or force to prevent such injury. But such measures should be under close and direct control of a doctor or a psychologist.
- If you are treated in violation of your rights or the rules of the institution, you have the right to make a complaint to an independent complaint committee. You can also call your lawyer (see above).

Finally find out what the possibilities and conditions are for an early release from the institution. The staff should provide you with that information but if necessary you can also ask your lawyer about it.

If you meet those conditions make a request – with the support of your lawyer if necessary – for early release.

---

[34] See article 37, under c CRC and General Comment No. 10, par. 28c.

[35] See General comment No. 10, par. 28c.

[36] See Havana Rules No. 59.

Some Concluding Remarks

This draft is written from the perspective of the juvenile. But much more can be said about the rights of young people in juvenile justice. For instance, the respect for and protection of these rights require that juvenile justice is carried out by well-informed and properly trained professionals such as police officers, prosecutors, judges, lawyers and probation officers. Special services should be developed – probation, alternative measures – to contribute to the realization of the objectives of juvenile justice. It may require specific legislative measures and regulations, e.g., regarding the quality of treatment in institutions, but certainly the allocation of adequate financial resources.

Many states undertake efforts to establish juvenile justice in accordance with the CRC via legislation and projects. The major challenge for the coming years is the full implementation of all the good plans and intentions. This is a challenge states can only meet if they get as much support as possible from UN agencies such as UNICEF and the inter-agency coordination panel on juvenile justice,[37] from NGOs and juvenile justice experts and with the maximum participation of children themselves, parents and the media.

---

[37] See "Protecting the rights of children in conflict with the law" – Programme and advocacy experiences from member organisations of the inter-agency coordination panel on juvenile justice – (2005). The members of this panel are the OHCHR, UNICEF, UNDP, UNODC, Casa Alianza, Defence for Children International, Penal Reform International, Save the Children UK, Terre des Hommes and World Organization against Torture.

Chapter 3
Young People's Rights: The Role of the Council of Europe

Frieder Dünkel

The Recommendation on "New Ways of Dealing with Juvenile Delinquency and the Role of Juvenile Justice"

The Recommendation of the Council of Europe on *"New Ways of Dealing with Juvenile Delinquency and the Role of Juvenile Justice"* (see http://www.coe.int) of the year 2003 pursues the following paramount goals:

1. The prevention of offending and re-offending
2. The rehabilitation and reintegration of offenders
3. Regard for the needs and interests of victims of crime

The strategic approach incorporates the following perspectives:

The juvenile justice system has to be treated as a component of a wider community-based strategy for the prevention of juvenile delinquency, that takes into account the wider family, school, neighbourhood and peer group context within which offending occurs (No. 2 of the Recommendation). Resources should in particular be targeted towards addressing serious, violent, persistent and drug- and alcohol-related offending where possible (No. 3). There is a need for the development of more suitable and effective measures of prevention and reintegration that are tailored to young migrants, groups of juveniles, young girls, and children and young people under the age of criminal responsibility (No. 4).

Sanctions should – as far as possible – be based on scientific results of what works, with whom and under which circumstances (No. 5).

The consequences for ethnic minorities require particular policy attention. Therefore, the persons in charge are obliged to compile so-called *impact statements* (No. 6).

The Recommendation proposes the following "new responses":

The expansion of the range of suitable alternatives to formal prosecution should continue. The principle of proportionality is to be upheld, and the voluntariness of the offender must be regarded (No. 7). Regarding serious, violent and persistent juvenile crime, (proportional) community sanctions should be further developed

F. Dünkel (✉)
Rechts- und Staatswissenschaftliche Fakultät, Universität Greifswald, Greifswald, Germany

J. Junger-Tas and F. Dünkel (eds.), *Reforming Juvenile Justice,*
DOI: 10.1007/978-0-387-89295-5_3, © Springer Science + Business Media, LLC 2009

(this can also imply the inclusion of the parents into the criminal responsibility of their children, so long as this is not counterproductive), especially such measures that incorporate elements of reparation and restoration to the victim (No. 8, 10).

The recommendation to expand community sanctions in cases of serious crime is remarkable in that emphasis is usually placed on the necessity of imprisonment in this context. However, experiences with suspended sentences as well as with community education-/treatment programmes within the framework of the proba- tion or youth welfare services have shown that positive results can be achieved with repeat and/or violent offenders or groups of offenders (see Dünkel 2003a pp. 89, 96). Insofar, juveniles who were viewed as traditional clientele of the juvenile prison system 20 or 30 years ago can now be successfully supervised in the community.

With regard to the extended phases of (school and vocational) education and transi- tion into adulthood, the sanctions of juvenile criminal law should be applicable to young adults according to their degree of maturity and development (No. 11). This matches the stated positive experiences that have been made in Germany, and mirrors contemporary legal reform in, for example, Lithuania, Slovenia, Serbia and Austria (see Dünkel 2008a; 2008b and below chapter 13).

Incidentally, the recommendations repeatedly emphasise the need for "risk assessment, evidence-based interventions and empirical evaluation". Although aspects of "neo-correctionalist" thinking (for example regarding parental liability) can also be observed, the Recommendation Rec (2003) 20 remains adherent to the tradition of a moderate justice system that prioritises education (key term: 'mini- mum intervention') and that emphasises community-based interventions also in cases of more serious offending. This should serve as a mental note for counter- reforms in a more repressive direction.

The implementation of the 2003 Recommendation is to be executed in close collaboration with the local prevention and intervention agencies and should take quality standards into account. Continuous "*monitoring*" and the *dissemination* of good practices also belong to the recommended strategies.

It remains to be seen to what extent the Recommendation shall influence the reforms in Europe, especially in the Central and Eastern European countries. Unfortunately, one can assume that there shall be problems with the funding of sci- entific evaluations. The importance of evidence-based criminal justice policy can, however, not be valued highly enough. Only by this means can we effectively coun- ter the populist trends in juvenile justice policy that are being publicised by the party of the late Jörg haider in Austria, Silvio Berlusconi in Italy and Le Pen in France.

The European Rules for Juvenile Offenders Subject to Sanctions and Measures of 2008

In January 2006 the Committee of Ministers of the Council of Europe decided the new *European Prison Rules* (EPR, vgl. Council of Europe 2006). At the same time the *Committee on Crime Problems* (CDPC) set up a further expert group which was to draft European Rules for juveniles under community sanctions and measures and deprived of their liberty. The terms of reference explicitly referred to community sanctions and sanctions with deprivation of liberty and thus went beyond the scope of the EPR. But also with regard to deprivation of liberty the new Rules are more comprehensive than the EPR as they cover all forms of deprivation of liberty such as pre-trial detention, detention in (closed) welfare institutions, youth imprisonment and psychiatric juvenile facilities.

The Rules have been drafted until April 2008, and after the final discussions in the CDPC they have been accepted by the Committe of Ministers on 5 November 2008 as *"European Rules for Juveniles Subject to Sanctions and Measures"*. (Rec (2008) 11).

The Rules are structured in eight parts. In the same way as the EPR they start with "Basic Principles" which concern the imposition and execution of community sanctions and all forms of deprivation of liberty. Rules on the scope of application and definitions also belong to Part I. The most important issue in that respect is that the scope of application is extended to young adults of 18–21 years of age (as far as national law provides the application of juvenile law or sanctions or special rules for the execution of sanctions or measures for this age group). The second part deals with community sanctions and measures, while Part III covers issues regarding the deprivation of liberty. Part IV concerns "legal advice and assistance" and Part V is dedicated to "complaints procedures, inspection and monitoring". Questions related to staffing are dealt with in Part VI, and those related to evaluation and research as well as to work with the media and the public are contained in Part VII. The closing Rule 142 requires the Rules to be regularly updated.

The preamble formulates the following general directive: "The aim of the present Rules is to uphold the rights and safety of juvenile offenders subject to sanctions or measures and to promote their physical, mental and social well-being when subjected to community sanctions and measures or any form of deprivation of liberty.

Nothing in these Rules ought to be interpreted as precluding the application of other relevant international human rights instruments and standards that are more conducive to ensuring the rights, care and protection of juveniles. In particular, the provisions of Recommendation Rec (2006) 2 on the European Prison Rules and of Recommendation R (92) 16 on the European Rules on Community Sanctions and Measures shall be applied to the benefit of juvenile offenders in as far as they are not in conflict with these Rules."

This statement makes it clear that the present Rules do not go beyond the guarantees formulated in earlier Recommendations and Rules concerning the human rights of offenders. This must be interpreted as a formal prohibition of any discrimination or restriction of rights and legal guarantees for juveniles, for example, with regard to educational needs. Basic Principle 13 in the same way requires: "Juveniles shall not have fewer legal rights and safeguards than those provided to adult offenders by the general rules of criminal procedure."

The 20 "basic principles" are as follows:

1. *Juvenile offenders subject to sanctions or measures shall be treated with respect for their human rights.*
2. *The sanctions or measures that may be imposed on juveniles as well as the manner of their implementation shall be specified by law and based on the principles of social integration and education and on the prevention of re-offending.*
3. *Sanctions and measures shall be imposed by a court or, if imposed by another legally recognised authority, they shall be subject to prompt judicial review. They shall be determinate and imposed for the minimum necessary period and only for a legitimate purpose.*
4. *The minimum age for the imposition of sanctions or measures as a result of the commission of an offence shall not be too low and shall be determined by law.*
5. *The imposition and implementation of sanctions or measures shall be based on the best interests of the juvenile offenders, limited by the gravity of the offences committed (principle of proportionality) and take account of their age, physical and mental well-being, development, capacities and personal circumstances (principle of individualisation) as ascertained when necessary by psychological, psychiatric or social inquiry reports.*
6. *In order to adapt the implementation of sanctions and measures to the particular circumstances of each case, the authorities responsible for the implementation shall have a sufficient degree of discretion without leading to serious inequality of treatment.*
7. *Sanctions or measures shall not humiliate or degrade the juveniles subject to them.*
8. *Sanctions or measures shall not be implemented in a manner that aggravates their afflictive character or poses an undue risk of physical or mental harm.*
9. *Sanctions or measures shall be implemented without undue delay and only to the extent and for the period strictly necessary (principle of minimum intervention).*
10. *Deprivation of liberty of a juvenile shall be a measure of last resort and imposed and implemented for the shortest period possible. Special efforts must be undertaken to avoid pre-trial detention.*
11. *Sanctions or measures shall be imposed and implemented without discrimination on any ground such as sex, race, colour, language, religion, sexual orientation, political or other opinion, national or social origin, association with a national minority, property, birth or other status (principle of non-discrimination).*
12. *Mediation or other restorative measures shall be encouraged at all stages of dealing with juveniles.*
13. *Any justice system dealing with juveniles shall ensure their effective participation in the proceedings concerning the imposition as well as the implementation of sanctions or measures. Juveniles shall not have fewer legal rights and safeguards than those provided to adult offenders by the general rules of criminal procedure.*
14. *Any justice system dealing with juveniles shall take due account of the rights and responsibilities of the parents and legal guardians and shall as far as possible involve them in the proceedings and the execution of sanctions or measures, except if this is not in the best interests of the juvenile. Where the offender is over the age of majority the participation of parents and legal guardians is not compulsory. Members of the juveniles' extended families and the wider community may also be associated with the proceedings where it is appropriate to do so.*

15. *Any justice system dealing with juveniles shall follow a multi-disciplinary and multi-agency approach and be integrated with wider social initiatives for juveniles in order to ensure a holistic approach to and continuity of the care of such juveniles (principles of community involvement and continuous care).*
16. *The juvenile's right to privacy shall be fully respected at all stages of the proceedings. The identity of juveniles and confidential information about them and their families shall not be conveyed to anyone who is not authorised by law to receive it.*
17. *Young adult offenders may, where appropriate, be regarded as juveniles and dealt with accordingly.*
18. *All staff working with juveniles performs an important public service. Their recruitment, special training and conditions of work shall ensure that they are able to provide the appropriate standard of care to meet the distinctive needs of juveniles and provide positive role models for them.*
19. *Sufficient resources and staffing shall be provided to ensure that interventions in the lives of juveniles are meaningful. Lack of resources shall never justify the infringement of the human rights of juveniles.*
20. *The execution of any sanction or measure shall be subjected to regular government inspection and independent monitoring.*

The following comments are largely based on the commentary to the Rules which have been drafted by the experts of the Council of Europe since 2007 (see Dünkel et al. 2007; Dünkel 2008a; 2008b).

Rule 1 corresponds to Rule 1 of the EPR. As stated in the Preamble, the *European Rules on Community Sanctions and Measures* of 1992 are of particular relevance as well. Human rights issues arise not only when deprivation of liberty is used, but also when community sanctions and measures are applied. Both full-scale deprivation of liberty and lesser restrictions of liberty can be intrusive and may violate human rights if the principle of proportionality contained in Rule 5 is not applied. It is a basic standard of all international instruments that the human rights of juveniles have to be protected in the same way as it is the case for adults. The *United Nations Convention on the Rights of the Child* as well as the recommendations of the Council of Europe in the field of juvenile justice emphasise this issue. It should be noted that Rule 1 refers to protecting not only human dignity, but all human rights of juvenile offenders both deprived of their liberty or under community sanctions and measures. It should be clear that, in addition, other international instruments such as the *United Nations Rules for the Protection of Juveniles Deprived of their Liberty* of 14 December 1990 (the so-called Havana Rules) have also played an important part in the development of these Rules.

Rule 2 refers to the fact that all juvenile justice and welfare systems are based on the principles of social integration and education with regard to imposing and executing community sanctions and measures and sanctions of deprivation of liberty. This leaves much less space, and in some countries no space at all, for the principle of general deterrence or other (more punitive) aims that are a feature of the criminal justice system for adults.

In the field of juvenile justice it is recognised that the personalities of juveniles are still developing and open to positive influences. Emphasis must be placed on the possibility of reintegrating young persons. This may be achieved in some cases only by intensive educational or therapeutic efforts. The rule on social integration would therefore not allow long-term security measures or life sentences that aim solely at protecting society from juvenile offenders and do not give them the prospect of release within a reasonable period. (See in this respect the case law of the European Court of Human Rights: *T. v. the United Kingdom* [GC], no. 24724/94, 16 December 1999; *V. v. the United Kingdom* [GC], no. 24888/94, ECHR 1999-IXT).

The emphasis that is placed on the major aim of education for the prevention of re-offending is important. In most international instruments education is not clearly defined. This is problematic as the term "education" may be misused as can be seen by repressive forms of authoritarian education, for example, military-style detention regimes that do not correspond to the European concept of human rights and dignity. On the one hand, the aim of preventing re-offending is modest, for it does not seek to achieve more than law-abiding integration into society. On the other hand, it is ambitious, for it is connected to the term social integration and therefore aims at promoting the juveniles' personal and wider social development, and their taking responsibility for their behaviour. Education therefore should be understood as including measures such as enhancing their communication skills or requiring them to make reparations, for instance, writing appropriate letters of apology. Equally, society has to enable these changes to take place. It is important that the opportunities for learning and the interventions chosen to achieve these goals should be evidence-based and should contribute to the development and differentiation of the capacities of perception, interpretation, decision-making and responsible action.

The restriction of the power to impose sanctions and measures to a court or to another legally recognised authority – as stipulated in *Rule 3* – enshrines the principle of legality. Prompt judicial review where the imposition is decided by another authority is a further guarantee in this regard. Detention only for a legitimate purpose follows the requirements set by the European Court of Human Rights in its interpretation of Article 5 of the ECHR. It further relates to Rule 2, which emphasizes the primary goals of any sanction or measure imposed on juvenile offenders.

It is important that all sanctions and measures imposed on juveniles be of determinate duration because of the need for legal certainty and realistic prospects for reintegration into society. Where the sanctions or measures are open-ended this can be achieved by making them subject to regular review. The principle of proportionality applies both to the imposition and to the implementation of sanctions and measures. This principle should be applied at every stage of the procedure, so that juveniles are not subject to unnecessary restrictions.

The principle of minimum intervention in Rule 3 refers to the sentencing stage. Sanctions and measures should be imposed "*for the minimum necessary period*". Rule 9 contains the same idea but for the level of the execution of sanctions and measures, and Rule 10 emphasises this idea with regards to deprivation of liberty (see below).

Rule 4 stipulates that the law should set a minimum age for any type of intervention resulting from an offence. This includes the determination of the age of criminal responsibility as well as the age from which more punitive penal measures can be taken. It follows directly from the universally recognised principle of legality: the condition for any criminal liability is that the criminalized behaviour and the possible offender must be described by law. The principle of legality applies in the same way to other types of intervention.

The age of criminal responsibility has to correspond to "an internationally acceptable age" (see United Nations, Committee of the Rights of the Child, General Comment No. 10 (2007), para. 32, CRC/C/GC/10, 25 April 2007). Although it might be difficult to find a general European consensus, such a minimum age should not be too low and should be related to the age at which juveniles assume civil responsibilities in other spheres such as marriage, end of compulsory schooling and employment. The majority of countries have fixed the minimum age between 14 and 15 years and this standard should be followed in Europe. Criminal responsibility for juveniles of less than 12 years exists only in a few countries such as England and Wales and Switzerland (see chapter 13, Table 1).

In any case, very young offenders who are formally criminally liable should not be admitted to juvenile penitentiary institutions. In some countries the age for admission to such institutions is 15 (as in Switzerland) or 16, whereas the general age of criminal responsibility might be lower, usually between 12 and 14 years.

Rule 5 provides that all sanctions and measures must be subject to what is in the best interests of the juvenile, and this needs to be established in every individual case. This implies regular assessments by social workers, psychologists, psychiatrists or other professionals. On the other hand, the best interests of the juvenile should not be an excuse for excessive or disproportionate interventions. Measures that promote social integration are generally in the best interests of the juvenile.

This Rule contains two further interrelated principles. The principle of individualisation is inherent in traditional juvenile justice. When a sanction or a measure is imposed, the age, physical and mental well-being, development, capacities and personal circumstances of the offender shall be taken into consideration. Information about these individual circumstances of the juvenile will usually be obtained from psychological, psychiatric or social inquiry reports and therefore a multi-agency approach as indicated in Rule 15 is necessary. The principle of proportionality serves as a corrective to avoid extended educational sanctions or measures that cannot be justified in terms of the gravity of the offence. The principle of individualisation should, therefore, *not* be used to justify interventions that are disproportionately severe with respect to the offence.

Rule 6 stipulates that in the implementation of sanctions and measures a certain degree of discretion must be given to the implementing authorities in order to meet the individual circumstances of each case. This should, however, not lead to serious inequality of treatment. There should be careful documentation of the sentencing practice as well as of the implementation of sanctions and measures. To avoid discrimination, particular attention must be paid to identifying local, cultural, ethnic and other differences and determining whether a different treatment would be justified in order to achieve the same results of social reintegration, education and prevention of re-offending.

Rule 7 prohibits any violation of human dignity. Overcrowding in institutions and harsh, military-type regimes, solitary confinement, depriving juveniles of social contacts are examples of what should be avoided. Equally, some forms of community work can also stigmatise juvenile offenders and would not be consistent with this rule (special uniforms which identify them as offenders, etc.).

Rule 8 corresponds to Rule 102.2 of the EPR. There should be no forms of implementation of sanctions or measures that aggravate their afflictive character, for example, by hard and degrading work either in prisons or as a form of community service. Therefore, different regimes in juvenile penitentiary institutions which are (for punitive reasons) related to the gravity of the offence are not allowed. Overcrowding is one of the well-known circumstances that can endanger the well-being and physical or mental integrity of detained juveniles. An undue risk of physical or mental harm can be caused by exposing detained juveniles to other detainees who are dangerous or violent. Conditions of detention that are not sufficiently stimulating and social or sensory deprivation of any kind are prohibited by Rule 8. As far as community sanctions are concerned, special emphasis should be given to avoiding stigmatising or humiliating conditions (see also Rule 7 above).

Rule 9 refers to the principle of the speedy implementation of sanctions and measures. Undue delay is undesirable also because it undermines the effectiveness of the interventions. Rule 9 relates to Rule 5 and limits community sanctions or measures as well as deprivation of liberty to the minimum necessary. Therefore, review schemes must be provided by law that can shorten the execution of a sentence where continued enforcement does not seem to be necessary for the social integration of the juvenile offender. All countries have introduced early release schemes concerning imprisonment. Community sanctions and measures can also be adjusted in order to lessen their negative impact, or their duration may be reduced. The principle of minimum intervention also better protects human rights and preserves social ties while not increasing the risks posed to society.

Rule 10 reflects No. 37 of the UN Convention on Children's Rights, Rule 17 of the Beijing Rules and the Council of Europe's Recommendation No. R (87) 20 concerning "Social Reactions to Juvenile Delinquency" as well as Recommendation Rec (2003) 20 on "New Ways of Dealing with Juvenile Delinquency and the Role of Juvenile Justice". It follows from Rule 9 on minimum intervention and emphasises that deprivation of liberty should only be a measure of last resort: normally other, less intrusive sanctions should have been tried first. The Beijing Rules give examples of what is meant by the provision that deprivation of liberty shall be limited to "exceptional cases": Deprivation of liberty shall be restricted to older juveniles involved in violent or persistent serious offending. Many national legislations have responded to this idea by raising the age for being sentenced to youth custody or youth imprisonment to a minimum of 15 or 16 years, whereas the general age of criminal responsibility might be lower (see Table 3.1 and the commentary to Rule 4 above).

Furthermore, deprivation of liberty is also to be restricted to the minimum necessary period. This is important as it prevents detention from being unnecessarily prolonged, for instance, in order to complete educational and treatment programmes or other forms of interventions. Instead, there should be provisions so that juvenile offenders who have been released early can complete such programmes outside of the institution. Even where the initial deprivation of liberty is also linked to other goals, for instance, retribution, it must be clear that preparing the juvenile for reintegration into society becomes increasingly important as the implementation of the sanction progresses ("progressive principle"). The final decision remains with the judicial authority that has the legal power to order the deprivation of liberty.

The problem of pre-trial detention is already emphasised by Rules 16–18 of the Recommendation Rec (2003) 20. It reflects the empirical evidence that pre-trial detention is used extensively in many countries, for longer than justified and for purposes that are not provided by law; for example, as a form of crisis intervention or for reducing public concern. Therefore, Rule 16 of Rec (2003) 20 states: "When, as a last resort, juvenile suspects are remanded in custody, this should not be for longer than six months before the commencement of the trial." In addition, Rule 17 of the above Recommendation clearly outlines that "where possible, alternatives to remand in custody should be used for juvenile suspects, such as placements with relatives, foster families or other forms of supported accommodation. Custodial remand should never be used as a punishment or form of intimidation or as a substitute for child protection or mental health measures." The present Rules incorporate these restrictions on pre-trial detention by requiring that "special efforts must be undertaken to avoid pre-trial detention".

The principle of non-discrimination laid out in *Rule 11* is a basic principle in all human rights instruments of the Council of Europe and the United Nations (see, for example, art. 14 of the ECHR and Rule 13 of the EPR). It does not mean that formal equality should be the ideal if it would result in substantive inequality. Protection of vulnerable groups is not discrimination, nor is treatment that is tailored to the special needs of individual juvenile offenders. Therefore, this principle is not infringed by special positive measures aimed at addressing juvenile offenders or groups of juvenile offenders with specific needs.

Rule 12 emphasises mediation and other restorative justice measures that have become important forms of intervention in juvenile welfare and justice systems. In many countries recent national legislation gives priority to mediation and restorative justice as methods of diversion from formal proceedings at various stages in the juvenile justice process. These strategies should be considered at all stages of dealing with juveniles and be given priority because of their special preventive advantages for the juvenile offenders as well as for the victims and the community.

Rule 13 includes the right to be informed, to have access to legal remedies, to legal assistance, complaints procedures and other procedural rights and safeguards (see also Rule 15, Recommendation Rec (2003) 20). The principle of effective participation in this case refers to the stage of imposition as well as of execution of sanctions and measures. Independently of which specific model of criminal investigation and procedure is followed, the juveniles and their parents or legal guardians must be informed about the offence or offences the juveniles are alleged to have committed and the evidence against them. The juveniles have the right to legal defence counsel also in purely welfare proceedings. In cases where deprivation of liberty is possible, a legal defence counsel must be allocated to the juveniles from the outset of the procedure. The Rule makes it clear that there is no justification for giving juveniles lesser rights than adults. Therefore regulations that restrict the right to appeal or complaints procedures with arguments of education cannot be justified. Other examples refer to issues of data protection: The more comprehensive social inquiry reports and case records within the juvenile justice and welfare system should not be transferred to criminal records that could possibly disadvantage juvenile offenders in their later adult life. Juvenile criminal records should include only serious sanctions and interventions in order to prevent stigmatisation as far as possible.

Rule 14 emphasises the rights and responsibilities of parents and legal guardians to participate at all stages of investigations and proceedings. This is already inherent in the general principle of effective participation. However, it is important to stress the parents' or legal guardians' individual rights of participation. Nevertheless, these rights can be restricted if parents or guardians act against the best interests of the juvenile. The need for such restrictions should be assessed by psychologists or other professional staff of the juvenile welfare authorities and formally decided by the judicial authorities. While the participation of parents or legal guardians of juveniles is generally mandatory, this is not the case for young adults who have reached the age of civil majority. Nevertheless, their participation may still be desirable, especially if the young adults still live with them. Even if the juveniles' parents and guardians live abroad, attempts should be made to contact them. Where these parents and guardians cannot participate, their place should be taken where appropriate by an appointed representative. Restrictions may also be imposed where required by ongoing criminal investigations, but only for the period for which it is strictly necessary.

Proceedings against juveniles and the execution of resulting sanctions and measures take place in a wider context in which family members and the wider community may have a role to play where this is applicable and can have a positive impact on the juvenile and society. One example of such community involvement is the execution of a community sanction or measure where the local community is by definition involved. Reintegration after deprivation of liberty also necessarily supposes acceptance by and interaction with the local community. This too is subject to the principle that such involvement must be in the best interests of the juvenile. The corollary of Rule 14 is that juveniles have a right to have contact with the members of their family.

The characteristics of juveniles require a specific multi-disciplinary and multi-agency approach. This is emphasised by *Rule 15*. The key disciplines to be included are psychology, social work and education. The multi-agency approach is a normal form of co-operation between youth welfare and justice agencies in many countries. Social workers, the police, school and vocational training authorities, prosecutors and juvenile judges as well as lay organisations of juvenile welfare should work closely together in order to act in the best interests of the juvenile. The multi-agency approach should involve as fully as possible agencies and organisations outside the justice system, for they may be socially and environmentally closer to the juvenile. In this context the principle of through care is of major importance.

The principle of "end to end" offender management where a community-based social worker or probation officer maintains contact with the offender throughout the sentence is of particular value in providing continuity of care. Discharge arrangements should be planned carefully so that continuity of care is ensured. Institutions for the deprivation of liberty must work closely together with aftercare services and other relevant welfare agencies. However, data protection concerns must be borne in mind when cooperating in this way.

Rule 16 emphasises the rights to privacy and data protection. Juvenile offenders and their families have specific rights to privacy to protect them from negative stigmatisation. This recognises the need to help juveniles in their development to adulthood. Rule 16 places a duty on the state to provide the necessary protection for juvenile offenders and their families. In particular, the identity of juveniles and their families should not be communicated to anyone who is not legally authorised to be informed thereof.

Legal authorisation to receive information must be limited strictly to persons and institutions that require particular information related to a specific case. This should not lead to the public disclosure of entire lists of names of specific juvenile offenders. It follows too that only information that is necessary for this purpose should be collected in the first place.

Rule 17 deals with young adult offenders. Recommendation Rec (2003) 20 states in Rule 11 that "reflecting the extended transition to adulthood, it should be possible for young adults under the age of 21 to be treated in a way comparable to juveniles and to be subject to the same interventions, when the judge is of the opinion that they are not as mature and responsible for their actions as full adults". Similarly, Rule 3.3 of the Beijing Rules states: "Efforts shall also be made to extend the principles embodied in the Rules to young adult offenders." Rule 17 continues in the same vein. Young adults in general are in a transitional stage of life, which can justify their being dealt with by the juvenile justice agencies and juvenile courts. Particularly in the past 15 years, many countries have taken into consideration this extended period of transition by either providing the possibility of applying educational measures to young adult offenders or at least by providing for special mitigation of their sentences (see, for a summary, Pruin 2007; Dünkel and Pruin 2008). Applying sanctions or measures provided under the juvenile criminal law does not automatically mean that young adults will receive milder sanctions than adults over the age of 21; but where appropriate, they should benefit from the variety of educational sanctions and measures that are provided for juvenile offenders. It is an evidence-based policy to encourage legislators to extend the scope of juvenile justice to the age group of young adults. Processes of education and integration into the social life of adults have been prolonged and more appropriate constructive reactions with regard to the particular developmental problems of young adults can often be found in juvenile justice legislation (see for example the special emphasis given to mediation, and family conferencing in many new juvenile justice laws).

Rule 18 corresponds to Rule 8 of the EPR and places the staff of juvenile welfare and justice agencies or institutions at the centre of caring for juvenile offenders as they need special and intensive assistance. Rule 18 is strongly related to Rule 15 emphasising the co-operation of different agencies involved (multi-agency approach). All staff in the field of juvenile welfare and justice must be suitable for working with juveniles and be specially trained or experienced in developmental and educational matters. Regular in-service training and supervision should be provided. Positive role models are particularly important, as in many instances staff has to play the role which is normally taken by members of the juvenile's family. The standards of care and accountability apply not only when staff is employed on a permanent basis but also when execution is delegated to, or commissioned from, other agencies.

Rule 19 is related to Rule 18 and is designed to clarify that juvenile welfare and justice agencies must receive the necessary funding in order to achieve the required educational and social integration goals. The different agencies must be equipped in a way that enables them to provide the appropriate standard of care to meet the distinctive needs of juveniles. This can also mean that services are allocated according to different needs and risks posed by offenders. The rule corresponds to Rule 4 of the EPR. It conveys the message that lack of resources can never justify the infringement of human rights of juveniles. By imposing sanctions or measures on juvenile offenders the state intervenes at an age where normally the family is responsible for the juvenile's upbringing. If the state partially replaces the parents it must guarantee that its interventions are meaningful, positive, and effective.

Rule 20 reflects the necessity of regular government inspection as well as of independent monitoring. This Rule corresponds to Rule 9 of the EPR. Independent monitoring by persons or institutions that are not controlled by state agencies is an essential and important element of democratic control as it may guarantee effective supervision of the general juvenile justice system that is independent from individual complaints procedures. The Rule envisages monitoring by recognised bodies such as boards of visitors or accredited NGOs, ombudsmen and other similar agencies. An effective individual complaints procedure available to juveniles concerning the imposition and execution of sanctions and measures complements the inspection and monitoring mechanisms.

Chapter 4
Criminal Responsibility of Adolescents: Youth as Junior Citizenship

Ido Weijers and Thomas Grisso

Children below a certain age are too young to be held responsible for breaking the law. There is wide consensus about this principle, which is spelled out in the Convention on the Rights of the Child and in other international standards, such as the Beijing Rules for juvenile justice. The Convention calls for nations to establish a minimum age "below which children shall be presumed not to have the capacity to infringe the penal law". And since the beginning of this year (2008) it sets 12 as the minimum age, explicitly. Worldwide, though, there is continuing debate about the appropriate age. This debate too often tends to arise when exceptional cases involving children who have committed heinous offences are given prominent coverage by the media. Sometimes this has far-reaching consequences.

In England, children have become fully accountable for offending at 10 since the murder of two-year-old James Bulger by two young boys, both 10, in 1993. In New South Wales, the 1999 manslaughter trial of an 11-year-old boy for throwing his 6-year-old companion into a river attracted widespread comment and the NSW Attorney-General started a review of the age of criminal responsibility of children. In Japan, the minimum age was lowered from 16 to 14 in 2001 following public outrage over the brutal beheading of a little boy by a 14-year-old in 1997. The murder of another youth by a 12-year-old in 2003 in Nagasaki prompted the discussion again. In the USA, the state of Arkansas lowered the age at which young people could be tried as adults for murder to age 11, after an 11-year-old and a 13-year-old killed a youth with rifles at the entrance to their school. In the Czech Republic the minimum age is 15, but the Minister of Justice is considering lowering the age for particularly serious crimes, since in August 2006, six boys under the age of 15 robbed and killed an elderly woman and in February 2007 a 14-year-old boy confessed to the rape and murder of a classmate.

Experts working in this forensic field usually operate lists of criteria for assessing whether a young person could be found to be criminally responsible. They consider biological criteria such as constitutional abnormality, physical development,

I. Weijers (✉)
Faculty of Social Sciences – Pedagogic, University of Utrecht, Utrecht, The Netherlands

T. Grisso
Department of Psychiatry, University of Massachusetts, Worcester, Ma 01655, USA

J. Junger-Tas and F. Dünkel (eds.), *Reforming Juvenile Justice*,
DOI: 10.1007/978-0-387-89295-5_4, © Springer Science+Business Media, LLC 2009

brain damage, endocrinal and mental disorders, and sociological–psychological criteria concerning milieu, mental–moral maturity, neurotic tendencies and the significance of puberty for the act. They also consider personality factors such as contacts with others, structure of relationships, feeling of self-worth, frustration tolerance, and usually they analyse possibly stressful events and the situation at the moment of the offence. From their professional, diagnostic focus on individual stories, many of them will emphasise that there can be no universal checklist or overarching criteria for criminal responsibility or maturity.

Others have suggested though that it might very well be possible to say something in general about the age of criminal responsibility. Several authors seem to be convinced that by the age of 14 young persons are generally mature enough to be held criminally responsible (that is, in juvenile court) unless there is some exceptional circumstance, such as considerable developmental delay. Some even go further. They state that the understanding of the wrongfulness of punishable acts can already be presumed for 12- or 10-year-old children, as long as there is no extraordinary set of circumstances.

Another point of view has been expressed recently by the Scottish Law Commission, the official law reform body in Scotland. In Scotland the lower age limit of criminal responsibility has remained 8 years since the thirties, which is strikingly low in comparison with other European countries. However, instead of recommending a higher minimum age, the Commission proposed abolition of the rule that a child has no criminal capacity below a certain age (Scottish Law Commission 2002).[1] The Commission had three arguments for this proposal (Maher 2005). First, it argued that today 8-year-old children have a greater understanding of the world than children of this age had in the past. This might suggest, in its opinion, that there could be a case for lowering the age in the Scottish rule. Second, the Commission argued that if an age of criminal responsibility was a matter of applying developmental psychology, then why was there such disparity in the ages adopted in different countries? Finally, it quoted the findings of the well-known Kilbrandon Committee, that stated that the principle that children below a certain age are too young to be held responsible for breaking the law was not based on any empirical data concerning children's understanding: "The legal presumption by which no child under the age of 8 can be subjected to criminal proceedings is not therefore a reflection of any observable fact (…) It is clear, therefore, that the 'age of criminal responsibility' is largely a meaningless term" (Committee 1964, 73).

This chapter intends to throw new light on the question of the age of criminal responsibility by bringing together some criminological findings, data from empirical research and theoretical insights. It will present an overview of the international state of affairs concerning legal regulation of the criminal responsibility of children. Then in order to obtain some idea of the often opaque, or at least not transparent,

---

[1] This recommendation, however, was clearly not inspired by a call to be tougher on youth crime. The Commission confirmed the characteristic rule in Scots criminal law, that no child under the age of 16 should be prosecuted for any offense except on the instructions of the Lord Advocate (Criminal Procedure Act 1995, c. 46, § 42).

reality concealed behind these rules, several practical implications from a variety of perspectives and experiences will be discussed. This is followed by an overview of findings from developmental studies. It will become clear that, contrary to the conclusions of the Scottish Law Commission, recent research provides relevant scientific data concerning children's understanding. Next, a conceptual framework for the evaluation of these findings will be discussed. The chapter will conclude with some suggestions for guidelines for the age limits in criminal law. We start, however, with a short historical introduction, which will make clear that "the age of criminal responsibility" is a layered concept with different meanings.

Historical Introduction

The principle that children below a certain age may not be held responsible for breaking the law is not a modern idea that just emerged with the Convention on the Rights of the Child or the Beijing Rules. On the contrary, a special concern for the treatment of young offenders can be found throughout history. Children were punished less severely, or not at all. In classical Roman law children under the age of seven were regarded as not criminally responsible for their acts. This did not suggest a physical incapacity to commit offences, but an incapacity to be held responsible for them. For an act to be regarded as criminal and imputed to the perpetrator, it had to have been committed with *dolus* or "deliberately". *Dolus* or malice aforethought required a certain mental maturity as well as a certain life experience such that the person's judgement could be guided by their understanding. Children under seven could not be guilty of criminal acts because they did not have *dolus capacitas* or capability for evil on purpose.

In later Justinian Roman law a new category became legally relevant, generally between 7 and 12 (girls) or 14 (boys). The very young children could not be guilty of criminal acts under any circumstances, whereas the criminal responsibility of these older children was dependent on whether they were *doli capax*, which meant that evidence could be presented to determine whether they could fully understand the gravity of their offending.

The use of more than one age limit has remained characteristic of the treatment of young offenders for centuries. In Roman law these limits were founded on the idea of being incapable of evil. In Common law a somewhat similar development can be found, founded originally on the idea of the wrongfulness of punishment which gradually evolved towards the notion of mental incapability. In ancient Anglo-Saxon law young age was regarded as a reason for an exception from severe punishment. The law had to protect the young against punishment that would be out of proportion considering their age. From the principle that children under a certain age should generally be punished more mildly than adults, two different age levels of criminal responsibility subsequently emerged. There was an age of absolute criminal incapacity, often called the "age of discretion", which due to the influence of Roman law became fixed at seven. Under the age of seven a child could never be punished (that is, by a court; of course they could be punished by their parents and teachers), and there was an age of conditional criminal responsibility for older children. This implied that they normally would not be punished, but that punishment was possible under certain circumstances, that is, if the child had sufficient criminal capacity. This capacity was dependent on the child's ability to distinguish between good and evil.

The *doli incapax* presumption has been operated in several countries for centuries, both in Common Law and in Civil Law countries. It became very influential in continental Europe at the beginning of the nineteenth century with the introduction of the Code Pénal. It became known as the *"discernement"* principle, which presumed that children above a certain minimum and up to a certain upper age limit normally would not be subject to prosecution proceedings unless that presumption could be rebutted in a specific case. The prosecution had to adduce evidence and the judge had to decide that this child possessed the requisite understanding and knowledge to fully realise that its actions were seriously wrong.

The establishment of special juvenile justice systems at the turn of the nineteenth and twentieth century implied the introduction of another age limit. In general, special juvenile justice systems confirmed the lower age limit, below which children were considered too young to be held responsible for breaking the law under any circumstances, although in many cases they also raised this limit. However, they also introduced an upper age limit, beyond which young people were considered old enough to be prosecuted for breaking the law, like an adult. Generally, the new juvenile justice systems implied that children could be prosecuted in a special youth court, according to special youth procedures with special youth sanctions. In several countries, though, the *doli incapax* presumption remained intact, which meant that, normally, children were not brought into the youth court immediately after attaining the lower age limit of the juvenile justice system.

This resulted in two different implications for the lower age limit of criminal responsibility. In some jurisdictions children from this age can be prosecuted in juvenile court; in others, children are prosecuted some years later than this age in juvenile court, because of (a version of) the *doli incapax* presumption. We will come back to this point in Practical Implications. Some jurisdictions, however, did not establish a special juvenile justice system. This is the case in the Scandinavian countries in particular. Here a third variation of the lower age limit of criminal responsibility can be found, that has to be distinguished again from a fourth variation, where the age of criminal responsibility means that a person of that age can be held fully responsible in criminal court, as an adult. In the Scandinavian countries, on the other hand, where 15 years is recognized as the age of criminal responsibility, special legislation still applies for juveniles until they reach 21 years.

Legal Regulations

The historical outline points to a rather complex and diverse set of concepts concerning criminal responsibility and the appropriate age. This complexity and great diversity is typical for this field. Countries vary far more widely in juvenile than in adult justice systems, as Michael Tonry and Anthony Doob have rightly observed (Tonry and Doob 2004: VII). "Whatever else a sentence was said to accomplish, it would be seen unambiguously as punishment by the community and by the person subject to it. Sentencing systems in many countries have changed in the last thirty years – sometimes dramatically – but the focus of the sentence is more likely to be on the severity of punishment, rather than its purposes" (Tonry and Doob 2004: 3).

This statement may be too strong in some cases, in particular for continental Western Europe – think for instance of the special treatment tradition for forensic psychiatric patients in the Netherlands. The point being made by Tonry and Doob, however, is clear and true: juvenile justice systems do not have these basic similarities. This holds for the age boundaries, sentences and educational measures, and it is even more striking from a wider perspective. There is a huge variety in definitions and purposes of juvenile justice. This is easily illustrated by the phenomenon of the "status offences". These imply behaviour that is prohibited only because of a person's status as a minor. Although this is well known in some jurisdictions, it has always been completely unacceptable in others. There is an enormous range of formal and purported normative differences. Juvenile justice systems vary widely in their structural details and in their policy premises, in their age jurisdictions and particularly in their practical implications and elaborations of these age jurisdictions.

These upper age jurisdictions vary worldwide between 15 and 18, with one exception (Japan: 20; Austria lowered its age for adult criminal court jurisdiction recently from 19 to 18). This is only superficially a small margin. In fact, these small margins are profoundly relativised by a wide variety of options to transfer or waive young offenders to adult criminal court (see chapters. 4 and 5 in this volume).

Looking at the lower age limits of criminal responsibility worldwide, however, we find extreme contrasts. At one extreme there is 6 years in North Carolina and at the other extreme 16 years of age in Belgium. Among the 100 countries and states for which we have been able to collect data, three main groups emerge: 12 countries and 3 American states have 7 years; 11 American and 7 Australian states and 7 countries have 10 years; and 21 countries have 14 years as their age of criminal responsibility (see Table 4.1).

Europe and the Rest of the World

There are interesting differences between continents. In Europe, the absolute lower age limit below which children cannot be held criminally responsible varies from 8 (Scotland) to 16 (Belgium).[2] The dominant European picture, however, is represented by the large group of countries where 14 is the age of criminal responsibility. Overall, this results in 13 years as the average and typical age of criminal responsibility in Europe as shown in Table 4.2.

---

[2] In Belgium children cannot normally be held criminally responsible before their 18th birthday, but in the case of murder or manslaughter they can be held criminally responsible from their 16th birthday.

Table 4.1 Lower age limit of criminal responsibility worldwide

Country/State	Age	Country/State	Age
North Carolina	6	Ukraine	10
Egypt	7	Vermont	10
		Victoria	10
Ghana	7	Western Australia	10
India	7	Wisconsin	10
Malawi	7	Brazil	12
Maryland	7	Canada	12
Massachusetts	7	Colombia	12
New York	7	Jamaica	12
Nigeria	7	Korea, Republic	12
Pakistan	7	Morocco	12
Singapore	7	Netherlands	12
South Africa	7	Peru	12
Sudan	7	Portugal	12
Arizona	8	Turkey	12
Bermuda	8	Uganda	12
Indonesia	8	Algeria	13
Kenya	8	France	13
Scotland	8	Greece	13
Sri Lanka	8	Israel	13
Zambia	8	Poland	13
Bangladesh	9	Uzbekistan	13
Ethiopia	9	Albania	14
Iran	9	Armenia	14
Philippines	9	Austria	14
Arkansas	10	Bosnia-Herzegovina	14
Australian Capital Territory	10	Bulgaria	14
Colorado	10	China	14
Cyprus	10	Croatia	14
England	10	Estonia	14
Fiji	10	Germany	14
Guyana	10	Hungary	14
Hong Kong	10	Italy	14
Ireland	10	Japan	14
Kansas	10	Latvia	14
Louisiana	10	Lithuania	14
Malaysia	10	Romania	14
Minnesota	10	Russia	14
Mississippi	10	Serbia	14
Nepal	10	Slovenia	14
New South Wales	10	Spain	14
New Zealand	10	Taiwan	14
Pennsylvania	10	Vietnam	14
Queensland	10	Czech Republic	15
South Australia	10	Denmark	15
South Dakota	10	Finland	15
Switzerland	10	Iceland	15
Tanzania	10	Norway	15
Tasmania	10	Sweden	15
Texas	10	Slovakia	15
		Belgium	16

Table 4.2 Youngest age for juvenile court jurisdiction and adult criminal court jurisdiction in Europe (European Sourcebook 2006)

Country	Youngest age	
	Juvenile court	Criminal court
Scotland	8	16
Cyprus	10	18
England	10	18
France	10	18
Ireland	10	18
Switzerland	10	18
Netherlands	12	18
Portugal	12	16
Greece	13	18
Poland	13	17
Albania	14	18
Austria	14	18
Bosnia-Herzegovina	14	18
Bulgaria	14	18
Germany	14	18
Hungary	14	18
Italy	14	18
Croatia	14	18
Latvia	14	18
Lithuania	14	16
Romania	14	18
Serbia	14	18
Slovenia	14	18
Spain	14	18
Czech Rep.	15	18
Denmark	15	15
Finland	15	15
Norway	15	15
Sweden	15	15
Slovakia	15	18
Belgium	16	18

On the other side of the world, in Australia, the lower age limit was raised (following the example of the United Kingdom) from 7 to 8 and then to 10 years. The last jurisdictions to come into line were the Capital Territory and Tasmania, in which the minimum ages were until recently 8 and 7 respectively. This means that Australia is now the only continent with uniform legal regulations on the lower age limit of criminal responsibility.

There is more variation on this point in America than in Australia, but less than in Europe. There is considerable variation across states in the USA, yet there is a clear general trend. Instead of raising the lower age of criminal responsibility, as has been the case in Australia and in Europe, in the USA the trend across the states has been to lower both the minimum and the maximum jurisdictional limits

(Bishop and Decker 2006). The age of criminal responsibility is 6 in North Carolina, 7 in Maryland, Massachusetts and New York, 8 in Arizona, and 10 in 11 other states (Table 4.3).[3]

This does not mean, though, that children of this age are automatically prosecuted. It is often concluded that the minimum age in the United States is "typically" 10, but this holds only for these 11 states. Much more typical for the United States is that the vast majority of states do *not* have a minimum age for criminal responsibility. Currently, although all have jurisdiction over truancy beginning at ages five, six or seven, the juvenile codes in 33 states do not indicate a minimum age of jurisdiction for delinquency cases (Bishop and Decker 2006). This means in fact, that we do not know the typical lower age limit of criminal responsibility in the United States.

We encounter similar problems in Asia, Africa and the rest of the world. We have data from 31 European countries, but we have far less data from other continents (13 in Africa and 15 in Asia, as is shown in Tables 4.4 and 4.5).[4]

Nonetheless, from the data we have collected a rather clear picture emerges: the European average level of 13 years is not typical in the rest of the world. The average of this selection of 100 countries and states is 10 years of age, which corresponds with the typical age of criminal responsibility in Australia (and in our selection of Asian countries). In our selection of American states and African countries the

Table 4.3 Youngest age for juvenile court jurisdiction and adult criminal court jurisdiction in the United States (Juvenile Offenders and Victims: 2006 National Report, 103)

State	Youngest age	
	Juvenile court	Criminal court
North Carolina	6	16
New York	7	16
Massachusetts	7	16
Maryland	7	18
Arizona	8	18
Arkansas	10	18
Colorado	10	18
Kansas	10	18
Louisiana	10	17
Minnesota	10	18
Mississippi	10	18
Pennsylvania	10	18
South Dakota	10	18
Texas	10	17
Vermont	10	18
Wisconsin	10	17

[3] The majority of states use age 17 as the maximum age of juvenile court jurisdiction, ten states use 16 and three states use 15.

[4] Since a lot of data from African and Asian countries were collected relatively long ago, there may have been changes since the year of collection.

Table 4.4 Age of criminal responsibility in Africa (UN, Implementation of UN Mandates on Juvenile Justice in ESCAP, 1994)

Country	Age
Nigeria	7
South Africa	7
Sudan	7
Kenya	8
Ethiopia	9
Ghana	9
Tanzania	10
Morocco	12
Uganda	12
Algeria	13
Egypt	15

Table 4.5 Age of criminal responsibility in Asia (UN, Implementation of UN Mandates on Juvenile Justice in ESCAP, 1994)

Country	Age
Bangladesh	7
Pakistan	7
Singapore	7
Thailand	7
Indonesia	8
Sri Lanka	8
Philippines	9
Hong Kong	10
Nepal	10
India	12
Korea, Republic	12
China	14
Japan	14
Vietnam	14

average age is nine. This might indicate that international conventions such as the European Convention for the Protection of Human Rights and Fundamental Liberties and the United Nations Convention on the Rights of the Child are taken seriously in both Western and Eastern Europe.

Practical Implications

What does this overview of national legal regulations on the lower age limit of criminal responsibility tell us? What is the reality behind these rules? In the "Historical Introduction" above we pointed to the different meanings of the notion of "the age of criminal responsibility", which made clear, in particular, that these regulations do not necessarily indicate when a youth can be prosecuted. One of the other striking differences hidden behind these rules has to do with the extent of conformity or discrepancy between legal regulations in the field of criminal law and other regulatory fields in countries and states. This is what Franklin Zimring called a "test of the quality of any punishment policy": does juvenile justice policy say the same things about the nature of growing up as the legal rules that govern the advancement to adult status in other legal categories (Zimring 2000, 285)? To give just two examples: in Hong Kong, 7-year-old children are viewed as criminally responsible (with rebuttable presumption of *doli incapax* until 14), but young persons may marry only when they are 16 and they need parental consent to marry until they are 21; in several American states, youths aged younger than 10 are held responsible for violations of the criminal law but the minimum drinking age is 21.

This section will focus on the actual implications of the legal regulations. We do not have enough data to survey the implications of the age boundaries for penal liability of children in all these 100 countries and states. This section will therefore just present some intriguing, not immediately obvious findings, concealed behind the rules. First, we will look at two phenomena that indicate a recent tendency of indifference to the importance of absolute lower age limits. Then, we will study two phenomena that point to the acknowledgement of a special legal status for youths.

Skirting the Rules

There is a strong tendency in several countries to relativise the legal regulations set out in the age lists above. "Nipping crime in the butt" to fight "physical and moral degeneration of the neighbourhood" is one of the strong and explicit motives. This has been an avowed aim of British New Labour, in particular, since the mid-nineties. Inspired by the "broken windows" theory, developed in the USA by Wilson and Kelling, it held that zero-tolerance policing was required to achieve "public safety and the re-generation of social life in Britain". From this perspective the Home Office stated in 1997 in its consultation paper *Tackling Youth Crime*, that "children under ten need help to change their bad behaviour just as much as older children" (pp. 98–99).

From the same perspective the Crime and Disorder Act 1998 introduced two new interventions directed towards very young children. First, local authorities were provided with general local curfews in their area for children under ten (Bottoms and Dignan 2004).[5] Second, the magistrates court was provided with a power to impose a Child Safety Order on a child under ten. There have always been child protection measures for cases of parental neglect or other situations where there is grave concern about the family circumstances of children. The crucial new thing is that a Child Safety Order implies punitive interventions both for the child

---

[5] There has been reluctance on the part of the local authorities to invoke this power. By the end of 2002, not a single child curfew order had been applied for.

and for his parent. The child can be placed under the supervision of a social worker or member of the local youth offending team for between 3 and 12 months and must participate in any intervention deemed necessary to prevent the behaviour recurring. The parent of the child may be subject to a "parenting order" and required by the court to take appropriate care and control of the child as well as fulfilling other conditions, as deemed necessary. The child safety order is founded in civil law as the child is under the age of criminal responsibility. The behaviour of the child which may prompt an order is offending and antisocial behaviour, so it is clear, according to various commentators, that the order represents an attempt to circumvent the minimum age of criminal responsibility (Fionda 2005; Rutherford 2000).[6]

In the Netherlands a similar intervention for children under the age of criminal responsibility (which is 12 in this country) was created in the same period, though it is founded in criminal law. This intervention has been called *Stop*. It has nothing to do with child protection and does not address specific problems of the child or the family. It is inadequate as an educational intervention and explicitly not meant as such. It is a variation of *Halt*, the very popular light punishment for first offenders.[7] Children carry out up to 20 h of work, training and/or restorative activities for *Halt*. The Guidelines of the Board of the Procurator General advise that nearly all cases of police intervention with children should be referred to *Halt*, which implies that the traditional police caution has almost vanished (van der Laan 2006). *Stop* introduced this approach for children under 12 nationwide in 2001. These young children may be ordered to participate for a maximum of 10 h in '*Halt*-like' activities. Since these children are under the age of criminal responsibility, *Stop* requires parental consent. *Stop* is operating now almost everywhere in the Netherlands, but it has been seriously criticised on principle right from the start (Bruins 1999; Quispel 2000).

Stop depends on police discretion. Police discretion is a rarely studied phenomenon, but it probably exists in many countries. New Zealand, for instance, has an age of criminal responsibility of ten, but that does not rule out earlier police intervention. Younger children can get warnings, they may be asked to write apologies, or do community work or reparation, follow a program and they may receive a curfew or some other restriction (Morris 2004).

The Child Safety Order, *Stop* and police-directed interventions for very young children are clearly all attempts and accepted practices to skirt the legal regulations on the age of criminal responsibility as an absolute bar to prosecution. This implies a conflict with article 40.3.a of the Convention on the Rights of the Child, which does not set a specific minimum age of criminal responsibility but demands the establishment of a minimum age "below which children shall be presumed not to

---

[6] Once again, there has been resistance on the part of social workers and youth offending teams to invoke this power. It is generally thought that children under ten should be dealt with within the essentially separate English child protection system (Newburn 2002; Bottoms and Dignan 2004).
[7] *Halt* is known to be not particularly effective, mainly because it does not address nor even assess the specific needs of children (Ferwerda et al. 2006).

have the capacity to infringe the penal law". Child Safety Orders, *Stop* and police discretion were generally created for petty offences and antisocial behaviour. *Stop* is explicitly meant as a minimal intervention (which raises questions both about its justification and its effectiveness, of course). The Child Safety Order and the imposition of programmes and curfews may intervene at a deeper level, but much more questionable are the interventions that are specifically directed at serious offending. That will be discussed in the next section, in which we will look at the new transfer policies in the United States.

Transfer and Mandatory Sentencing

The trial of Nathaniel Abraham in 1999 in Oakland County, Michigan, for first-degree murder made this young boy into a "poster child for the troubled state of American juvenile justice" (Tanenhaus 2004, XXIII). Two years before, when Nathaniel was only 11, he had stolen a rifle and shot an unknown person from a hilltop more than 200 ft from his victim. Abraham had confessed to firing the rifle, but denied aiming at anyone. The prosecutors depicted him as a premeditated killer who knew what he was doing. Amnesty International reprinted an AP photo of the African-American child on the cover of its report entitled *Betraying the Young* (Nov. 1998). The trial, which Court TV broadcast in its entirety, received international attention.

The judge could decide to sentence Abraham to a juvenile sentence, or as an adult, or to use a staggered sentence first in a juvenile detention centre and retain the possibility of imposing an adult sentence later. This case made clear, to many people outside the United States in particular, that during the last decades of the past century a major shift had occurred in the American juvenile justice system, as part of the "get tough" reforms for serious offenders. Statutes had been passed that circumvented the traditional mode of transfer – a waiver hearing in juvenile court. New "statutory exclusion" and "prosecutorial waiver" statutes had shifted the responsibility for transfer from the judiciary to the legislative and executive branches and in addition many states had instituted blended sentencing (Bishop and Decker 2006).

This development has important implications for the question of the age of criminal responsibility, since most states have minimum ages for these new statutes, but several do not. Statutory exclusion can be used in eight states at any age (Delaware, Florida, Idaho, Illinois, Mississippi, Nevada, Pennsylvania and Wisconsin). In Florida this can be applied in cases of auto theft and when a youth has been in court three times before. In Pennsylvania it can be applied at any age with prior adjudication and in Idaho in cases of arson. Prosecutorial waiver or "direct file" can be used at any age in Georgia in the case of capital offences and in Nebraska for any felony (Feld 2000).[8] It is clear that these statutes are in fundamental

---

[8] In Texas, blended sentencing is available in juvenile court to include youths as young as 10 years of age (Redding and Howell 2006).

conflict with the Convention on the Rights of the Child. They show a distressing indifference to the recognition of absolute lower age limits in criminal law and of the special needs of youths on trial.

The Age of Prosecution

There is another perspective at work in the field of criminal law, though. This can be demonstrated by studying three phenomena. First, we will look again at the age of prosecution, then at special court proceedings (and their absence) for youths and then at special provisions (and their absence) for the execution of sentences for young offenders.

Despite different circumventing strategies, the age of criminal responsibility is understood in general as denoting a complete bar to prosecution. However, as we said in our historical introduction, this does not necessarily mean that youths will be prosecuted from that age. Many countries do not prosecute youths as soon as they reach this minimum age. They operate a typical compromise, combining two different age levels with more or less discretion. They use the age of criminal responsibility as the upper limit of absolute criminal incapacity and as the beginning of a period of *conditional* criminal responsibility. A well-known formula for this solution is still the use of the *doli incapax* presumption for that period, that holds unless it is rebutted. According to this presumption, youths will not be prosecuted in principle, until they have reached a certain age, some years after the age of criminal responsibility. In practice, there are great differences, both in the period of the presumption and in the actual application of this presumption, which can imply a fundamental change to the principle itself. Different elaborations of the *doli incapax* presumption can be discerned.

A classical version can be found in Ireland, where the age of criminal responsibility is still 7 and where the presumption holds for children from 7 to 14. On raising the minimum age to 12 with the introduction of the Children Act 2001, this presumption was established in principle for children aged over 12 but under 14. However, this aspect was never enacted. This means that in Ireland the old situation, with large discretion for the prosecution and the court and few exact rules as to how the presumption may be rebutted, still continues (Seymour 2006).

Another version can be found in Australia. Here the age of criminal responsibility has been raised to 10 recently and the *doli incapax* presumption applies until the age of 14 years. The meaning of the presumption is limited in practice in that not many prosecutions of very young offenders aged 10 or 11 are pursued, unless the offence is very serious (George Urbas, ANU, personal communication, March 2007). This version also implies that there are formal caution mechanisms that the police can use for more minor crimes. However, the presumption does not give any certainty of non-prosecution of children aged 12 or 13, nor are serious offences normally excluded from prosecution by this modernized version of the presumption.

Another, rather "thin" version is presented by New Zealand, which raised the age of criminal responsibility from 7 to 10 in 1961. Offences committed by those under age 14 became the concern of newly created children's boards, intended to keep them out of the courts. Since the enactment of the Children and Young Persons Act of 1974, New Zealand has distinguished between the age of criminal responsibility (10) and the age of prosecution (14). The Children, Young Persons and their Families Act 1989 introduced family group conferences in New Zealand's youth justice system. Since then the police have been able to choose between a warning, a diversion, a training programme, a curfew, a referral to a family group conference or being charged in the youth court (which may result in a court referral to a family group conference). The only difference in the response to children under 14 and older children is that the older children can be sent to youth court, while this is impossible for children under 14. However, in the case of manslaughter or murder, children aged 10 to 14 can be prosecuted and will be dealt with in adult criminal courts (Morris 2004). We will come back to this type of reasoning in our conclusions.

In England and Wales the *doli incapax* presumption has been abolished. In 1994 Laws J published fierce criticism of it.[9] New Labour responded in 1997 in its consultation paper on youth justice, *Tackling Youth Crime*, suggesting that this presumption prevented youths being held accountable for their actions. One year later, the Home Office paper, *No More Excuses*, announced the abolition of the presumption. The Home Secretary, Jack Straw, made clear that he wanted to break with the history and philosophy of youth justice in England and Wales, which he branded as an "excuse culture" (Bottoms and Dignan 2004). The abolition of the *doli incapax* presumption with the introduction of the Crime and Disorder Act of 1998 was a clear example of breaking with that culture.

This development in England and Wales contrasts sharply with the vicissitudes of the *doli incapax* presumption in Germany. The first striking difference is that in Germany the age of absolute criminal incapacity ends and the age of conditional criminal responsibility starts exactly where full criminal responsibility used to start in England, namely, the age of 14 (Crofts 2002). Full criminal responsibility starts in Germany only at 18 years of age. Another difference has to do with the assessment of the criminal responsibility of the youth. In England and Wales no proof is required of the child's moral evaluation of the act, while in Germany this is a necessary, though not a sufficient, condition for the criminal responsibility of the young person (Crofts 2002). The main difference, of course, is that the principle of an age of conditional criminal responsibility as such has been abolished in England and Wales and remains intact in Germany. However, there is a wide discrepancy between theory and practice. Although the German Youth Court Act doubts that young people have the capacity for criminal responsibility, in practice, they are generally presumed

---

[9] "This presumption is a serious disservice to our law (…) the effect of the presumption is then that a defendant under 14 is assumed to possess a subnormal mental capacity, and for that reason to be *doli incapax*. There can be no justification for such a bizarre state of affairs" (1994, 3 All ER 190, 197, quoted in Fionda, 2005, 15).

to be criminally responsible by the age of 14. Contrary to the Act, exculpation of youths between 14 and 18 is the exception, not the rule (Crofts 2002).

Variations on the German model can be found all over Europe, in the West and the East. In the Czech Republic, for instance, the age of criminal responsibility is 15, but responsibility from age 15 is conditional, depending on the youth's maturity (Válková 2006). Slovenia, to take another example, has a similar system of two age limits. Yugoslavia's first Criminal Code and Criminal Procedure Code (1929) contained provisions pertaining to young offenders. They were divided into two groups: younger (14–17) and older juveniles (17–21). The younger ones were considered relatively irresponsible, which implied that the court could impose a sentence or educational measures only if their maturity was proven. This division remained intact after the Second World War and it was further elaborated with the new legislation of Slovenia in 1995 into four categories: children under 14 who could never be held criminally responsible, young minors (14–16) against whom only educational measures may be applied, older minors (16–18) and young adults (18–21) (Filipcic 2006).

Finally, we will look at a rather exceptional juvenile justice system: Scotland. Here the response to juvenile offending is still based on the legacy of Kilbrandon (1964). In the view of this committee the referral of children to the criminal courts was best understood as a failure in their social education. It recommended the removal of those under 16 years from adult criminal procedures, except for the most severe offences. The welfare of the child should be the paramount concern in decision-making about children, whether they were involved in offending or in need of care and protection. The distinctive Children's Hearing System was a direct result of the deliberations of the committee. A crucial part of this system is the use of two concepts of the age of criminal responsibility. One concerns a rule on criminal capacity, and the other a rule on immunity from criminal prosecution. In Scotland, a child under the age of 8 years cannot be guilty of any offence, as they are considered to lack the mental capacity to commit a crime. The age at which an offender becomes subject to the adult system of prosecution and punishment is 16 years. Children below this age can be prosecuted only on the instructions of the Lord Advocate (Burman et al. 2006).

We may conclude, on the one hand, that Scotland's high place on the list tells us nothing about its strong and almost exclusive welfare orientation. Until recently, children under 16 could not be prosecuted in Scotland. In recent years, though, policy has shifted from child welfare to public safety. Since coming to office in 2001, the First Minister has spearheaded a number of "get tough" initiatives. Most typical of that shift was the introduction in 2004 of the Antisocial Behaviour Act. It is feared that this will impact exponentially on youth and that the new Act represents a new system of social control over children that parallels and cuts across the work of the Children's Hearings system. Some fear the end of an era (Burman et al. 2006). Finally, it is important to note, on the other hand, that the very great majority of 16- and 17-year-old offenders are prosecuted in Scotland in the adult criminal court (Bottoms and Dignan 2004). This is exceptional from a European point of view. Nowhere else in Western Europe are 16- and 17-year-olds routinely dealt with in adult criminal courts (Whyte 2001).

Clearly it is important to know, in addition to the lower age limit from which children can be held responsible for breaking the law, the age at which youths can be prosecuted. It could even be argued that the latter age is more important in fact than the formal age of criminal responsibility.

Court Procedures

Studying another vital dimension of the criminal law system's image and experience – the court proceedings – the observer is touched again by fundamental differences. Some countries, such as the United States, England and Australia, operate juvenile justice systems that are, in their procedures and their outcomes, criminal courts for young offenders. The present American juvenile judge is incomparable with the pioneers of a century ago, who compared themselves with doctors or psychologists, working in direct contact with youth and addressing primarily the problems and needs of the child. English judges have never been in that position. This has little to do with their personalities or characters, but primarily with the court structure, that is with the adversarial tradition that dominates court procedures, even in the youth court (Weijers 2004).

This is a clear contrast with continental Europe, where the inquisitorial tradition is still dominant, certainly in youth courts. Several countries, notably Scotland, Belgium and the Scandinavian countries, have no courts at all for dealing with young offenders under the age of criminal responsibility. They operate systems that are based primarily on child welfare premises, though all with different foci, emphases, and implications. In Denmark, Finland, Iceland, Norway and Sweden offences of adolescents under age 15 are handled outside the criminal justice system; 15-year-olds and older children are dealt with in adult criminal courts. In Scotland this holds for 16-year-olds and in Belgium for 18-year-old youths (apart from the very serious cases, see chapter 5). Other European countries, such as Germany, France, Switzerland, and the Netherlands, have hybrid systems, combining criminal court formalities and rituals with some special procedures, and combining substantive criminal court sentencing and a retributive orientation (proportionality) with a welfare and prevention orientation for young offenders.

We will not develop this dimension further here, but it will be clear that the implications of appearing in court for adolescents are far-reaching (Grisso 2000; Grisso et al. 2003; Masten and Coatsworth 1998; Morris and Giller 1977).

Scientific Evidence

Whether delinquent adolescents should be considered less blameworthy than adults when they engage in illegal behaviours is determined by society's perceptions of adolescents' decision-making capacities. If adolescents are believed to have less mature decision-making capacities than adults, they may be deemed to be deficient in their abilities to consider the consequences of their illegal acts or to avoid engaging in them. This could be relevant in arguments to discount adolescents' degree of culpability when sentencing.

Where is the evidence that adolescents are any different in their decision-making capacities than adults? One of the sources of guidance for society's laws and policies about adolescents' culpability is scientific evidence. An argument for reduced culpability would be supported, at least by some, if there were empirical evidence that adolescents' decision-making capacities were less mature than those of adults.

Before examining that evidence, it is helpful to frame the potential scientific evidence in two ways. First, one should not necessarily expect to find that *most* adolescents have less mature decision-making capacities than most adults. Adolescence typically is identified as the age range from 11 or 12 to 17 or 18, after which individuals are classed as adults (especially for purposes of legal responses to criminal conduct). The concept of development inherently refers to a process of growth. If growth in decision-making abilities is occurring across that age span, it is probably not meaningful to ask whether adolescents in general are different from adults, especially since the differences between adolescents and adults are likely to diminish in the upper age range of the adolescent group. This translates the basic question into at least two, more specific questions. Does growth in decision-making abilities occur during adolescence? If so, what are the approximate ages during adolescence when decision-making abilities are, and are not, significantly different from those of persons that society considers to be "adults"?

Second, one needs to define decision-making within the context of the question of legal culpability. In formal terms, decision-making typically is construed as requiring knowledge (information about the matter about which a decision must be made) and requisite cognitive abilities to process the information in some logical fashion. In everyday life, however, other human factors influence the degree to which knowledge and cognitive capacities actually are applied to decision-making. For example, one may know the consequences of a behaviour, and one may have the cognitive ability to weigh those consequences before acting. Yet neither of these types of abilities will come into play if an individual is deficient in the capacity to delay action long enough for them to be employed, or if the individual discounts the importance of the decision and therefore does not apply his cognitive capacities effectively.

Consider, for example, the following hypothetical situation (from Scott and Grisso 1997). An adolescent is "hanging out" with his friends, when one of them suddenly suggests that they rob a passer-by to get money to buy beer. Others immediately agree and begin moving in on the passer-by. The adolescent goes along with them, having "chosen" to do so not because of some deliberate application of knowledge and cognitive processing, but rather because he does not want to lose standing with his friends. He might literally have knowledge that the act is wrong, as well as the capacity to think of optional ways to extricate himself from the situation, but peer acceptance is very important to him, the event happens quickly, and he has difficulty projecting the course of events as they might unfold. The immediate, concrete gains (peer acceptance, money, excitement) might weigh differently from if he were in circumstances that allowed him to think through the longer-range negative consequences without the emotional qualities of the situation.

This example includes a class of variables that are not usually found in discussions of formal decision-making, but that are relevant for any consideration of adolescents' culpability for bad decisions. They include what have been called "psychosocial factors" that may still be developing during adolescence and that can influence youths' capacities to employ knowledge and cognitive abilities when responding to decision choices. These psychosocial factors have been categorized in recent US literature as (a) susceptibility to peer influence, (b) attitudes toward and perceptions of risk, (c) future orientation and (d) capacity for self-management (Cauffman and Steinberg 2000a; 2000b; Scott et al. 1995; Steinberg and Cauffman 1996). If these psychosocial characteristics are developmental in nature, and if they are still maturing during adolescence, then they represent ways in which adolescents' abilities to make decisions may be different from adults' abilities, in ways that are relevant for laws and policies involving reduced culpability in adolescence.

What, then, is the scientific evidence regarding the ages of adolescence at which cognitive and psychosocial characteristics related to decision-making are substantially different from those of adults? Comprehensive reviews of the evidence have been provided recently by Steinberg and Scott (2003) and Scott and Grisso (2005). The following synthesis of the evidence draws upon those reviews.

Cognitive Abilities

Developmental psychology has established quite good evidence that adolescents in their younger teen years differ a great deal from adults in several cognitive and intellectual ways that influence their decision-making capacities (see generally, Keating 1990; Steinberg 2002). They are still acquiring general knowledge about the world through education and experience, and the ability of younger adolescents to remember, attend to, and process information is not yet that of most adults (Siegler 1997).

In addition, intellectual development during adolescence involves progressive improvements in basic information processing skills, including organisation of information, sustained attention, short- and long-term memory, and verbal fluency. Early adolescence is characterised by gains in deductive reasoning and abstract thinking (for general reviews, see Flavell 1993; Siegler 1997).

The same cumulative research, however, suggests that formal intellectual abilities required for decision-making tend not to increase markedly after about ages 15 to 17. On standardised intelligence tests, for example, the absolute level of cognitive ability or functioning that is required to attain an "average" score for one's peers increases progressively through mid-adolescence, but reaches an apex at an "adult" level of performance around the age of 16. Examining research on the logic of adolescents' decisions about a number of life choices (e.g., medical care), reviewers have asserted that, by mid-adolescence, many youths describe the consequences of hypothetical choices or offer their reasoning about them in ways that are not very different from adults' performance on the same tasks (Weithorn and Campbell 1982; Fischhoff 1992).

From a cognitive perspective, therefore, there is good reason to believe that youths in their early teens on average do not have the knowledge or cognitive capacities of adults whom we hold fully culpable when they make decisions about illegal behaviours. Those differences typically are less significant or non-significant, however, when comparing older adolescents (ages 16–17) to adults.

Psychosocial Abilities

As noted earlier, examining decision-making about illegal behaviours often requires looking beyond cognitive abilities to various psychosocial factors that influence decisions. These psychosocial factors may cause adolescents to make choices differently from adults (or to make different choices from what they themselves would make when they mature), because those factors influence the importance that they attach to various possible consequences of their decisions. To the extent that these psychosocial factors change as a result of development across the adolescent years, they are important to consider when weighing adolescents' culpability for illegal behaviours.

There is considerable evidence that development in adolescence involves changes in the degree to which decisions are made based on *peer influences*. For example, in studies in which adolescents are given the hypothetical choice of an antisocial act suggested by their peers or choosing a more socially acceptable act on their own, the attractiveness of the peer-recommended act increases from about ages 10–14, then gradually decreases across older adolescent age groups (Berndt 1979; Steinberg and Silverberg 1986). This parallels Moffit's (1993) theory about the reason why many delinquent youths in middle adolescence desist from delinquency as they reach older adolescent ages; in middle adolescence they are more likely to be led by delinquent peers and more likely than adults to place emphasis on peer acceptance when making choices, a tendency that decreases as they approach adulthood.

There is evidence that adolescents' *future orientation* undergoes changes across adolescence. Many studies have found that when adults' and adolescents' thoughts about the potential consequences of their choices are examined, adolescents tend more often to focus on immediate rather than long-range possibilities (Gardner and Herman 1990; Greene 1986; Grisso et al. 2003; Halpern-Felsher and Cauffman 2001; Nurmi 1991). If this difference is found in laboratory studies, it is likely to be accentuated in real life, because in stressful situations, time to consider longer-range consequences is naturally attenuated by the need for a quick reaction.

Many studies have demonstrated that *willingness to take risks* changes across adolescence. Adolescents on average are more willing to take risks for the sake of experiencing novel and complex sensations (Arnett 1994). Several studies have concluded that adolescents tend to weigh risks differently from adults, with a greater emphasis on anticipated gains than possible losses or negative risks when making choices (Benthin et al. 1993; Furby and Beyth-Marom 1992; Gardner 1993).

Finally, compared to adults, adolescents appear to be more susceptible to manifesting *impulsive responses* to emotional arousal (Greenberger 1982), even into later adolescent years (Steinberg and Cauffman 1996). Moreover, they have a tendency to greater and more rapid mood swings, suggesting greater difficulty in modulating or regulating their moods and impulses (Larson et al. 1980).

Neuroscientific Evidence

Recent studies involving magnetic resonance imaging of the brain have produced evidence of continued brain maturation through and well beyond the adolescent years. These changes primarily involve continued myelination and "pruning" of neural networks, structural changes that make for more efficient neural functioning. What is of special interest is that the areas of the brain that are continuing to mature through adolescence appear to have functions related to the psychosocial developmental factors previously reviewed. For example, around the time of puberty there are changes in the limbic system, which plays a role in emotional arousal (Dahl 2001). In addition, examination of the prefrontal cortex across adolescence indicates that this area is continuing to develop through the early and middle adolescent years (Geidd et al. 1999). The prefrontal cortex is known to regulate emotions and control impulses, promote planning, and contribute to the consideration of risks before acting.

Although there is as yet no evidence directly relating degrees of brain maturation to actual behaviours and decision-making of adolescents, there is an obvious parallel between these brain functions and the behavioural and psychosocial deficits in adolescents' decision-making described earlier. This creates a strong hypothesis that lesser maturity of adolescents' decision-making capacities may be linked to brain structures that also have not yet reached adult maturity (Spear 2000).

Values and Limits of the Evidence

While the evidence for adolescents' lesser maturity in decision-making abilities is significant, there are limits to the usefulness of existing research when applied to policy regarding adolescents' culpability or blameworthiness.

First, research on adolescents' decision-making is incomplete. Only a few studies have been performed for some of the psychosocial factors that appear to differentiate adolescents' and adults' decision-making capacities. Moreover, for obvious reasons, we have virtually no studies of adolescents' decision-making in actual situations in which they make illegal choices. Regarding research on maturation of the brain, no studies have yet examined the link between the degree of maturation of particular areas of the brain and actual decision-making behaviour of adolescents. The evidence we have is considerable, therefore, and relevant for the purpose of guiding law and policy, but it is not immune from challenge.

Second, almost all of the research on adolescents' decision-making capacities has been performed with "normal" adolescent samples, but the population of adolescents about whom we are most concerned in legal and policy analyses are delinquent youths. In contrast to adolescents in general, adolescents encountered in the juvenile justice system have a much higher prevalence of mental disorders and developmental disorders (generally reported as about 70%: Grisso 2004; Teplin et al. 2002; Wasserman et al. 2002; Vermeiren 2003), and the average level of measured intelligence of youths in juvenile justice custody is not IQ = 100, but about 85 (Grisso 2004). Mental disorders, lower intelligence, and significant developmental disabilities can be expected to further delay the maturation of cognitive and psychosocial abilities, so the differences between *delinquent* adolescents and adults may be greater than existing studies based on adolescents in general would suggest.

Adolescence as Junior Status in Law

The child is unfinished relative to a human telos, that is to the concept of the accomplished nature of the fully grown human being that is the crucial agent in law: the autonomous individual. The child in law is regarded as not yet fully autonomous or fully morally and legally responsible. Children do not fully know what they are doing. They may know what they are doing in that they are correctly apprised of the relevant facts, without being able to really grasp the moral and legal importance of these facts (Archard 2001).

Children below a certain age are too young to be held responsible for breaking the law. They cannot fully perceive themselves as citizens, or as subjects to the law. If they do something wrong, they perceive this as a wrong against their parents, the wider family or their teacher. Their reasoning is not yet adequate, their notions of law, state and citizenship need further maturity, and they lack experience with the law (Berti and Andriolo 2001; Helwig and Jasiobedzka 2001; Ruck et al. 1998; Otterspoor-Kousemaker 1983; Adelson 1971).

The lower age limit of criminal responsibility is understood as denoting a complete bar to state interference, regardless of any behaviour committed by the child, even when such behaviour would result in a (serious) offence if committed by an older person. This is grounded in the idea that children lack the capacity to form criminal intent or to fully understand the moral and legal implications of their actions. The idea is that children under the age of criminal responsibility may understand (or not) that what they are doing or have done may be naughty or mischievous, but they are unable to fully understand their actions as a criminal offence, that is, as actions against the law, implying the legal consequences of those actions. They do not understand themselves as citizens, as subjects to the law, but as children who have to obey their parents and teachers. For that reason we have had lower age limits in law for centuries. Criminal responsibility requires a perception of the law, of acting and wrongdoing in the perspective of the law and the state. It requires a capacity to really grasp the legal impact of our actions, "to know what we are responsible for and what our prospective responsibilities are" (Cane 2002, 54).

The view of the child as "becoming" implies, though, that the child is not simply viewed in law as completely irresponsible. Children are viewed as beings with a growing responsibility and a growing awareness of their position as subjects to law. Our modern view of childhood is a developmental one. The normal youth acquires moral and legal autonomy step by step, developing from extreme dependence and vulnerability in infancy to near independence, partial self-sufficiency and growing maturity in adolescence. The developmental view implies that adolescence presents a fascinating and troubling stage in law. Adolescents are too young to be held fully responsible for breaking the law, but too old to be held completely non-responsible. The special status which we normally attribute to adolescents in law may be understood as a junior status, a junior citizenship.

The findings in the last paragraph concerning adolescents' lesser maturity in decision-making abilities may be seen as underpinning the age-old intuition that adolescents deserve a special status in criminal law. In this stage, roughly between 12 and 18 years, the question of the young person's responsibility becomes increasingly problematic, urging countries to develop age levels in their jurisdictions. In many fields of law this has resulted in age boundaries, like 16, 18 or 21, from which age young persons are viewed as fully, morally and legally responsible agents. From that age on young persons are allowed to get married without parental approval, to make contracts on their own, to drive a car, to leave school, etc.

Conclusions

We may conclude, first, that there is no evidence that today children under 12 have a greater understanding and more cognitive abilities than children had in the past. On the contrary, there appears to be strong evidence to recommend 12 as the age below which we should presume absolute lack of criminal responsibility.

Second, we may conclude that the age of criminal responsibility is far from a meaningless term. We have argued that the age at which youths can be prosecuted may be viewed as more important in fact than the formal age of criminal responsibility. But we have argued also that concerning the formal age of criminal responsibility there are good empirical data concerning children's understanding. It is true that existing studies do not provide a specific age at which decision-making abilities have reached adult maturity. But it is equally true that for the "average" youth some findings are clear: formal cognitive abilities appear to mature by middle adolescence, many psychosocial abilities mature somewhat later, and brain development may continue into early adulthood.

Third, at present, one finds the strongest evidence for adolescent immaturity in a range of factors related to decision-making for adolescents aged 15 and under as a group. Fourth, there are indications that similarly immature decision-making abilities exist among youths aged 16 and 17 whose development is delayed by disabilities, but further research is needed to test this.

Reviewing this evidence, Steinberg and Scott (2003) considered it sufficiently strong to argue for US laws that recognise lesser penalties for offences during adolescence, and a reduction in the practice of trying adolescents as adults. The United States Supreme Court's recent decision to abolish the death penalty for crimes committed before age 18 (*Roper v. Simmons* 2005) was based in part on the American Psychological Association's digest of the same evidence presented in this brief review.

Finally, something we should not accept on the basis of the same evidence without very good additional reasons is the idea that adolescent offenders normally should be handled in a juvenile justice system or in a welfare system, but that they should go to adult criminal court if they have committed something very serious, such as manslaughter or murder. An adolescent has the same degree of capacity to form criminal intent, no matter what crime he commits. Regarding substantive law, there need to be very strict rules and explicit justification by the judge should be required to justify breaches of the sentencing limits of the juvenile justice system for the older adolescent who has committed a very serious crime. Regarding procedural law, it is hard to imagine convincing justifications for breaches of the normal, protectionist juvenile justice procedures. The same holds for the implementation of sentences in adult detention situations. This leads us on in fact to the next two chapters of this volume.

Chapter 5
Parental Responsibility for Youth Offending

Raymond Arthur

Introduction

In Shakespeare's *The Merchant of Venice* Lancelot declares that "the sins of the father are to be laid upon the children". Here Lancelot is paraphrasing an old biblical concept that the son pays for the sins of his father. The youth justice system in England and Wales has sought to reverse this ancient adage and instead seeks to hold parents accountable for the delinquency and offending of their children. This view of parents' being responsible for their children's offences is one that has also found favour throughout history. For example, Aristotle asserted that in order to be virtuous "we ought to have been brought up in a particular way from our very youth". Diogenes of Sinope believed that "if the child swears, slap the parent". This belief has also permeated the rulings of the judiciary, for example the United States Supreme Court held in *Eddings v. Oklahoma* (1982) that "... youth crime ... is not exclusively the offender's fault, offences by the young also represent a failure of family".

This chapter will examine the laws which hold parents responsible for the crimes of their children in England and Wales and also in other jurisdictions such as Scotland, Ireland, Australia and the USA. The chapter will consider the association between parenting and youth offending and assess whether these laws are an effective means of preventing youth offending. The chapter will then investigate the duty of the state to provide support to families in crisis. I will consider the effectiveness and availability of policies that strengthen the family, and examine whether supporting families, rather than penalising them, would be a more effective response to youth offending.

R. Arthur (✉)
School of Social Sciences and Law, University of Teesside, Middlesbrough, Tees Valley, UK

J. Junger-Tas and F. Dünkel (eds.), *Reforming Juvenile Justice*,
DOI: 10.1007/978-0-387-89295-5_5, © Springer Science+Business Media, LLC 2009

Parental Responsibility Laws in England and Wales

Fining Parents for Their Children's Offences

The Children and Young Persons Act 1933 was the first Act to empower the courts to require parents to pay the fines of a juvenile offender. The Criminal Justice Act 1982 extended this power to allow courts to order parents to pay a juvenile offender's fines or compensation. Section 87(3) of the Anti-Social Behaviour Act 2003 allows for the issuing of Fixed Penalty Notices to parents of offenders between the ages of 10 and 16. Section 144 of the Serious Organised Crime and Police Act 2005 introduced Parental Compensation Orders. A Parental Compensation Order is a civil order that requires a parent to compensate, up to a maximum of £5,000, any person whose property has been taken or damaged by a child. Such an order may be made by a magistrate where a child under 10 years of age has taken or has caused loss or damage to property in the course of acting in either an antisocial manner or in a way that would have been a criminal offence had the child been over 10 years of age. A Parental Compensation Order can only be made if it would be desirable in the interests of preventing repetition of the offending behaviour. Section 137 of the Powers of the Criminal Courts (Sentencing) Act 2000 provides that in the case of a child under 16 years of age, a criminal Compensation Order that has been made under Section 130 must be paid by the parent, unless the parent cannot be found or it would be unreasonable to do so. When the child is aged between 16 and 17 years then the power to make the order against the parent is discretionary.

Parental Bind-Over

The first law in England and Wales which held parents directly responsible, as opposed to financially liable, was enshrined in the Criminal Justice Act 1991. The most significant aspect of the 1991 Act was the introduction of the parental "bind-over" which allowed for the parent to be "bound over" by the court to exercise control over an offending child. The Criminal Justice and Public Order Act 1994 extended this power to include parents having to ensure their child's compliance with the requirements of a community sentence. Failure to meet the terms of the bind-over could result in a fine of £1,000. This was the first time that parents were fined for their failure to control their children's behaviour. In relation to a young person between 10 and 16 years of age, this power must be exercised where the court is satisfied that it would be desirable in the interests of preventing the commission of further offences by the offender. If the court is not satisfied that it would be appropriate to impose a bind-over on the parents of an offender under 16 years, it must state openly why it is of this opinion (Section 150(1) Powers of Criminal Courts (Sentencing) Act 2000).

Parenting Order

The Crime and Disorder Act 1998 introduced the "parenting order" enabling the court to require the parents of every convicted juvenile offender to attend parenting programmes and if necessary to control the future behaviour of the juvenile in a specified manner. The parenting programmes deal with issues such as experiences of parenting, communication and negotiation skills, parenting style and the importance of consistency, praise and rewards. The parenting order requires a parent to attend these sessions once a week for a maximum of 12 weeks. Since the Anti-Social Behaviour Act 2003 this can include attendance on a residential course. Parents may also be required to apply control over their child; for example, they may be ordered to ensure their child attends school or avoids associating with particular individuals who are adversely affecting their behaviour. The 1998 Act empowers the court to impose a parenting order in the following circumstances: where a child safety order has been made in respect of a child; where a sex offender order is made on a child or young person; where a person is convicted of an offence under Section 443 (failure to comply with a school attendance order) or Section 444 (failure to secure regular attendance at school of a registered pupil) of the Education Act 1996; or where a referral order or an antisocial behaviour order has been made. An antisocial behaviour order is a civil order made against a person who has engaged in antisocial behaviour. A referral order is given to a young person who pleads guilty to an offence provided it is the young person's first time in court. The relevant condition that has to be satisfied to justify making a parenting order is that the order is desirable in the interests of preventing any repetition of the kind of behaviour that led to the order being made and the prevention of further offending by the child or young person. Should a parent fail to comply with the requirements of the order he or she may be liable to a fine of up to £1,000. The Anti-Social Behaviour Act 2003 increased the circumstances in which a parenting order can be made. Section 26 empowers Youth Offending Teams (YOTs) to apply to the courts for parenting orders where the YOT suspects that the parent is not taking active steps to prevent the child's antisocial or criminal-type behaviour, and it is clear that this behaviour will continue. YOTs comprise representatives from the police, probation, education and health authorities and the local authority. Under the Crime and Disorder Act 1998 the YOT has primary responsibility for providing a multi-agency service for children and young people who are involved in offending behaviour and working with young offenders in order to prevent further offending. Local education authorities are also empowered to seek a parenting order where a child has been excluded from school for serious misbehaviour. Section 24 of the Police and Justice Act 2006 allows registered social landlords to apply for a parenting order where they have reason to believe that a child is engaged in antisocial behaviour. Registered social landlords provide low cost housing for people in housing need. Parenting orders can thus be made even where a child has not committed an offence, been charged with an offence or been issued with an antisocial behaviour order.

Parenting Orders in Other Jurisdictions

The Crime and Disorder Act 1998 precluded the use of parenting orders in Scotland. However parenting orders, similar to those in England and Wales, were introduced in Scotland in the Anti-Social Behaviour (Scotland) Act 2004. The Scottish Executive decided to introduce the parenting orders as a 3-year pilot running from 2005 to 2008 before rolling them out across Scotland (Scottish Executive 2004). The Scottish parenting order is a civil order that requires parents to engage in counselling and guidance sessions in order to prevent their children engaging in antisocial and offending behaviour. Ireland introduced similar laws in the Children Act 2001 which allows courts to order the parents of juvenile offenders to participate in courses to improve their parenting skills, to undergo treatment for alcohol or drug abuse and to supervise their child where their child has been convicted of an offence. A number of parental responsibility laws have also been introduced in Australia. In 1994 the New South Wales government introduced laws similar to those of the English parenting order, which were replicated in Western Australia and Southern Australia. Parental responsibility laws, similar to those enacted in England and Wales, are also popular in the United States of America. In 1988 California enacted its Street Terrorism and Prevention Act which fines and imprisons parents for failing to adequately supervise their children. In 1994 St. Clair Shores, Michigan, was the first municipality to adopt a Parental Responsibility Ordinance which allows parents to be fined up to $100 for failing to control their children's actions or seek professional assistance. Amongst other things, parents have to take measures to ensure that their children will not be tempted into crime and keep their children from destroying property and handling stolen goods. Similarly, Alabama and Wyoming laws require that parents who fail to help their child comply with court-ordered terms be held in criminal contempt and fined or imprisoned. Louisiana parents may be fined or imprisoned, or both, for failure to control their children. Hawaii's statute is particularly stringent and fines or imprisons parents for the child's curfew violation. Arkansas and Colorado require parents to take parental responsibility training courses. A New Mexico statute directs parents to participate in probation or treatment programmes. Pennsylvania requires the parent to attend treatment, counselling, education or rehabilitation. Oregon and Idaho statutes require parents to sign contracts with the court agreeing to adhere to probation provisions (Harris 2006).

All of these laws are based on the premise that much youth lawbreaking and antisocial behaviour is attributable to parents' failure to exert control over their children. These laws consider all parents of young offenders as willfully negligent and aim to reduce youth crime by forcing parents to assume responsibility for their children. In the next section I will examine the causal links between parenting and youth offending and assess whether these laws actually address the underlying causes of youth offending, or whether parental responsibility laws are based on a simplistic and limited understanding of the causal links between parenting and youth offending.

Parenting and Youth Offending

The recognition that there may be a link between parenting and family circumstances and the chances that a child becomes involved in juvenile offending is not a new one. One of the most ambitious projects to investigate why some young people commit crime, and to assess how far criminality can be predicted, was the Cambridge study in delinquent development undertaken by D.J. West in 1961 (West 1969; 1973; 1982; West and Farrington 1977). A sample of 411 working class boys aged eight was selected from six primary schools in Camberwell, London. They were contacted again when aged 10, 14, 16, 18, 21, 25 and 32 to examine which of them had developed a delinquent way of life. West outlined five major factors which had a significant association with the likelihood of children becoming offenders. The five key factors were as follows:

1. Having parents considered by social workers to have performed their child-rearing duties unsatisfactorily. Of 96 such boys, 32.3% became juvenile offenders. The unfavourable features that contributed to the general rating of "unsatisfactory" parental behaviour included marital conflict, the dominance of one parent over the other in decision-making relating to children, inconsistency between the parents in their handling of the child, attitudes of indifference, positive rejection or neglect, over-strict or erratically varying discipline and harsh methods of enforcement.
2. Having a parent with a criminal record. Of 103 such boys, 37.9% become juvenile offenders, compared with 14.6% among the rest of the sample.
3. Coming from a large-sized family, defined as four or more other surviving children born to the boy's mother prior to his tenth birthday. Of 99 such boys, 32.3% became juvenile offenders.
4. Having below average intelligence on testing, defined as IQ of 90 or less on Raven's Progressive Matrices Test. This test measures non-verbal intelligence. Of 103 such boys, 31.1% became juvenile offenders, compared with 15.9% of the rest of the sample.
5. Coming from a low-income family. Of 93 such boys, 33.3% became juvenile offenders, compared with 16.7% among the rest of the sample. Income was categorised taking into account a number of circumstances including number of children, housing conditions, family possessions, style of living and whether the family was supported by social agencies. Most of the families classified as poor were existing at a level similar to those who qualify for, or were actually receiving, National Assistance at that time, so the degree of material deprivation among them was quite severe.

Most of West's predictors for juvenile involvement in offending behaviour relate to the family and issues of parenting. These risk factors have emerged consistently in the most rigorous empirical research on the causes of juvenile crime in projects elsewhere in England and in the United States, Scandinavian countries, New Zealand, China, Taiwan, and Hong Kong (Arthur 2007a). In particular, the following negative family factors were found to be predictive of youth involvement in antisocial and offending behaviour: parental rejection, inadequate supervision and inconsistent discipline by parents, family conflict, marital discord, disrupted and broken families, physical violence, teenage parents, family criminality, inadequate prenatal care, child abuse and poverty. The evidence strongly suggests that parents have a central role to play in preventing the onset, development and perpetuation of criminal careers. The American criminologist Hirschi characterised the nature of the parent–child relationship as a 'bond of affection' whose strength can later determine the degree of resistance to breaking the law, "the important consideration is whether the parent is psychologically present when temptation to a crime appears" (Hirschi 1969). Thus it would seem that the most logical place to begin preventing juvenile offending behaviour is the family.

However, the fact that parental behaviour is related to youth offending does not provide sufficient reasons for imposing sanctions on parents. The challenges that confront children who are engaging in antisocial and offending behaviour, their families and the various professionals who work with them are complex, deep-rooted and multi-faceted. A key feature of the risk factors investigated in this chapter is their interconnectedness. Reviews of risk factors for problem behaviour such as substance abuse, mental health problems and school dropout suggest that most of the risk factors for youth offending behaviour also predict these problems. Similarly problems such as mental health issues, poor school attendance and drug abuse are predictive of juvenile offending. Accordingly, delinquency, school problems, psychological problems, drug use and family problems cluster around the same individuals. For instance, Graham and Bowling found that for both males and females the odds of offending amongst those who truanted were more than three times greater than those who had not truanted (Graham and Bowling 1995: 42). Ball and Connolly also found a reciprocal relationship between delinquency and truancy and school exclusion (Ball and Connolly 2000). Truancy and school exclusion may be both a cause and a consequence of juvenile offending behaviour. Schools may use exclusion to respond to problematic behaviour, including persistent non-attendance and offending behaviour; therefore it is difficult to determine which behaviour causes which.

Strong links have also been established between mental health problems in children and young people and juvenile offending. The term "mental health problems" is used generically to cover a range of types and severity of psychological and psychiatric difficulties and disorders that are experienced by children and young people. Rutter found that the rate of mental health problems is high in young offenders, particularly persistent young offenders (Rutter 1990; Rutter and Smith 1995; Rutter et al. 1998). Screening of 10–17-year-olds attending a city centre youth court revealed disturbingly high levels of both psychiatric and physical morbidity, including learning difficulties, mood disorders, mental illness and frequent use of alcohol and illicit drugs (Farrington et al. 1996). Many research studies have also found evidence of a strong association between juvenile substance abuse and antisocial behaviour in young people. Indeed worldwide almost every survey of these behaviours has found some form of association between them (Howard and Zibert 1990; Huizinga et al. 1994; Inciardi and Pottieger 1991). The Youth Lifestyles

Survey supports the finding that juvenile drug use and juvenile offending are associated (Flood-Page et al. 2000). Of the serious and persistent offenders aged 12–17, 38% of males and 20% of females admitted using drugs in the last 12 months, compared with 7% of males and 4% of females of the rest of the cohort. The Youth Lifestyle Survey found that 75% of persistent offenders reported lifetime use of drugs (Goulden and Sondhi 2001). In addition to raised general prevalence rates, the survey also suggests that the rates of use of drugs such as crack and heroin are significantly higher among young serious and persistent offenders than they are in the general population. Hammersley et al. (2003) examined a sample of 293 young people who were clients of 11 YOTs in England and Wales between summer 2001 and summer 2002. The group was highly delinquent, and most had committed multiple types of offences repeatedly. Substance use amongst the sample exceeded the rates of the Youth Lifestyles Survey offender group and the British Crime Survey group. Most of the sample had consumed alcohol (91%), cannabis (86%) and ecstasy (44%). Drug use was highest amongst the most frequent offenders and lowest in the less frequent offenders. Over half of the sample agreed that alcohol or drugs had been associated with their offending and 44% said that they sometimes committed crimes to get money for drugs or alcohol.

Poverty is another persistent feature in the lives of young offenders. The links between economic deprivation and juvenile offending are well established in academic criminology and are vividly evidenced in many seminal and defining studies. What emerges from the official crime figures and longitudinal research is that children from low income, working class families are more likely to become juvenile offenders than those from comfortable middle class homes (Bartol and Bartol 1998). For example in the *Newcastle 1,000 Family Study* three generations of families were studied over a 30-year period (Kolvin et al. 1990). The more deprived the family, the more likely it was that their children would offend. The findings showed that one in six children living in more affluent districts became offenders compared to one in three in the poorest neighbourhoods.

The evidence shows that many youths entering the youth justice system have serious multiple problems in terms of their school achievement, psychological health, alcohol and drug abuse. Most of these problems are preceded by the family problems discussed throughout this chapter. For example the family has an important role to play in children's school adjustment, attendance and performance. Parents' involvement in school and monitoring of school performance lessens the likelihood of school failure and associated outcomes such as delinquency (Smith and Stern 1997). Graham and Bowling found that school truants usually had a poor relationship with one or both parents, family members in trouble with the law, low attachment to family and were poorly supervised in that their parents frequently did not know where their child was, whom they were with or what they were doing (Graham and Bowling 1995).

Certain groups of children are at greater risk of developing mental health problems than others. Children who do not do well at school whether because of low IQ or a specific learning disorder are at an increased risk of mental health problems which may be as high as 40% (Graham 1986). The Audit Commission found that

9% of children with mental health problems were looked after by the local authority, compared with 0.5% in the general population (Audit Commission 1999). Poor and inconsistent parenting is linked with mental health problems in young children and adolescents. Poor supervision, erratic and/or harsh discipline, parental disharmony, rejection of the child and low involvement in the child's activities have been consistently shown to contribute to mental health problems in children (Cleaver et al. 1999; Farrington 1994). The lives of youth with mental health problems are often characterised by chronic residential instability and difficult family relationships. These children are more likely to come from low income families, to have previously lived outside the home and to come from reconstituted or single parent families (Frensch and Cameron 2002; Quinn and Epstein 1998; Wells and Whittington 1993). In the Office for National Statistics study 47% of children assessed as having a mental health disorder had a parent who was likely to have a mental health problem, such as anxiety or depression (Office for National Statistics 2000).

Research also indicates that the risk factors for substance abuse and delinquency overlap substantially; these include poor parental supervision, a disrupted family background, poor psychological well-being, difficulties in school, school exclusion, truancy, low educational achievement, having been abused, having been in care, parental divorce or separation or having a family member with a criminal record (Bennett 2000; Collinson 1994; Hawkins et al. 1995; Lloyd 1998; Newburn 1999). These studies suggest that substance abuse and delinquency develop together in a common "causal configuration". Therefore associations between juvenile offending and drug use may exist because of the shared antecedents of drug abuse and delinquency, rather than because drug use causes offending. Similarly, the stress caused by poverty is believed to diminish parents' capacity for supportive and consistent parenting. Economic hardship has a growing and devastating effect on families and influences children through its impact upon parents' behaviour towards children. Families living in poverty are often unable to provide the necessary emotional support and stimulation critical to healthy child development. Low family incomes and poor housing can also lead to weaker parental supervision and control. Accordingly, economic and environmental factors collaborate to make it more difficult to be an effective parent. Economic hardship can contribute to parental conflict and poor parenting and consequently to delinquency and other behavioural problems among the children in these families. Low income and lack of full-time employment have also been shown to increase the likelihood of abuse by parents. Also living in disadvantaged settings can lead to the belief that economic survival through conventional channels is not possible (Guerra et al. 1995; James 1995).

The obvious conclusion from this analysis is that the tangled roots of youth crime lie to a considerable extent inside the family. The connection between the difficult family circumstances which plague increasing numbers of children and their subsequent offending behaviour cannot be ignored or denied. Similarly, the fact that there is an increasing convergence in the explanations offered for offending behaviour by the young and for childhood problems such as drug abuse, poor educational attainment and poor mental health cannot be ignored. These findings emphasise the need for prevention policies and interventions to avoid a narrow focus on parents and to take into account the family, social and contextual factors that are frequently associated with juvenile offending. These family problems need to be viewed as a "web of causation" rather than as a single causal factor. Given the need to make families function better, the objective of delinquency prevention laws must be to develop and provide the environment, the resources and the opportunities through which families can become competent to deal with their own problems. The family should be assisted in guiding and nurturing the child, through the provision of resources and support services which equip them to be good parents, reduces their isolation and promotes the welfare of parents and their children. Do parental responsibility laws actually achieve this?

Parenting Orders in Practice

Developing the skills of parents to deal with difficult and challenging behaviour of their children can be vital in restoring family relationships and providing the structure and support that a young person requires to change its behaviour and desist from further offending behaviour. Ghate and Ramella (2002). evaluated the effectiveness of parenting programmes. Around 800 parents and 500 young people provided information for the national evaluation. The researchers found significant evidence of positive change in parents who participated in the programmes, including improved supervision and monitoring of their children's activities, a reduction in the frequency of conflict with their children and an improved ability to cope with parenting in general. There was also considerable evidence of positive change for young people during the time their parents participated in the programme. Young people reported improved supervision and monitoring by their parents, reduction in the frequency of conflict with their parents and improved relationship with their parents. In the year after the parents left the programme the reconviction rates of young people had fallen by over 30%, offending had dropped by 56% and the average number of offences per young person reduced by 50%. It seems that the parenting programme helped to "apply the brakes" on a sharp downward course for young people. Scott et al.'s (2006) study also showed that parenting programmes improved several aspects of parenting in important ways such as increasing sensitive responding to children, improving the use of effective discipline and decreasing criticism. The study showed that the intervention had lasting effects on the parent–child relationship for at least 6 months after the intervention had ended. This evidence relates to parenting programmes in general; many of the participants will have been there voluntarily. Although the supportive aspects of the parenting order are attractive, evidence indicates that using compulsion and the threat of fines and imprisonment is not an effective way to change the behaviour of parents and their children.

According to Ghate and Ramella's evaluation of parenting programmes, voluntary participants were more likely to have positive expectations of the intervention than those whose attendance was court ordered, who were less likely to have found

the programme helpful (Ghate and Ramella 2002). Field (2007) found in his interviews with a range of youth justice practitioners in Wales that many YOTs in Wales
had marginalised parenting orders. Parenting orders were generally seen as being
unhelpfully coercive and so YOTs discouraged magistrates from using them where
parents had not agreed to participate voluntarily. Field's findings echo the views
expressed by the Magistrates' Association when parental bind-overs were introduced. The Magistrates' Association opposed parental bind-overs on the grounds
that such orders were likely to exacerbate existing pressure on vulnerable families
and would thus be "counterproductive, leading to an increase in family breakdown"
(Ashford and Chard 2000). Similar views emerged from earlier research carried out
in the USA. In 1948 a juvenile court judge in Ohio examined the effectiveness of
laws that held parents responsible for their children's offending. He analysed the
results of 1,027 cases from 1939 to 1946 and concluded that punishing parents
accomplished very little and did not decrease the juvenile offending rate (Alexander
1948). Similarly, a study conducted by the Children's Bureau found that between
1957 and 1962 delinquency rates in 16 states with laws that punished parents for
delinquency were slightly higher than the national average, suggesting that these
laws were ineffective in reducing youth offending (Freer 1964). Barry Krisberg, the
president of the National Council on Crime and Delinquency, sharply criticised
parental responsibility laws and described them as "dangerously naïve" (Smith 1995):

> Most of these laws are a complete waste of time … it's country club criminology. It sounds
> good in the suburbs but in reality it's an empty threat because if you carry it out you just
> further endanger and pull apart families (Applebome 1996).

Concern has also been expressed that parental responsibility laws contradict fundamental principles of criminal liability (Commission on Families and Wellbeing of
Children 2005; Hollingsworth 2007). Customarily a crime requires proof of a
physical act (*actus reus*) and the requisite mental state (*mens rea*). The accused
must have either acted voluntarily or failed to act under circumstances imposing a
duty to act. Parental responsibility laws enforce a form of strict liability on parents
in that parents are liable even if they exercised reasonable care. The court does not
need to prove that the parents were at fault to make the order. The parent has
not been convicted of any offence, and in some circumstances the child may not
have been convicted of any offence, but both parent and child are subject to sanction.
A graphic illustration of this issue is provided in the English case of *Bryant v
Portsmouth City Council* (2000). This case concerned a grandmother who took in
her two grandsons when they were aged 4 and 5 years old and reared them. By the
time of the proceedings the boys were two teenagers over whom the grandmother
could exercise no control. The boys engaged in a range of antisocial behaviour over
a period of 10 years, including throwing stones at, and spitting at neighbours;
assaulting and threatening neighbours; spraying graffiti; and damaging property.
A suspended possession order under section 84 of the Housing Act 1985 was made
against the grandmother on the grounds that she had "allowed" the boys to engage
in antisocial behaviour. The effect of this order was that the grandmother's home of

over 30 years could be repossessed. The Court of Appeal took note of the fact that the grandmother could not exercise control over the boys, nor did she encourage or tolerate the boys' behaviour or give them permission to behave in this way. However, Simon Brown LJ felt it was inappropriate and unnecessary to examine the grandmother's parenting skills and assess whether she could have been more successful in disciplining and controlling the boys. Simon Brown LJ held that because she had "signally failed to prevent" their behaviour, she was in fact "allowing" them to behave antisocially and therefore had to accept responsibility for their conduct. Parental responsibility laws do not require that a clear link be established between the parents' actions and the offence committed. *Bryant* illustrates that it is no defence to parents to argue that they attempted to supervise their children properly.

One of New Labour's driving themes since 1997 has been the need for joined-up government. Yet parental responsibility laws serve to fragment the government's approach to both tackling youth crime and supporting families in crisis. In 1997 the government stated in *No more Excuses* that "as they develop, children must bear an increasing responsibility for their actions, just as the responsibility of parents gradually declines" (Home Office 1997). The government believed that:

> to prevent offending and reoffending by young people we must stop making excuses for youth crime. Children above the age of criminal responsibility are generally mature enough to be held accountable for their actions and the law should recognise this.

Yet parental responsibility laws are built upon the idea that parents have caused their children to offend. Rather than parental responsibility decreasing when the child is held criminal responsible, both parent and child are held legally liable regardless of the actual or indeed presumed capacity of the child, and consequently there is no diminution in parental responsibility as the child gains responsibility (Hollingsworth 2007). Kempf-Leonard and Peterson (2002: 445) express this contradiction succinctly:

> If youths are to be processed using adult criteria and held responsible for their delinquent actions as individuals capable of making rational decisions, it is an incompatible dichotomy to hold parents responsible for these capable youths as well.

Parental responsibility laws not only reduce the responsibility of the child but obscure the fact that the government can be implicated in the causes of antisocial and criminal behaviour. The case of *Bryant* provides a good example of the growing trend of holding parents and guardians responsible for their children's antisocial and offending behaviour, while ignoring the role of government. In *Bryant* the court were willing to impose culpability upon the grandmother without any reference to the prevalence of family difficulties, poverty, social exclusion, or the state's responsibilities under the Children Act 1989 to provide adequate care and protection for children in need and their families. In the next section I will examine the state's family support duties and powers and consider whether the state is complicit in allowing young people to engage in antisocial and offending behaviour and question whether the state should be permitted to wash its hands of its youth crime prevention responsibilities?

The Duty of the State to Support Families in Crisis

In September 2003 the government produced a Green Paper on children at risk *Every Child Matters* which focussed on, amongst other things, early intervention, effective prevention and supporting parents and carers. Providing high-quality services for children and their families was seen as an essential step in preparing young people for the challenges and stresses of life and giving them real opportunities to achieve their full potential (Chief Secretary to the Treasury 2003). *Every Child Matters* followed on from the 1998 consultation document *Supporting Families*, which outlined a programme of measures to strengthen the family as the "foundation on which our communities, our society and our country are built" (Home Office 1998). These documents are underpinned by the Children Act 1989 which recognises the importance of supporting high-risk families in order to prevent delinquency and youth offending. Schedule 2 of the 1989 Act requires local authorities to take reasonable steps to encourage children in their area not to commit criminal offences. *Guidance* suggests that such reasonable steps might involve advice and support services for parents, the provision of family support services, family centres, day care and accommodation, and health care and social care (Department of Health 1991). The 1989 Children Act provides a framework for local authorities to provide established types of family support and services to young offenders and their families, including family support; access to play and leisure opportunities; training parents in effective child rearing methods; preschool intellectual enrichment programmes; positive opportunities for physical, emotional, social and intellectual development in childhood; alcohol and drug programmes; providing families and young people with access to behaviour modification models such as anger management and conflict resolution; and the provision of day care and providing respite breaks and family holidays (Arthur 2002; 2005).

Various studies have observed that staff are concerned about the limited resources to provide support to families under stress. For example the Social Services Inspectorate *Inspection of Children's Services* found that arrangements to deliver child and adolescent mental health services on an integrated basis were poorly developed (Cooper 2002). This is a finding which is confirmed in the Consultation Document *Youth Matters* in which the government admits that existing social services for teenagers in England and Wales do not amount to a coherent modern system of support for young people (Secretary of State for Education and Skills 2005). Existing services are failing to meet the needs of young people because the various organisations providing services and help for young people do not work together as effectively or imaginatively as they should, with the result that money and effort are wasted; and not enough is being done to prevent young people from drifting into a life of crime or poverty (Arthur 2007b). In July 2006 the Department of Health conceded that only half of Primary Care Trusts are able to provide access to mental health specialists for teenagers with learning disabilities and that there is no emergency help for teenagers suffering a "psychotic crisis" or severe depression (Revill 2006). According to a joint report published by the Health

Care Commission and HM Inspectorate of Probation one in three YOTs still did not have access to a designated mental health worker in 2006. Also mental health service provision for 16–17-year-olds remained particularly problematic (Healthcare Commission, HM Inspectorate of Probation 2006). Similarly, a national audit of family services conducted in 2001 found a real shortage of support for parents of teenagers (Henricson 2001). These findings are of concern because it means that there is very little early intervention to address the problems of this age range, such as mental health, substance abuse or offending behaviour. If such problems are not addressed at an early stage, the children and young people in question may find themselves precipitate into care or into juvenile offending systems.

The Office for Standards in Education, Children's Services and Skills (Ofsted) *Narrowing the gap* report found that actions to reduce offending and re-offending and to manage the reintegration of young people who offend back into the community are not as effective as they could be, reflecting the need for more effective multi-agency work (Ofsted 2007). Partner agencies were found to lack a clear shared understanding of their roles in relation to safeguarding. Thresholds governing access to social care services are set too high, with no shared understanding of their purpose and application. A common area of weakness was found to be the inequality of provisions between different areas and different groups of children and young people. This includes poor ongoing monitoring and assessment of the physical and mental health needs of vulnerable groups – in particular children and young offenders, especially as they make the transition to adulthood. Concern has also been expressed that Sure Start, the Labour government's most expensive investment in social policy, is failing to help the most disadvantaged and excluded families. Sure Start provides a one-stop service for children under six and their families in deprived communities. The first evaluation of Sure Start found that children in areas where the Sure Start programme runs do less well than children in poor areas without the scheme (Belsky et al. 2006; National Evaluation of Sure Start 2005). In response to this a programme of new children's centres is being rolled out across the country as part of Sure Start. However, there are fears that this expansion will dilute the original purpose of Sure Start leading to what its architect, Norman Glass, has called "a severe cut in the funding per head" from £1,300 per child to just £25 (Glass 2005; 2006). Sure Start has also been accused of serious failings in the way its programmes work with minority groups and has been branded a "substantial wasted opportunity" (Craig et al. 2007).

The National Evaluation of the Children's Fund in its detailed case studies of 18 Children's Fund Partnerships highlighted the tensions within local authorities between balancing responses to immediate pressing needs with longer term preventive strategies (National Evaluation of the Children's Fund 2004). The Children's Fund, delivered through 149 Children's Fund partnerships in England, aims to demonstrate how the point of intervention by services to support children and families can be shifted from acute need towards earlier interventions. This report highlighted that there was still "a road to travel in influencing the wider preventative agenda in the local authority". The National Evaluation of the Children's Fund found that despite the Children's Fund being an allocated preventive programme, partnerships still needed to work hard to keep prevention high on the local agenda and avoid services being pulled towards meeting only the most acute needs. Even though some authorities were actively engaged in local developments around children's trusts and were prioritising prevention, many others felt less included in local developments around collaborative working and were concerned about the future priority for preventive services. There was also widespread concern about the sustainability of voluntary sector involvement once the Children's Fund dried up.

Staff shortage is also a serious problem undermining the delivery of services to young people at risk of engaging in offending behaviour. The second *Safeguarding Children* report found regular difficulties in recruiting and retaining skilled and experienced social workers (Social Services Inspectorate 2005). As a result of the shortage of resources local authorities are having to operate high thresholds and small safety nets, turning away people who desperately need help. Several studies drew attention to the fact that families were sometimes offered services inappropriately, drawing from a pool of existing services that did not meet families' needs rather than providing services based on assessment of needs (Statham et al. 2001). Resource constraints compel local authorities to target particular groups; consequently, they do not have the resources to provide the assistance many children need. The result is that local authorities are hesitant to commit expenditure to prevention and the reasons behind young people's offending behaviour are not addressed. The tensions between prevention and early intervention on the one hand, and meeting immediate acute needs on the other, require an increase in funding if gaps in services are to be bridged.

Evidence also suggests that those most in need of support are the least likely to access it. Analysis from the Millennium Cohort Study showed that poorer families were less likely to receive a visit from health visitors than those families with higher incomes (HM Government 2006). Feedback from parenting programmes such as Webster Stratton's Incredible Years and Triple P shows that parents value extra support such as parenting classes. Yet not all parents who need these services can access them; the principle of progressive universalism is not yet being met with respect to support for parents (Leung et al. 2006). The Child Poverty Review identified a number of potential barriers to engagement of those most in need of support: a fear or mistrust of statutory services and concerns that children's services might take away children from parents if they are seen to have problems (HM Treasury 2004). There is a lack of readily accessible information about what services are available. Parents may recognise that they need some support, but they do not know where to get help (HM Treasury, DFES 2007). Many services are perceived to cater for "failed" or "struggling" families, and this stigma may deter parents from accessing support that they know is available.

A progressive approach to youth crime prevention is ultimately bound up with the perusal and resourcing of mechanisms for social justice. The government must ensure that social justice extends to all members of society. According to this view the state must acknowledge that it, as well as the offender, has some responsibility for youth crime and that society can justifiably punish young offenders and their families for their crimes only to the extent it has fulfilled its obligations to those young people and their families as members of society. Social investment in family offers a promising prospect for both reducing crime and maximising the human capital that the young represent. Parental responsibility laws reduce the responsibility of both the child and wider society, encourage a blaming culture that does not take account of the full circumstances, and leads to ineffective punitive sanctions rather than the holistic support-based interventions which are required.

Conclusion

For many children in trouble, offending is but one problem amongst many, which combine and interlock to form a complex network of disadvantage and difficulty. Farrington, summarising the lessons to be learned from the Cambridge Study of Delinquent Development, believes that addressing the wider social problems is likely to be the most effective way of preventing offending (Farrington 1986a). This chapter has argued that the state, and particularly the local state, has a crucial role to play in social justice. The state must ensure that the likelihood of offending is reduced by ameliorating the familial and socioeconomic conditions which generate or underlie much of the offending in the first place. However, the findings from this chapter were disturbing as the evidence suggests that local authorities are failing to fulfil the youth crime prevention role envisaged for them in the Children Act 1989. While there exist pockets of effective and innovative practice in local areas, the resourcing of preventive efforts simply does not match the scale of the problem. At a macro level policy trends have served to promote rather than reduce criminality. Youth work has found itself vulnerable to cuts in local authority spending. Increases in family breakdown have coincided with reductions in the ability of local authorities to undertake preventive social work. As a result overburdened local authorities are reluctant to take on the youth crime prevention responsibilities of the Children Act. The effect of this is that the very parents who have been denied assistance and support from state agencies are also the targets of parental responsibility laws (Goldson and Jamieson 2002).

Statutory parenting interventions that are of relatively short duration and which come at a comparatively late stage in young people's lives are unlikely to offer a quick fix for the complex circumstances that might give rise to criminal or antisocial behaviour (Goldson and Jamieson 2002). A change in political vision has to be made from short term and supposed immediate gains to one in which long-term investment in the lives of children is accepted. This chapter has shown that attempts to modify youthful offending by punishing parents are not effective. Instead more money should be invested in projects that would attempt to stop offending behaviour by working with offenders and their families. What is required is a shift beyond penalising families to protecting families from the social, economic and political forces that conspire to induce children into engaging in antisocial and offending behaviour.

Chapter 6
Juvenile Transfer in the United States

Donna M. Bishop

Children and Adolescents in the Early Juvenile Court

From its inception in 1899 and throughout most of its 100-year history, the American juvenile court was firmly rooted in the doctrine of *parens patriae*. Nascent ideas about differences between young people and adults were especially influential in the creation of a separate juvenile court, whose establishment coincided with the emergence of the fledgling discipline of developmental psychology and with what has come to be known as the child study movement. Two ideas that were advanced in the child-study literature were especially influential (Ryerson 1978: 28–29). The first focused on "childhood innocence". Greatly influenced by Darwin's theory of evolution, some argued that children were amoral from birth but were destined to evolve naturally into moral and law-abiding adults. From this perspective, children and adolescents lacked sufficient maturity to be held criminally responsible for their bad acts. Their misdeeds were normal and temporary and would be naturally outgrown in due course, so long as corrupt or misguided adults did not bungle natural processes of development. Thus, Richard Tuthill, the first juvenile court judge in Chicago, warned of "brand[ing] [a child] in the opening years of its life with an indelible stain of criminality" and of placing a child "even temporarily, into the companionship of men and women whose lives are low, vicious, and criminal" (Tuthill 1904: 1–2). Those who shared Tuthill's view supported a diversionary rationale for the juvenile court: the court would shield youth from criminal convictions and from adult correctional institutions, where exposure to depraved adults might derail their natural development (see also Zimring 2000).

Others claimed that children were naturally inclined from birth to be good and moral (Ryerson 1978: 29–31). They might occasionally commit bad acts, not out of a desire to do harm, but out of ignorance of the rules that it was incumbent on adults to teach them. Benjamin Barr Lindsey, the first judge of the Denver Juvenile Court, espoused this view. He was instrumental in the passage of a landmark legislation

D.M. Bishop (✉)
College of Criminal Justice, Northeastern University, Boston, MA, USA

J. Junger-Tas and F. Dünkel (eds.), *Reforming Juvenile Justice*,
DOI: 10.1007/978-0-387-89295-5_6, © Springer Science + Business Media, LLC 2009

to impose penalties on parents and guardians for "contributing to the delinquency of a minor". Lindsey claimed that juvenile delinquents were not only blameless for their behavior, but were also victims, deserving of sympathy and guidance (Harris 1914: 311). Such a view of childhood innocence supported a rehabilitative or interventionist rationale for the court.

Another core idea on which the juvenile court was founded is that children are more malleable than adults. Nathan Oppenheim, a leading pediatrician of the period, explains: "[The child] is in no way really like an adult, since his condition is one of continuous change (Oppenheim 1898, p. 9)...[H]e is so plastic that his daily surroundings mould him as surely as a warm hand shapes a piece of wax" (Oppenheim 1898, p. 83). Malleability, together with immaturity, provided strong justification for coerced but non-punitive intervention. With naive optimism (some would say arrogance) about their "child saving" abilities, pioneers in the juvenile court movement sought to shield young people from the harshness of the criminal process, and to "substitute constructive efforts for the purely negative and destructive effects of the customary punishments" (Travis 1908, p. 187).

For much of the juvenile court's history, proceedings were informal and nonadversarial. Proof of the offense – which might be seen as a logical and necessary predicate to an inquiry into the child's needs and circumstances – was often handled in a peremptory way. In many jurisdictions standards of proof were low, if the court acknowledged any at all. There was little concern about protecting children from erroneous adjudications of delinquency because the upshot of such an error would presumably be the delivery of benign treatment from which the child might profit anyway. The benign nature of juvenile court intervention was also reflected in the scope of the court's authority, which included youths accused of crimes, status offenders, and those who were believed to be "at risk" for delinquency.

Judge Julian Mack, who became presiding judge of the Cook County juvenile court in 1904, set forth the primary focus of the juvenile court in an influential law review article:

> [The criminal court] put but one question, "Has he committed this crime?" It did not inquire, "What is the best thing to do for this lad?" It did not even punish him in a manner that would tend to improve him; the punishment was visited in proportion to the degree of wrongdoing evidenced by the single act.... Why is it not just and proper to treat these juvenile offenders, as we deal with the neglected children, as a wise and merciful father handles his own child whose errors are not discovered by the authorities? Why is it not the duty of the state, instead of asking merely whether a boy or a girl has committed a specific offense, to find out what he is, physically, mentally, morally, and then if it learns that he is treading the path that leads to criminality, to take him in charge, not so much to punish as to reform, not to degrade but to uplift, not to crush but to develop, not to make him a criminal but a worthy citizen (Mack 1909, p. 107).

The realization of Mack's vision "to understand" and "to uplift" was best served, it was believed, through the establishment of a warm, avuncular relationship between the judge and the child. Because the judge needed to understand the child's problems and needs, it was essential that the child be encouraged to talk freely. Thus, defense counsel was seen not only as unhelpful but as obstructive of the court's purposes. Procedural informality would best serve the objectives of understanding the child and planning his/her treatment. The child met with the judge in a setting that was less formal and threatening than a standard courtroom. Softer language – petition, adjudication, disposition – replaced the stigmatizing lexicon – complaint, indictment, prosecution, conviction, sentencing – of the criminal court.

Ideal meets Reality: At its inception, the juvenile court was a fragile institution whose future was very much dependent on public support. It soon became apparent that the behavior of some young offenders – especially violent youth and chronic offenders – threatened to erode that support (Tanenhaus 2004, p. 42). Commission of a serious violent act neither transforms a young person into a fully responsible adult nor renders him a poor candidate for juvenile intervention, but the public tended to view young violent offenders not as immature children, but as sophisticated and adult-like, and pressed for harsh punishments.[1] One commentator explains:

> The apparent philosophy behind statutes concerning juvenile offenders is that a child has not reached a degree of intellectual and emotional development that would qualify him as fully responsible for his acts. The laws, however, embody an obvious contradiction: for when the offense is too obnoxious or repugnant, complete responsibility is placed upon the child and he must face the full weight of the law (Banay 1947, p. 13).

Persistent recidivists posed at least as great a challenge for the court. Their failure to respond to the court's interventions suggested that young people might be more intractable than juvenile court advocates had made them out to be.

One solution, which was used from the start, was to transfer these "problem cases" to the criminal court. While transfer was inconsistent with the juvenile court's foundational principles, it was politically expedient. So, for example, we find that only 1 year after the juvenile court was established in Chicago, Judge Tuthill quietly and without fanfare referred 37 boys to the grand jury as "not fit subjects" for juvenile court. Other juvenile courts quickly followed suit. By relinquishing authority over a few, judges attempted to placate the public and preserve the juvenile court's diversionary and rehabilitative commitments to the vast majority of young offenders.

Although the boundaries of juvenile court jurisdiction were permeable from the start, by the mid-1920s the court had done much to shore up its perimeter and to fortify its legitimacy as an institution. This was accomplished in a number of ways. In some jurisdictions, juvenile court proceedings were open to the public so that the community might see the good that the court was doing on behalf of young people. Judges and probation officers used these proceedings as opportunities to educate the public, and also gave lectures that underscored the plight of poor, especially immigrant children. There was great faith that education would energize the public to ensure that conditions facing children would be improved (Breckenridge and Abbott 1912, p. 11). A real boost to the court's legitimacy came in 1923 with the publication of the first *Juvenile Court Standards* (United States Children's Bureau 1923). The standards set national norms for the court's broad jurisdiction over children and

---

[1] Such an illogical response is no less likely today than it was in the 1910s. Indeed, it is more common now than it was a century ago.

over parents who failed their obligations, highlighted the need for ancillary court clinics to assess each child, emphasized the notion of individualized treatment tailored to the needs and circumstances of each child, and established a presumption that children should be retained in the community under the supervision of the juvenile court. With time came also the creation of an organizational infrastructure (paid probation staff, court psychiatric clinics, foster care, mother's pensions, and specialized residential placements) that simultaneously brought to the court both greater resources and greater legitimacy. Although transfer to criminal court became established practice, juvenile court judges waived only a tiny proportion of the young people brought before them.

1960s–1990s: Crisis and Change

In the ensuing years, idealistic visions of individualized assessment and benign and effective treatments fell far short of being realized. The lack of procedural safeguards for children, and the broad scope of the court's authority over delinquent and pre-delinquent youth – viewed as essential to the child-saving mission – led to arbitrariness and abuses of power. Probation and institutional corrections programs were chronically understaffed, and their personnel were poorly paid and poorly trained (President's Commission on Law Enforcement and the Administration of Justice 1967). The plight of juvenile offenders was finally revealed in the 1960s and early 1970s, when the juvenile court came under the scrutiny of the United States Supreme Court in a series of cases that brought about a "due process revolution." *In re Gault* (1967, p. 87) – by far the most celebrated of these cases – the Supreme Court admonished that "Under our Constitution, the condition of being a boy does not justify a kangaroo court". It extended to children a right to counsel, a privilege against compelled self-incrimination, a requirement that proof of guilt be established "beyond a reasonable doubt," and other rights associated with the adversarial adult system. In the wake of these decisions, juvenile court proceedings began to look a lot like their criminal court counterparts.

In the 1970s, another challenge to juvenile justice appeared, this time from the academic community. A series of negative appraisals of juvenile treatment programs was published (e.g., Lipton et al. 1975; Wright and Dixon 1977; Sechrest et al. 1979), prompting what has been called "the decline of the rehabilitative ideal". Other researchers countered that negative assessments reflected methodological flaws in the research, weak evaluation designs, and poor program implementation, rather than the absence of viable treatment methods (e.g., Palmer 1991; Lipsey 1992; Fagan and Forst 1996), but these responses drew little attention. The interventionist rationale for the juvenile court was seriously undercut.

Capping the trends that led to a transformation in juvenile justice policy in the last 20 years was a surge in juvenile violence that began in the mid-1980s and extended through the early 90s. There was a virtual explosion of youth gun violence, much of it committed by young minority males in the nation's largest cities. The media responded to this violence with very heavy and sensationalized coverage. Media portrayals of young offenders also shifted sharply: the traditionally rather benign images of needy but redeemable juvenile offenders gave way to menacing portraits of savvy, cruel, and remorseless adolescent "superpredators," who were forecast to increase in numbers to 270,000 by the year 2010 (DiIulio 1995). DiIulio (1995, p. 23) claimed that "Americans are sitting atop a demographic crime bomb."

What ensued was a "moral panic" that politicians used to their advantage. Electoral politics began to revolve around efforts to outdo one's opponents in the race to "get tough" on juvenile crime. The underlying assumptions about youth that had animated the juvenile court movement were sharply challenged. Conceptions of juvenile offenders as adult-like, incipient career criminals legitimized a different set of penal responses. For young offenders who did not even approach "worst cases," legislators touted the utility of criminal punishment both as a deterrent and as a means of protecting a fearful public. What followed was an unprecedented series of transfer reforms.

The Criminalization of Juvenile Justice

Beginning in the 1980s, juvenile justice policy in the USA dramatically shifted away from the *parens patriae* mission to nurture miscreant youths, replaced by schemes in which punishment played an increasing role (Torbet et al. 1996). Loss of faith in the distinctiveness of youth – indeed, the near convergence of adolescence and adulthood – legitimated the criminalization of delinquency.

Historically, youth could be transferred to criminal court only if the juvenile court judge determined, after a full investigation and an adversarial hearing, that the child posed too much of a danger to the public or was no longer amenable to treatment in the juvenile justice system. With the increases in youth crime in the 1980s and the ensuing panic over superpredators, legislatures in the federal jurisdiction and every state save one responded by altering their laws to expedite the removal of young offenders to criminal court. Because juvenile court judges were perceived to be too conservative in the application of juvenile waiver proceedings, alternative procedures were established that either stripped juvenile court judges of their responsibility for transfer decisions or that sharply restricted their discretion.

In many states, authority to choose the forum in which a case would be tried was shifted to the prosecutor, who was permitted to make transfer decisions without a formal hearing or any possibility of review. Many states also statutorily excluded certain (most often violent) crimes or offense/prior record combinations from juvenile court jurisdiction, quite without regard to the offender's age. In some states, this meant that children as young as ten would automatically be tried as adults. Juvenile court judges' hands were tied by other statutes that created mandatory or presumptive waiver. The effects of all of these revisions were amplified by the creation of "once an adult, always an adult" provisions, which required that youths who had been transferred be treated as adults for any subsequent offenses, no matter how

Table 6.1 Facts about transfer in the USA

I. Lower limit of criminal court jurisdiction
18th birthday, 39 states
17th birthday, 10 states
16th birthday, 2 states
II. Jurisdictions instituting transfer reforms during the 1990s[a]
Traditional discretionary waiver (45)
Mandatory waiver (15)
Presumptive waiver (15)
Statutory exclusion (29)
Prosecutorial direct file (15)
Blended, juvenile courts can impose criminal sentences (15)
Once an adult, always an adult (34)
III. Minimum age for transfer
No minimum (23 states)
Age 10, 2 states
Age 12, 2 states
Age 13, 6 states
Age 14, 16 states
Age 15, 1 state
IV. Youth under 18 tried in the Criminal Justice System
Estimated 220,000 annually (including states that define adulthood at an age lower than 18)
75% have no prior arrests
Many non-violent offenders
Minorities greatly overrepresented, especially among those transferred via statutory exclusion and mandatory waiver

Source: Patrick Griffin 2003

[a]Numbers do not add to 51 because some had multiple reforms

minor. Finally, some states lowered the minimum age of criminal court jurisdiction, in effect transferring all youths of a given age to criminal court for prosecution and punishment as adults. As a result of all these changes, it is estimated that approximately 200,000 offenders under 18 are tried in American criminal courts annually, many of whom are neither particularly serious nor particularly chronic offenders, and some of whom are not yet in their teens.

A summary of The Criminalization of Juvenile Justice is presented in Table 6.1. There we see that, for purposes of the criminal law, 12 jurisdictions have set the boundary of "adulthood" at an age lower than 18.[2] In ten states, all juveniles are considered adults at their 17th birthdays. In two, they become adults when they turn 16. Remarkably, only one state prohibits transfer of offenders under age 15; 22

---

[2]Ironically, though in every state children aged 14–16 are routinely held to adult standards of criminal responsible, they are not adults for other purposes. For example, young people cannot vote or make medical decisions without parental consent until they are 18. Owing to concerns about the immaturity of their decision-making, they are not permitted to drink until they are 21.

set the minimum age at 14 or 15. In 27 states, even pre-teens are eligible for adult prosecution.

Today, only one state continues to rely exclusively on judicial waiver. All the rest permit or require youths to be removed from juvenile court jurisdiction without investigation or review of the need for transfer. Fifteen states have instituted mandatory waiver. Twenty-nine exclude certain offenses from juvenile court jurisdiction by statute. In 15 states, prosecutors may choose which cases shall be tried in criminal and which in juvenile court. Thirty-four states have adopted "once an adult, always an adult" provisions. And more than half the states have also adopted "blended sentencing," which provides for a combination juvenile–adult sentence. At the extreme, the juvenile court in Texas is authorized to sentence youths to up to 40 years in the state penitentiary.

Sentences imposed on youths who are convicted in criminal court are not mitigated by virtue of the offender's age. Indeed, research shows that the sentences adolescents receive are *harsher* than those imposed on comparable adult defendants. Even extreme penalties are not deemed to be inconsistent with youth. Until the Supreme Court's decision in *Roper v. Simmons* (2005), the death penalty could be imposed on offenders as young as 16. And today, in contravention of the U.N. Convention on the Rights of the Child,[3] at least 2,225 individuals are serving sentences of life without possibility of parole for offenses they committed as juveniles (Human Rights Watch, Amnesty International 2005).[4] Only three other countries (none in Europe) permit such sentences, and they have been imposed in only about a dozen cases (Human Rights Watch, Amnesty International 2005, p. 5). On the world stage, the USA stands alone by virtue of the harshness with which it responds to its juvenile offenders.

In sum, over the past two decades, the United States has embraced "get tough" policies that expand the reach and bite of transfer laws and increase the punitive powers of juvenile courts. Ideological, jurisdictional, and procedural transformations have promoted the substantive and procedural convergence of the juvenile and adult systems. This convergence has been supported by a loss of confidence in rehabilitation and, more important, by challenges to the basic ideas of youthful immaturity and malleability that provided the critical jurisprudential underpinnings of the juvenile court.

---

[3] The U.N. Convention on the Rights of the Child [CRC] recognizes the special needs of children and their potential for rehabilitation. Because sentences of life without possibility of parole flatly contradict the idea that children have the potential to change, the CRC provides (Article 37a) that "Neither capital punishment *nor life imprisonment without possibility of release* shall be imposed for offences committed by persons below eighteen years of age."

[4] Sixty percent of these youths were first offenders. The vast majority were convicted of murder, but more than one quarter were convicted of felony murder, where a youth participated in a robbery or burglary during which a co-defendant committed murder without his knowledge or intent (Human Rights Watch, Amnesty International 2005, p. 1 f.).

Towards a Revitalized Juvenile System and Reversal of Transfer Reforms

Despite the punitive policy reforms of the last two decades, I argue that the substantive rationale for the juvenile court is stronger today than ever before. We no longer need to rely on a vague "mathematics of maturity" grounded in politics and popular opinion to justify a separate system of juvenile justice. Advances in neuroscience, developmental psychology, and criminological research provide a strong rationale for a juvenile justice system that is resistant to threats of encroachment by the criminal justice system. These advances support the following conclusions:

- Adolescents are less culpable than adults. On grounds of fairness, they should not be held to adult standards of responsibility.
- Transfer to the criminal justice system exacerbates the risk of recidivism. On utilitarian grounds, it cannot be justified except in the most exceptional of circumstances.

On Account of Their Immaturity, Adolescents Are Less Culpable Than Adults and Should Not Be Held to Adult Standards of Responsibility

In the past 20 years, significant advances have been made in our understanding of adolescence. Especially relevant is the body of research on changes that take place in qualities of decision-making and judgment as youths make their way through adolescence to the early adult years. Breakthroughs have been made in our understanding of cognitive differences (differences in reasoning and understanding) between adolescents and adults, and psychosocial differences – differences in social and emotional functioning that affect the exercise of these cognitive capacities (Cauffman and Steinberg 2000a). Although, to be sure, there is wide variation among individuals, it can generally be said that "individuals at the point of entry into adolescence are very different than are individuals who are making the transition out of adolescence" (Steinberg and Cauffman 2000, p. 383).

Cognitive Development: Legislators and the general public tend to greatly overestimate adolescents' cognitive maturity. Although laboratory research indicates that by about the age of 14 or 15 adolescents know right from wrong and have the ability to process information and to make decisions that is roughly equal to that of adults, it does not follow that youths should be held to adult standards of criminal responsibility. Laboratory research findings can be misleading. All subjects have the benefit of the same information, and the research setting is most often relaxed, unhurried, quiet, and free of distractions. As a consequence, laboratory research depicts cognitive performance under ideal conditions, which may bear little relation to decision-making in the real world. As Scott and Steinberg (2003, p. 812 f.) explain, "findings from laboratory studies are only modestly useful…in understanding how youths compare to adults in making choices that have salience to their lives or that are presented in stressful unstructured settings (such as the street) in which decision makers must rely on personal experience and knowledge."

In the real world, people base decisions and judgments on the information they possess. Unlike the laboratory, where all subjects have the same information, people in the real world have acquired, through education and experience, different amounts of information about what options are available, and the nature and consequences of those options. Decision-making is generally better when we have the benefit of previous experience, particularly if the kind of decision we are called on to make is one that we have made before. In the words of Professor Zimring (2005, p. 17), "Being mature takes practice." Thus, despite the fact that their capacities for understanding and reasoning may be equal to adults, by virtue of their relative lack of education and experience, teens are less likely than adults to be cognizant of all of their options, to recognize and appreciate the consequences of the alternatives, and to weigh the costs and benefits of the alternatives in ways that produce positive outcomes.

In addition to cognitive development, psychosocial factors are also influential in the exercise of good judgment. Psychosocial factors refer to things such as risk perceptions, time perspective, and responsiveness to others that influence our preferences and, ultimately, the decisions that we make. Researchers have identified multiple psychosocial factors that are especially salient during the teen years, and which contribute to the characteristic immaturity of adolescent decision-making. Psychosocial development lags behind cognitive development – it continues to develop throughout adolescence and into the early adult years – and it appears to have a biological base. Before turning to a discussion of those psychosocial factors believed to be most important to the adolescent years, we take a brief excursion into the biological roots of psychosocial development.

Neuropsychological Research: Advances in neuroscience have produced an exciting new body of knowledge which reveals significant differences in the psychosocial maturity of adolescents and adults that are rooted in biochemical structures and processes of the brain. Research has focused especially on two areas of the brain. One involves the limbic and paralimbic regions, which are sensation- and reward-seeking areas of the brain that are activated by external stimuli (Brownlee 1999). The other region of the brain that is especially important to judgment and decision-making involves the prefrontal and parietal cortices. This region is often described as the "executive" or "cognitive control" center because it is the portion of the brain that is responsible for foresight, planning, strategic thinking, and self-regulation (Dahl 2004; Giedd 1999; Goldberg 2001; Sowell et al. 2001; 2002). Importantly, the frontal region regulates the expression of impulses emanating from the limbic region.

Development of the executive center of the brain occurs gradually, and is generally not complete until people reach their early twenties.[5] This means that even though young people may have developed adult-like capacities for understanding and reasoning by mid-adolescence, they do not acquire adult-like capacities for regulating their impulses until much later.

For reasons that are not entirely clear, the limbic regions become more easily aroused and more active with the onset of puberty. Both the intensity and lability of mood that we associate with adolescents are presumably manifestations of this change in functioning. The limbic system of adolescents is often bursting with emotions and impulses. The frontal lobes do not keep pace, but continue to develop at a much slower rate. Consequently, during the period between the onset of puberty and the maturation of the frontal cortices some 8–10 years later, individuals frequently have considerable difficulty modulating their emotions. When teens are emotionally aroused (e.g., in the company of friends, on dates, in situations of stress or excitement or danger), the executive center of their brains is not able to effectively rein in their impulses. This may account for the high rate at which teens make poor judgments, e.g., to drive after drinking, to engage in unprotected sex, to ride a motorcycle without a helmet, and to engage in other risky behaviors. Adolescents may understand the risks, but they do not have the tools to self-regulate. As neuroscientist Debra Yergulon-Todd explains, "[g]ood judgment is learned…[and] you can't learn it if you don't have the necessary hardware" (Brownlee 1999). Adolescents are simply not equipped to respond to stressful situations in the same ways as adults: They see fewer options, their time perspective is shortened, and their ability to foresee more distal consequences is limited (Mulvey and Peeples 1996). At other times, when they are not in a state of emotional arousal or stress – conditions more akin to the experimental laboratory setting – the reasoning and planning capacities of their brain can work more effectively. It is only in the early twenties, when frontal lobe development "catches up," that individuals reach mature adulthood and are better able to check emotions and impulses. It is then that they become less likely to "act without thinking" or to engage in risky and thrill-seeking behaviors, and more capable of delaying gratification, resisting external

---

[5]Longitudinal research using magnetic resonance imaging (MRI) and other sophisticated scanning techniques (e.g., PET scans, MRS) have provided images of brain functioning at rest and during various tasks, during regular intervals through adolescence and into adulthood. Using these technologies, Dr. Elizabeth Sowell, Dr. Jay Giedd, and others have shown that the prefrontal cortex undergoes dramatic changes during the adolescent years, and is one of the last areas of the brain to reach maturity. The gray matter thins in a pruning process that tightens the connections among neurons. In the same areas where gray matter thins, white matter increases through a process called "myelination." The accumulation of myelin around brain cell axons forms an insulating sheath, which increases communication among cells and allows the executive center to process information more efficiently and accurately. More important perhaps, the myelination process eventually completes the circuitry that integrates the executive center with other regions of the brain so that greater control is exerted over the social and emotional impulses originating in the limbic region (see Giedd et al. 1999).

pressures, and channeling negative emotions in constructive ways. Gur sums up the neuroscientific evidence nicely when he says: "The evidence is strong that the brain does not cease to mature until the early twenties in those relevant parts that govern impulsivity, judgment, planning for the future, foresight of consequences, and other characteristics that make people morally culpable.... Indeed, age 21 or 22 would be closer to the 'biological' age of maturity" (Gur 2002).

Psychosocial Development: In the past 20 years, especially through the work of the MacArthur Research Network on Adolescent Development and Juvenile Justice, developmental psychologists have identified psychosocial factors that contribute to the immature and impetuous character of much adolescent decision-making. In many instances these nonbiological aspects of development can be linked to and may interact with biological underdevelopment of regulatory controls. Although different scholars give these factors somewhat different labels, the following four categories capture them fairly well: (1) susceptibility to external influence, (2) risk orientation, (3) time orientation, and (4) impulse control (e.g., Scott and Steinberg 2003, p. 813 ff.). I briefly discuss each one below.

Susceptibility to External Influence: Scientific research confirms popular wisdom that adolescents are very much influenced by their peers. As part of the transition from dependence on the family of origin to independent adult living, adolescents spend a great deal of time in the company of peers, and much of their behavior – including most delinquent behavior – is committed in groups. Adolescence is also a time of identity development, and peers often provide the contexts in which teens "try out" new identities. Teens frequently imitate friends' speech, clothing, hairstyles, and other behaviors to gain acceptance and approval, and as symbols of friendship and belonging. Peers also influence one another more directly, sometimes pressing each other to engage in risky behaviors. There is considerable research evidence that, in the company of peers, the probability of engaging in risky behaviors is amplified: the desire for peer approval and fear of ridicule and rejection prompt teens to engage in acts that they would not commit alone (Warr 2002). Gardner and Steinberg (2005) recently demonstrated the effects of peers on risky behaviors in a laboratory study in which subjects played a video driving game of "Chicken" both alone and with friends. Subjects had to decide what to do when they approached an intersection where the signal light had turned yellow – either stop the car safely or try to beat the red light and risk a crash. The researchers found that the presence of peers more than doubled the risks taken by 13–15-year-olds, while it had a lesser effect on 18–22-year-olds, and no effect at all on those aged 24 and older. (It should be noted that these patterns of peer influence correspond closely to the course of development of the executive center of the brain.)

Risk Orientation: Perhaps in part because of the hyperactivity of their limbic systems, adolescents are more likely than adults to engage in risky behaviors (e.g., delinquency, unprotected sex, smoking, drinking), and, as we have just seen, the probability of engaging in risky behaviors is magnified when young people are in the company of peers. Furby and Beyth-Marom (1992) suggest that, relative to adults, youths give insufficient consideration to consequences, amplify rewards, minimize risks, and frequently perceive themselves as invulnerable to negative outcomes – the "personal fable" ("It may happen to others, but it won't happen to me.").

Time Orientation: Faced with a situation that calls for a decision, adolescents tend to give more consideration to short-term consequences, and less to long-term ones. Partly due to their lesser life experience, their time perspective is more limited than that of a typical adult. Furthermore, in the analysis of costs and benefits, they tend to discount whatever long-term consequences they do see. As a result, they tend, more so than adults, to opt for immediate gratification – e.g., postponing their homework to hang out with friends, spending their money now on things that they will forget about in a week instead of saving for something that will be much more meaningful. As most parents who have weathered the teen years know, adolescents tend to need things "this minute" and urgently ("I've simply got to have it.").

The foreshortened time perspective of adolescents is also implicated in their involvement in delinquency. Before committing crime, delinquent youths seldom consider the prospect of being caught and incarcerated, or the length of time they might be incarcerated. When they are sentenced to a term of years, it is difficult for them to project what that will mean in terms of life opportunities and life experiences forgone. The perceived difference between a sentence of 5 years and 10 years is a lot less meaningful to a teen than to an adult. Temporal perspective, then, may have important implications for differences in the extent to which adolescents and adults can be deterred by threats of legal sanctions.

Impulse Control: Compared to adults, young people have lesser ability to restrain their impulses. For reasons related in part to limbic system arousal, they experience emotional urges more intensely, and the underdevelopment of the frontal lobes means that they have lesser capacity to restrain these urges or divert them into prosocial outlets. There are additional psychosocial reasons for youths' impetuosity. They lack experience that would help them to think before acting, they are subject to pressures to act from peers, and their identities are still forming and fragile. Consider, for example, that for young boys, adolescence is the stage when there is a major focus on masculine identity. It should not be surprising that challenges to identity – insults, slurs on a boy's reputation for toughness – are often the triggers for episodes of impulsive violence (e.g., Fagan and Wilkinson 1998). When situations are stressful and emotions are high ("hot cognitions"), adolescent judgment is severely impaired relative to the situation of "cold cognitions," where emotions are calm and consequences are more readily apparent and considered. When cognitions are hot, adolescents are less sensitive to contextual cues that might temper their decisions.

These observations are borne out by a recent national study that compared nearly 1,000 adolescents and several hundred adults in their decision-making capacities as trial defendants. It was found that 16-year-old adolescents were less responsible, had less perspective (ability to consider different viewpoints and broader contexts of decisions), and were less temperate (able to limit impulses and evaluate situations before acting) than the average adult. It was not until age 19 that improvements in "judgment" reached adult levels (Cauffman and Steinberg 2000b).

Transfer to the Criminal Justice System Exacerbates the Risk of Recidivism and Cannot Be Justified Except in the Most Exceptional of Circumstances

Prompted in large measure by the widespread transfer reforms, over the past 10 to 15 years criminologists have conducted several studies for the purpose of assessing the comparative effectiveness of juvenile vs. criminal court processing of adolescent defendants. To date, seven studies have been carried out in demographically diverse jurisdictions, over a substantial time period, and using very different methodologies (Bishop et al. 1996; Fagan 1996; Fagan et al. 2007; Lanza-Kaduce et al. 2002; 2005; Myers 2001; Podkopacz and Feld 1996; Winner et al. 1997). Some of the studies have used fairly weak research designs while others are methodologically sophisticated. Regardless of the methodology used, all have produced very similar results. Such consistency of findings is rather unusual for social science research and gives us greater confidence in the findings.

Briefly stated, the research shows that young people who are transferred to criminal court for prosecution and punishment as adults are more likely to re-offend than equivalent young offenders who are processed in the juvenile court system. Transferred offenders re-offend more quickly, at higher rates, and commit more serious crimes than their counterparts who are retained in the juvenile system. These ill effects are especially pronounced among violent offenders and among first offenders (those most often targeted by automatic transfer laws) (Bishop et al. 1996; Fagan 1996; Lanza-Kaduce et al. 2002; 2005). Importantly, the negative effects of transfer are found among those who receive sentences in the community (e.g., adult probation) as well as those who are incarcerated in adult jails and prisons, although these effects are exacerbated among those who are incarcerated (Fagan 1996; Fagan et al. 2007). A recent review of this body of research conducted by the national Centers for Disease Control (CDC) reported that the overall median effect across studies was "a 34% relative increase in subsequent violent or general crime for transferred juveniles compared with retained juveniles" (CDC 2007, p. 7). The CDC report concluded that "transferring juveniles to the adult system is counterproductive as a strategy for preventing or reducing violence" (CDC 2007, p. 8).

The explanation for these rather robust findings remains unclear. However, we have quantitative data on juvenile and adult correctional institutions that provide some insights into the ways in which the juvenile and adult systems differ. When combined with qualitative research on young people in the juvenile and adult systems, we can begin to identify sources of negative effects. In the early 1980s, Forst et al. (1989) interviewed 140 adolescent male offenders in four states, all of whom had been convicted of serious violent crimes. Fifty-nine had been processed in juvenile courts and confined in training schools while the rest had been transferred and incarcerated in prisons. More recently, Bishop and her colleagues (Bishop et al. 2000; Lanza-Kaduce et al. 2002) interviewed 150 serious and chronic adolescent male offenders in Florida, half of whom had been transferred to criminal court and confined in state prisons, the balance of whom had been prosecuted in juvenile court and incarcerated in "maximum risk" juvenile commitment facilities. Still more recently, members of the MacArthur Foundation Research Network interviewed matched samples of adolescent inmates who were confined in juvenile correctional facilities in New Jersey and California, and adult institutions in New York and Arizona ($N = 425$). All three studies found that adolescents had quite different experiences in and reactions to the juvenile and criminal justice systems. Taken together, they suggest that the criminogenic effect of the criminal justice system is related to exposure to harsh and dispiriting conditions in adult prisons and to formidable problems of reintegration.

Official records data indicate that youths who are sentenced to incarceration by the criminal courts most often serve their sentences in adult correctional facilities where they are housed together with the general population of adult inmates (31 states), with youthful offenders up to age 21 or 25 (7 states), or some combination of the two (5 states) (Library Information Specialists 1995). Prison inmates are older, more often violent, and often have lengthy criminal histories and prior experiences with incarceration. Consequently, when juveniles are transferred to criminal court and institutionalized with adults, they are exposed to an older, more seasoned and more violent group of offenders over an extended period.

Official data also reveal organizational differences between juvenile and adult institutions. Adult facilities tend to be much larger than juvenile ones. The average daily population in institutions for adults is 700, compared to approximately 70 in juvenile facilities. And staffing patterns differ markedly in the two systems. Given their larger size, prisons must accord a much higher priority to security concerns: Nationally, two thirds of the personnel in adult correctional facilities are custody or security staff, and the ratio of security staff to inmates is 1:4 (BJS 1997). In contrast, the ratio of security staff to inmates in juvenile institutions is 1:11 in training schools, and much higher still in smaller residential placements (Parent et al. 1994). Additionally, there are many more opportunities for counseling, education and training by professional staff in juvenile correctional facilities.

Qualitative research indicates that adult prisons are rather like warehouses. Their core mission is custody, not treatment. Youths in adult correctional facilities are much less likely to receive counseling and other therapeutic services, education, or vocational training. They have much idle time which is spent in the company of older, more seasoned inmates at a critical period in adolescent identity development. The Florida researchers reported that in the institutional world of the adult prison, youths were more likely to learn social rules and norms that legitimated domination, exploitation, and retaliation. Youths routinely observed both staff and inmate models who exhibited these behaviors and reinforced illegal norms. Others in the inmate subculture taught them criminal motivations as well as techniques of committing crime and avoiding detection. The Florida researchers also reported that prison staff engaged in negative shaming: Custodial staff most often treated inmates with disdain and hostility, and clearly communicated messages that youths were irredeemable and incapable of change.

The Florida researchers also found that relations between staff and youths in juvenile correctional institutions were most often described in very positive terms.

The general sense of youths' comments was that most staff cared for them and believed in their potential to become productive and law-abiding adults. Staff was credited with being skilled at modeling and teaching appropriate behaviors, and providing helpful guidance about personal matters. To be sure, some staff were described as having little interest or concern for youths. However, only a small fraction of staff in juvenile institutions were characterized in this way. Similarly, Forst et al. (1989) found that, compared to staff in prisons, staff in juvenile facilities were more involved in counseling, more concerned about youths' adjustment, more encouraging of their participation in programs, more helpful in assisting them to understand themselves and deal with their problems, and more facilitative of improved relationships with their families. Juvenile program staff was also rated significantly more highly than prison staff in terms of helping youths to set and achieve goals, to improve relationships with peers, to feel better about themselves, and to acquire skills that would be useful upon release.

Both Forst et al. (1989) and the Florida researchers found that juvenile facilities were generally organized around a therapeutic model – most often, a cognitive–behavioral one – which provided core principles that governed staff behavior and staff–resident interactions. Staff in juvenile programs were expected to model self-discipline, social skills, and strategies for problem-solving and impulse control. Even line staff was trained in treatment methodologies and were expected to integrate them into daily activities on a more-or-less ongoing basis. Significant incentives for staff – salary enhancements and promotions – were linked to therapeutic skills.

All three studies reported a stronger treatment orientation in juvenile institutions compared to adult ones. Programs in juvenile institutions addressed mental health needs, learning deficits, and social skills deficits, and were designed to facilitate adolescent development (social competencies, prosocial identity, decision-making, planning). According to the MacArthur research group, in terms of youth's ratings of fairness, counseling and therapeutic services, educational and job training services, and program structure, adult correctional facilities fared significantly worse than juvenile ones. They also reported that organized gangs were the dominant social group in adult prisons, while loosely organized groups of peers dominated in juvenile facilities; that youths in adult correctional facilities experienced a greater sense of danger, and that those confined in adult facilities had significantly higher rates of depression, and scored significantly more poorly on measures of overall levels of mental health functioning than youth in juvenile correctional institutions.

Those who are transferred to the adult system also must deal with the greater stigma that attaches to a criminal conviction. This is true of those who are placed on probation in the community as well as those who are sentenced to incarceration. Felony convictions must be reported on employment applications, making it more difficult to obtain jobs. Those convicted of felonies in adult court are barred from military service and many other forms of public employment. They may be denied access to student loans and educational opportunities. They are frequently ineligible for low-cost public housing. They also have more difficulty reintegrating into conventional social networks. Most youths who engage in delinquency will desist from crime by early adulthood as they move into jobs and marriages that give them a sense of place and purpose, while those prosecuted in the criminal justice system carry a stigma that may severely limit legitimate work and social opportunities, and impair their life chances for a very long period of time. Stigmatization and obstruction of conventional opportunities certainly make re-offending more likely.

In sum, the factors contributing to the criminogenic effects of transfer are complex and include the multiple negative effects of incarceration in the adult system (e.g., exposure to negative shaming, opportunities for criminal socialization, modeling of violence) and the stigmatization and opportunity blockage that flow from a record of criminal conviction. Compared with the criminal justice system, the juvenile system is more reintegrative in practice and effect.

Implications for Policy

On grounds of both fairness and practicality, then, juvenile offenders are best retained in the juvenile justice system, which is better equipped to respond to adolescents in ways that promote positive youth development. Neuroscientific research and research in developmental psychology clearly support the conclusion that, except in rare cases, it is inappropriate to hold adolescents to adult standards of criminal responsibility. Significant legal support for this conclusion was recently provided by the United States Supreme Court in the case of *Roper v. Simmons* (2005). In that case, the Supreme Court banned capital punishment for persons who were under the age of 18 at the time of their offenses. In assessing the constitutionality of the death penalty, the Supreme Court inquired whether such a penalty was consistent with "evolving standards of decency." It looked at the states and at international standards – including the International Convention on the Rights of the Child – and concluded that the death sentence for minors is inconsistent with contemporary notions of decency. The Court also ruled that the death penalty is a disproportionate sentence for minors. The Court accepted neurobiological and social science evidence of the immaturity of adolescents, their greater susceptibility to external pressure, and their greater capacity for change. The linchpin of the Court's decision was that these differences between youths under 18 and adults render youths less culpable than adults. Although the decision in *Roper* was a narrow one that applies only to cases involving capital punishment, the logic of the Court's opinion arguably extends beyond such cases and is consistent with the view that few offenders under 18 deserve to be treated as adults.

Beyond considerations of fairness, research also supports the conclusion that, on utilitarian grounds, expansive transfer policies are both imprudent and harmful. Instead of deterring young offenders, it appears that prosecution and punishment as an adult is criminogenic. Compared to retention in the juvenile system, transfer has deleterious effects on youths to whom it is applied and only increases the risk to public safety. When transfer statutes are applied broadly, incapacitative gains reaped in the short run are quickly nullified over the long term.

Because young people generally do not achieve adult-like maturity until their late teens or early twenties, a more fair and rational policy would set the lower limit of criminal court jurisdiction at age 18 (or even 21) and would severely restrict the transfer to criminal court of youths who have not reached that boundary. For offenders under that age limit, transfer should not be permissible in the absence of a careful psychosocial assessment and a determination that a young defendant possesses the requisite cognitive and psychosocial maturity to be held to adult standards of responsibility. To ensure that the application of transfer law is properly restricted, it is essential that responsibility for transfer be returned to juvenile judges in a system of discretionary waiver. Legislative exclusion statutes, mandatory waiver laws, and prosecutorial transfer provisions need to be repealed.

There is much to be said for the idea of raising the age of the juvenile court's continuing jurisdiction to age 24. Such a course would remove much of the incentive to transfer youths who are nearing the current upper limits of the juvenile court's continuing jurisdiction (usually 18, or 21) and would enhance the prospects of rehabilitation in intensive, long-term treatment programs while young people are still going through periods of significant neuropsychological development.

Sound juvenile justice policy would also include a focus on "evidence-based treatment," and would ensure that juvenile correctional programs are well funded. Meta-analyses of program evaluations have identified many effective programs, some of which, when staffed appropriately and implemented well, can substantially reduce the risk of re-offending, even among serious and violent offenders (Lipsey and Wilson 1998). These programs focus on building social skills, enhancing educational and vocational competencies, improving interpersonal relationships, and other aspects of positive youth development.

These policy recommendations are not beyond reach. There are many signs that the pendulum of juvenile justice policy has begun to swing away from the "get tough," punitive approach to children and adolescents that has defined American juvenile justice for the past two decades. For example, a national poll of American voters conducted in 2007 showed that 90% of respondents are concerned about youth crime, but that an equal proportion support rehabilitative services and treatment (Krisberg and Marchionna 2007). Eighty percent believe that spending tax dollars on enhanced rehabilitation services is cost-effective, while nearly three quarters feel that incarcerating juveniles in adult correctional facilities only promotes further crime. Two thirds of those polled oppose the incarceration of persons under 18 in adult jails and prisons. These results are consistent with those of numerous other state polls, and should be considered by lawmakers whose preferences are too often guided by media accounts of high-profile juvenile crimes and the short-lived fear-driven pressures to toughen penalties that they tend to engender. Elected representatives need to know that they can support treatment of serious offenders in the juvenile justice system without jeopardizing their chances of re-election (Nagin et al. 2006).

There are other hopeful signs of change. Research on adolescent brain development and on the negative consequences of transfer has received considerable publicity. So too has the decision in *Roper v. Simmons*. The heavy financial burden associated with maintaining the nation's overcrowded adult jail and prison facilities has also produced an openness to change. Taken together, these developments have already prompted some legislators to soften their approach to youth crime.

Last year the Connecticut legislature raised the age of criminal court jurisdiction from 16 to 18, and the North Carolina legislature has recently ordered a study of the feasibility of doing the same. Florida, which led the nation in transfers just a few years ago, has reduced their number by more than two thirds. At the same time, the legislature provided substantially increased funding for juvenile treatment programs and adopted an evidence-based approach to juvenile programming.

In 2006, the Colorado legislature abolished sentences of life without possibility of parole for juveniles, and legislatures in several other states are considering similar steps. In several states, legislation that excluded drug offenses from juvenile court jurisdiction has been repealed. And, led by the MacArthur Foundation – which has been responsible for funding much of the research on adolescent development –, four states have been identified as sites for Models for Change, an effort to develop more effective and developmentally appropriate juvenile justice systems. Although it is too soon to tell whether the tide has turned, there are signs that support for progressive reform consistent with foundational principles of the juvenile court is gaining momentum.

Cases Cited

In re Gault, 387 U.S. 1 (1967).
Roper v. Simmons, 543 U.S. 551 (2005).

References

Banay, Ralph S. 1947. Homicide among children. *Federal Probation* 11: 11–20.
Bishop, Donna M., Charles E. Frazier, Lonn-Lanza-Kaduce, and Lawrence Winner. 1996. The Transfer of juveniles to criminal court: Does it make a difference? *Crime and Delinquency* 42: 171–191.
Breckenridge, Sophonisba Preston, and Edith Abbott. 1912. *The Delinquent Child and the Home*. New York: Charities Publication Committee.
Brownlee, Shannon. August 9, 1999. Inside the teen brain. *U.S. News and World Report*, pp. 44–48.
Cauffman, Elizabeth, and Laurence Steinberg. 2000a. Researching adolescents' judgment and culpability, in Thomas Grisso and Robert G. Schwartz, eds., *Youth on Trial: A Developmental Perspective on Juvenile Justice*. Chicago: University of Chicago Press, pp. 325–343.
Cauffman, Elizabeth, and Laurence Steinberg. 2000b. (Im)maturity of judgment in adolescence: Why adolescents may be less culpable than adults. *Behavioral Sciences and the Law* 18: 741–760.
Centers for Disease Control and Prevention, U.S. Department of Health and Human Services. November 30, 2007. Effects on violence of laws and policies facilitating the transfer of youth from the juvenile to the adult justice system. *Morbidity and Mortality Weekly Report* Vol. 56, No. RR-9. Atlanta, GA: CDC.
Dahl, Ronald E. 2004. Adolescent brain development: A period of vulnerabilities and opportunities. *Annals of the New York Academy of Sciences* 1021: 1–22.
DiIulio, John. November 19, 1995. The coming of the Super-predators, *The Weekly Standard* 1: 23–29.

Fagan, Jeffrey. 1996. The comparative advantage of juvenile versus criminal court sanctions on recidivism among adolescent felony offenders. *Law and Policy* 18: 77–119.

Fagan, Jeffrey, and Deanna L. Wilkinson. 1998. Guns, youth violence, and social identity in inner cities, in Michael Tonry and Mark Moore, eds., *Youth Violence—Crime and Justice: A review of Research, Vol. 24*. Chicago: University of Chicago Press, pp. 105–188.

Fagan, Jeffrey, Aaron Kupchik, and Akiva Liberman. 2007. Be careful what you wish for: Legal sanctions and public safety among adolescent felony offenders in juvenile and criminal court. Columbia Law School, Pub. Law Research Paper No. 03-61. Available at SSRN: http://ssrn.com/abstract=491202

Furby, Lita, and Ruth Beyth-Marom. 1992. *Risk-Taking in Adolescence: A Decision-making Perspective*. Washington, DC. Carnegie Council on Adolescent Development.

Gardner, Margo, and Laurence Steinberg. 2005. Peer influence on risk taking, risk preference, and risky decision making in adolescence and adulthood: An experimental study. *Developmental Psychology* 41: 625–635.

Giedd, Jay, et al. 1999. Brain development during childhood and adolescence: A longitudinal MRI study. *Nature Neuroscience* 2: 861–863.

Goldberg, Elkhonon. 2001. *The Executive Brain: Frontal Lobes and the Civilized Mind*. New York: Oxford University Press.

Griffin, Patrick. 2003. *Trying and sentencing juveniles as adults: An analysis of state transfer and blended sentencing laws*. Pittsburgh, PA: National Center for Juvenile Justice.

Gur, Ruben C. 2002. Declaration of Ruben C. Gur, Ph.D., in *Patterson v. Texas*. Petition for Writ of Certiorari to U.S. Supreme Court, J. Gary Hart, Counsel. Available at http://www.abanet.org/crimjust/juvjus/patterson.html

Harris, Thomas LeGrand. 1914. Ben B. Lindsey. in Mary Griffin Webb and Edna Lenore Webb, eds., *Famous Living Americans*. Greencastle, IN: Charles Webb and Co., pp. 300–312.

Human Rights Watch/Amnesty International. 2005. *The rest of their lives: Life without parole for child offenders in the United States*. New York, NY: Amnesty International. Available at http://hrw.org/reports/2005/us1005/

Krisberg, Barry, and Susan Marchionna. 2007. Attitudes of US voters toward youth crime and the justice system. Oakland, CA: National Council on Crime and Delinquency. Available online at http://www.nccd-crc.org/nccd/n_pubs_main.html

Lanza-Kaduce, Lonn, Jodi Lane, Donna M. Bishop, and Charles E. Frazier. 2005. Juvenile offenders and adult felony recidivism: The impact of transfer. *Journal of Crime and Justice* 28: 59–78.

Lipsey, Mark W. 1992. Juvenile delinquency treatment: A meta-analytic inquiry into the variability of effects, in *Meta-Analysis for Explanation*, Thomas D. Cook, Harris Cooper, David S. Cordray, Heidi Hartmann, Larry V. Hedges, Richard J. Light, Thomas A. Louis, and Frederick Mosteller, eds.,. New York: Russell Sage Foundation.

Lipton, Douglas, Robert Martinson, and Judith Wilks. 1975. *The Effectiveness of Correctional Intervention: A Survey of Treatment Evaluation Studies*. New York: Praeger.

Mack, Julian W. 1909. The juvenile court. *Harvard Law Review* 23: 104–122.

Mulvey, Edward P., and Faith L. Peeples. 1996. Are disturbed and normal adolescents equally competent to make decisions about mental health treatments? *Law and Human Behavior* 20: 273–286.

Myers, David L. 2001. *Excluding Violent Youths from Juvenile Court: The Effectiveness of Legislative Waiver*. New York, NY: LFB Publishing.

Nagin, Daniel S., Alex R. Piquero, Elizabeth S. Scott, and Laurence Steinberg. 2006. Public preference for rehabilitation versus incarceration of juvenile offenders: Evidence from a contingent valuation study. *Criminology and Public Policy* 5: 627–652.

Oppenheim, Nathan. 1898. *The Development of the Child*. New York: The MacMillan.

Palmer, Ted B. 1991. The effectiveness of intervention: Recent trends and current issues. *Crime and Delinquency* 37: 330–346.

Podkopacz, Marcy R., and Barry C. Feld. 1996. The end of the line: An empirical study of judicial waiver. *Journal of Criminal Law and Criminology* 86: 449–492.

President's Commission on Law Enforcement and the Administration of Justice. 1967. *Task Force Report on Juvenile Delinquency and Youth Crime*. Washington, DC: U.S. Government Printing Office.

Ryerson, Ellen. 1978. *The Best Laid Plans: America's Juvenile Court Experiment*. New York: Hill and Wang.

Scott, Elizabeth S., and Laurence Steinberg. 2003. Blaming youth. *Texas Law Review* 81:799–840.

Sechrest, Lee B., Susan O. White, and Elizabeth D. Brown, eds. 1979. *The Rehabilitation of criminal Offenders*. Washington, DC: National Academy of Sciences.

Sowell, Elizabeth R., et al. 2001. Mapping continued brain growth and gray matter density reduction in dorsal frontal cortex: Inverse relationships during postadolescent brain maturation. *Journal of Neuroscience* 21: 8819–8829.

Sowell, Elizabeth R., et al. 2002. Development of cortical and subcortical brain structures in childhood and adolescence. *Developmental Medicine and Child Neurology* 44: 4–16.

Steinberg, Laurence, and Elizabeth Cauffman. 2000. A developmental perspective on jurisdictional boundary, in Jeffrey Fagan and Franklin E. Zimring, eds., *The Changing Borders of Juvenile Justice*. Chicago: University of Chicago Press, pp. 379–406.

Tanenhaus, David S. 2004. *Juvenile Justice in the Making*. New York, Oxford University Press.

Torbet, Patricia, Richard Gable, Hunter Hurst IV, Imogene Montgomery, Linda Szymanski, and Douglas Thomas. 1996. *State Responses to Serious and Violent Juvenile Crime*. Pittsburgh: National Center for Juvenile Justice.

Travis, Thomas. 1908. *The Young Malefactor: A Study in Juvenile Delinquency: Its Causes and Treatment*. New York: Thomas Y. Crowell and Co.

Tuthill, Richard S. 1904. History of the children's court in Chicago, in *Children's Courts in the United States: Their Origin, Development, and Results*. New York: The International Prison Commission.

United States Children's Bureau. 1923. *Juvenile-Court Standards: Report of the Committee Appointed by the Children's Bureau, August, 1921, to Formulate Juvenile-Court Standards, Adopted by a Conference Held under the Auspices of the Children's Bureau and the national Probation Association, Washington, DC, May 18,1923*. Publication no. 121. Washington, DC: U.S. Government Printing Office.

Warr, Mark. 2002. *Companions in Crime: The Social Aspects of Criminal Conduct*. Cambridge, UK: Cambridge University Press.

Winner, Lawrence, Lonn Lanza-Kaduce, Donna M. Bishop, and Charles E. Frazier. 1997. The transfer of juveniles to criminal court: Reexamining recidivism over the long term. *Crime and Delinquency* 43: 548–563.

Wright, William F., and Michael C. Dixon. 1977. Community treatment of juvenile delinquency: A review of evaluation studies. *Journal of Research in Crime and Delinquency* 19: 35–67.

Zimring, Franklin E. 2000. The common thread: Diversion in juvenile justice. *California Law Review* 88: 2477–2495.

Zimring, Franklin E. 2005. *American Juvenile Justice*. New York: Oxford University Press.

Chapter 7
Transfer of Minors to the Criminal Court in Europe: Belgium and the Netherlands

Ido Weijers, An Nuytiens, and Jenneke Christiaens

The transfer of youths from the juvenile to the criminal court was common in large parts of the world throughout the past century. Right from the start, judicial waiver mechanisms to remove very serious cases from the juvenile court formed part of the juvenile justice system in many countries. It was and is still viewed by many as a 'safety valve' for the juvenile courts, and for the juvenile justice system as a whole. The idea was that by offering this safety valve for extremely serious cases that happen only rarely, the special treatment of the mass of young offenders could be saved. There has been little if any research into these mechanisms until recently, when, alarmed by reports from the United States, some researchers in Western Europe started to investigate this phenomenon.

There is, of course, a wide variety of factors that can be taken as indicators of the state of affairs in juvenile justice. The transfer of minors to adult criminal court can be taken as one such relevant indicator, a standard, and so a comparison between the United States and Western Continental Europe may be interesting. This chapter will present the findings of two recent studies, carried out independently from each other in Belgium and in the Netherlands. It will start by explaining the two different answers that were developed in Western continental Europe for the problem of the extremely serious cases: the 'strict' systems and 'flexible' systems. Second, it will present the findings of two 'flexible' systems, the Belgian and the Dutch systems, and compare these. As was made clear in chapter 4, in the United States the primary and explicit focus of reform efforts was to increase the number of youths tried as adults. In these two European countries the opposite can be found. In so far as the response to serious crime by minors can be taken as a relevant indicator of the state of affairs in juvenile justice, this study suggests that there is a wide gap between what has happened in the last few decades in the United States and on the European continent. Finally, the chapter will present some conclusions and recommendations for the future.

I. Weijers (✉) and A. Nuytiens
Faculty of Social Sciences – Pedagogic, University of Utrecht, Utrecht, The Netherlands

J. Christiaens
University of Gent, Section Penal Law and Criminology, Gent, Belgium

J. Junger-Tas and F. Dünkel (eds.), *Reforming Juvenile Justice*,
DOI:10.1007/978-0-387-89295-5_7, © Springer Science+Business Media, LLC 2009

Europe

In Western continental Europe the upper limit of penal liability within the juvenile justice system is 18 years of age. In some countries this upper limit is absolute, which means that minors can never be brought before an adult court. In others, this limit is flexible, which implies that it can be lowered in certain cases and that minors can get adult sentences and (in some countries) even be sentenced by an adult criminal court.

This has resulted in two strategies in Europe for responding to the problem of very serious crimes committed by minors. First, there is the *strict* model, in which a fixed upper age limit is operated for juvenile justice; this means that trial under the ordinary criminal law is ruled out. In this model, therefore, the problem of the criminal-law response to very serious crimes committed by minors is dealt with within the juvenile justice system itself, through high maximum sentences for certain offences. Substantive, procedural and correctional aspects all remain within the juvenile justice system.

Germany is a striking example of this model. In Germany, juveniles only come under the youth justice system from the age of 14. The German *Jugendgerichtsgesetz* (JGG) distinguishes educational measures, disciplinary measures and punishments. The punishments vary from a minimum of 6 months up to a maximum of 5 years' youth detention, unless the juvenile has committed a crime punishable in the adult criminal law with a prison sentence of more than 10 years, in which case the maximum term of youth detention is 10 years (par. 18 JGG).[1]

Austria also operates the strict model, also with 14 years as the lower age limit for juvenile justice. For the majority of offences committed by juveniles, there is no minimum term of detention; the maximum punishment under juvenile criminal law is half of the maximum for the same offence under adult criminal law. For very serious offences, however, which under general criminal law carry a life sentence or 20 years as maximum sentence, detention of between 1 and 10 years can be imposed under the juvenile justice system for 14- to 16-year-olds and between 1 and 15 years for 16- to 18-year-olds (par. 5 No. 2 öJGG).[2]

Switzerland is another country that operates this model. Switzerland used to be known for the very young age at which criminal responsibility started, namely, 7 years, but that has now been raised to 10 years. However, while this means that *educational* measures can be taken from the age of 10, criminal penalties can only be imposed from the age of 15 years. The maximum custodial sentence for minors is 1 year, but there is a maximum of 4 years for young people aged 16 and over who have committed very serious crimes (Art. 24 JStG). Despite appearances to the contrary, due to the low minimum age limit, Switzerland therefore has an exceptionally

---

[1] Albrecht 2004; Dünkel 1990.

[2] For young adults (18 to 20 years) the penalties available in that case vary from 5 to 20 years' detention, see Jesionek 2001.

lenient juvenile justice system, certainly as far as the maximum penalties are concerned.[3]

The second model in operation in Europe is one in which a flexible upper limit is coupled with relatively low maximum penalties in the juvenile justice system. While in this *flexible* model the majority of juveniles who appear in court are guaranteed a relatively low maximum penalty, exceptions are made for very serious cases. In principle, if the court considers it to be necessary and fair, sentences from adult criminal law can be imposed.

This model operates in the Netherlands. The general rule in Dutch criminal law is that all young people aged between 12 and 18 years are dealt with under the juvenile justice system. Departures from this general rule are possible, however. Article 77b of the Penal Code allows courts to try suspects who were 16 or 17 years old at the time of the offence under ordinary adult criminal law, if they find grounds to do so in 'the seriousness of the crime, the personality of the offender or the circumstances in which the crime was committed'. In addition, Article 495b paragraph 2 of the Penal Code allows a court to depart from the principle of trying minors behind closed doors, if in its opinion 'the importance of hearing the case in open court must outweigh the importance of protecting the privacy of the suspect, his co-accused, parents or guardian.'

Belgium operates this model too. The Belgian Youth Protection Act (WJB) offers a broad range of measures that can be imposed for a diverse range of problematic or troublesome behaviour. What is remarkable about Belgium is that, as a rule, these measures can also be imposed in response to criminal offences. However, the Belgian Youth Protection Act also provides for another drastic intervention in response to very serious crimes, that is the transfer (Art. 38 WJB) for 16- and 17-year-olds. This means that the juvenile is transferred to the ordinary adult criminal justice system.[4]

This model is also found in France. The foundations of French juvenile criminal law were laid down in 1945 in the *Ordonnance relative à l'enfance délinquante*. The minimum age is 13. The youngest offenders and those who have committed the least serious offences can be dealt with by the *juge des enfants* (Art. 8 Ord.). Thirteen- to sixteen-year-olds who are accused of more serious offences have to appear before the *Tribunal pour enfants* (Art. 3 Ord.), while 16- to 18-year-olds are tried by the *Court d'assises des mineurs* (Art. 20 Ord.). All these courts hear cases behind closed doors and work with a rather informal approach geared to the young person (Art. 8, Art. 14 and Art. 20 Ord.). As far as the very serious crimes are concerned, both the *Tribunal pour enfants* and the *Court d'assises des mineurs* can impose heavy sentences on minors, namely, half of the maximum sentence for the offence under general criminal law up to a maximum of 20 years. Where this maximum is already very high, the *Court d'assises des mineurs* can furthermore impose

---

[3] Rehberg 2001; Zermatten 2004.

[4] Nuytiens et al. 2005.

a sentence from general criminal law upon offenders aged between 16 and 18, if the circumstances and personality of the offender call for this (Art. 20-2 Ord.).[5] Apart from that, the sentence should (in the first instance) be served in a separate young offenders-institution or -section. There have been various proposals in France in recent years to make it easier to try minors under the ordinary criminal law, most recently by Minister for Justice Clément following months of pressure from his colleague Minister Sarkozy for Home Affairs. President Sarkozy has announced new initiatives.

An extreme version of the flexible model can be seen in England and Wales, where juvenile delinquents can be tried by a variety of courts. In addition to the usual Youth Court, in some cases, for example if a minor has committed a criminal offence with one or more adults, the case will be heard in the Magistrates' Court. Where very serious crimes are concerned – murder, manslaughter – then the trial will be held on indictment in the Crown Court. A Crown Court trial is a very formal and public hearing which amounts in fact to normal criminal proceedings (Art. 53 Children and Young Persons Act).[6] This was for that matter the essence of the European Court's criticism of the trial of the two very young offenders in the Bulger case, which was judged to be in breach of Article 6.1. (right to a fair trial) of the European Convention on Human Rights. From a substantive perspective also, this amounted to a trial under the ordinary criminal law. While the maximum sentence in the current English juvenile criminal law is 2 years, in the case of grave crimes – crimes carrying a maximum sentence of 14 years in general criminal law – the court can go much further. For grave crimes in England and Wales, very long prison sentences are possible for children from the age of 10 years, which appear to match the maxima in the ordinary criminal law.[7] Minors who are convicted of murder can be given an indeterminate sentence, which in practice may eventually amount to life.

Following this brief review, we can anyway conclude for the time being that the situation in Europe is completely different from that in the United States. In the strict model, transfer to the adult criminal justice system is completely impossible. In the flexible system, it is possible but it is the court that decides on the penalty to be imposed on the juvenile, and not the prosecutor. We have to note also, however, that both models show a great variety of forms and a large range from severe to lenient in the responses to serious offending by juveniles. Furthermore, there are still more variants in Europe. There are countries that have no separate juvenile justice system at all, especially in Scandinavia, where however separate maximum penalties are laid down for juvenile offenders, such as 7 years in Denmark and 10 years in Sweden.[8] Finally, Scotland stands out as having a completely different approach: here children are tried under the general criminal law from their 16th birthday (see chapter 4 and 13.

---

[5] Renucci 1998, p. 106.

[6] Bottoms and Dignan 2004.

[7] Stump 2003, p. 191.

[8] Fourteen years if an offence is committed with an adult offender.

The following sections will examine in more detail how the Netherlands and Belgium respond to very grave offences committed by minors. What is the policy on this issue and how is it implemented in practice?

The Netherlands

The Netherlands has been shaken in the past few years not only by a political killing (Fortuyn 2002) and a murder which smacked of terrorism (van Gogh 2004), but also by a number of appalling crimes of violence involving juvenile offenders, some with fatal outcomes, which have forced themselves into Dutch public consciousness. Several really shocking cases dominated the news for weeks in short succession around the end of 2003 and early 2004. In October 2003, a 43-year-old female drug addict was kicked to death by a group of young men on a square in Amsterdam. A month later the public was again shaken by the cold-blooded murder of a 16-year-old girl in Bemmel whose body was then set on fire. Two months after that, the attack on the deputy head of a school in The Hague, who was shot through the head by a pupil in broad daylight in the school canteen, which was full at the time, caused further public outrage. Minors were involved in all these cases and each one of them was tried under the general criminal law.

The option to make such an exception to juvenile criminal law has existed since the introduction of the separate juvenile justice system in 1901. On a parliamentary initiative an amendment was adopted which created the opportunity to impose an adult penalty from the age of 16 years in some cases at the discretion of the court. The decision and reasons for the decision were, in other words, left entirely to the court. This judicial discretion remained untouched for over half a century. It was only in 1965 that conditions were attached to it. The criteria were worded in very general terms as 'the seriousness of the offence' and 'the personality of the offender'. They were applied cumulatively: so there had to be both a serious offence and something in the offender's personality which justified making an exception to the limits of the juvenile criminal law.

The lowering of the age of majority in civil law from 21 to 18 years provided the occasion for a review of all the rules based on this age limit. An advisory committee proposed raising the upper age limit of juvenile criminal law, arguing for a single system of juvenile justice which would apply from the age of 12 to 24 years.[9] It would, of course, have to be possible to make exceptions to this, because in the committee's opinion there could be circumstances in which it would be desirable to apply the general criminal law to young people aged between 16 and 24 who had committed a serious crime. In the view of the advisory committee, the personality of the offender should be the deciding factor. The committee also proposed to

---

[9] Anneveldt Committee 1982, p. 16.

increase the maximum term of youth detention for 16- to 18-year-olds from 6 to 12 months. The extension of the system to include 18- to 24-year-olds would be accompanied by a new maximum sentence of 18 months for this age group. Under the age of 16 the maximum should be kept at 6 months.

The government, however, put aside this sound proposal for a juvenile justice system up to the age of 24 years which had been so long in the preparation. Even the grounds for the exceptions to applying juvenile criminal law to 16- and 17-year-olds were interpreted differently from what the committee had proposed: there was certainly no decisive role for the personality of the offender, the criteria became alternatives rather than accumulative, and a third, separate criterion, 'the circumstances in which the offence was committed', was added. Finally, the committee's proposal on maximum sentences was disregarded. Contrary to the committee's recommendations, sentences were made more severe across the whole range. For 12- to 16-year-olds, the maximum was increased from 6 months to a year; for 16- and 17-year-olds it went up to 2 years. Since 1995, therefore, Dutch juvenile courts have been able to impose much heavier sentences within the framework of the juvenile justice system. How far has there also been a need on top of that for more flexible arrangements for transfer to the adult criminal justice system since then?

In Practice

Following the shocking events in late 2003, early 2004, and especially the prolonged and lurid attention given to them in the media, it was suggested from many quarters, including professional experts, that more and more minors were being tried under the general criminal law in the Netherlands. This was the reason for investigating the practice on this point in the Netherlands. If we look at the available figures for the past 10 years, however, we see that, contrary to expectations, there has actually been a considerable *decrease* in the trial of minors under general criminal law. While in 1995 there were 16% of all cases dealt with by the juvenile courts, in 2004 it was only 1.2%. Even when we look at absolute figures for recent years, there is a clear decrease to be seen (Table 7.1).

Table 7.1 Guilty verdicts in courts of first instance in criminal cases against 12- to 17-year-olds

Year	All cases (12–17)	General criminal law (16–17)	%
1998	7,798	206	2.7
1999	8,291	198	2.4
2000	8,930	170	1.9
2001	8,489	205	2.4
2002	9,531	204	2.1
2003	10,462	174	1.7
2004	11,584	143	1.2

Source: OMDATA

We are forced to conclude that the amendment to the law in 1995 brought about a spectacular turnaround. The percentage of all minors who appeared in court who were tried under general criminal law has been reduced more than tenfold in 10 years and it seems likely that this downward trend is set to continue. A conclusion that can be drawn from this is that one component of the package of amendments in 1995 – the heavier maximum sentences – has given courts so much scope that they have much less need to use the option to apply general criminal law. Evidently, the other part of the package of amendments – making trial under general criminal law easier by allowing alternative rather than accumulative grounds and the addition of a third separate ground 'circumstances in which ...' – has not prompted courts to make extra use of Article 77b of the Penal Code.

The general trend, therefore, is for decreasing use of general criminal law, but is that the case all over? If we break this information down by the different district courts, major local differences emerge. This is clearly illustrated by a comparison of data from the district courts for two periods: 2000–2001 and 2003–2004 (Table 7.2).

Over the whole country the falling trend is obviously confirmed: from 417 cases in the first period there has been a decrease to 355 in the second period. However, while for example in Den Bosch there was a dramatic decrease over the 4 years from 60 to 15, in Zutphen over the same period the trend is in completely the opposite direction: an increase from 5 to 35 cases! These are the two extremes but the rest of the picture is also far from unequivocal.

Table 7.2 Comparison of court decisions on the application of general criminal law to minors in the periods 2000–2001 and 2003–2004

Court	2000–2001	2003–2004
Amsterdam	62	60
Den Bosch	61	15
The Hague	52	26
Rotterdam	34	19
Utrecht	27	29
Assen	27	10
Breda	26	23
Arnhem	24	27
Zwolle	20	26
Dordrecht	12	23
Almelo	11	13
Maastricht	11	13
Groningen	9	8
Haarlem	8	11
Roermond	8	4
Alkmaar	7	1
Leeuwarden	7	5
Middelburg	6	6
Zutphen	5	35
Total	417	355

Source: WODC

If we analyse the data from the same source by type of offence, a new and intriguing fact comes to light. We assumed that the main reason for applying adult criminal law to minors would be that they had committed serious crimes, especially crimes of violence. However, that turned out to be the case in only a minority of these cases. Less than 30% of these cases concerned crimes of violence, over 40% concerned property crimes, just under 15% were for vandalism and public order offences and almost 10% were offences against the Opium Act. While we would expect that the decrease in these cases since 1995 would be coupled with a strong concentration of cases involving serious violence, based on these court data this turned out not to be the case. That raises the question again as to whether the other part of the package of amendments in 1995 – the relaxation of the option to apply general criminal law – does not perhaps offer too much scope for it to be used too readily.

Another surprising outcome of our research into Dutch practice emerged from the analysis of 5 years of court judgements, which was that in total sentences of 2 years or more were only imposed 83 times on juvenile offenders; that comes down to an average of 16 or 17 cases a year. This means that over the past 5 years, with 65,085 court cases against juvenile suspects, in less than 0.13% of cases was a sentence imposed which exceeded the maximum sentence that can be imposed under juvenile criminal law. That is remarkable, because the reason for having the option of transfer is that it provides a safety valve for very serious crimes which would call for a heavier sentence than is customary and possible under juvenile criminal law.

The Case Files[10]

To make a proper assessment of the issue of minors who are tried under the general criminal law, more information was needed than could be obtained from the figures of CBS/WODC and the court statistics. Not only do these figures give no information about what sanctions were imposed, they also leave us in the dark about the role of experts and the grounds of the courts' decisions. This information can only be obtained by studying case files. It was with great difficulty, due to the poor administration systems at the courts, that we eventually managed to gather together 62 useable files from 13 courts spread over the whole country for the period 1999–2005. That averages out at only eight case files per year. Clearly this gives us a biased picture of practice with regard to the application of Article 77b of the Penal Code, because the cases we examined are almost certainly the most serious 5% to 10%.[11]

These 62 case files correspond in one respect with the overall picture of when the general criminal law was applied. Here too the ratio between crimes of violence and property crimes turns out to be opposite to what we expected. In this collection

---

[10] For further details, see Weijers 2006.

[11] The overwhelming majority of the accused were 17 years old (55 cases), while nine offenders were probably 16 at the time of the offence.

Table 7.3 Most important offences

Art. 310 Penal Code	Theft	23 x (Art. 310 + 6 cases Art. 311)
Art. 312 Penal Code	Robbery	17 x
Art. 289 Penal Code	Murder	11 x
Art. 287 Penal Code	Manslaughter	9 x (of which 2 x Art. 288)
Art. 317 Penal Code	Extortion	9 x
Art. 242 Penal Code	Rape	7 x
Art. 140 Penal Code	Criminal organisation	5 x
Art. 250 Penal Code	Forcing someone into prostitution	4 x

of files, the greatest number concerned theft – 23 cases (Art. 310 Penal Code and in six cases Art. 311 Penal Code) and 17 cases of robbery (Art. 312 Penal Code), whether or not combined. Only after that came homicide: 11 cases of murder (Art. 289 Penal Code) and 9 cases of manslaughter (Art. 287 Penal Code, plus in two cases Art. 288 Penal Code) (Table 7.3).

One of the questions that our case file study aimed to throw light on was the role of experts' reports: did the courts follow the reports or in applying Article 77b of the Penal Code did they regularly take decisions against the advice of the behavioural experts? First of all we needed to ascertain how often there was an expert report. It turned out that there had been expert's reports in three-quarters of these cases. In a quarter of the cases there were two or more different reports and in some cases there were three or even more. Despite the fact that in the main there was no lack of reports, in only half of the cases were we able to find out what the courts had done with the advice in the experts' reports. Where we were able to establish this, it turned out that the courts followed the advice in three-quarters of cases, and in the other quarter they did not. These findings seem to justify the conclusion that in cases where an expert opinion is produced, the court follows the advice in most cases.

The next question concerned the grounds for the courts' decisions. As we have already stated, Article 77b of the Penal Code offers three grounds for this article to be applied: the seriousness of the offence, the personality of the offender and the circumstances in which the offence was committed. The first rather remarkable discovery here was that there was no explanation to be found in the documents in the case files in a quarter of the cases. The next striking discovery was that in all the documents where the court did provide an explanation, the prime ground given was *always* the seriousness of the offence. Finally, in almost half of these cases, all three grounds were given. In all these cases, this was confined to an obligatory mention, without any further explanation or supporting reasons. This was also true of those cases where two or more grounds were given: there was usually a complete absence of any detailed explanation.

Finally, we wanted to know what penalties the courts actually imposed in this selection of serious Article 77b Penal Code cases. We found that detention in a youth custody centre was imposed in eight cases (13%) (usually in combination with a prison sentence). The average sentence was over 4 years. The maximum was 12 years, followed by seven cases of 8 years [and two cases of 8 years' detention followed by detention under a hospital order (*TBS*)]. The minimum was 6 months.

We are therefore able to conclude that the range of sanctions imposed by the application of Article 77b of the Penal Code was very broad. Furthermore, it was found that even within this selection punishments were imposed which in fact lie within the scope of juvenile criminal law, certainly when the reduction in the sentence that is customary in general criminal law in the Netherlands but not in juvenile criminal law is taken into account. In this sample of serious cases, the courts found it necessary to try the suspects under general criminal law but in almost half of the cases they then imposed a penalty which, in terms of its length or severity, could also have been imposed under the juvenile justice system.[12] That raises questions about the ratio and justification for these decisions. When viewed in that light especially, the poor or complete absence of explanations by the courts in the majority of cases is a serious omission.

As far as the strategy of the courts was concerned, three tracks can be distinguished. First, there were the cases where the safety argument was decisive in the decision to apply the general criminal law. That was the case, for example, in the case of a 17-year-old girl who was convicted of murdering her ex-partner. The expert witnesses warned that she had a seriously disturbed personality structure and psychopathic character structure as well as an extremely limited moral sense. She was given 8 years' detention followed by detention under a hospital order. Precisely the same sanction was imposed on the murderer of Maja Bradaric, who was killed and burned in November 2003 in Bemmel near Nijmegen. These were cases involving very serious crimes, where the court concluded based on the expert reports that in view of the personality of the offender account had to be taken of the risk of repetition of the offence which, despite treatment, could remain a serious risk for a very long time. In short, these offenders needed to be securely locked up and above all *given treatment* for a sufficient period of time.

Second, there were cases where the court judged that the offence was so serious as to justify the application of the general criminal law, even though the risk of repetition was not considered to be very high. In these cases the court decided to impose lengthy prison sentences, sometimes against the advice of the expert witnesses. One such case became known as the 'Veghelse honour killing': the oldest son of a Turkish family was put under severe pressure by his father to avenge his sister's elopement. The boy, who had no criminal record and was not known for any problems, was given a loaded pistol by his father and then he went to his school, a regional training centre where the boy who had eloped with his sister turned up, and fired wildly in all directions, fortunately without killing anyone. The Den Bosch District Court probably wanted to set an example. It felt that the seriousness of the offence justified trying the boy under adult criminal law, and he was sentenced to 5 years' imprisonment for attempted murder and attempted manslaughter.

Third, there were a number of cases where the offences were relatively minor and consequently relatively lenient sentences were imposed. A typical case concerned

---

[12] In the case files we only found nine cases where the Public Prosecutor had demanded a different sentence. In seven of these cases the prosecutor had demanded a heavier sentence and in two cases a lighter one.

a minor who had broken into 15 houses within a space of a few months and had also taken part in circulating forged money. This boy had previously been sentenced to 8 months' suspended youth detention and in that framework had taken part in an intensive social rehabilitation program. However, he soon got involved in another spate of burglaries and the Zwolle District Court stated 'that this conduct on the part of the accused gives us reason to be very gravely concerned about the future'. As was often the case in this third category, there was no expert report and therefore no personality investigation. Nevertheless, the court concluded that the seriousness of the offence, the circumstances *and* the personality of the accused provided grounds for applying adult criminal law. The young man was sentenced to 18 months in custody, of which 6 months was suspended, and to pay ¤ 2,000 Euros in compensation.

This is an example of a penalty that could easily have been imposed within the juvenile criminal justice system. That would also have seemed the logical course of action given the relative seriousness of the offences: no violence or threat of violence was used in the burglaries and the offender did not use, or indeed have in his possession, any weapons. The circumstances also did not seem to directly justify the transfer decision, and finally the assessment of the offender's personality was questionable.

Two conclusions, one positive and one negative, can be drawn from this research. The positive conclusion is that the number of transfers of minors to the general criminal law has fallen sharply in the Netherlands and will probably decrease even further. On the other hand, it is a cause for concern that a large proportion of the remaining transfers take place without being supported by adequate statements of reasons for the decision.

Belgium

The age of criminal responsibility in penal law was raised in Belgium from 16 to 18 by a recent amendment to the 1965 Youth Protection Act (YPA). Since then, delinquents under the age of 18 have been sentenced in the Youth Court. However, there is one exception to this rule. Since 1965, the Youth Court has been able to transfer a juvenile offender, aged 16 or over, to the Public Prosecutor with the intention of having the young offender sentenced in the Adult Court.[13] In this case, the young offender ends up in the general criminal justice system and is treated as an adult. Penalties from penal law can be imposed, except the death penalty.[14] Hence, the most severe punishment that can be imposed on transferred offenders is life imprisonment. Because transferred offenders are treated as adults, they serve their detention in prison (Nuytiens et al. 2005).

---

[13] Theoretically, the Public Prosecutor can still dismiss the case or propose mediation. In practice, this only happens occasionally. This is not surprising, because in most cases it is the Public Prosecutor who demanded transfer.

[14] Since the death penalty was abolished in 1996, this restriction has lost its relevance.

The 1965 YPA considers transfer to be an exceptional decision. This is why (1) the Youth Court is obliged to explain a transfer decision in detail; and (2) two inquiries are compulsory before the Youth Court can decide to transfer a young offender to Adult Court. First, for the purpose of obtaining relevant information on the personality of the young offender, the Youth Court is obliged to order a medical-psychological examination. This inquiry is carried out by a psychiatrist, a psychologist or a multidisciplinary team of experts. Second, a social inquiry must be accomplished in order to gain sufficient information on the home background of the youngster (e.g. school career, family). This inquiry is carried out by social workers of the Youth Court's social service.[15]

According to the YPA, the main motivation for transfer is whether or not the intervention options at the disposal of the Youth Court (the youth protection measures) are still adequate, that is, whether the youngster is still likely to benefit from these interventions. In line with the protective and rehabilitative philosophy of YPA, the personality of the minor is crucial in this judgement.[16] However, transfer criteria are not explicitly listed in the YPA. Hence, neither the seriousness of the offence nor juvenile justice antecedents are criteria for transfer according to the YPA. Nevertheless, the Youth Court can take into account the nature or gravity of the offences, as well as the juvenile justice history of the youngster, if it provides information concerning the personality of the young offender.[17]

The 1965 YPA was modified profoundly in 2006, and the legal framework for transfer to Adult Court was altered substantially as part of a thorough reform of the juvenile justice system.[18] The most important changes are illustrated in Table 7.4.

While the lower age limit has not been altered, significant changes concerning the grounds and criteria for transfer, the authorised court dealing with transferred offenders, as well as the limits and the execution of punishments, have been implemented.

Table 7.4 Legal framework for transfer decisions

	1965	2006
Age	≥16 years	≥16 years
Grounds	Personality	Personality, maturity and environment
Criteria	None	Serious offence(s)
		OR
		At least 1 Youth Court measure
Court	Adult Court	Adult Court
		OR
		Extended Youth Court
Punishment	No death penalty	No life sentences
	Prison	Youth Detention Centre or prison

[15] Van Dijk et al. 2005.

[16] Nuytiens et al. 2005.

[17] Goiset 2000.

[18] The 2006 Act will be put into operation gradually. The entire Act has to be fully operational in 2009.

Whereas the 1965 YPA did not define criteria for transfer, the 2006 Act explicitly defined two non-cumulative criteria. First, an offence-based criterion was introduced; transfer is now restricted to young offenders who have committed serious offences. More specifically, these are rape, sexual assault involving violence or menaces, assault or battery causing death or severe injuries, violent theft, murder and attempted murder, manslaughter and attempted manslaughter. Second, a criterion concerning the juvenile's criminal record was introduced. The 2006 Act postulates that young offenders can only be transferred if the Youth Court has already imposed at least one youth measure in the past. The grounds for the transfer decision still have to be reasoned in terms of the personality of the youngster. However, two cumulative variables are added: the young offender's degree of maturity and his environment.

Another important change has occurred, concerning the court that deals with transferred offenders. Before the law was amended, transferred offenders were sentenced in the Adult Court. More specifically, they were tried in the Correctional Court or in the *Court d'assises*,[19] depending on the gravity of the offence(s). The 2006 Act created a new jurisdiction, the 'Extended Youth Court', within the Youth Court. In contrast to the Youth Court, presided over by only one professional juvenile judge, the Extended Youth Court is presided over by two juvenile judges and one judge of the Correctional Court. While the most serious crimes will still be sentenced in the *Court d'assises*, other offences will be handled by the Extended Youth Court.

In both cases, however, the youngster will be tried according to the rules of penal law, and prison sentences can be imposed, though the 2006 Act restricts prison sentences to a maximum of 30 years; life sentences can no longer be imposed. Another innovation is the fact that transferred offenders serve their sentences in specific youth detention centres for transferred offenders. However, this 'prerogative' is only guaranteed for transferred offenders who are still minors at the time of sentencing. For youngsters who have already turned 18, detention in a youth centre is only guaranteed if there is sufficient space. On top of that, youngsters who disturb the peace in the youth centre can still be transferred to prison. While this legal amendment is promising, there are reasons, though, tobe sceptical. First, the youth detention centres still have to be built, and budgets are tight. Second, the option of detention in youth facilities is not obligatory but depends on the availability of places.

The Practice

According to the 1965 YPA, transfer of young offenders to Adult Court has to be considered to be an exceptional decision. Recent statistics show that the use of transfer is indeed limited in practice. Research shows that only 1% of the Youth

---

[19] This court, where professional judges are assisted by 12 laymen, deals with the most serious offences.

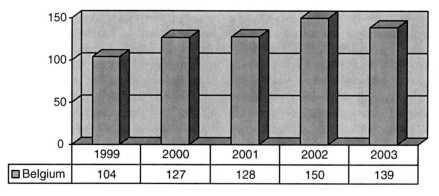

Fig. 7.1 Absolute number of transfers in Belgium: 1999–2003

Court's decisions concern transfer to Adult Court. It is more accurate to say that transfer decisions amount to 3% of all judgements.[20] As the graph above illustrates, the absolute number of transfer decisions made by the Youth Court has fluctuated between 104 and 150 in recent years. The figures do not show a huge (Vanneste 2001) increase but rather suggest stagnation.[21] Of course, it remains to be seen whether the recent amendment to the law will affect the application of transfer in the future (Fig. 7.1).

It is remarkable that the application of transfer shows significant geographical variation. First, transfer is used far more often in the French-speaking part of Belgium. Second, it seems that in 1999, 2000 and 2001, 86% of all transfer decisions were pronounced in only 7 of 27 court districts. On top of this, the figures show that the Brussels Youth Court was responsible for 47.1% of all transfer decisions! Of course, we have to take the huge case load of this district into account. Figures are only significant if we put them in context, in this case, if we relate them to the total number of decisions taken by the Youth Court.[22]

The Files

Between 2003 and 2005 (before the recent amendment to the law), we carried out some fieldwork on the practice of transfer. An analysis of files in the Youth Court and in the Adult Court was conducted in order to paint a picture of the profile of transferred offenders and their criminal careers. In addition to this, interviews with

---

[20] Vanneste 2001. The Youth Court can take preliminary decisions as well as final decisions. The transfer decision can only be imposed as a judgement.

[21] Nuytiens 2006.

[22] Ibidem.

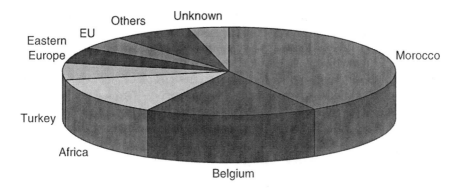

Morocco	Belgium	Africa	Turkey	Eastern-Europe	EU	Others	Unknown
87	35	29	13	12	10	16	8

Fig. 7.2 Ethnic origin of transferred juveniles

juvenile judges were conducted in order to gain more insight into the decision-making process concerning transfer.[23]

From an analysis of the files of 210 transferred[24] offenders in 5 Belgian Youth Courts,[25] where transfer has been used relatively often between 1999 and 2001, we can paint a picture of the personal and socio-economic profile of these offenders. A large majority (94.3%) of the population consisted of males. As far as their ethnic origin is concerned, it is striking that almost three-quarters of them did not originate from an EU[26] country. More specifically, we found that youngsters originating from Morocco were highly overrepresented (41.4%). Young gypsies and asylum-seekers were also overrepresented: of the 157 non-EU youngsters, 35 (22.3%) were gypsies or asylum-seekers (Fig. 7.2).

The greater share of the juveniles were not performing well at school; most of them were attending vocational schools (64.7%) or special education (7.1%). It is striking that 10% had never attended secondary school, and some had never even been to school at all. The latter group was entirely made up of gypsies. Another indication of problematic school careers was the high number of drop-outs (at least[27] 30.8%) and juveniles who had repeated one or more grades (at least 29.9%). The number of

---

[23] Nuytiens et al. 2005; Nuytiens et al. 2006.

[24] Transferred between 1999 and 2001.

[25] Antwerp, Brussels, Charleroi, Mechelen and Mons.

[26] We noted that (1) the categories were constructed before some new member states joined the EU; and (2) the category 'Africa' did not include the North African countries (Morocco, Algeria, Tunisia and Mauritania).

[27] We noted that problems can exist without being reported in the files. This goes for the other variables as well.

truants (at least 44.1%) and youngsters expelled from school (at least 44.8%) appeared to be very high as well. Despite the fact that juvenile judges have to base their decision on the personal and contextual situation of the young offender, for 11% of the transferred offenders information concerning their school situation was lacking.

The analysis of files showed that transferred offenders often lived in large families and that a lot of youngsters were living in problematic familial environments. The problems reported were of a financial as well as of a social nature.[28] Moreover, it seems that at least 34.1% of the population had one or more siblings with judicial antecedents.[29] Finally, at least 14.2% of the youngsters' fathers had come into contact with the judicial authorities.

The young offenders were also having to cope with personal problems. According to the medical-psychological reports, half of the transferred youths denied, minimised or justified their deviant behaviour, and lacked empathy with their victim(s). Other frequently mentioned descriptions were: immature, dangerous, aggressive, mistrustful, spoiled and so on. A large proportion of the transferred population were suffering from psychiatric disorders. Most frequently mentioned were: neurotic personality (15.7%), antisocial personality disorder (14.6%), depression (13.1%) and behavioural disorder (7.8%). In addition, experts often estimated the chances of these young people developing some kind of personality disorder as high. Based on the medical-psychological inquiries, we could conclude that a large proportion of the transferred population suffered from psychological and/or psychiatric problems.

Exploring the time span between the first contact with the Youth Court and transfer, it appeared that young offenders with a long history in juvenile justice were not overrepresented. On the contrary, most of them had been transferred rather quickly: the time span between the first contact with the Youth Court and transfer was 1 year or less for 19% of the youngsters; 21.5% came into the category of 1 to 2 years; and another 19% had spent 2 to 3 years in the youth justice system before transfer. The longer the history, the fewer youngsters were situated in the categories. Maybe this is not surprising: transfer can affect only young offenders aged 16 or over. Transferred offenders come into contact with the Youth Court at a rather advanced age. The greater share of the transferred youngsters were either aged between 14 and 15 (40%) or aged between 16 and 17 (26.2%) at the first contact with the Youth Court. Only 9.5% were younger than 12 when this happened.

Before transfer to the Adult Court, one in four young offenders had already been convicted of one to five offences by the Youth Court. Remarkably, 20% of all transferred offenders had never been convicted of other offences prior to transfer. In contrast, 'multi-recidivists', defined as young offenders convicted of 20 or more

---

[28] For 18% of the families, a financial problem was reported (e.g. debts, living on benefits). For 24.8% of the families, intra-familial aggression was reported (e.g. incest, physical or mental abuse). For 17.1% of the families, drug abuse of the parent(s) was reported. For 26.1% of the families, a health care problem was reported (physical or mental problems of the parents). It was striking that many of the parents were living on social security due to health problems.

[29] The sibling had come into contact with the Youth Court (welfare reasons and/or offending-related reasons) and/or with the Criminal Court.

offences before transfer, accounted for only 8%. However, we do have to take into account the large number of missing values (18.1%).

Finally, we looked at the nature of the offences committed. The analysis of the files revealed that more than 75% of the offences committed before transfer were property offences. Moreover, 75% of the offences resulting in the transfer decision were also property offences. However, an in-depth analysis of the Youth Court files showed that a lot of these property offences involved aggravating circumstances, that is, physical or psychological violence (e.g. threatening the victim), or were of a violent nature (e.g. extortion, vandalism). This population was not committing white-collar crime. The majority of the offences concerned were so-called 'street crimes', offences that are very visible and alarming for citizens.

As the next table illustrates, the most serious offences, punishable with long-term imprisonment under the Belgian Penal Code, were relatively rare. For example, manslaughter and murder accounted for less than 1%. Of all the serious offences, the greater part concerned property offences with aggravating circumstances (burglary, theft involving threats/violence). Remarkably, however, there were more serious offences committed by transferred youngsters in the 'offences for which transferred' category than in the 'offences judged before transfer' category. This indicates that their criminal careers had developed over time and their offences had become more serious (Table 7.5).

Decision Mechanisms

The analysis of files revealed some remarkable findings. These findings can be better understood by analysing the decision-making process concerning transfer. Through interviews with juvenile judges[30] we found that several factors influenced the transfer decision. According to the judges, the most decisive factor was the attitude of the young offender. Transfer was more likely for youngsters who adopted a negative attitude (e.g. no regrets) and who were responsible for the failure of previously imposed youth measures. These elements are obviously related to the

Table 7.5 Offences committed before and after transfer

	Offences judged before transfer	Offences for which transferred
Burglary	28.8%	35.9%
Theft with aggravating circumstances	16.3%	21.9%
Rape/sexual harassment	0.8%	1.9%
Manslaughter/murder	0.15%	0.7%
Hostage	0.15%	0.7%
Arson	0.3%	0.4%
Other offences	53.5%	38.5%

[30] We interviewed 11 juvenile judges of the Youth Court and 6 juvenile judges of the Court of Appeal.

young offender's personality. The interviews revealed that objective elements also played a role in the decision-making process. The seriousness of the offence(s) and the protection of society were considered especially important factors. For juvenile judges, violence against persons, especially repeated crimes of violence, were considered to be very serious.

It seemed that judges were deciding whether or not to transfer a young offender on the basis of personality- and offence-related aspects. In these cases, it was the young offender and his actions that brought the Youth Court to a transfer decision. However, there seemed to be a group of young offenders who were transferred to Adult Court more readily as a result of a lack of options within the juvenile justice system. Several judges indicated that the lack of available and enforceable youth measures was a decisive factor, or at least a catalyst. The lack of space in youth institutions, in particular, put a lot of pressure on the judges. One judge stated that 'You have to give a youngster every chance until he turns 18, but since the number of beds in the institutions has been reduced (…) these youngsters do not get the chances they deserve. They are forced into recidivism, and the only thing left to do is to conclude that the youth measures are no longer useful.'[31]

Furthermore, certain groups are practically systematically expelled from the juvenile justice system. Several judges indicated that, for example, young offenders dealing with psychiatric problems are sometimes transferred because of the lack of suitably adapted measures within the juvenile justice system. One judge declared that 'Within the juvenile justice system there is no possibility of detention. Sometimes a youngster is transferred to Adult Court in order to obtain detention in penal law. In that case, we reason as follows: the youth measures are not useful because the young offender is mentally ill.'[32] Juvenile judges indicated that gypsies and asylum-seekers were also transferred more often, due to the lack of effective youth measures for these groups; it is very difficult to work with these youngsters because, in general, they speak neither French nor Dutch.

It is clear that these structural deficits influenced the decision-making process. Judges were not making decisions exclusively on the grounds of what was best for the young offender, but they were taking account of the availability of youth measures as well.

Penal Career

In order to paint a picture of what happens to the young offender once he is transferred to Adult Court, the Criminal Court files of the exact same offenders were analysed. Leaving out the missing values (13%), it appears that transfer did not lead to penal consequences in 11.6% of all cases. This is due to the fact that the

---

[31] Nuytiens et al. 2005, p. 196.

[32] Ibidem, p. 215

transfer decision was annulled by the Court of Appeal or due to the dismissal of the case (Public Prosecutor) or acquittal by the penal authorities.[33] Eventually, the Criminal Court passed judgement in at least 75% of all transferred cases.

The analysis of the Criminal Court files showed that transfer decisions that did lead to a penal conviction often resulted in non-conditional suspended prison sentences (28%) or conditional suspended prison sentences (=probation) (25.6%). Actual (nonsuspended) prison sentences were less often imposed (17.4%). More specifically, it seems that long-term imprisonment (>5 years) occurred very rarely: detention of 6 years was imposed five times, and detention of 8 years was imposed only once. Finally, one young offender was sent to prison for 28 years.

As the figure below shows, other sentences were rare (Fig. 7.3).

At first sight, nonsuspended prison sentences were relatively rare. However, on taking a closer look, it appeared that most of the suspended prison sentences (75%) and probation sentences (54.6%) were only partially suspended. This means that part of the prison sentence was suspended while the remaining part had to be served. Taking this information into account, it turns out that more than half of the transfer decisions led to a sentence involving a period in custody! However, we do have to note that in Belgium, due to overcrowded prisons, short-term prison sentences are not always enforced. Our research showed that more than a quarter of the imposed custodial sentences on transferred offenders were not enforced.

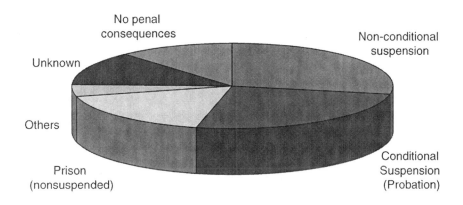

Non-conditional suspension	Conditional Suspension (Probation)	Prison (nonsuspended)	Others	Unknown	No penal consequences
82	75	51	13	38	34

Fig. 7.3 Sentences imposed on transferred Juveniles

---

[33] Another reason is that the Adult Court was of the opinion that the offences had already been punished by means of a former judgement.

Follow-up research revealed that the transfer decision (and in a lot of cases the subsequent prison sentence) did not deter the youngsters. Within a period of 4 to 6 years, at least 51.1% were convicted again in Adult Court for offences committed as adults. This means that more than half of the transferred youngsters relapsed into crime within a relatively short time span.

Three conclusions can be drawn from our research. First, the application of transfer in practice has always remained limited, and recent figures suggest stagnation. Second, the profile of the transferred population is surprising. Transfer is not only used for the young offenders for whom transfer was conceived, namely, the 'serious offenders'. Interviews with juvenile judges revealed that the option of transfer is very often used to compensate for the shortcomings of the youth justice system. Third, long-term prison sentences are rarely imposed on transferred offenders. However, we have to note that, notwithstanding this observation, our research found that at least 73.4% of all transferred offenders ended up in prison at least once within 4 to 6 years following transfer. This was as a result of (1) preventive custody; (2) convictions for offences committed as juveniles and/or (3) convictions for offences committed as adults. A large number of transferred offenders relapsed into crime within short time span.

Conclusions and Recommendations

Despite differences in the legal frameworks, the transfer practices in Belgium and in the Netherlands show remarkable similarities. Notwithstanding significant geographical variation inside both countries, the overall use of transfer is very moderate. Whereas in Belgium the numbers are rising slowly but not alarmingly, in the Netherlands the numbers are clearly falling. The most important conclusion is that the use of transfer is at a very low level in both countries.

Another, rather worrisome conclusion though is that transferred offenders end up in adult prison in both countries. More possibilities within the juvenile justice system are needed, so that the serving of punishments in prison can be avoided. In Belgium, the recent amendment to the law partly fulfils this need, but in the Netherlands alternatives are not yet available.

Finally, another, both more surprising and more worrisome conclusion is that in both countries many of the transferred offenders do not appear to belong to the category of 'serious offenders'. This is partly due to vague or absent legal criteria. For that reason, stricter legal criteria on transfer are needed. In Belgium, the recent amendment to the law seems to partly fulfil this need, but again, this is not the case in the Netherlands.

Chapter 8
The Prevention of Delinquent Behaviour

Josine Junger-Tas

It is useful for the purpose of pursuing a practical policy to make a somewhat artificial distinction between opportunistic and persistent delinquent behaviour. The largest group of juvenile delinquents consists of opportunistic offenders: they commit essentially offences with a high nuisance value, such as vandalism, shoplifting, petty theft and fighting. This type of behaviour is heavily dependent on a 'good opportunity' and characterizes young people aged 14–18. Once the responsibilities of adulthood appear such behaviour is quickly abandoned. Prevention policies that reduce opportunities to commit crime through environmental design, technical measures and greater supervision and control have been shown to be effective in this respect. Together with more formal interventions, such as diversion, mediation and alternative sanctions, this appears to be an effective response to such crime. In general, we need not to be too much concerned about these youthful groups of impulse offenders, because most of them – with a little help of the community and the authorities – will not persist in criminal behaviour.

There is, however, a very small group of serious and persistent offenders. These young people start committing delinquent acts at an early age, the delinquency becomes gradually more serious, re-offending is considerable and criminal behaviour continues well into adulthood. If persistent delinquency is defined by being known to the criminal justice system for five or more offences, the size of this group is estimated at 6% to 7% of the juvenile population (Wolfgang et al. 1972; Tracy et al. 1990; Farrington and West 1990), but they commit more than half of all offences. Prevention policies should therefore be addressed to this persistent delinquent young people.

Where this group of young offenders is concerned our interventions are not very successful. We try to treat them in young offender institutions but the level of re-offending remains extremely high. Truly effective treatment programs are rare. Moreover, even when treatment effects can be shown they are quickly lost as soon as the young people return to their criminogenic environment. There is substantial evidence for the lack of treatment efficacy in earlier (Cornish and Clarke 1975;

J. Junger-Tas (✉)
Willem Pompe Institute, University of Utrecht, Utrecht, The Netherlands

J. Junger-Tas and F. Dünkel (eds.), *Reforming Juvenile Justice*,
DOI: 10.1007/978-0-387-89295-5_8, © Springer Science+Business Media, LLC 2009

Lipton et al. 1975) and in later research (Lipsey 1992; Lipsey and Wilson 1993; MacKenzie 1991; MacKenzie and Souryal 1992). There are a number of reasons that might explain the lack of success in treating these young offenders. One important reason is of course our still imperfect knowledge about what are effective treatment methods. Many treatment interventions are rather based on 'common sense' notions and good intentions than on proven efficacy, although it should be observed that there have been some improvements (Andrews et al. 1990a,b; Lösel 1995), which point to the effectiveness of cognitive behaviour training programs.

Another reason is that treatment covers a relatively short period in their life, after which they return to the peer group and 'usual' activities in their neighbourhood.

However, by far the most significant reason seems to be the fact that the intervention comes at such a late stage, when the young people reach the peak of their criminal activities. By that time there has been a long history of behaviour problems, truancy, fighting and delinquency. Crime has become a rewarding 'way of life' – at least for the time being.

This does not mean that all interventions are useless. But research has shown that influencing the behaviour of young children is far more effective than trying to do this with adolescents. Young children are more malleable, while people as they grow older become more tenacious and resistant to change (Olweus 1979; Huesmann et al. 1984; Eron 1990; Gottfredson and Hirschi 1990). This is not to say that after a specific age change is impossible (Sampson and Laub 1993; Laub and Sampson 2003): behavioural change is possible at all ages but my conjecture is that such change in adolescents and adults is more realistically determined by what they perceive as their own interest as well as by situational factors.

Now if policymakers would want to address the problem of preventing serious and persistent criminal involvement of juveniles, a number of preliminary questions would have to be answered. First, does there exist some basic understanding and consensus about the fundamental causes of criminal behaviour? Second, is it possible to predict persistent delinquency with some degree of certainty? Third, if the answer to these questions is positive, are there programs available that can effectively address the conditions that are related to persistent delinquency and that demonstrate positive outcomes in terms of later criminal involvement? And if so, how does one solve the ethical aspects related to interventions in the lives of families? These are the problems I will discuss in this chapter.

Causes of Serious Delinquent Behaviour

It is clear that there are a number of interacting causal factors, which are linked in specific ways to constitute a probability model. In fact one might call it a risk model which predicts later criminal behaviour in terms of greater or lesser degrees of probability. In order to structure the different causal elements I have distinguished factors related to the behaviour of the child, to the family, to the family's environment and to the interrelationships between the different factors.

Risk Factors in the Child

Developmental psychologists have demonstrated the stability of temperamental factors such as social introversion and extroversion, assertiveness, impulsiveness, person-orientation, IQ and ADHD (Attention Deficit/Hyperactivity Disorder), some of which are wholly or partly innate. Children differ in the responses they arouse in their parents and in fact they make a very active contribution to the child-raising process. For example, children with behavioural problems are difficult to socialize. Some parents simply give up trying, thereby fostering aggressive and anti-social behaviour. Some basic biological factors, such as age and gender, are related to criminal behaviour: boys commit considerably more offences than girls and as we know criminal behaviour reaches a peak in adolescence and then falls with increasing age.

Research has shown that aggressive behaviour and anti-social tendencies are very stable characteristics and have a great influence on later behaviour (Olweus 1979; Huesmann et al. 1984; Loeber 1991). They may lead to behaviour problems in the family but also to learning difficulties and problem behaviour at school (Barnum 1987). In longitudinal research in England it was found that children who showed persistent delinquent behaviour were defined by their schoolteacher as troublesome and lying before the age of 10. They had a low IQ and performed poorly at school. They were impulsive and hyperactive and unpopular with their schoolmates. At the age of 14 they were more aggressive than other pupils and at the age of 18 they differed from their age group in a large number of factors: they drank more, were more often drunk and aggressive, they smoked and gambled more, used drugs more frequently and were more often convicted of a road traffic offence (Farrington and West 1990). They also were more often involved in road accidents, a finding that has been confirmed in Dutch research. Junger et al. (1995) found a great number of factors that were equally related to delinquency and to being involved in a road accident.

Although there is general agreement that hereditary factors have only a weak link with delinquency (Rutter and Giller 1983; Loeber and Stouthamer-Loeber 1986a), anti-social behaviour is a cause of children being rejected at school as well as of school failure. That failure makes them easily attracted to and influenced by deviant friends (Patterson 1994), although it is important to bear in mind that half of the children with behavioural problems in their youth will simply 'grow out of them' as they approach adulthood and will never become involved in criminal behaviour. However, what research shows is that such children are at greater risk of developing such behaviour. Whether or not this happens depends on a number of other conditions. Unfavourable conditions in this respect are: children who display problem behaviour in several environments, for example both at school and within the family; children with frequent and severe problem behaviour from an early age on; children who show a varied pattern of problem behaviour, such as various forms of theft and aggression; and children who are not only hyperactive but have also difficulty in concentrating (Loeber 1991; Loeber et al. 1998).

We may conclude this section by stating that there are a number of factors in the behaviour of the child itself which can increase the risk of subsequent deviant and/ or delinquent behaviour. This means that there might be a degree of '*early propensity for criminality*'. However, it should be borne in mind that these factors do not automatically and necessarily give rise to later criminality. Whether this happens depends on the interaction between child factors and environmental factors, which could be called '*interactive continuity*'.

In this respect the family plays a central role. Other important causes of continuity in criminal behaviour are structural disadvantage and ever-declining opportunities for social integration, which result from penal interventions and labelling. Examples of this type of '*cumulative continuity*' are the reduced chances of ex-inmates in the labour-, housing-, and marriage market (Sampson and Laub 1993; Kroese and Staring 1993).

Parents and Family

To a degree parents fulfil their upbringing task for the benefit of the community, for if they are successful socializers the risk that their child develops a criminal career is considerably smaller than if this is not the case. This places a great responsibility upon the parents' shoulders. Some have defined the socializing task as follows: first, parents should care sufficiently about their children to invest in their upbringing; second, they should continuously guide and monitor the child's behaviour; third, it is essential that they recognize deviant and delinquent behaviour; and fourth, they should punish the child if he shows unacceptable and/or delinquent behaviour, using in a consistent way appropriate, non-violent and effective disciplining methods (Hirschi 1994; Patterson 1994).

There are a number of *structural family risk factors*. One such factor is teenage motherhood, in particular because teenage mothers usually have little education, have a low income, are welfare dependent, live in criminogenic neighbourhoods, and more often than not have to raise their child without the support of another adult (Morash and Rucker 1989). In the United Kingdom, these children are more commonly victims of physical neglect and the mothers show little maternal care, inadequate supervision and inconsistent discipline (Farrington and West 1990). Later delinquent behaviour appears not so much to be related to biological factors but rather to the absence of a father, lack of supervision and guidance by the mother and problems at school.

Little evidence has been found for the thesis that mother's employment is a criminogenic factor. In fact no harmful effects on the children have been found, provided the mother has arranged for adequate care and supervision during her absence (Glueck and Glueck 1950; Hirschi 1969; Riley and Shaw 1985; Junger-Tas et al. 2003a).

A structural factor which has given rise to much research is the broken home as a result of divorce or desertion. This is an important point in view of the fact that many children have experienced divorce or will do so in the future. If such disruption of the family were to have serious consequences in terms of the children's behaviour, the future would look bleak indeed. Part of the problem seems to be due to the increasing number of one-parent, generally mother-headed, families. The hypothesis is that such families are seriously handicapped in their child-raising task. As the possible link between a broken home and delinquency has been the subject of long-standing research this allows us to draw some conclusions on this matter.

First, comparisons between families with two biological parents, families with one parent and families with one step-parent show that children in families with a step-parent display more problems as well as delinquent behaviour than children from either of the other groups (Johnson 1986; Hirschi 1969; Morash and Rucker 1989; Junger-Tas et al. 2003a). This suggests that it is not so much the family's structure but its quality that could be of decisive importance.

Second, there is a clear – although weak – link between the broken family and delinquency (Nye 1958; Wilkinson 1980; Rankin 1983). A survey of the research carried out in the 1990s shows a difference in delinquent involvement between children from complete and incomplete families of 13% to 15% (Wells and Rankin 1991). The delinquency relates mainly to what in my country is termed 'problem behaviour', that is difficult behaviour at home, poor school achievement, truancy, running away from home and using drugs. The relationship with serious criminal behaviour is not strong (Wells and Rankin 1991; Rutenfrans and Terlouw 1994). Most delinquent behaviour occurs in two-parent families where the parents are continually fighting, in particular when they use violence. This is also true for one-parent families where the mother feels little affection for her children. There is little delinquency in harmonious, complete families or in one-parent families with a warm and affectionate mother. It is worth mentioning that the effect of the break up of the family on the children's behaviour has not changed since the first studies were conducted 60 years ago. It appears to be constant over time.

In fact *qualitative factors* are of considerably more importance than the structure of the family, in particular the control of children and the relationship between parents and children.

Inadequate supervision of children is one of the strongest predictors of criminality (Farrington and West 1990; Rutter and Giller 1983; Rutter et al. 1998; Junger-Tas et al. 2003a). Poor parental child-rearing method, in terms of supervision and discipline, and criminality of parents or siblings are significantly related to delinquent behaviour (Farrington 1996). Interestingly, according to a Home Office survey, children whose parents provide little structure and discipline feel that their parents do not care enough about them (Riley and Shaw 1985). However, delinquent young people do not easily accept their parents' control (Junger-Tas et al. 2003b), such juveniles often have a bad relationship with their father, which suggests that good parent–child relationships are an important pre-condition for effective supervision.

Another risk factor is inconsistent discipline, often accompanied by severe and violent disciplining methods, such as bad language, threats, blows and kicks. Criminality or heavy drinking of the father have an adverse effect on child-raising methods: such fathers use more often violence and inconsistent discipline than other fathers. Mother's alcohol abuse and irregular work pattern particularly affects the supervision of her children (Sampson and Laub 1993). Research has shown that both too little control and extreme control and discipline are related to higher rates of delinquent behaviour. Punishing children too often, too severely and too forcefully, using violence even appears to foster delinquent behaviour. In this connection it should be remembered that violence in the family differs from other violence in three respects. It usually occurs within relationships that are of a lasting nature, between parents or between parents and child. In contrast to violence between strangers, the violence is often repeated, with one of the parties being weak and vulnerable compared to the assailant. Finally, the violence takes place in private and is therefore invisible and difficult to detect (Reiss and Roth 1993). Where children are concerned, boys are more often physically maltreated, while girls are more often victim of sexual abuse (Straus et al. 1980). Abuse and neglect are strongly related to income: the lower the income the greater the risk to the children (Sedlak 1991). Physical abuse not only has medical consequences but also gives rise to a greater risk of suicide (or attempted suicide) and depression. Parents who suffer from depression tend more often to maltreat their children. Violence in the family is often passed on from one generation to the other (Straus et al. 1980). Moreover, people who were abused or neglected as children run later a much higher risk of being arrested for a crime of violence than people who did not have this experience (Widom 1989).

Apart from the control aspects, the quality of the relationship between parent and child is of great significance. Strong negative feelings by the child towards his or her parents are related with criminal behaviour. The most important elements in this respect are: acceptance, respect and faith in the child; good communication between parents and child about thoughts, feelings and problems; the absence of conflict, both between parents and between parents and children. It is interesting to note that none of these factors are related to family structure. However, they are all associated with the development of pro-social behaviour in the child (Cernkovich and Giordano 1987). In this regard internal family dynamics appear to be more important than family structure in the production of norm-conform behaviour.

A survey of all family studies carried out up until the 1980s led to a classification into four models of 'families at risk' (Loeber and Stouthamer-Loeber 1986b). In the *neglecting family* parents devote little time to their children and do hardly supervise them. Such parents do not check where their children are, who they are associating with and what they are doing. In the *conflict family* there are constant rows between parents and between parents and children, often accompanied by violence. Verbal and physical disciplining methods are ineffective. The child is frequently rejected by his or her parents and in turn withdraws from them. The child learns that conflicts can only be resolved by violent means. The *deviant family* tolerates or secretly encourages delinquent behaviour, such as fighting, handling of stolen goods, theft, either openly or surreptitiously. In this case the parents are criminal and aggressive and the children risk developing serious criminal behaviour, including violent crime. In the *disintegrated family* marital conflicts, both before and after the divorce, are related with considerable child-raising problems and with inconsistent discipline.

The Family Environment

As we all know crime rates are higher in urban environments than in rural areas. Other problems, such as behavioural-, emotional- and psychological problems, also occur more frequently in big cities than in the country (Rutter 1980). The reason is not that criminal or problematic people disproportionately migrate to cities, but studies have shown that families in big cities are more often affected by serious problems, such as unemployment, poor housing, psychiatric disorders, marital difficulties, alcoholism and criminality (Rutter 1980).

Neighbourhoods are important in this respect. An area which is dilapidated, where many of the houses are boarded up and drug dealing goes on openly, where vandalism is the order of the day and rubbish and dirty needles lie around everywhere, is not a suitable environment for children to grow up. Such areas cause fear among residents, reduce social control and invite crime. It is in these areas that many unemployed and poor families live, among which many of different ethnic origin. Young people hang around and form groups or gangs. School drop-out, unemployment and boredom easily lead to a collective search for leisure opportunities as well as for the commission of offences. Among the structural background factors that are associated with delinquent behaviour of children are: poor and overcrowded housing, the break up of the family, welfare dependence, poverty, ethnic origin, high resident mobility, irregular employment, alcoholism or drug abuse of (one or both) parents, criminality of (one or both) parents (Laub and Sampson 1988; Wikström 1998; Wikström and Butterworth 2006).

The quality of the school – its instruction and education – is also important. Poor school achievement, a low level of ambition, a dislike of school, repeating classes and truancy have been shown to be linked with criminal behaviour (Sampson and Laub 1993; Junger-Tas et al. 2003a).

Finally, the peer group has a great influence on the behaviour of young people. The relationship between having delinquent friends and a person's own criminal behaviour is exceptionally strong and, of course, much of this behaviour is group behaviour. It is not self-evident that young people are drawn into delinquent peer groups by chance. There are indications that young people who have a poor relationship with their parents and are school failures tend to join a delinquent peer group through a process of self-selection: juveniles in a marginalized social position seek out similar youths, because they feel at ease with their equals (Junger-Tas 2003b; Sampson and Laub 1993).

Crime and Other Adverse Outcomes

It is useful to be aware that a number of socio-demographic and socio-economic factors that are related to criminal behaviour are also associated with physical illness, mental disturbance and all kinds of accidents. For example boys commit more offences than girls, and have more accidents as well because they tend to take more risks. Another factor is ethnicity: children from ethnic minority groups are more likely to be victims of a road accident and mortality among young minority children is higher than among children of the population of origin (Junger 1990; Cummings et al. 1994). Although it is not entirely clear why this is the case, the higher mortality rates may be due to their poor social-economic situation and the lack of parental supervision. Low income and a low level of education are related to fatal accidents by fire, road accidents, and accidents in the home, drowning and burns. The same is true when the parents – the mother in particular – have an alcohol problem (Rivera 1995). In addition, delinquents take great risks on the road and are more often victim of road and other accidents (Gottfredson and Hirschi 1990; Junger et al. 1995; Yoshikawa 1994). Mortality among delinquents is also higher. This is partly due to the fact that they are more prone to alcohol and drug abuse than non-delinquents (Stattin and Romelsjö 1995).

Child factors, such as a difficult temperament, behavioural problems and concentration difficulties, also present a greater risk of accidents and injuries, although it is not a very strong link. The link is stronger for adolescents who have discipline problems at school, frequently drink alcohol and use soft drugs (Rivera 1995).

Family factors which are good predictors of criminality also predict psychological and psychiatric disorders. Among these are low socio-economic status, a large family, criminality of the father, marital conflict, family violence, psychiatric disorder of the mother and intervention by Child Care authorities. Children who grow up in a family with one of these risk factors run no greater risk of developing a disorder than other children, but children in families with two risk factors run four times as high such a risk. That risk is multiplied with each additional risk factor (Rutter 1979). Delinquents are more frequently admitted to hospital than non-delinquents for illnesses, injuries and accidents (Farrington 1995). They also have more mental disorders, such as schizophrenia and depression, and are at greater risk of committing suicide (Fergusson and Lynskey 1996). Dutch research among young adult inmates revealed affective disorders, anxiety disorders and schizophrenia among a third of them and addiction problems among two thirds (Bulten et al. 1992). Two thirds of a group of 73 young people brought before the public prosecutor and referred for a social and medical report were found to have a psychiatric disorder (Doreleijers 1995).

Even if children from such risk families do not later become involved in a life of crime they often lead miserable lives. A London longitudinal study found that among a group of working class boys some of the men for whom a criminal career had been predicted had not developed such a lifestyle by the age of 32 (the so-called false positives). But they were social failures in terms of employment, housing, having a partner or children, alcohol consumption and mental health. Most of them led a solitary and marginal existence (Farrington 1988).

A Global Causal Picture

Of course all of the mentioned factors do not carry equal weight and we cannot just add them up. Some of them are of greater significance than others and some facilitate others. Moreover, some of them are related to delinquency in an indirect rather than any direct way (Sampson and Laub 1993; Wikström and Butterworth 2006).

For example, one might ask whether structural background factors are more important than internal family factors, or whether risk factors within the child are more decisive than the parents' upbringing (the 'nurture or nature' discussion). The answers to these questions are of particular importance if one wants to design effective preventive interventions.

First, evidence shows that specific family factors are the most powerful predictors of later criminal behaviour. These are the *degree of supervision, the degree and nature of discipline* and the *emotional bond* between the parents and the child.

Second, research suggests that structural background factors do not have a direct relationship with criminality, but operate via family processes (Sampson and Laub 1993). These factors facilitate or hinder the proper functioning of the family. If there are social and financial problems, stressful living conditions and little support in bringing up the children, it is difficult for parents to fulfil their role in a satisfactory way. This is all the more true when there is only one parent. Similarly, unemployment or mother's employment, a large family, ethnic minority status, alcohol abuse and parental criminality affect the ability of parents to raise their children so that they will become pro-social adults. Furthermore these factors also have a strong impact on *school achievement* due to the fact that the parents are unable to support their children, to check their homework, or to teach them the importance of school and education.

Finally, a deficient upbringing does not only lead to school failure but also to the children associating with a delinquent peer group. For all these reasons socialization and family processes are of crucial significance in bringing about criminal behaviour.

However, as mentioned before, child factors should not be discarded because some children are considerably more difficult than others. The main factors in this respect are *impulsive and disruptive behaviour, being resistant to discipline and early aggressive and/or anti-social behaviour.* These have indeed a powerful and independent effect on later criminality, which is why some have called them the best predictors of delinquency (White et al. 1990). However, given the fact that there is a continuous interaction between child factors and parent factors it would be very difficult, if not impossible, to disentangle both types of factors. For example a very troublesome, moody and difficult child might arouse impatience and harsh disciplining methods in parents. Therefore, it is not surprising that a relationship has been found between children's disruptive behaviour and inconsistent and harsh discipline of parents. On the other hand, there are findings showing that increased supervision by the mother – regardless of all other factors – leads to a reduction in delinquent behaviour (Sampson and Laub 1993; Wikström and Butterworth 2006). In other words parental factors seem to be more important determinants of pro-social or delinquent behaviour than child factors. This is why preventive measures which target only the child would seem insufficient. The role of the family is so crucial that it will have to be included if lasting results are to be achieved.

Prediction and Prevention

How easy is it to predict criminal behaviour and how certain can we be that those predictions will prove true if nothing is done? Is this a sufficient basis for social intervention? These questions are of crucial importance if judicial authorities want to contribute to a preventive family and youth policy. Traditionally judicial authorities do not intervene unless there are serious problems, and then they do so either by a civil child protection measure or – for those over 12 years of age – through juvenile penal law. Preventive intervention, although it does presuppose the presence of serious (behaviour) problems in the family and at school, which constitute a risk of subsequent delinquency, does not presume the presence of the delinquent behaviour itself. Therefore, there needs to be compelling reasons for the judicial authorities to be associated with a preventive policy of this kind. One of those reasons might be the fact that serious youth criminality is reasonably predictable. Another reason might be that in this regard early intervention achieves considerably better results than later intervention.

The essential question is, therefore, how accurate are predictions of future delinquent behaviour? One of the major problems with respect to the prediction of criminality is the question of what exactly we want to predict. If we define delinquency by self-report data, the base rate – that is the number of young people defined as delinquents – will be very high. But if the definition refers only to boys who are known to judicial authorities for at least five serious offences, the base rate will be rather low. A definitional choice has to be made in terms of the number of known offences or the number of convictions that define 'serious and chronic' delinquency. According to that definition offending is a relatively rare event. For example, only 6% of a group of boys from inner London became systematic offenders. Although 70% of this group were defined as 'very troublesome' at the age of 8–10, only 19% of these turned into repeated offenders (Farrington 1987). In other words, there is considerable over-prediction, leading to a large number of 'false positives' – young people for whom criminal behaviour was predicted but who did not develop such behaviour – and also under-prediction, leading to 'false negatives' – young people for whom criminality was not predicted but who did develop criminal behaviour. One of the first prediction instruments came from the Glueck and Glueck's study (1950). Their prediction table was based on five family variables: discipline of the boy by the father, supervision by the mother, affection for the boy of the father and of the mother, and family cohesiveness. Although the prediction instrument was later heavily criticized, mainly on methodological grounds, it is of some interest to observe that the screening variables have been confirmed in later research as fundamental for the prediction of criminality.

Prediction research is faced with a number of problems. Most research has been retrospective in nature, that is, predictive factors are looked for when the criminality is already known. Furthermore, very often selective samples have been used, such as children referred to a clinic for behaviour problems, first-offenders, or boys identified because of their persistent delinquent behaviour. Another problem is that some of the predictive factors have been found to be more important at an early age than they are later on, while others, such as a lack of parental supervision, become more important with age (Farrington 1987; Loeber and Stouthamer-Loeber 1986a).

Better predictions are achieved using prospective longitudinal research. Although research shows a large degree of continuity in a person's behaviour, many children undergo a sort of 'maturation process', as a result of which earlier predictions based on risk factors do not materialize. However, this 'drop-out phenomenon' is not spread evenly among young people. Children who manifest problem behaviour at an early age, in more than one setting (e.g. at home and at school), and children with more than one form of problem behaviour are at greater risk of developing delinquent behaviour than children who are difficult only at home, whose problem behaviour appears at a somewhat later age or shows less variation (Loeber 1987). *The accumulation of risk factors is therefore crucial to accurate prediction.* An interesting finding in longitudinal research is also that if circumstances change radically, behaviour also changes (Sampson and Laub 1993; Laub and Sampson 2003). A related question is at what age we should predict. Of course, prediction at a later age has a stronger predictive accuracy than predictions at an early age. For example, the best predictor for persistent offending is the number of previous convictions. However, once this stage is reached there is very little to achieve in terms of preventing criminal behaviour. Different meta-analyses conducted in the United States have shown that early intervention programs with young children have considerably more effects than treatment programs of delinquent adolescents (Tremblay and Craig 1995). Therefore, it would seem to me that what we first and foremost need is accurate prediction methods for young children.

Predictions of criminal behaviour are generally based on statistical probability calculations and can therefore never be perfect. This means that overzealous prevention policies, under which individual children and families are selected only on the basis of the statistical risk of subsequent delinquent behaviour, would be arbitrary and stigmatizing. According to Leblanc (1997), this type of predictions should lead to primary prevention policies, which are universal programs such as Head Start, which has the ambition to address all poor and deprived families in the United States, or more cost-effective programs which address all children and families in specific cities and neighbourhoods.

The selection of predictors should be based on multiple informants and multiple settings. It is not sufficient to rely on only one data-source, such as the parents or the child. Data obtained from more than one source, such as parents, teachers, children and their peer group, are considerably more reliable (Patterson 1994).

If the objective is to screen potential chronic and serious offenders on an individual basis, one would need additional information, such as clinical data provided by social and health services, or by child care authorities. These may lead to more targeted preventive interventions, which leads to the ethical question of voluntary or compulsory participation in prevention programs, a question I will turn to in a later section.

All in all there is a large consensus about the different variable domains, the information sources and the accumulation of risk factors, that are most important in prediction, but there is still a lot of work to be done to devise screening instruments for policymakers and practitioners (Leblanc 1997). The use of specific screening instruments will of course also depend on the population examined, the precise criterion variable, the objectives of the screening and the policy implications of the screening's results.

Early Prevention for Families and Children

It is clear that any crime prevention policy which targets families and children will need to take a broad approach. It will not suffice to tackle only one element of the causal chain, because the causal factors mentioned in this chapter are interrelated in complex ways. Many prevention programs here and abroad have not been set up with the specific objective of crime prevention. Most of them have the aim of improving the educational achievements of specific groups of children. Other prevention projects are addressed to parents and attempt to make them more effective child-raisers. A third group of programs attempt to improve dysfunctional behaviour in children. Only a small number of programs have the specific purpose of reducing and preventing anti-social, aggressive and delinquent behaviour in children. A number of meta-analyses of treatment programs have been carried out in the United States. Table 8.1 presents some results of meta-analyses of treatment programs aimed at improving adaptive behaviour of parents and children (Trembly and Craig 1995). These analyses show that early interventions with young children have considerably more effect than treatment of juvenile delinquents. The different projects may be distinguished by target group – parents or children –, by intervention type – parent training or (pre)school projects – and hybrid forms which involve both parents and children. The goals of the projects vary from the prevention of delinquency to the prevention of factors that are closely related to subsequent criminality, such as cognitive deficiencies, behavioural problems and inadequate parenting (Tremblay and Craig 1995; Welsh and Farrington 2006; Beelmann and Raabe 2007).

Table 8.1 Selected meta-analysis results of treatment studies

Type of treatment	Mean effect size	Number of studies
Treatment for Juvenile delinquents (Lipsey 1992)	.18	443
Cognitive Behaviour Therapy with dysfunctional children (Durlak et al. 1991)	.53	64
Parent training (Cedar and Levant 1990)	.33	26
Head Start – Early educational Program (Administration for Children, Youth and Families 1983)	.34	71
Cognitive behavioural modification strategies with children (Duzinski 1987)	.47	45

Source: Tremblay and Craig 1995, p. 157

It is important to point out that many of the experimental programs, either in the United States or elsewhere, have a number of shortcomings. The treatment was frequently administered to small target groups (from less than a hundred to a few hundred experimental subjects), the allocation of children to experimental or control group was not always based on random allocation, the population was sometimes heterogeneous, the implementation of the program did not always follow the design, a number of studies were plagued by the problem of attrition, that is some of the experimental subjects got 'lost' over the years, and the test measurements were not always reliable (Tremblay and Craig 1995). Moreover, as far as Europe is concerned, thorough evaluations are rare. Usually people content themselves with interviewing some key figures – who often have a stake in the program – or simply renounce all effect evaluation, merely pointing out the problems associated with measuring treatment effects.

In fact all this makes the similarity of the results achieved by these programs all the more striking. This fact alone should give us confidence in the value of this type of approach. The following results appear in a great number of effect studies.

- Parent training schemes have an impact on problem behaviour and anti-social behaviour in the children of the parents concerned;
- A significant effect of guidance and treatment of young teenage mothers is that the incidence of physical abuse and neglect of their children is considerably less among them than among comparable families who have not been treated;
- Cognitive skills and social competence programs affect children's learning and behavioural problems. The improvement of problem behaviour in turn affects learning ability and, as a consequence, delinquent behaviour;
- In general, the effectiveness of intervention programs increases as the age of the target group falls, from adolescents to toddlers (Tremblay and Craig 1995);
- Early intervention programs which target more than one risk factor have cumulative effects (Yoshikawa 1994). The best example is the Perry Pre-school project where pre-school training of infant children was combined with weekly contacts with parents, in order to improve their caretaking skills. The study showed long-term effects on delinquent behaviour as well as on a broad range of social and economic factors during adolescence and in adulthood (Schweinhart et al. 2005; see for an overview on the effectiveness of early intervention programmes also Lösel and Beelmann 2005; 2006; Welsh and Farrington 2006; Beelmann and Raabe 2007; Krüger 2009).
- Some treatment programs of adolescents have also been shown to be effective, on the condition that they directly address the young people's acute problems at school and at home and provide additional incentives to motivate them to participate. More research is needed in this area;
- Preventive intervention programs have significant benefits other than the mere reduction of criminal behaviour: the education level rises, labour participation increases, incomes are higher, welfare dependence is reduced, and physical and mental health and general well-being increase;
- In order to achieve long-term effects, preventive intervention projects must be of relatively long duration. Most researchers claim a treatment period of at least 2 years.

In conclusion it seems clear that administrative and judicial authorities should take a great interest in prevention policies that target children and their families. Such a policy would have three important goals.

The first goal is to realize that, just as situational crime prevention has become an integral part of national and local policies, whether it is in questions of town planning, social housing or public transport, crime prevention should also become a permanent part of any youth policy. Youth welfare should not be exclusively concerned with improving health, reducing learning disabilities and increasing recreational options. It is also important to prevent a sizable minority of young people, both of native and immigrant origin, from drifting gradually in a life of crime. The prevention of juvenile delinquency should be integrated into all national, provincial, urban and neighbourhood planning as a natural concern and responsibility.

The second goal is to ensure that prevention programs which target children should also target their parents, because it is not only cognitive skills and social competence that need to be developed, but also the necessary caretaking skills of parents. Guidance and monitoring, supervision and control are essential elements of effective socialization that is socialization which prepares the child for effective participation in social institutions, such as school and society as a whole. Appropriate parent training has a positive impact on these skills.

The third goal is to complement programs that support families and promote school achievement: they are most effective by an environment which creates the conditions for happy family life and good parenting. Considerable efforts have to be made by both state and local government to support parents and families in their upbringing tasks. Crèches, nurseries and pre-school centres should be available for working mothers as a matter of course. Schools should open their buildings for after-school activities, such as sports, music, and theatre, so that children would not have to hang around on the streets till their parents come home. In the evening the schools should be open for adult activities, including courses and parent training. Experiments in this field in middle-class schools have been quite successful, but in deprived neighbourhoods there is a pressing need for funding such arrangements by the local government. In addition, more attention should be paid to the difficulties of migrant families and their children: special programs for these children – cognitive and social competence training – *and* their parents – language courses and parent training – should be available free of charge. Moreover, the state as well as the local government must create unskilled and lower skilled jobs for young people who cannot pursue a higher education. There is still a need for such jobs, for example, in the service sector, the security sector and in the health and welfare service. Also of importance are good housing policies.

Early Intervention: For Whom?

A policy of early preventive interventions regarding children and families is faced with an ethical dilemma. Most of the studies in this field do not discuss this dilemma, but of course, in experimental programs it is easy to ignore this question.

However, if one wants to develop preventive policies there is no escape and one has to deal with it. The dilemma is based on the question whether one is justified to intervene in the lives of people on the basis of predictions that have statistical validity on an aggregated level but much less so on an individual level. More precisely the question is on what scientific and moral grounds we can offer training programs to groups and to individual families at risk on a voluntary basis and to what extent would we be justified to make participation in these programs compulsive.

In this regard there are a number of considerations in order.

First, it might be stated with reasonable certitude that it is possible to identify groups of families presenting so many risk factors that their children run a considerable risk of developing a criminal and marginal life. This is the determining factor which entitles the community to undertake specific preventive action.

Second, it would be incorrect to claim that the responsibility for this situation lies wholly and exclusively with the families themselves. Therefore, as mentioned above, special efforts on the level of the state and the local government are paramount to improve the conditions for adequate family life. It is only when the authorities recognize their own responsibilities and act upon them by taking adequate measures that they are justified to require compulsive participation in training programs.

Third, given the fact that the predictive validity of the risk factors that have been found in prospective research is not perfect and thus cannot be stretched too far, it seems reasonable to state that compulsive participation in training programs for individual families and children should take place only exceptionally and in specific cases only.

If all these conditions are met a three track approach could be considered.

The first track would consist of a general preventive approach in deprived neighbourhoods. Together with measures taken by local government this would be a universal approach addressed to the resident families. The offer of cognitive stimulation programs to children aged 4–8 and of parent training can be made through the school and by home visitors. By working through the school *all* children are reached. In addition, social competence programs, such as the 'Good Behaviour Game', can also be presented in school. Another advantage is that in this way it is easier to reach parents. Experience of school principals in this respect has learned that most parents are sensible to the argument of 'improving the chances for their children for a better future'. Moreover, parent training programs have been designed which join positive interactions among trainer and parents and effective didactic methods. Once parents attend they usually like the program. Offering a modest financial incentive might help increasing attendance of some (ethnic minority) groups. Such a general approach can be extended to secondary schools in an effort to prevent school drop-out and improve social functioning of pupils.

The second track is concerned with families where there are indications of serious problems or where these problems threaten to arise. Here a more outreaching approach would seem to be in order. It should be emphasized that in this case statistical predictions are not sufficient and clinical evidence would be needed (Leblanc 1997). For example, teachers may signal children with excessive aggressive and anti-social behaviour if they have reason to suspect child abuse. The health services in the Netherlands are working with diagnostic instruments for measuring the physical and psycho-social health of all young children which come routinely to their attention. Based on the outcomes of such examination the city of Rotterdam is offering special assistance and parent programs to families at risk. This city also conducts anonymous youth surveys in a random sample of municipal (primary and secondary) schools in order to detect serious problems. The results are presented to the schools which are invited to consider taking special preventive measures. Although in some of these cases identification of individual families and children at risk has taken place, participation in preventive programs remains voluntary. However, there is a fair amount of persistent efforts to convince parents to participate.

The third track is compulsory treatment. When families are known to the authorities for incidents of child abuse, alcohol and drug abuse; when young teenage mothers are living on their own with social benefits but without a social network; when there is serious anti-social behaviour of the child and the threat of a supervision order or the child might be taken in care, preventive intervention is the only realistic alternative.

The fact that authorities are usually not too keen on taking official – and thus stigmatizing – measures would seem to justify a certain amount of pressure on families to participate in preventive programs. In some cases this could take the form of a conditional child care measure or some kind of diversion.

The State of the Art

It is important to recall that originally the objective of prevention programs in most of the Western world was not to prevent serious and violent criminality. Their main goal was to improve the life of mothers and their young children in deprived neighbourhoods by addressing the health and educating skills of the mother and the cognitive development of the child, such as the programs that were developed and evaluated by Olds and his colleagues (1986; 1988). Only when longitudinal research showed the stability of early anti-social and aggressive behaviour (Olweus 1979; Huesmann et al. 1984; Loeber 1991; Farrington and West 1990) did one consider the importance of the prevention of later criminal behaviour. In the Netherlands there was a similar development. Programs such as early edu-cation and parent training have been developed out of concern for children's permanent lags in education, young people's lack of labour participation and inter-generational poverty.

Early Intervention

It is interesting to note a shift in the focus on prevention from the Ministry of Justice to the Ministry of Public Health and Welfare. Great sums of money are invested by the ministry's research fund into different kinds of prevention research programs, such as an extensive test of the Olds program, including parent training. The program has been adapted to Dutch culture and will be evaluated by an experienced research unit of the Sophia Children's Hospital (Erasmus University Rotterdam). More generally, research on the development of young children is encouraged and ways are looked for to improve screening methods of (very) young children and their mothers, so as to detect eventual psycho-social family or child problems. In this respect, it is the local health authorities, administered by the local authorities, who seem to play an increasingly important role. Local health care is organized in so-called 'consultation offices' where babies aged 0–2 are regularly examined – free of charge – and small children aged 2–4 are remaining under medical control. This is a universal program reaching about 95% of all families. The consultation offices have to follow a recently established 'Basic health care' program which is increasingly standardized, making sure that it is uniformly applied. At the same time considerably more focus is placed on screening for early psycho-social family problems and anti-social child behaviour. In addition, many of the existing parent training programs, focused essentially on the transfer of educational skills to assist parents, have been developed and are administered by these offices. One of the problems with the original training programs was its voluntary character. Parents who ideally should be reached from a perspective of crime prevention, that is multi-problem families or families under a civil supervision order, were not reached, as appeared from reviews of participating parents (Bakker et al. 1997). However, in the framework of civil and penal interventions parent training may now selectively be imposed on parents whose children are persistent truants, or in the case of families under a supervision order. In addition, the Minister of Justice, considering that parents have considerable responsibility for the actions of their children, is examining the possibility (taking the UK as a model) to impose parent training as a measure on parents when their children have committed an offence.

What may be concluded is that in terms of prevention programs for families and young children there has been undeniable progress since the late 1990s. At the same time parent training is increasingly used by the child care and juvenile justice system as some sort of parent disciplining measure.

School Programs

With respect to early education, we have actually a number of tested programs at our disposal. For example, a Dutch version of the Perry pre-school project (Schweinhart et al. 1993; 2005) as well as Slavin's 'Success for All' (Slavin et al. 1990; 1993) have both been carefully tested and found effective (Lesemann et al. 1998; 1999). Both have been introduced in Dutch schools under the names of *Kaleidoscoop* and *Piramide.* In addition, there are three other original Dutch programs (*Kea, Opstap* and *Overstap)* focused on the improvement of cognitive development of primary school pupils, which have also been found effective (Kook 1996; van Tuijl 2002; Wolfgram 1999). Two American social competence programs, the Good Behavior Game (Kellam et al. 1998), a program for primary school pupils, and Skills for Life for secondary school students, have been adapted to Dutch culture and both have been extensively tested and found effective (van Lier 2002; Gravesteijn 2003).

In the late 1990s the Ministry of Education made a start with introducing tested early education programs in all schools situated in deprived areas. For budgetary reasons it was a gradual approach and at the end of the last century one third of all target schools was reached. However, since then decentralization policies made local authorities responsible for primary education and actually we do not know what has been left of these policies. This is all the more uncertain since the ministry considerably reduced school budgets for extra educational assistance to deprived children.

Several programs are set up to get persistent truants and drop-outs back to school or into an apprenticeship. These young people are referred to one of the programs by the education authorities. Most of them have considerable problems with their parents, such as neglect and abuse, alcohol abuse, incest, as well as at school, such as conflicts with teachers and pupils, alcohol and drug abuse, gambling, delinquency, and a lack of social skills and self-confidence. Careful screening is the basis of a treatment plan, combining instruction with monitoring and assistance. Most participate for a term of 6–12 months, the majority of which takes up school again or joins the labour market. The program is followed by several months of after-care and monitoring. What is remarkable is that these programs are supported by the local community, the police, childcare agencies and labour organizations. Although the programs have not been scientifically evaluated, they seem quite successful in helping troubled youth to resume their education or to get a job. Finally, many communities create so-called *large schools* in deprived neighbourhoods, which also exist in the Scandinavian countries. The first large schools were created by local communities in the 1990s in two major Dutch cities, but at this moment there are more than 600 primary large schools and about 300 secondary large schools. The Ministry of Education's goal is to double the number of such schools by 2010. Their objective is to improve the effectiveness of the education process, the enlargement of the school's functions, to relate home, school and leisure and to reinforce pupils' social competence. To achieve this communities have reintroduced social work in the school, lengthened the school day with recreational activities, involved neighbourhood residents, included the offer for parent training and social competence programs for pupils. Most of such primary schools assemble at the same location crèches, a kindergarten, a special education school, after-school programs and parent training, as well as in some cases a sports organization, leisure and cultural organizations. In addition, they have close contacts with the local library, the music school, social work and Child care organizations and the police. According to the community's characteristics, large schools emphasize different programs, such as early education, a reading and book club, a cooking club or cultural activities. Parent participation and close coordination of all organizations and programs are required to guarantee the success of these schools.

Community Programs

In 1999 both the Ministry of Justice and the Ministry of Public Health and Welfare funded the implementation and evaluation of the American program *Communities that Care* (Hawkins et al. 1992a; Catalano and Hawkins 1996), a very structured and rational prevention model. The program is based on research on *risk factors* and *protective factors* in families, schools and the neighbourhood, in relation to behaviours such as delinquency, drug abuse, violence, school drop-out and teen pregnancy. Priorities for preventive action are based on careful analysis of risks and protections in the family and the community and are followed by the input of effective intervention programs addressed to the selected risk factors. Communities that Care (CtC) was piloted in four sites,[1] two of which were (very) deprived neighbourhoods in Amsterdam and Rotterdam. Since the funded experimental period was no more than 4 years, and since the introduction of such an elaborate program was not without considerable practical difficulties, the accompanying research had to be limited to an evaluation of the implementation process.

The interim results of the DSP process evaluation in 2004 (DSP Research Group 2004) showed that the main results in the short term refer to output data, that is to information on the possibility of directing, administrating and controlling the operation of relevant organizations and service providers. Several conclusions were drawn concerning the number of different organizations involved in CtC and the share of social service providers, the extent of mutual collaboration and the degree of support by community leaders. It appeared to be considerably more difficult to involve residents and young people in the CtC process. So far the Dutch outcomes did not differ from what has been found in the Unites States:

- Increase in the quality of planning and decision taking
- Greater collaboration among service providers
- More coordination in programming preventive interventions
- Greater focus of prevention efforts on risk and protective factors
- Greater use of demonstrated effective and promising approaches
- More involvement of young people and other citizens in preventive interventions

The Verwey-Jonker institute in Utrecht was commissioned to conduct an effect evaluation of the four existing pilots as well as two new sites.[2] This study was recently completed. The main outcomes of that study as far as the young people in the studied neighbourhoods are concerned are the following:

- The situation in the experimental neighbourhoods is improved
- Alcohol and drug abuse, truancy and violence have significantly decreased
- However, results on community improvement are expected in 5–10 years

All in all researchers conclude that CtC is a valuable instrument for youth policies to be implemented by local communities.

What is interesting to note though is that Amsterdam wants to spread CtC to only some other parts of the city, while Rotterdam wants to introduce it in the whole city. It is also of importance to note that 1 of our 13 provinces (South Holland) has adopted CtC as a provincial program that will be introduced on a large scale.

---

[1]Amsterdam, Rotterdam, Zwolle and Arnhem.

[2]Leeuwarden and Almere.

Conclusions

Reviewing the main developments in the last 5 years in terms of prevention research and prevention policies, the question is to what extent there have been changes and to what extent one could – cautiously – discover some new trends. In that respect I have three comments.

First, it may be said that the principles of evidence-based interventions have gained considerable ground, as is testified by numerous examples. As far as research is concerned the main progress is undoubtedly to be found in the public health field: it is there that research standards are highest, the best effect evaluations are found and the first longitudinal studies have started. However, progress may also be noted in criminology. For example, the Dutch Ministry of Justice has followed the British model, introducing an Accreditation Commission. Also prompted by budget cuts the Dutch ministry realized that it was impossible to continue funding all kinds of projects and interventions, most of which had no demonstrated effects. The ministry is determined to put together a pool of effective, or at least promising programs (to be evaluated as soon as possible), so as to know what interventions to use in the criminal and juvenile justice system on one side, and have better control over spending on the other. Another example is a survey done by the Dutch *National Youth Institute* of all existing effective and promising prevention programs in the Netherlands (Ince et al. 2004). Furthermore, the same institute is setting up a data-base of all Dutch effective interventions in the field of (psycho-social) health and juvenile justice. Finally, although this has taken some time, practitioners have increasingly realized that for their program to be accepted good quality research has to demonstrate its effectiveness.

Second, it seems to me that there is some difference in focus between the United States and Europe as far as prevention is concerned. Reading the US literature the main focus is on programs to put in place in specific risk situations and addressed to individual children or youths, while the trend in Europe is to think rather in terms of broad national or local policies. This is illustrated for example by the Dutch Consultation offices, which cover the whole country and produce national rates of infant and young children's health. It is also demonstrated by initiatives of the Ministry of Education, such as introducing early education programs in all schools in deprived neighbourhoods or in the *Large schools*, initiatives which may contribute to assist numerous children to succeed their school career. Another example are the initiatives of schools for technical and vocational training to modify their curriculum (promoting job-training), and to connect with the business community around the schools so as to allow pupils to get jobs. Again, one should train practitioners to put in place registration systems, so as to have at least some control over what they try to achieve, but it is the difference in focus that I find of interest here.

This brings me to my third point, a nagging problem for which we have not yet found a satisfying solution. I am referring to the dissemination of effective interventions into standing practice. For example, a social competence program for primary schools, the *Good Behaviour Game*, has been implemented in the Netherlands with great care as well as been evaluated in an excellent study (van Lier 2002). Now what will happen if a great number of schools would wish to adopt this program? Although there is an implementation manual for practitioners, taking into account the way teachers usually operate to maintain order and discipline, it is clear that they would need careful and continuous training in how to apply the game. This is true for many programs if one wishes to guarantee program fidelity and treatment integrity, but unfortunately in practice this is not always possible, if only for reasons of cost-effectiveness.

The problem has been considered in the United States and Canada and, based on Lipsey's work, Howell discusses this from the standpoint of local juvenile justice interventions (Howell 2003, pp. 216–223). Lipsey conducted a meta-analysis of practical juvenile justice programs that had a rehabilitative orientation but were *not* research demonstration projects (Lipsey 1999, cited by Howell), finding that nearly half of them reduced recidivism by 10–24%, while some of the best programs reduced recidivism by 20–25%. In this respect, the following characteristics were all important: (1) the provision of services, (2) a sufficient amount of services, (3) relating these to the relevant target group, and (4) a distinct role for the juvenile justice system. The more of these characteristics an intervention realized, the greater the reduction in recidivism. Howell then pleads (Howell 2003, p. 221) for a pragmatic approach by which program principles and guidelines for effective interventions resulting from previous evaluations are taken up by communities and used in practical program development. This might then lead to what is called evidence-based practices, or best practices. Although this problem has not yet been really dealt with in many countries, it seems to me that more reflection is needed if we want to improve prevention policies.

An effective preventive policy is a long-term investment. Even if we achieve some successes in the short-term, we cannot expect immediate improvements in the safety and the living conditions of inner city neighbourhoods. However, we should not allow that inner city areas deteriorate to the point where alcoholism, drug abuse, drug dealing and crime become endemic. This would mean that we would accept that some population groups end up in totally marginal and dead-end situation. In such areas violence and crime would be at a very high level and the local community would be permanently threatened by sudden outbreaks of serious violence and rioting. To prevent this to happen is the main challenge of our time.

Chapter 9
Diversion: A Meaningful and Successful Alternative to Punishment in European Juvenile Justice Systems

Frieder Dünkel

Diversion: Historical Aspects and International Instruments

Since the 1960s particularly in North America[1] and across Europe, *tendencies in juvenile criminal policy* have emerged that were based on the notions of the subsidiarity and proportionality of state interventions against juvenile offenders, and which were voiced in many international human rights instruments, such as in the UN standard minimum rules for the administration of juvenile justice of 1985. More specifically, these developments also involve the *expansion of procedural safeguards* on the one hand, and the *limitation* or *reduction of the intensity of interventions* in the field of sentencing on the other hand. One major element of this philosophy was the idea of diversion, that is, to avoid possibly stigmatising state interventions in favour of a more lenient and with regard to future social integration more appropriate approach.

In spite of heavy criticism in the early 1980s, blaming 'net-widening' effects and informal social control that would even surpass formal social control of the youth courts (see for example Austin and Krisberg 1981, 1982; Kerner 1983), diversion has continued its 'triumphant' expansion due to national and international developments in juvenile crime policy in the 1980s.

The concept of non-intervention or better: avoiding formal prosecution was developed in combination with efforts of decriminalisation (particularly of

---

F. Dünkel
Rechts- und Staatswissenschaftliche Fakultät, Universität Greifswald, Greifswald, Germany

---

[1] In 1967 the US *President's Commission on Law Enforcement and Administration of Justice* in its final report stated: '*The formal sanctioning system and pronouncement of delinquency should be used only as a last resort. In place of the formal system, dispositional alternatives to adjudication must be developed for dealing with juveniles, including agencies to provide and coordinate services and procedures to achieve necessary control without unnecessary stigma. Alternatives already available, such as those related to court intake, should be more fully exploited. The range of conduct for which court intervention is authorized should be narrowed, with greater emphasis upon consensual and informal means of meeting the problems of difficult children*', see President's Commission on Law Enforcement and Administration of Justice 1967, p. 2; see also Heinz 2005, p. 168.

J. Junger-Tas and F. Dünkel (eds.), *Reforming Juvenile Justice*,
DOI:10.1007/978-0-387-89295-5_9, © Springer Science+Business Media, LLC 2009

so-called status offences) and deinstitutionalisation (from youth custody and residential homes).

The present chapter focuses on diversion in the field of juvenile justice. It has, however, to be emphasised that the expansion of diversion is also seen in the general criminal law for adults, sometimes influenced by the experiences in juvenile justice. The rise of prosecutorial power across Europe in order to cope with overloaded criminal justice systems is described by Jehle and Wade (2006). Their report includes in depth descriptions of the general system of diversion (for adult offenders) in England and Wales, France, Germany, the Netherlands, Poland and Sweden.

Particularly in the area of juvenile justice, many international recommendations since the mid-1980s emphasised that diversion should be given priority as an appropriate and effective strategy of juvenile crime policy. It repeatedly has been dealt with in international human rights instruments such as

- The United Nations Standard Minimum Rules for the Administration of Juvenile Justice of 1985 (so-called Beijing Rules, see Rules No. 11.1–11.4).
- The Council of Europe's Recommendation on Social Reactions to Juvenile Delinquency of 1987, Rec. (87) 20 (see Rules No. 2 and 3).
- The Convention on the Rights of the Child of 1989 (see Article 40 (2) b).
- The United Nations Guidelines for the Prevention of Juvenile Delinquency of 1990 (so-called Riyadh-Guidelines, see Rules No. 5 and 6).
- The United Nations Standard Minimum Rules for Non-custodial Measures (so-called Tokyo-Rules, see Rule No. 5).
- The Council of Europe's Recommendation on 'New ways of dealing with juvenile delinquency and the role of juvenile justice' of 2003 (Rec. (2003) 20, see Rules 7, 8 and 10).
- The Council of Europe's 'European Rules for Juvenile Offenders Subject to Sanctions and Measures' of 2008 (Rec. (2008) 11, see Rule 12).

A definition of diversion can be as follows: Diversion is the dismissal of the case when the offence is of a minor gravity and if formal proceedings do not seem to be appropriate. Diversion follows the procedural principle of 'expediency' (in contrast to a strict principle of 'legality' which demands formal proceedings and court decisions in any case). It regularly is a decision of the prosecutor, as its main aim is to avoid formal court proceedings. In many countries diversion can also be adjudicated by the judge, if after an accusation the case seems to be appropriate for a dismissal (e.g. because of reparation efforts by the offender in the meantime).[2]

---

[2] The second report of the US *Advisory Commission on Criminal Justice Standards and Goals* in 1973 had defined the term 'diversion' as follows: '... *the term "diversion" refers to formally acknowledged and organized efforts to utilize alternatives to initial or continued processing into the justice system. To qualify as diversion, such efforts must be undertaken prior to adjudication and after a legally prescribed action has occurred. In terms of process, diversion implies halting or suspending formal criminal or juvenile justice proceedings against a person who has violated a statute, in favour of processing through noncriminal disposition or means*' (Advisory Commission on Criminal Justice Standards and Goals 1973, p. 73).

Theoretical Background

There are six theoretical assumptions which can be seen as the basis for diversion:

1. To avoid (unnecessary) stigmatisation. This aspect is related to the so-called labelling approach. The concept of diversion thus reflects the views of labelling theory which stresses the possible negative effects of stigmatisation by formal sanctions of the youth court. Judicial interventions often impede rather than encourage social integration of young offenders. The empirical evidence or at least plausibility of possible negative consequences of state interventions has promoted the recognition of the principle of subsidiarity and of the last resort of imprisonment since the beginning of the 1960s.
2. The principle of giving priority to education instead of punishment ('educative diversion').
3. The principle of proportionality as a limitation of state intervention (minimum intervention model). This aspect is related to a 'constitutional' or 'human rights approach' that wants to avoid disproportionate sentencing. This approach sets clear limits to 'excessive' educational efforts based only on an assessment of educational needs which are not justified by the seriousness of the committed offence.
4. The 'economic' base of diversion is related to the pragmatic consideration of reducing or limiting the courts' case load (see in general Jehle and Wade 2006). It can be shown that an increase of cases in the criminal justice system needs to be compensated by diversionary or other bureaucratic strategies that make the 'input' manageable.
5. The criminological base of diversion is the evidence of the episodic and petty nature of most juvenile crimes. Criminological research has well demonstrated that juvenile delinquency is a ubiquitous and passing phenomenon, linked to age. Even so-called (repetitive) career offenders abandon their criminal lifestyle when entering the age of an adult of over 20 or 25 years. The episodic and petty nature of most juvenile crimes supports the concept of diversion, that is, the avoidance or reduction of state intervention. This strategy is accompanied by strengthening the educational interventions in the family and/or the social peer group, etc.
6. The perspective of sociology of law: The advantage of non-intervention or less severe punishment (e.g. probation instead of imprisonment) lies in the increased expectations of future norm conformity, which are expressed by the competent punishing authority to the offenders in question. The violator of the norm is under the pressure of a special (informal) obligation as he has been given a 'social credit' which contributes to a higher compliance with the norm (see Raiser 2007, p. 235 f.; Spittler 1970, p. 106 ff.).

Legal Provisions for Diversion

Diversion has always been an option of (juvenile) prosecutors in countries that follow the procedural principle of '*expediency*', that is, the dismissal of the case where it seems to be appropriate in view of the (petty) nature of the crime and not opposing purposes of punishment such as special or general prevention. Examples are Belgium, France, the Netherlands and French speaking Swiss cantons. On the other hand, countries following the procedural principle of *'legality'* traditionally did not provide for diversion in their general criminal procedure law. Examples were Austria, Germany, Greece, Italy, Portugal, German speaking Swiss cantons and most Eastern European countries. Most of these countries have relaxed the legality principle particularly in the field of juvenile law and provide large exceptions of the principle making extensive use of informal procedures, as can be shown by the German example below.

In the field of juvenile justice countries following the traditional *welfare model* have facilitated diversionary strategies because of the wide discretionary power of the juvenile judge. Examples are Belgium, Poland, Portugal, and Scotland, whereas countries underlining the *justice approach,* including juvenile prosecutions, have had more difficulties. Examples are Austria, Greece and Italy. However, Austria with its reforms of 1988 and 1993, and Greece with the recent reform of 2003 have introduced diversion, particularly in connection with restorative practices (mediation, etc.). Juvenile justice reforms particularly in these countries have been the forerunner of a more liberal system enlarging the possibilities for diversion, as has been the case, for example, in Austria and Germany.

Diversion has been introduced and extended in almost all European countries, but with certain variations (see also Dünkel and Pruin in this volume, Table 9.1). The Recommendations of the UN (Beijing-Rules, Riyadh-Guidelines, etc.) and of the Council of Europe (of 1987 and 2003, see above) can be seen as specific backgrounds of this development. However, some more restrictive tendencies appeared in some countries in the 1980s (see for example the Netherlands) and 1990s (England/Wales: 1998). In the Netherlands (contrary to what happened in Germany) non-intervention without any sanction has been reduced in favour of diversion with interventions (minor obligations like community service, etc.). In England the system of police cautioning has been restricted by limiting it to a first and then 'final warning' and thus excluding repeated diversionary decisions.

Examples of Diversion in Practice: The Case of Germany

In the case of crimes the interventions of the German JJA are characterised by the principle of 'subsidiarity' or 'minimum intervention'.[3] This means that penal action should only be taken if absolutely necessary. Furthermore, sanctions must be limited

---

[3]The application of the JJA is restricted to crimes defined by the general penal law (StGB). The Juvenile Welfare Act (JWA) is applied when a child or juvenile in his personal development seems to be 'in danger' and needs help or measures provided by the JWA. The measures are chosen according to the estimated educational needs. They are not imposed in an 'interventionist' style, but offered and taken according to a request of the parents. In part, the measures are the same as the ones provided by the JJA (e.g. social training courses and special care). The residential care order exists in both laws, too. If the authorities of the youth welfare department want to bring a child or juvenile to a home (against the parents' will), they must ask the family court judge for a specific order (according to § 1631b Civil Code, *Bürgerliches Gesetzbuch*). Such homes are usually open facilities.

by the principle of proportionality. The legislative reform of the JJA in 1990 underlines the principle of juvenile court sanctions as a last resort ('*ultima ratio*'). Therefore the primary sanctions of the juvenile court are educational or disciplinary measures.

The most important response to petty offences is the dismissal of the case without any sanction. In this context one should emphasise that police diversion, such as the British 'cautioning', is not allowed in Germany. The underlying reasoning is the abuse of police power that occurred under the Nazi regime. Therefore all forms of diversion are allowed only at the level of the juvenile court prosecutor or the juvenile court judge. The police are strictly bound by the principle of legality. All criminal offences have to be referred to the public prosecutor. This situation differs from the one in England where police cautioning plays a considerable role.

The 1990 reform of the Juvenile Justice Act in Germany extended considerably the legal possibilities for diversion. The legislature has thus reacted to the reforms that have been developed in practice since the end of the 1970s (see Bundesministerium der Justiz 1989; Heinz in Dünkel et al. 1997). The law now emphasises the discharge of juvenile and young adult offenders because of the petty nature of the crime committed or because of other social and/or educational interventions that have taken place [see § 45 (1) and (2) JJA]. Efforts to make reparation to the victim or to participate in victim–offender reconciliation (mediation) are explicitly put on a par with such educational measures. There is no restriction concerning the nature of the offence; felony offences ('*Verbrechen*') can also be 'diverted' under certain circumstances, for example a robbery, if the offender has repaired the damage or made another form of apology (restitution/reparation) to the victim.[4]

Four levels of diversion can be differentiated. Diversion without any sanction ('*non-intervention*') is given priority in cases of petty offences.

Diversion with measures taken by other agencies (parents, the school) or in combination with mediation is the second level ('*diversion with education*'). Dismissal of the case after *educative measures* have been taken is provided in particular after efforts for reparation/restitution to the victim in the framework of mediation have taken place. Mediation as a particular educational measure is given special attention by the legislator [see § 45 (2) JJA].

The third level is '*diversion with intervention*'. In these cases the prosecutor proposes that the juvenile court judge impose a minor sanction, such as a warning, community service (usually between 10 and 40 h), mediation ('*Täter-Opfer-Ausgleich*'), participation in a training course for traffic offenders ('*Verkehrsunterricht*') or certain obligations such as reparation/restitution, an apology to the victim, community service or a fine [§ 45 (3) JJA]. Once the young offender has fulfilled these obligations, the juvenile court prosecutor will dismiss the case in co-operation with the judge.

The fourth level includes the introduction of levels one to three into juvenile court proceedings after the charge has been filed. Fairly often in practice the juvenile court judge is faced with the situation that the young offender has, in the meantime (after

---

[4] The situation is different in the general penal law for adults (>18- or 21-years old) where diversion according to §§ 153 ff. of the Criminal Procedure Act is restricted to misdemeanours. Felony offences (i.e. crimes with a minimum prison sentence provided by law of 1 year) are excluded.

the prosecutor has filed the charge), undergone some educational measure like mediation, and therefore a formal court procedure seems unnecessary. Section 47 of the JJA enables the judge to dismiss the case in these instances.

Already before the law reform the discharge rates (diversion) in West Germany had increased from 43% in 1980 to 56% in 1989. This steady increase continued to 69% in 2003 and 68% in 2006 (see Heinz 2008; Heinz in Dünkel et al. 1997 and Fig. 9.1). It should be stressed that the increase concerns particularly diversion without intervention [according to § 45 (1) JJA], whereas the proportion of diversion combined with educational measures remained stable or recently even slightly declined (see Fig. 9.1).

However, there are large regional disparities, which have not been eliminated. The discharge rates varied in 2006 between 57% in Saarland, 62% in Bavaria and 81% in Hamburg and 88% in Bremen. Apparently in all the federal states of Germany discharge rates in cities are higher than in the rural areas (see Heinz and Storz 1994). This contributes to the rather stable conviction rates and case-load of juvenile court judges.

It is interesting to compare the diversion practice in East and West German states. It had been presumed that the penal culture in East Germany would be more severe and repressive. However, calculations of diversion rates gave evidence of an even wider extended diversion practice in the new federal states with an overall rate of 75% (Mecklenburg-Western Pomerania and Brandenburg even 78% and 76%; see Figs. 9.2 and 9.3; see also Heinz 2008; Dünkel et al. 2003). Again, the 'economic' strategy of controlling the input and workload of the juvenile courts is evident.

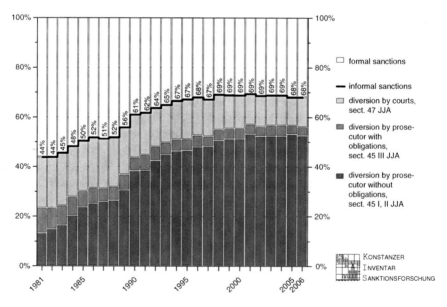

Fig. 9.1 Diversion rates (dismissals by prosecutors or courts) in the juvenile justice system of Germany, old federal states, 1981–2006

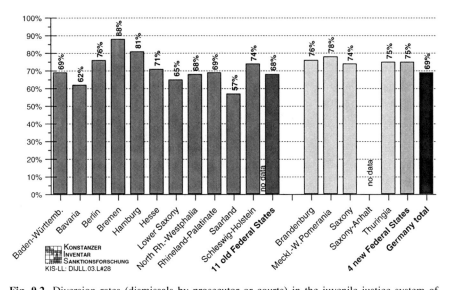

Fig. 9.2 Diversion rates (dismissals by prosecutor or courts) in the juvenile justice system of Germany, in comparison of the federal states, 2006

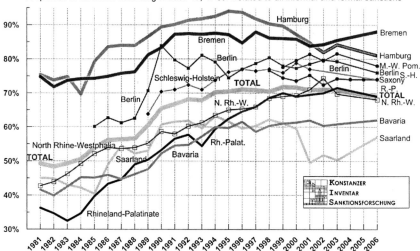

Fig. 9.3 Diversion rates (dismissals by prosecutor or courts) in the juvenile justice system of Germany, in comparison of selected federal states, 1981–2006

There is, however, also another explanation that seems to be plausible. The expanded diversion rates could also be a reaction to a difference in reporting behaviour. More petty offences might be reported to the police in East Germany, which are later excluded from further prosecution by the juvenile court prosecutors.

The overall diversion rate for Germany in 2006 was 69% (see Fig. 9.2).

There are several aspects of the explanation for the 'triumphant advance' of diversion in Germany that might explain it: The practice in Germany was strongly influenced by the wide-spread acceptance of labelling theory in the 1970s. Furthermore, this development was supported by the educational ideal ('education instead of punishment', derived already from the Juvenile Justice Act of 1923) and the constitutional principle of proportionality[5] which emphasises the necessity of applying to juvenile delinquency the mildest reaction which may be justified. The 'triumphant advance' of the diversion movement, however, was probably primarily due to the fact that it proved to be a useful strategy for coping with increasing crime rates and because it stabilised the case load of the juvenile justice administration (the pragmatic 'economy' of diversion). On the other hand, the Recommendations of the United Nations and the Council of Europe mentioned above have had some influence as well.

The pragmatic results of diversion can be shown with respect to the practice in the different federal states of Germany. Interestingly the relatively high police-registered general crime rates for juveniles and young adults in the northern and north-eastern states like Bremen, Berlin, Hamburg, Schleswig-Holstein, Mecklenburg-Western Pomerania or Brandenburg, in comparison with those of southern states like Bavaria or Baden-Württemberg, diminish if we compare the ratios of court-sentenced young persons (always calculated per 100,000 of the age group). The ratio of *sentenced* young offenders in the southern states is even higher than in the above mentioned northern states (see Fig. 9.4). This is primarily a result of very distinct and different diversion styles as has been shown above. The pragmatic result for the northern states is that the juvenile courts' case load is stabilised on an even lower level than that of the mentioned southern states.

The Practice of Diversion in Other European Countries

Diversion is a wide-spread practice in many European countries. It is seen as cost saving and effective, balancing the case load of juvenile courts. Although some more repressive rhetoric can be observed in some countries, claiming for 'punishment in the community' (England and Wales), the overall dominance of diversion as well as alternatives to custody and residential care seem to be a still prevailing strategy.

England and Wales have a form of police diversion (*cautioning*). The Crime and Public Disorder Act of 1998 has restricted police diversion insofar as *after a first*

---

[5] In Germany, this general principle is enshrined into the Constitution (see Art. 20 Basic Law, *Grundgesetz*), which guarantees this principle with regards to all state interventions.

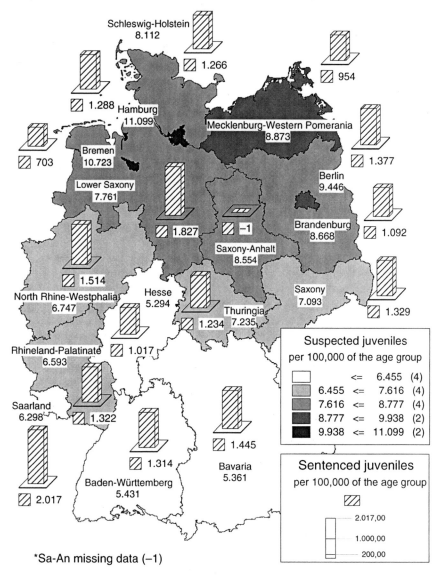

Schleswig-Holstein
8.112
1.266
954
1.288
Hamburg
11.099
Mecklenburg-Western Pomerania
8.873
703
Bremen
10.723
1.377
Lower Saxony
7.761
Berlin
9.446
1.827
-1
Brandenburg
8.668
1.092
Saxony-Anhalt
8.554
1.514
North Rhine-Westphalia
6.747
Hesse
5.294
Thuringia 7.235
Saxony
7.093
1.329
1.234
Rhineland-Palatinate
6.593
1.017

Suspected juveniles
per 100,000 of the age group

	<= 6.455	(4)
	6.455 <= 7.616	(4)
	7.616 <= 8.777	(4)
	8.777 <= 9.938	(2)
	9.938 <= 11.099	(2)

Saarland
6.298
1.322
1.445

Sentenced juveniles
per 100,000 of the age group

2.017,00
1.000,00
200,00

1.314
Bavaria
5.361
Baden-Württemberg
5.431
2.017

*Sa-An missing data (−1)

Fig. 9.4 Suspected and sentenced German juveniles in a comparison of the federal states in 2006

caution only one further caution is possible (*final warning*); after that a formal court hearing is obligatory.

The 'high time' of minimum intervention were the 1970s and 1980s. Diversion rates for 14–16-years-old juveniles went up from 24% to 73% (males) and 39% to 90% (females). In 1992 the maximum age for juvenile justice was raised from the 17th to the 18th birthday, therefore statistics from then on refer to the age group of

15–17-years-old juveniles. In 1992 the rate for 15–17-year-old male juveniles was 59%, the one for female juveniles even 81%. The rate dropped to 47% and 69% in 2005 (see Dignan 2009). The influence of the 1998 reform law seems to be rather limited as already before that year diversion rates were dropping (see Bottoms and Dignan 2004). Nevertheless it has to be stated that diversion in England still is a wide-spread option, which characterises the day-to-day policing of juvenile delinquency.

Austria had a remarkable juvenile law reform in 1988, introducing different forms of diversion without and with intervention (see Jesionek 2001; Bruckmüller 2006; Bruckmüller et al. 2009). Diversion with intervention includes minor fines and particularly victim–offender mediation. An interesting form of non-intervention is the immunity for 14- and 15-year-old offenders in case of a moderate and non-serious misdemeanour if there are no convincing reasons urging the court to enforce juvenile penal law to prevent the offender from committing further acts [§ 4 (2) 3 Austrian Juvenile Justice Act, JGG]. This form of decriminalisation is an equivalent to procedural diversion in other countries. The pettiness of the offence and 'minor guilt' result in the decision that the facts are not qualified as an offence. There are no statistical data giving evidence on the practice in this respect, but it seems to be of rather limited importance. Much more important are withdrawals of charges with regards to non-intervention because of the pettiness of the offence according to § 6 Austrian JGG. In 2004, 4,767 (31.0%) cases were dropped correspondingly without intervention, another 7,275 (47.3%) juveniles received a diversionary intervention. 3,336 (21.7%) juveniles between 14 and 18 years of age were convicted, in most cases to a fine or suspended sentence, only 693 (4.5%) to a partly or totally unconditional youth prison sentence. This means that diversion covers 69% of all decisions taken by juvenile prosecutors or judges (which are very similar to the above mentioned German practice which, importantly, includes 18–21-year-old young adults). Mediation as diversionary measure increased from 712 cases in 1988 to more than 2,500 cases in 1999, but then decreased to 1,610 cases in 2004. Nevertheless it still counts for 10.5% of all informal or formal sanctions in the juvenile justice system (own calculations of percentages according to Bruckmüller et al. 2009).

Belgium maintained its purely welfare approach also in the law reform of 2007. So juveniles under the age of 18 (with small exceptions for serious crimes and offenders aged 16 and 17) are not criminally responsible. Nevertheless Belgian law provides also several possibilities to escape formal court proceedings. Diversion implies a wide range of rehabilitative (educational), retributive sanctions and restorative measures. The term 'retributive' is used in the context of community service orders accompanying restorative measures and as such reinforcing 'the punitive features of the intervention' (van Dijk et al. 2006, p. 196). Victim–offender mediation has become a major issue in the 1990s, and family group conferences have been implemented in the new legislation as a further means of diversion from formal proceedings (first experiments with such conferences had started in 2001). Statistical data indicate that community sanctions such as community service are preferably imposed by the juvenile judges, whereas about 85% of the mediation cases were referred to mediation centres by the Public Prosecutor, only 15% by the judge (van Dijk et al. 2006, p. 199).

Exact statistical data are difficult to obtain, but it seems that more than 70% of the cases are dealt with informally by diversionary measures.

Greece, a country where prosecution was guided by the principle of legality, has introduced a new rule in the Criminal Procedure Act (Article 45a) in 2003 which provides for diversion if the prosecutor estimates that a court hearing is not necessary because of the petty nature of the crime and/or the personality of the juvenile (under 18, see Spinellis and Tsitsoura 2006). The prosecution is conditionally suspended and the minor can be obliged to fulfil certain educational measures (with special emphasis on reparation or compensation to the victim). After the fulfilment of these obligations the prosecutor definitely discharges the case.

The law reform of the *Czech Republic* in 2003 extended the possibilities of non-prosecution in the sense of diversion considerably. The Czech Penal Code provides for diversion in the following ways:

- Conditional dismissal of the case (with a probationary period of 6 months up to 2 years),
- Mediation and abandonment of criminal prosecution, no further action (see Válková 2006).

Both forms can be applied on the prosecutorial level as well as by the courts. Judges still seem to be reluctant to apply these measures. In 2000 only 10% of the cases have been diverted, followed, however, by a considerable increase, which resulted in 2006 in about 18% of cases being conditionally dismissed (see Válková and Hulmáková 2009). Particular difficulties and reservations of the juvenile prosecutors were observed with respect to diversion with no further action or in combination with restorative measures (mediation), which counted for less than 100 cases per year in 2004–2006.

Another country with a recent juvenile justice reform is *Serbia* (see Škulić in Dünkel et al. 2009). The new juvenile justice law came into force on 1 January 2006 and introduced for the first time diversion with educational measures. Until 2006 only the general rules of prosecutorial discretion applied. These allowed prosecutors to dismiss a case under the principle of expediency. It was the declared aim of the new law to extend the scope of application of diversionary measures also to more serious crimes (and not as before restrict it to petty offences). The offender's efforts to reach an agreement with the victim or to apologise, pay reparation, etc. is particularly emphasised as a condition of diversion (very similar to the German law).

According to article 7 of the Law on Juveniles diversion orders may include:

- A settlement with the injured party, for example, by compensation of the damages, apology, work or otherwise (the detrimental consequences should be alleviated either in full or in part);
- Regular attendance of school or work;
- Engagement, without remuneration, in the work of humanitarian organisations or community work (welfare, local or environmental work);
- Undergoing regular check-ups and drug and alcohol treatment programs;

• Participation in individual or group therapy at a suitable health institution or counselling centre.

All orders should be completed within 6 months. The practice – as in most countries which recently extended the legal possibilities for diversion or educational measures – is rather limited, but developing with the implementation of the growing infrastructure for such measures.

The Scandinavian countries can choose among a large range of diversionary disposals. Although they have no specific juvenile justice system or specialised juvenile courts, there exist specific sentencing rules for juveniles and to a limited extent also for young adults (see for an overview Stoorgard 2004). Sweden has a particular regulation of 'diversion' providing for the transfer of a juvenile to the youth welfare board as a 'sanction' of the criminal court. All Scandinavian countries allow for much discretion of prosecutors and courts enabling them to apply diversionary measures. Mediation has gained particular importance in Norway and Finland (also for minors under the age of criminal responsibility, see Stoorgard 2004, p. 194 f.). Recently the Scandinavian countries have extended the scope of alternative sanctions such as community service (Finland 1996; Sweden 1999) or stipulating specific conditions in connection with a withdrawal of charges, the so-called youth contracts (Denmark 1998; Norway on an experimental base in 2000). Whether these measures have increased the number of juveniles diverted from courts is not clear (see Stoorgard 2004, 196 ff.). Some researchers suspect that the increase of social control compared to traditional forms of diversion has no impact on lowering the recidivism rate of those undergoing the new sanctions and measures (see Kyvsgard 2004, p. 382). Although in parts of Scandinavia diversion is used more reluctantly in the last 10 years, it is still a priority for first-time offenders. Sentencing practice in Denmark relies rather on fines (mostly so-called ticket fines without a formal court hearing). In 2000 64% of juveniles aged 15–17 years were fined, 11% received a withdrawal of charge and 20% a suspended and 5% an unconditional prison sentence (see Kyvsgard 2004, p. 174). Although the proportion of withdrawals (diversion) has decreased by about half, they were replaced by fines and not by more severe punishments. Therefore it may be said that the sentencing practice in Denmark has not really changed very much.

The same is true for the *Netherlands*, although a more repressive rhetoric may be observed since the mid-1990s. In the 1980s more than 70% of all cases have been diverted. The rate of court indictments has been rather stable, although it has slightly increased from less than 30% to 35% in 2003 (see van der Laan 2006, p. 155). Statistical data of all forms of diversion apparently are not complete, but the development of diversionary measures is impressing. Referrals to the so-called HALT-projects (police diversion: juveniles carry out up to 20 h of reparative or other types of activities) increased from about 1,100 cases in 1987 to more than 24,000 cases in 2005 (see van Kalmthout and Bahtiyar 2009). The total sanctioning practice seems to be rather moderate if one considers that out of 12,000 sentencing decisions by the juvenile judge in 2006 about 16% referred to a term in a juvenile institution ranging between less than 2 weeks to 3 months, and 1.4% in a prison sentence (according to adult criminal law, which is applicable for serious 16- and 17-years-old offenders (see van der Laan 2006, p. 156; van der Heide and Eggen 2007). A real getting tough approach is not visible, although diversion since the mid-1990s more often has been conditional than unconditional and in these cases more often has been combined with minor sanctions. The above mentioned increase of referrals to HALT-projects can be seen in the same line of challenging juveniles with reparative or other activities.

What Works with Diversion? Recidivism After Non-Intervention or After Punishment

There is empirical evidence that diversion 'works'. The recidivism rates are lower, or at least not higher, than after formal court procedures and convictions. The following German experiences are impressive in this regard.

The strategy of expanding informal sanctions has proved to be an effective means, not only to limit the juvenile court's workload, but also with respect to special prevention. The reconviction rates of those first-time offenders that were 'diverted' instead of formally sanctioned were significantly lower. The re-offending rates after a risk period of 3 years were 27% versus 36% (see Fig. 9.5 and Heinz 2005, 2006, 2008; Dünkel 2003a, p. 94). Even for repeat offenders the re-offending rates after informal sanctions were not higher than after formal sanctions (see Storz 1994, 197 ff.; Heinz 2005, p. 306). The overall recidivism rates in states like Hamburg with a diversion rate of more than 80% or 90% were about the same (between 28% and 36%) as in states such as Baden-Württemberg, Rhineland-Palatinate or Lower Saxony where the proportion of diversion at that time counted for only about 43–46% and the recidivism rate for 31–32% (see Fig. 9.6). Thus the extended diversionary practice has had at least no negative consequences concerning the crime rate and general or special prevention (see Heinz 2005, 2006). It also reflects the episodic and petty nature of juvenile delinquency.

Another important result concerning the 'effectiveness' of diversion has been obtained from the Freiburg birth cohort study. The study covered more than 25,000 juveniles from the birth cohorts 1970, 1973, 1975, 1978 and 1985. The proportion of diversion instead of formal punishment for the age groups of 14- and 15-years-old juveniles increased from 58% to 82%. Recidivism after 2 years (according to official crime records) was 25% for the diversion group and 37% for the juveniles formally sanctioned by the youth court (see Bareinske 2004, p. 188; Heinz 2006, p. 186). The difference of 12% in favour of diversion corresponds to the above mentioned earlier studies. The Freiburg birth cohort study demonstrates that the increase in the use of diversion as shown by Figures 9.1 and 9.3 above does not correspond to an increase of delinquency rates among juveniles. On the contrary, the recidivism rates of comparable delinquents (for different typical juvenile delinquent acts) were significantly lower when diverted as compared to those formally sanctioned by the youth court (see Bareinske 2004, p. 136 f.).

Similar results have been obtained with regards to self reported delinquency of juveniles diverted from the juvenile justice system as compared to those formally

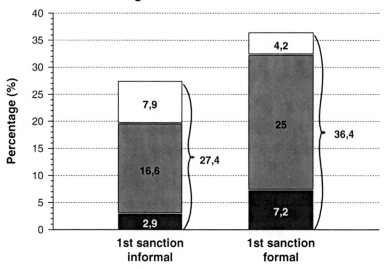

Informal and formal sanctions for reoffending according to the kind of the 1st sanction

Decisions after reoffending:		
informal only (diversion)	7,9%	4,2%
reconviction without imprisonment	16,6%	25,0%
imprisonment	2,9%	7,2%
total reconviction rate	19,5%	32,2%
total	27,4%	36,4%

Fig. 9.5 Rates of formal and informal sanctions after a first sanction for larceny and a risk period of 3 years (juveniles, cohort 1961)

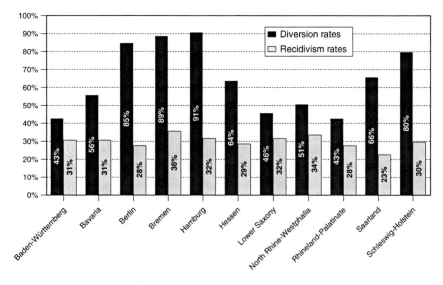

Fig. 9.6 Diversion rates and recidivism in comparison of the federal states in West Germany (simple theft, first-time offenders, birth cohort 1961)
Source: *Storz* 1994, p. 153 ff.; *Heinz* 2006, p. 184 ff.

sanctioned. The 'diversion group' reported less offences in the 3 years after being sentenced than the control group of formally sanctioned juveniles (see Crasmöller 1996). On this basis Crasmöller (1996, pp. 124 f., 132) therefore states that more repressive reactions contribute to an increase of further delinquency.

The most comprehensive and in depth study is the Bremen longitudinal study on juvenile delinquency and integration into the labour market by Schumann and his collaborators (see Schumann 2003a). Four hundred and twenty-four juveniles were contacted five times over a period of 11 years. The results revealed that the development of delinquent careers depended primarily on gender, attachment to delinquent peers and the kind of sanctioning by the juvenile justice system. Court sanctions had negative effects also with regards to the integration into the labour market (stable employment, see Prein and Schumann 2003, 200 ff.; Schumann 2003b, p. 213). On the other hand it seems that the juvenile justice system itself has less impact (no matter what sentencing decision is taken) compared to positive or negative developments in the life course such as successful school or work integration, good relations to pro-social friends, etc. or on the other hand negative experiences of exclusion in social life, attachment to delinquent peers, etc. Nevertheless, the Bremen longitudinal study also demonstrates that (prosecutorial) diversion instead of (court) punishment is an appropriate means to reduce juvenile and young adult delinquent behaviour (see Prein and Schumann 2003, p. 208).

The German results are confirmed by British empirical research demonstrating that reconviction rates of offenders with a conditional discharge had lower reconviction rates (39%) than those sentenced to fines (43%), probation (55%) or community service (48%, see Moxon 1998, p. 91). The evident methodological problems of comparing different sanctions (concerning the seriousness of different crimes, previous convictions, etc.) were addressed by controlling the different 'sanction groups' strictly with respect to key variables such as age, sex and previous criminal history.

Looking at the costs and the impact of different sentences and interventions it is evident that informal warnings and cautions are the least expensive measures. They are classified by Moxon (1998, p. 97) by 'low re-offending for first offenders'. 'Caution plus' is a combination with restorative justice schemes. Pure restorative justice is more expensive but 'promising in terms of re-offending'. There has to be, however, some caution in interpreting the comparison of different sanctions and interventions, since selection bias has to be seriously controlled and unfortunately this is not always the case. In general, we may conclude that the theoretical assumptions of diversion as an effective strategy can be confirmed by some empirical evidence, although further research 'what works, with whom under which circumstances' continues to be needed in this context.

Diversion and 'Zero Tolerance': A Contradiction?

Since the early 1990s the criminological debate has been strongly influenced by at first glance different and possibly contradictory approaches such as the idea of 'zero tolerance' as an 'effective' strategy to counteract delinquency (see for a critical comment as regards the underlying penal philosophy Hassemer 1998). Is diversion an old-fashioned strategy that should be abandoned after the claimed success of 'zero tolerance' strategies? First of all it should be noted that the effectiveness of zero tolerance strategies is more than doubtful, since there are many other explanations for the reduction in violence in New York and other American cities in the early 1990s (see for example Eisner 2003; see also the contributions in Dreher and Feltes 1997). Less drastic (and more citizen friendly) forms of community policing seem to be at least as 'effective' (see Skogan and Hartnett 1997). It should also be noticed that diversion and 'zero tolerance' are not necessarily a contradiction insofar as diversion does not mean tolerating delinquent behaviour. Diversion always aims at norm reinforcement through informal cautioning and often through minor informal sanctions or restorative procedures (see Sect. 'Theoretical Background' for the theoretical foundations). These strategies have been proven sufficient and effective (see Sect. 'What Works with Diversion? Recidivism After Non-Intervention or After Punishment') and therefore there is no need and no empirical-based justification for a more repressive juvenile justice system or police strategy. Furthermore the justification of diversion, because of the episodic and petty nature of juvenile delinquency and crime, holds even under the 'post-modern' conditions of the early 2000s.

Outlook

The main empirically ('evidence') based results and perspectives of diversion may be summarised by the following four theses:

1. Diversion is a meaningful and effective answer (particularly) to juvenile first and second time episodic offenders.
2. Diversion by 'non-intervention' should be given priority in most of these cases.
3. Diversion combined with restorative or educational measures is sufficient in many of the more serious cases.
4. Juvenile court dispositions should be preserved for persistent and/or more serious offenders.

These considerations are supported by international standard minimum rules and recommendations as can be shown by the actual Council of Europe's Recommendation 2003 (20) on 'New ways of dealing with juvenile delinquency and the role of juvenile justice.' Rule 7 of this recommendation states: 'Expansion of the range of suitable alternatives to formal prosecution should continue. They should form part of a regular procedure, must respect the principle of proportionality, reflect the best interests of the juvenile and, in principle, be applied only in cases where responsibility is freely accepted.' Rule 8 proposes that in order 'to address serious, violent and persistent juvenile offending, member states should develop a broader spectrum of innovative and more effective (but still proportional) community sanctions and measures. They should directly address offending behaviour as well as the needs of the offender.

They should also involve the offender's parents or other legal guardian (unless this is considered counter-productive) and, where possible and appropriate, deliver mediation, restoration and reparation to the victim'. So in summary there is no reason to give up a moderate and reasonable juvenile justice system which is based on the idea of education and more tolerance than is practised towards adult offenders.

Chapter 10
Restorative Justice and Youth Justice: Bringing Theory and Practice Closer Together in Europe

David O'Mahony and Jonathan Doak

Restorative justice can be viewed as a victim-centred approach which conceptualises criminal behaviour in a very different manner from which it has been traditionally conceived within orthodox models of criminal justice. In recent years, it has come to exert an increasingly strong influence over juvenile justice systems as policymakers have become increasingly concerned about the capacity of the traditional criminal justice system to deliver participatory processes and fair outcomes that are capable of benefiting victims, offenders and society at large.

In many jurisdictions, the orthodox criminal justice system has been conceived largely around the idea of protecting the public interest, in denouncing and punishing unacceptable behaviour and not furthering the private interests of individual parties. In the common law world in particular, many commentators have perceived a risk that these key objectives of the criminal justice system would be jeopardised if the public interest were to be 'compromised' by prioritising the reparative interest of victims and localised communities (Ashworth 1992; Buruma 2004). As Weisstub (1986, p. 205) has observed:

> Even if it is the case that we are encountering frustrations in delineating the terrain between public and private interests, to allow squatters and anarchists to run wild, they assert, would destroy any process we have made in gaining control over the process of resolving our conflicts. Their view is that introducing civil liberties into the criminal process is in effect to tribalise once again the relationship between victim and offender …. For in their perspective the long and short will be that the level of discretion of the participants in the system will be so enlarged that an *ad hoc* populism will replace the impersonal rigour of codified and judicially made law.

However, advocates of restorative justice conceptualise criminal behaviour in a very different way. Crime, they see, is first and foremost a violation of people and relationships, and the restorative process aims to make amends for the harm that has been caused to victims, offenders and communities (Zehr 2005). The retributive focus of the traditional justice system and the prioritisation of punishment and just deserts are thus not the primary goals of restorative justice. For many commentators,

D. O'Mahony (✉), and J. Doak
Department of Law, Durham University, Durham, UK;
Nottingham Law School, Nottingham Trent University, Nottingham, UK

J. Junger-Tas and F. Dünkel (eds.), *Reforming Juvenile Justice*,
DOI: 10.1007/978-0-387-89295-5_10, © Springer Science + Business Media, LLC 2009

the normative frameworks of the traditional criminal justice system are viewed as being largely ineffective, and even undesirable insofar as and they can be counter-productive in their failure to meet the needs of those most affected by crime (McCold 1996). By contrast, the restorative process looks to the individual needs of the parties through seeking to repair the injuries caused, restoring relationships, repairing harm, and through addressing the needs of the offender (Claassen 1996). In turn, restorative approaches are said to promote greater community protection and safety by promoting offender responsibility and removing the stigma of crime – aiming to restore and reintegrate the key stakeholders, including the victim, providing empathy and understanding for participants and ultimately (hopefully) reducing the likelihood of re-offending (Braithwaite and Mugford 1994).

Defining Restorative Justice

In spite of its growing popularity, restorative justice remains a contested concept, which has proved difficult to define in concise terms. One of the most widely accepted definitions is that provided by Marshall (1999, p. 5), who described it as 'a process whereby all the parties with a stake in a particular offence come together to resolve collectively how to deal with the aftermath of the offence and its implications for the future'. However, other commentators have argued that, as an alternative to associating the concept with a specific archetypal process, the term should be instead thought of as encapsulating a body of core practices which aim to maximise the role of those most affected by crime: the victim; the offender and potentially the wider community.

Zehr and Mika (2003) suggest that, in order for a practice to be labelled 'restorative', it should comprise a number of critical elements. The first is that crime should be conceptualised as a fundamental violation of people and interpersonal relationships. Victims and the broader community should be viewed as the primary stakeholders, since they are first and foremost affected by the offence. As such, the restorative process should seek to maximise their input in search for 'restoration, healing, responsibility and prevention' (2003, p. 41). The role of the state should therefore be circumscribed, and should be limited to investigating facts and facilitating the process. The second element is that violations create both obligations and liabilities: offenders are obliged to make amends for the harm that they have caused; and the broader community also has obligations to help victims and offenders restore themselves and thus maintain the general welfare of all its members. The third key element is that restorative justice seeks to 'heal' and put right the wrongs, so the needs of the victim are the starting point and offenders are encouraged to repair the harm insofar as possible. In this process there should be an exchange of information, dialogue and consent which provide for forgiveness and reconciliation. The process should therefore be rooted in and belong to the community.

In a similar vein, Dignan (2005) sees restorative justice as made up of three core features, and describes these as first putting right the harm caused by an offence.

The second relates to a balanced focus on the offender's personal accountability to those who have been harmed – including the victim and broader community – and on the victim's right to some form of reparative redress. The third is described as a process that is inclusive and non-coercive, that 'encourages participation by the key participants in determining how an offence should be dealt with' (Dignan 2005, p. 8).

There is thus a range of views as to what restorative justice actually means, but, as McCold (2000) has warned, there is also a danger of it being seen by some as meaning 'all things to all people'. This is highlighted by the fact that restorative justice programmes worldwide vary considerably in terms of what they do and how they achieve their outcomes – let alone the level of actual 'restorativeness' in terms of what is done. Practice often differs according to the situation and the manner in which programmes have developed in local areas. For instance, not all schemes accept all restorative principles in equal measure, and there is also considerable divergence on the extent to which schemes may be integrated into existing criminal justice structures. As such, there is no single 'prototype' format for practices that adopt the 'restorative' label. Programmes that seek to adopt restorative principles are diverse, covering areas like corporate crime (Braithwaite 2002); conflicts in prisons and schools (Nothhafft 2003; Robert and Peters 2003); domestic violence (Bannenberg and Rössner 2003); and serious violent crime (Umbreit et al. 2003). The restorative philosophy has also influenced the resolution of political conflicts: the South African Truth and Reconciliation Commission and the Gacaca courts of Rwanda are two such examples (see further Skelton 2002; Ironside 2002).

Schemes may also differ in relation to the degree of formality or legality. Some schemes are based in statute and require that offenders are dealt with through a strict legislative (restorative) framework. In such instances, considerable resources are often invested across a range of statutory agencies, and widespread training and a change in working culture of the police and prosecutor are required. By contrast, other schemes may be practice-led, 'voluntary' and may be much more informal. Typically, such schemes will lie on the fringes of the criminal justice system and may experience problems with resources and logistics.

It can be noted that, even where restorative interventions do become part of a formal juvenile justice system, the conditions for referring a young person may vary considerably, with some programmes taking referrals as diversionary interventions, or as a form of police caution, while others may be referred by the prosecutor or by the courts as an official form of disposal. Programmes can be led by different agencies, such as the police, an independent conferencing service, or even local community mediation organisations. Programmes also differ according to the level of victim involvement, with some using face-to-face meetings, while other use indirect mediation, or those that rarely involve victims. Even the nature of the offence and type of offender differ, with some schemes only taking first-time offenders who have committed relative minor offences, to others that consider a whole range of offences and individuals who have offended in the past. In essence, restorative practice with offenders is highly divergent and in considering how programmes operate one needs to be aware of their scope, range and intentions.

Nevertheless, in spite of the continuing divergence surrounding the scope and limits of restorative justice practice, there can be little doubt that there is a growing consensus at European and international levels about the desirability of developing initiatives grounded in restorative principles. International instruments increasingly view restorative interventions as a legitimate, if not superior, means of delivering justice. In placing a strong emphasis upon participation and reparation, international trends have certainly exerted a downward pressure upon national governments to develop policies based on restorative justice principles. At European level, Article 10(1) of the EU Framework Decision calls on Member States to promote mediation in criminal cases 'for offences which it considers appropriate for this sort of measure' and Article 10(2) calls on Member States to ensure that 'any agreement between the victim and the offender reached in the course of such mediation in criminal cases can be taken into account'. 'Mediation' itself is defined relatively broadly in Article 1(e) as 'the search prior to or during criminal proceedings, for a negotiated solution between the victim and the author of the offence, mediated by a competent person.' This definition would cover the vast majority of approaches taken by restorative practitioners within Europe.

In addition to the European Union, the Council of Europe has also recognised the value of restorative processes in recent years. In 1999, it issued a fairly detailed set of principles in its Recommendation (99)19 'Concerning Mediation in Penal Matters'. The Recommendation, which consists of 34 articles, recognises that there is a need for both victims and offenders to be actively involved in resolving cases themselves with the assistance of an impartial third party. These provisions generally reflect internationally recognised principles of best practice, including (inter alia), the importance of specific training, the principle of voluntariness, the need for judicial supervision, and the need to ensure that procedural human rights guarantees are safeguarded. In addition, Member States are called on to promote research and evaluation of mediation processes. It should be underlined, however, that this is a form of soft law that is non-binding on Member States. National governments are simply asked, in developing mediation schemes, to bear in mind the principles laid down in the Recommendation and to circulate the text as widely as possible.

The Council of Europe's Recommendation was adopted as the basis for part of the United Nations Vienna Declaration on Crime and Justice.[1] This instrument committed the Member States

> to introduce, where appropriate, national, regional and international action plans in support of victims of crime, such as mechanisms for mediation and restorative justice, and we establish 2002 as a target date for States to review their relevant practices, to develop further victim support services and awareness campaigns on the rights of victims and to consider the establishment of funds for victims, in addition to developing and implementing witness protection policies (at para. 27).

---

[1] *Vienna Declaration on Crime and Justice: Meeting the Challenges of the 21st Century* (UN Doc A/CONF.187/4).

Paragraph 28 of the Declaration further commits the member states to implementing restorative justice policies that are 'respectful of the rights, needs and interests of victims, offenders, communities and all other parties'. At a subsequent meeting, the United Nations Congress on Crime Prevention examined restorative justice in its plenary sessions and formulated a draft proposal for Basic Principles on the Use of Restorative Justice Programmes in Criminal Matters. The instrument was adopted by the United Nations in August 2002.[2]

The Basic Principles stipulate that restorative justice programmes should be generally accessible at all stages of the penal procedure; that they should be used on a voluntarily basis; that participants should receive all relevant information and explanation; and that differences in aspects such as power imbalances, age, and mental capacity need to be taken into account in devising processes. Core due process requirements should also be observed. Moreover, if restorative justice processes or outcomes are not possible or agreement cannot be reached, steps should be taken to support the offender to take responsibility for his actions to provide reparation to the victim and the community.

Restorative Justice in Practice

Against this backdrop, many jurisdictions have sought to make use of restorative interventions, albeit with variable degrees of success. While some have been relatively slow to respond to the international tide, restorative justice is beginning to permeate both law and practice in juvenile justice systems across Europe. Indeed, policymakers are becoming less insular in their outlook and are increasingly eager to move beyond formal international commitments, to practices where responses to juvenile offending are seen to work successfully elsewhere. The remainder of this chapter asks what can be learnt from the state of restorative justice practice, primarily within two of the United Kingdom's jurisdictions: England and Wales; and Northern Ireland. Four main forms of restorative justice are used here: victim–offender mediation; community reparation boards; police-led restorative cautioning; and family group conferencing. Each of these approaches is examined in turn and the chapter draws out lessons that can be learnt in promoting effective restorative interventions.

Victim–Offender Mediation

Most victim–offender mediation programmes within the criminal justice sphere have their roots in programmes that were developed in the mid-1970s, in places such as Ontario Canada. In Canada they were promoted by the Christian Mennonite

---

[2] ECOSOC Res. 2002/12.

movement with an emphasis on the values of personal reconciliation between victims and offenders. They bring together victims and offenders with a facilitator or mediator, who is usually professionally trained. The aim of mediation is to give victims and offenders a safe environment in which they are able to discuss the crime, its impact and the harm it may have caused, and to allow an opportunity to put right the harm caused. Some forms of victim–offender mediation limit the role of the offender and victim by using 'shuttle' type interactions or go-betweens, thereby limiting the victim's and offender's contact with each other. More commonly, however, the mediation takes place on a face-to face basis between victim and offender, with the mediator acting as a neutral facilitator.

Victim–offender mediation has proved very popular and is currently the most common form of restorative practice used across the United States (Dignan 2005). It has also developed into more general forms of dispute resolution and mediation services which can include neighbourhood disputes, especially where there has been a history of conflict between the parties that has not been resolved by other forms of intervention. It has also gained in popularity across many parts of Europe where it is currently the most dominant form of restorative justice practice (Miers 2001).

In the United Kingdom there have been a number of victim–offender mediation projects; however, these have mostly developed on an ad-hoc basis. Generally, they have been relatively small scale and are often local initiatives, rather than being 'mainstream' projects. This has largely been the result of a lack of specific legislation to formally establish them and the provision of little or no central funding, which has obviously impeded their development (Dignan and Lowey 2000). Although the Home Office funded a number of pilot projects in the 1980s, funding was not continued beyond the pilot phase (Davis 1992). Most of the schemes that operate today have been developed at a local level, through good working partnerships between criminal justice agencies such as probation, the police and social services. However, they continue to experience considerable logistical and resourcing difficulties, concerning which agencies should fund them and where their referrals come from.

Until recently, the future prospects for such restorative schemes seemed somewhat bleak, but in 2001, the Government undertook to fund a number of these voluntary schemes and offered financial backing for their evaluation as part of its Crime Reduction Programme. In particular, three voluntary schemes, facilitated by CONNECT, the Justice Research Consortium and REMEDI, are currently under evaluation by a team led by Professor Joanna Shapland at the University of Sheffield (Shapland et al. 2004; 2006). These schemes were established primarily to concentrate on cases involving adult offenders at different stages of the criminal justice process, from pre-sentence through to release from prison. They are largely typical of those operating on a local level around the country. Although the schemes mostly focus on adult offenders, convicted of serious offences, including assaults, robberies, burglaries and grievous bodily harm, results of the ongoing evaluation will undoubtedly carry important lessons for schemes that focus on juvenile offending.

Community Reparation Boards

Another restorative justice model that is more popular in the United Kingdom is that of community reparation boards. These boards have been commonly used in the United States, such as the Vermont Community Reparative Board since the mid-1990s (Dooley 1995). While the boards are primarily used for adult offenders convicted of non-violent offences, more recently their use has been extended to cover juvenile offenders. Such boards are typically composed of a small number of community representatives who hold face-to-face meetings with offenders who have been referred by the courts. The boards, with the offender, decide the sanction that should be imposed for the offence, monitor compliance and report back to the court on its completion. The main goal of the boards is to promote community involvement and empowerment in relation to offending and to promote offender responsibility and victim reparation (Bazemore and Umbreit 2004).

In the United Kingdom, one variation of the community reparation board is the youth offender panel. Under Part 1 of the Youth Justice and Criminal Evidence Act referral orders became a mandatory court disposal for first-time low-level juvenile offenders between the ages of 10 and 17. The Referral Order operates through diverting a young person away from court to a Youth Offender Panel. When a young person is referred by the court to a youth offender panel, it decides how the offending should be dealt with and what form of action is necessary. If the victim wishes they may attend the panel meeting and describe how the offence affected them. Parents are required to attend the panel meeting (if the young person is under the age of 16) and meetings are usually held in community venues. Somewhat contentiously, young people are not entitled to have legal representation at panel meetings, as this may hinder their full involvement in the process. However, a solicitor may attend in the capacity of a 'supporter' (Home Office 2002).

The Panel is intended to operate as a type of discussion forum, and seeks to offer the young person an opportunity to make reparation to the victim and community, take responsibility for their actions, and achieve reintegration into society. Although similar mechanisms in certain North American jurisdictions require that a young person must consent to taking part in such a programme, this is not the case with the English system of referral orders. The panel is thus a core disposal for low-level first-time offenders, although the actual disposal is the result of a contract that must be negotiated and agreed, and not simply imposed on a young person. Usually, a contract will contain specific offender-orientated interventions such as family counselling, mentoring, victim awareness sessions and drugs or alcohol programmes, which may be complemented by reparative measures, like a verbal or written apology or an offer to repair damaged property. The amount of reparation and length of the plan has to be proportionate to the seriousness of the offence and the young person must agree to the plan. In the event that there is no agreed outcome, the Youth Offending Panel will report back to the court, who will then reconsider how to deal with the young person.

Research looking at the operation of referral orders in 2000 and 2001 (Newburn et al. 2001) found that in the main the pilot areas successfully accomplished the implementation of the orders and that 'within a relatively short time youth offender panels have established themselves as constructive, deliberative and participatory forums in which to address young people's offending behaviour'. The orders were rolled out to the rest of England and Wales in April 2002 and based on early figures, it is likely there will be between 25,000 and 30,000 referral orders made per year (Youth Justice Board 2002).

Overall, Newburn et al. (2002) concluded that referral orders were working well and many young people played an active role in their panel meetings and were happy with their experience. They found that 84% of the young people felt they were treated with respect and 86% said they were treated fairly. The research found that 75% of the young people agreed that their plan or contract was 'useful' and 78% agreed that it should help them stay out of trouble (Newburn et al. 2002). Parents also appeared to be positive about the orders, and compared to the experience of the Youth Court, parents appeared to understand the referral order process better and felt it easier to participate (Newburn et al. 2002).

Despite these rather positive evaluation findings, a number of concerns have been raised concerning referral orders. Haines and O'Mahony (2006), for example, make the point that such orders raise questions in relation to informed consent as some young people and parents may feel forced into agreeing plans – especially if they are not given legal representation. They argue that children as young as 10-years old may feel they are being forced into what may be traumatic confrontations in a roomful of adults. Participants may even feel coerced into signing contracts involving serious deprivations of their liberty (Haines and O'Mahony 2006). Furthermore, they will not generally have the protection of any form of legal representation. Another concern raised by Ball et al. (2002) is that the discretion of magistrates is greatly curtailed in the legislation whereby minor first-time offenders had to be referred to panels. The danger in these circumstances is that magistrates make inappropriate use of absolute discharges for cases in which they feel are inappropriate to go before a youth offender panel, since that would be the only way to avoid a referral order. The research by Newburn et al. (2002) confirms this point as 45% of the magistrates interviewed felt that the lack of discretion in the legislation undermined their authority. Crawford and Newburn (2002) also found that some panels had difficulty devising suitable plans because of a lack of local resources and that panel members believed that adequate local facilities and resources were crucial to the success of panels.

More fundamental problems with the referral order especially with regard to their potential to be restorative centre around their low levels of victim involvement in the process. Newburn et al. (2002) note that a victim attended in only 13% of cases where at least an initial panel meeting was held. Such low levels of victim participation obviously greatly limit any chance of 'encounter, reparation, reintegration and participation' – regarded by some as the core ingredients of restorative justice (Van Ness and Strong 1997). Furthermore, research has yet to establish whether such orders are having any net-widening effects, such as unnecessarily drawing trivial offences and minor offenders further into the criminal justice system. The extent to which such orders are truly proportionate to the offence committed has been questioned, as has the likely longer term impact on recidivism, especially by comparison to other disposals (Mullan and O'Mahony 2002).

Police-Led Restorative Cautioning

Police-led restorative cautioning schemes have their roots in Australia where they were developed in the early 1990s, mostly as an alternative approach to traditional formal police cautioning. The approach spread and was taken up and used in various forms in New Zealand and America, particularly in Minnesota and Pennsylvania in the mid-1990s (McCold 1998). It then spread considerably and North American facilitators have promoted the approach and trained many facilitators worldwide (McCold and Watchel 1998).

In the United Kingdom restorative cautioning approaches have been used in a number of police forces, particularly by the Thames Valley police and more recently by the police in Northern Ireland. It has received much media attention in the UK and significantly it also caught the interest of the then Home Secretary Jack Straw. The approach is largely based around Braithwaite's ideas of 'reintegrative shaming' (Braithwaite 1989). In essence this approach seeks to deal with crime and its aftermath by attempting to make offenders ashamed of their behaviour, but in a way which promotes their reintegration into the community (Young and Goold 1999). It is different to the traditional police caution, which has been described by Lee (1998) as usually a 'degrading ceremony' in which the young person, most often a first-time and minor offender, is given a 'dressing-down' and good talking to by a senior police officer.

The process of reintegrative shaming, which is central to the restorative cautioning approach, attempts to deliver the police caution in a way that is not degrading – but rather as a 're-integrative ceremony' (Braithwaite 1989). This is achieved by first attempting to get the young person to realise the harm caused by their actions to the victim, but also to their family and even themselves. The focus is placed on the wrongfulness of the action or behaviour, rather than the wrongfulness of the individual. The process attempts to reintegrate the young person, after they have admitted what they did was wrong, by focusing on how they can put the incident behind them, for example, by repairing the harm through such things as reparation and apology. It thereby allows the young person to move forward and reintegrate back into their community and family. The whole process is usually facilitated by a trained police officer and often involves the use of a script or agenda that is followed in the conferencing process. The victim is encouraged to play a part in the process, particularly to reinforce upon the young person the impact of the offence on them, but as Dignan (2005) notes, restorative cautioning schemes have (at least initially) placed a greater emphasis on the offender and issues of crime control, than on their ability to meet the needs of victims.

Research by Hoyle et al. (2002) looking at the Thames Valley scheme have described the restorative approach as a significant improvement on the old-style and rather idiosyncratic approach to police cautioning. They found high levels of satisfaction with the process, both in terms of how conferences were facilitated and in terms of how fairly the participants were treated. Nearly all of the victims that attended the restorative cautions that were observed as part of their research expressed satisfaction with how their conference was handled and felt that it was a good idea, and some 71% said they felt better following the conference. The researchers also found that most of the victims who attended meetings said they felt differently about the offender as a result of the conference and just under 60% said the conference helped them to put the offence behind them.

However, it was also clear from the research that levels of victim participation were very low, only 14% of the cautioning sessions were attended by an actual victim (Hoyle et al. 2002). In an attempt to assess why victim participation was so low the researchers contacted a sample of non-attending victims. They found that most victims were invited but chose not to attend (52%). About a third of victims said they would have liked to attend but were unable, and only a small minority said they had not been invited or did not know about the caution. Hill (2002) notes that even victims who declined to take part in the caution often expressed an interest in knowing what would happen, or in providing some input as to how the crime affected them, but there was little evidence that police facilitators actively sought such input.

In Northern Ireland research looking at development of the police-led restorative cautioning scheme examined over 1,800 police case files and observed and interviewed participants involved in 70 restorative conferences (O'Mahony et al. 2002). The research found it to be a significant improvement on previous cautioning practice, and noted that the schemes were successful in securing some degree of reintegration through avoiding prosecution and instituting a process that prevented the young person from feeling stigmatised (O'Mahony et al. 2002). Furthermore, the process served to highlight the impact of the young person's offending on the victim and may even have helped foster better police–community relations – in these respects it was a substantive improvement in the quality of previous cautioning practice.

The research found that levels of victim participation were relatively low, with an actual victim attending in only 20% of the cases observed in one area. This obviously limited the restorative potential of such work, especially if the victim is unable to be part of the process. As such, the offender was often unable to experience the victim's perceptions first hand, or have their input into the process. Similarly, since many victims were not part of the process they were therefore unable to understand the incident from offender's perspective and see the person behind crime. In effect, low victim participation detracts from the restorative goals of conferencing, where ideally there should be a process of empowerment, dialogue, negotiation and agreement between all parties.

However, one of the key concerns to emerge from the Northern Ireland study was evidence of net-widening. The conferencing schemes were found to include some very young and petty offenders in what was a demanding process of accountability resulting in a police caution – which was sometimes considered disproportionate to the harm done. There was little evidence that the restorative cautions were being used as an alternative to prosecution, rather it appeared they were at times used for cases that would have been previously dealt with informally through such measures as a warning. Indeed the researchers noted that 80% of the cases examined were for offences concerning property worth less than £15 and it was not uncommon for considerable amount of police time and effort to be devoted to organising a caution where the young person had stolen a soft drink or a chocolate bar.

Despite these concerns, the research found the police to be enthusiastic and sincerely committed to the restorative process (O'Mahony and Doak 2004). They had been well trained and it was clear from the interviews with the young people and their parents involved in the process that they placed a high degree of confidence and support for the scheme. There was also evidence that it had other beneficial effects especially in terms of helping improve police/community relations, which have obviously been strained over the years of conflict (McEvoy and Mika 2002) – as such the restorative potential could even contribute to the broader social transition process of a society moving out of conflict (O'Mahony and Doak 2004).

Restorative Conferencing

Perhaps the best known restorative conferencing scheme is the family group conferencing model, first developed in New Zealand. The model was devised as part of a more general initiative which sought to address difficulties in the way young people were being treated in the criminal justice and welfare systems in New Zealand – particularly minority group offenders such as the Maori and Pacific Island Polynesians (Maxwell and Morris 1993). The model sought to develop a more culturally sensitive approach to offending that emphasises inclusive participation and collective decision-making, bringing together young people, their families and community to determine appropriate means of redress for victims (Morris and Maxwell 1998).

The family group conferencing scheme was brought into New Zealand under a reform agenda that emphasised diverting young people away from criminal justice interventions through police cautions or informal resolutions. The legislation made conferencing the main avenue of disposal for all but the few most serious offences like murder and manslaughter. In effect, family group conferencing became the main statutory method of disposal for young offenders being prosecuted. Young people can only be prosecuted if they have been arrested and referred by the police through a family group conference. The courts are required to send offenders for family group conferences and they have to consider the recommendations of the conference and generally do not deal with cases until they have had a conference recommendation (Morris and Maxwell 1998).

In the United Kingdom, the only jurisdiction to adopt a mainstreamed statutory-based restorative conferencing model for young offenders has been Northern Ireland. Youth conferencing was introduced following recommendations from the Criminal Justice Review Group (2000) that '… restorative justice should be integrated into the juvenile justice system in Northern Ireland' (2000, p. 205). The new youth conferencing system was introduced within a growing climate of restorative justice which saw the development of a number of community-based restorative schemes (McEvoy and Mika 2002). However, in spite of the burgeoning community restorative justice schemes, it was determined that for reasons of accountability, certainty and legitimacy the mode of restorative justice implemented should be based in statute and fully integrated into the formal justice system (O'Mahony and Campbell 2006). The new youth conferencing arrangements thus have statutory footing in Part IV of the Justice (Northern Ireland) Act 2002.

The introduction and mainstreaming of restorative interventions into the youth justice system in Northern Ireland signals a radical departure from previous responses to young offending. The new measures provide for two types of disposal, diversionary and court-ordered conferences. Both types of conference take place with a view to a youth conference co-ordinator providing a plan to the prosecutor or court on how the young person should be dealt with for their offence. A decision to hold a diversionary conference will be taken by the Public Prosecution Service. For the most part, these are not intended for minor first-time offenders, who are normally dealt with by the police by way of a warning or police caution. Rather, they are aimed at young offenders who would normally be considered for prosecution in the courts, but are deemed suitable for disposal by way of a restorative conference. Providing a conference plan is agreed and successfully completed, the young person will avoid a court appearance and criminal conviction. However, two key conditions are in place before a diversionary conference can be ordered. First, young person must admit to the offence; and second, he or she must consent to the process. If these conditions are not met the offence will be disposed of in the normal way through prosecution in the Youth Court.

Court-ordered conferences, on the other hand, are referred for conferencing by the court and like diversionary conferences the young person must agree to the process and they must either admit guilt, or have been found guilty in court. An important feature of the legislation is that the courts *must* refer all young persons for youth conferences, except for offences carrying a mandatory life sentence. The court *may* refer cases that are triable by indictment only or scheduled offences under the Terrorism Act (2000). In effect, the legislation makes conferencing mandatory except for a small number of very serious offences.

The format of the Youth Conference itself bears much similarity to the general model used in New Zealand (Maxwell and Morris 1993), though the Northern Ireland model places the victim much more at the centre of the process. It normally involves a meeting, chaired by an independent and trained youth conference facilitator (employed by the Youth Conferencing Service), where the young person will be provided with the opportunity to reflect upon their actions and offer some form of reparation to the victim. The victim, who is actively encouraged to attend, is allowed to explain to the offender how the offence affected them, in theory giving the offender an understanding of their actions and allow the victim to separate the offender from the offence. Following a dialogue a 'youth conference plan' or 'action plan' will be devised which should take into consideration the offence, the needs of the victim and the needs of the young person. The young person must consent to the plan, which can run for a period of not more than 1 year and which usually involves some form of reparation or apology to the victim. Ideally the plan will include elements that address the needs of the victim, the offender and the wider community, so as to achieve a restorative outcome (O'Mahony and Campbell 2006).

The Northern Ireland scheme has been subject to a major evaluation in which the proceedings of 185 conferences were observed and personal interviews were completed with 171 young people and 125 victims who participated in conferences (Campbell et al. 2006). The research findings were generally very positive concerning the impact of the scheme on victims and offenders and found it to operate with relative success. Importantly, the research showed that youth conferencing considerably increased levels of participation for both offenders and victims in the process of seeking a just response to offending. The scheme engaged a high proportion of victims in the process: over two-thirds of conferences (69%) had a victim in attendance, which is high compared with other restorative-based programmes (cf. Maxwell and Morris 2002; Newburn et al. 2002; O'Mahony and Doak 2004). Of these 40% were personal victims and 60% were victim representatives. Victim representatives were often used in cases where there was damage to public property or theft from a department store, where there was no directly identifiable victim. Personal victims, on the other hand, were used if there was a direct and identifiable victim, such as following an assault, or theft from a person. Nearly half of personal victims attended as a result of assault, while the majority (69%) of victim representatives attended for thefts (typically shoplifting) or criminal damage.

Victims were willing to participate in youth conferencing and 79% said they were actually 'keen' to participate. Most (91%) said the decision to take part was their own and not a result of pressure to attend. Interestingly, over three quarters (79%) of victims said they attended 'to help the young person' and many victims said they wanted to hear what the young person had to say and their side of the story: As one victim said, 'I wanted to help the young person get straightened out'. Only 55% of victims said they attended the conference to hear the offender apologise. Therefore, while it was clear that many victims (86%) wanted the offender to know how the crime affected them, what victims wanted from the process was clearly not driven by motivations of retribution, or a desire to seek vengeance. Rather it was apparent that their reasons for participating were based around seeking an understanding of why the offence had happened; they wanted to hear and understand the offender and to explain the impact of the offence to the offender (Doak and O'Mahony 2007).

Victims appeared to react well to the conference process and were able to engage with the process and discussions. It was obvious that their ability to participate in the process was strongly related to the intensive preparation they had been given prior to the conference. A considerable amount of work was put into drawing up plans for conferences, and victims felt generally well prepared. Only 20% of victims were observed to be visibly nervous at the beginning of the conference, by comparison to 71% of the offenders. They were also able to engage and play an active part in the conferencing process and 83% of victims were rated as 'very engaged' during the conference and 92% indicated they had said everything they wanted to during the conference.

Overall 98% of victims were observed as talkative in conferences and it was clear that the conference forum was largely successful in providing victims with the opportunity to express their feelings. Though most victims (71%) displayed some degree of frustration towards the young offender at some point in the conference, the vast majority listened to and seemed to accept the young person's version of the offence either 'a lot' (69%) or 'a bit' (25%) and 74% of victims even expressed a degree of empathy towards the offender. It is important to realise that while a minority of victims were nervous at the beginning of the conference, this usually faded as the conference wore on and nearly all reported that they were more relaxed once the conference was underway. Also, the overwhelming majority (93%) of victims displayed no signs of hostility towards the offender at the conference. Nearly all victims (91%) received at least an apology and more importantly 85% said they were happy with the apology. On the whole they appeared to be satisfied that the young person was genuine and were happy that they got the opportunity to meet them and understand more about the young person and why they had been victimised. On the whole, it was apparent, for the victims interviewed, that they had not come to the conference to vent anger on the offender. Rather, many victims were more interested in 'moving on' or putting the incident behind them and 'seeing something positive come out of it'.

For offenders it was clear that the conferencing process held them to account for their actions, for example, by having them explain to the conference group and victim why they offended. The majority wanted to attend and they gave reasons such as, wanting to 'make good' for what they had done, or wanting to apologise to the victim. The most common reasons for attending were to make up for what they had done, to seek the victim's forgiveness, and to have other people hear their side of the story. Only 28% of offenders said they were initially 'not keen' to attend. Indeed, many offenders appreciated the opportunity to interact with the victim and wanted to 'restore' or repair the harm they had caused. Though many offenders who participated in conferences said they did so to avoid going through court, most felt it provided them with the opportunity to take responsibility for their actions, seek forgiveness and put the offence behind them. Youth conferencing was by no means the easy option and most offenders found it very challenging. Most offenders found the prospect of coming face to face with their victim difficult. For instance, 71% of offenders displayed nervousness at the beginning of their conference, only 28% appeared to be 'not at all' nervous. Despite their nervousness, observations of the conferences revealed that offenders were usually able to engage well in the conferencing process, with nearly all (98%) being able to talk about the offence and the overwhelming majority (97%) accepting responsibility for what they had done.

It is important to emphasise the direct involvement of offenders in conferencing and their ability to engage in dialogue contrasts starkly with the conventional court process, where offenders are afforded a passive role – generally they do not speak other than to confirm their name, plea and understanding of the charges – and are normally represented and spoken for by legal counsel throughout their proceedings. Similarly, victims were able to actively participate in the conferencing process and many found the experience valuable in terms of understanding why the offence had been committed and in gaining some sort of apology and/or restitution. This too contrasts with the typical experience of victims in the conventional court process where they often find themselves excluded and alienated, or simply used as witnesses for evidential purposes if the case is contested (Zehr 2005).

Nearly all of the plans (91%) were agreed by the participants and victims were on the whole happy with the content of the plans. Interestingly, most of the plans agreed to centre on elements that were designed to help the young person and victim, such as reparation to the victim, or attendance at programmes to help the young person. Relatively few plans (27%) had elements that were primarily punitive, such as restrictions on their whereabouts, and in many respects the outcomes were largely restorative in nature rather than punitive. The fact that 73% of conference plans had no specific punishment element was a clear manifestation of their restorative nature, and, more importantly, provides an indication of what victims sought to achieve through the process. Clearly, notions of punishment and retribution were not high on the agenda for most victims, which cast doubt on the common assumption that victims of crime primarily seek vengeance: they were not (Doak and O'Mahony 2007).

Overall indications of the relative success of the process were evident from general questions asked of victims and offenders. When participants were asked what they felt were the best and worst aspects of their experience a number of common themes emerged. For victims, the best features appeared to be related to three issues: helping the offender in some way; helping prevent the offender from committing an offence again in the future; and holding them to account for their actions. The most positive aspects of the conferencing were clearly non-punitive in nature for victims: most seem to appreciate that the conferences represented a means of moving forward for both parties, rather gaining any sense of satisfaction that the offender would have to endure some form of harsh punishment in retribution for the offence. Victims and offenders expressed a strong preference for the conference process as opposed to going to court and only 11% of victims said they would have preferred if the case had been dealt with by a court. On the whole they considered that the conference offered a more meaningful environment for them. While a small number of victims would have preferred court, identifying conferencing as 'an easy option', this view was not held by the offenders. The offenders identified the most meaningful aspect of the conference as the opportunity to apologise to the victim, a feature virtually absent from the traditional court process. Yet, they also identified the apology as one of the most difficult parts of the process – underlining its importance.

A clear endorsement of victims' willingness to become involved in a process which directly deals with the individuals that have victimised them was evident in that 88% of victims said they would recommend conferencing to a person in a similar situation to themselves. Only one personal victim said they would not recommend conferencing to others. For the vast majority who would, they felt the process had given them the opportunity to express their views, to meet the young person face to face, to ask questions that mattered to them, to understand why the incident happened to them, and, ultimately, it appeared to help them achieve closure.

Research is underway to assess the impact of the scheme on recidivism rates. It is not expected that the success of youth conferencing will hinge on achieving marked reductions in re-offending. Previous research has shown such schemes can have positive impacts, but these are usually slightly better than traditional court-based sanctions. More significantly, the success of the process lies in its ability to deliver justice in a way which actively holds offenders to account for their actions, while giving victims a voice. The experience of restorative conferencing in Northern Ireland shows it produces high levels of satisfaction with both the process and outcomes for participants and ultimately it has been able to deliver a more just response to crime for many.

Conclusions

There is no doubt that restorative justice measures are becoming an important feature of youth justice developments internationally. Its ability to provide a useful and effective method for dealing with conflicts and disputes has made it an attractive model for criminal justice reform. In particular, its ability to engage victims in a meaningful process and provide them some form of reparation, as well as helping them to get over the effects of crime, are all highly desirable. International research shows that restorative justice can deliver high levels of satisfaction from victims in terms of the process they go through and how they are dealt with as individuals. Research also shows them to be satisfied with the outcomes from restorative interventions, as these usually attempt to directly address their needs. In relation to offenders, restorative justice measures offer a process that holds them to account. It requires them to face up to the consequences of their actions and see the impact of their behaviour on others. It also gives offenders the opportunity to make amends and put things right. Therefore, restorative justice in many respects empowers those who have been directly affected by crime and contrasts with more traditional models of criminal justice which have been criticised for marginalising victims and even offenders.

The experience of introducing restorative justice principles and practices into youth justice in the UK offers us an insight into its potential, but it also highlights some of the pitfalls when attempting changes such as this. The experience has been varied in terms of success, with some schemes flourishing and achieving very promising results, while others have struggled to provide services and have been criticised for drawing young and petty offenders into demanding schemes.

Overall, the UK experience shows that restorative justice schemes which are operated at the periphery of the criminal justice system often struggle to survive and experience considerable difficulty in providing services to victims and offenders. The victim–offender mediation programmes are a good example of this. While providing very valuable services to some victims and offenders, they are limited in what they can do and what services they provide by the fact that they have to operate on the periphery of the criminal justice system. As such, they have little control over the clients they are given, and the types of cases they are called to deal with. These decisions are made by criminal justice personnel, who apply their own judgement on whether restorative-based mediation will benefit. The schemes have also struggled to survive financially, with no established funding source and have had to work on a year to year, or month to month basis, unsure whether there will be the necessary funding to operate in the future.

Restorative schemes that have focused on low-level offending or first-time offenders have also experienced difficulties, such as the police-led restorative cautioning schemes. The introduction of restorative practices has improved the delivery of police cautions, by focusing them on principles of 'reintegrative shaming'. As such, these seek to condemn the criminal act rather than the young person and they have been evaluated positively. However, they have been criticised for sometimes being used for very minor offences, which may be better dealt with informally, such as through an informal warning. Furthermore, such schemes have been criticised for paying lip service to core restorative principles as they rarely involve meaningful victim participation. Similarly, the youth offender panels in England and Wales have been positively evaluated in relation to the experience of the young offender. However, they are mainly used for relatively minor offenders and there is little evidence that they properly involve victims in the process – which obviously limits their potential to deliver a restorative outcome.

On the other hand, the restorative youth conferencing arrangements in Northern Ireland have been very successful and there appear to be a number of core reasons behind this that are worth exploring. The first, and probably most important factor in its success, is the fact that it was mainstreamed within the criminal justice system. Unlike many other restorative programmes, the conferencing arrangements have been placed on a statutory footing at the centre of the criminal justice system. As such, the conventional system of prosecutions was entirely sidelined, and the new scheme was properly resourced and financed by the government. In practice, this meant that prosecutors, defence lawyers, and magistrates received training on how the new system would operate, while the new Youth Conferencing Service itself was overseen by experienced managers and staffed by well-trained facilitators.

Another factor, related to the first, is that the arrangements are mandatory in nature. Together, the Public Prosecution Service and the courts have a duty to refer the vast majority of cases to conferencing. Thus, there is little room or discretion to interfere with the statutory stipulations. Previous studies have shown that attitudinal resistance can act as a major obstacle to restorative justice initiatives (Mestitz and Ghetti 2004; Edgar and Newell 2006), thereby producing a chasm between law in the books and law in practice. The potential for this gap to expand is clearly exacerbated where decision-makers are given maximum scope for manoeuvre; this was clearly not the case with restorative youth conferencing in Northern Ireland.

The scheme is also victim-centred. In practice, this meant that considerable time and energy was invested by the Youth Conferencing through staff meeting, advising and reassuring victims about the process. It is well documented that criminal justice reforms designed to enhance the experience of victims are often undermined by the fact that their expectations are not properly managed (Erez and Tontodonato 1992; Sanders et al. 2001). Here, the close contact with the Youth Conferencing Service clearly helped to ensure that the expectations of victims were realistic, which led to the majority of victims stating that they were satisfied with the process and glad they had participated. Furthermore, while not all of the plans provided for material reparation, virtually all provided for some measure of symbolic recompense. Thus, in the eyes of the victim, not only were they given the opportunity to tell their story and have their feelings acknowledged, but they were also able to get something back, with the offender having made some form of amends. More fundamental is the question of whether victims should play an active role in criminal justice. The concern that victims might adversely affect conference outcomes by demanding retribution and harsh punishments was clearly not born out by the research. The overwhelming majority of victims contributed positively to the restorative dynamic of conferences and the research showed that victims can play an important part in a criminal justice process.

Another factor contributing to the success of the conferencing arrangements relates to the transitional context in which they were introduced. The fact that the scheme had been devised around the recommendations of the Criminal Justice Review Group meant that the reforms to the youth justice system were systemically interlinked with the peace process and the transition from the Northern Ireland conflict. Having invested so heavily in developing a new criminal justice system that sought support from all sections of the community, the government invested a considerable amount of effort and resources in ensuring that the recommendations of the Group were fully implemented.

The introduction of restorative youth conferencing in Northern Ireland has clearly had an impact beyond providing an alternative form of dispute resolution. The restorative philosophy has contributed to the very process of transition away from conflict towards stability and 'normalisation'. The success of the youth conferencing arrangements also highlights the importance of building any process of criminal justice reform around a set of certain core values and standards. Values such as reconciliation, inclusivity, accountability and healing, espoused in restorative justice theory and practice are values which, it is hoped, will influence governance and criminal justice reform in other jurisdictions.

Chapter 11
Community Sanctions and the Sanctioning Practice in Juvenile Justice Systems in Europe

Frieder Dünkel and Ineke Pruin

Introduction

There is a consensus all over Europe and worldwide that depriving young offenders of their liberty should be avoided wherever possible. This idea has been confirmed repeatedly by international standards of the United Nations (see for example the so-called Beijing Rules of 1985)[1] and the Council of Europe (see for example the Recommendation (2003)20 on "New ways of dealing with juvenile delinquency and the role of juvenile justice").

Juvenile justice systems therefore typically provide a variety of community sanctions that are less infringing on juveniles' rights and at the same time more educative and more promotional of social re-integration.[2] One appropriate way of dealing with less serious crime is to divert young offenders from juvenile courts and from possible stigmatisation or other negative effects of more serious justice interventions. This issue is covered in the chapter on diversion (see Dünkel in this volume) that highlights quite extensive diversionary practices (at least in some countries) which at the same time seem to be no less "re-integrative" than formal court proceedings, and which are in line with Rule No. 7 of Rec (2003)20 mentioned above.[3]

The following chapter focuses on the range of court dispositions and the sentencing practice at that stage. One has to be aware of the fact that in some countries these alternatives to imprisonment practically function for the remaining

---

[1] Standard minimum rules for the administration of juvenile justice, see United Nations, http://www.un.org/documents/ga/res/40/a40r033.htm. See in this respect particularly Rule 17.

[2] For the historical development see Jensen and Jepsen 2006: 452.

[3] Rule 7 states: "Expansion of the range of suitable alternatives to formal prosecution should continue. They should form part of a regular procedure, must respect the principle of proportionality, reflect the best interests of the juvenile and, in principle, apply only in cases where responsibility is freely accepted." See also the chapter on Restorative Justice by O'Mahony and Doak in this volume.

F. Dünkel (✉) and I. Pruin
Rechts- und Staatswissenschaftliche Fakultät, Universität Greifswald, Greifswald, Germany

J. Junger-Tas and F. Dünkel (eds.), *Reforming Juvenile Justice*,
DOI:10.1007/978-0-387-89295-5_11, © Springer Science + Business Media, LLC 2009

30% of cases that are not dealt with through diversionary procedures (including restorative conflict resolution, mediation, etc.). In its Recommendation of 2003 mentioned above the Council of Europe stresses the importance of also developing effective strategies for repeat (persistent) or serious offenders in the community (see Rule 8 of Rec (2003)20).

Sanction Systems in European Juvenile Laws

An overview of European juvenile justice systems demonstrates that historically such systems have tended to expand the variety of "alternative" court dispositions in order to reduce the use of different forms of deprivation of liberty. The idea of "deinstitutionalisation" started with respect to closed welfare institutions in the USA and Europe in the late 1960s. The experiment in Massachusetts in the early 1970s triggered abolitionist discussions concerning youth imprisonment in Europe.[4] Actually, in California there has been a surprising revival of the idea of closing down youth prisons.[5] The introduction of educational sanctions involving restitution, social training or educational courses, community service orders and other so-called intermediate sanctions is indicative of a strong movement for more constructive and educational response to juvenile delinquency. Whether alternative sanctions can contribute to an at least "reductionist" approach is an open and frequently discussed question, because creating more "alternatives" can also contribute to "net-widening" without any reduction in the application of liberty-depriving sanctions.[6] Without attempting to verify or reject this hypothesis, we want to describe the different approaches that can be found in Europe, and how often and in what way the juvenile courts are using such community sanctions.

Table 11.1 shows the variety of juvenile court dispositions or judicial diversionary measures in selected European countries. The information was taken from a European comparative project funded by the European Union (2007–2008).[7]

Community sanctions can be imposed either as a diversionary measure or as a formal sanction. In many countries both possibilities are available. The legal principles for choosing between different court dispositions regularly follow two major principles. One is that deprivation of liberty should be a measure of last

---

[4]See, for example, Schumann et al. 1986.

[5]See *The Record* from April 25, 2007; in July 2008 the State watchdog commission recommended that California phase out its antiquated juvenile prisons (run by the Department of Corrections) by 2011, replacing them by regional county lockups; see http://thinkoutsidethecage2.blogspot.com/2008/07/closing-juvenile-prisons-in-california.html.

[6]See Gibbons and Blake 1976; Nejelski 1976; Austin and Krisberg 1981, 1982.

[7]See the AGIS project JLS/2006/AGIS/168. Methodology: Juvenile justice experts from 34 European countries were asked to write a national report about their juvenile justice system following an outline developed by Prof. Frieder Dünkel, Greifswald. The country reports will be published in 2009 (see Dünkel et al. 2009).

Table 11.1 Diversionary and court dispositions in European juvenile justice systems

	Austria	Bulgaria	Croatia	Cyprus	Czech Rep	Denmark	Engl/Wal	Finland	France	Germany	Greece	Ireland	Kosovo	Latvia	Lithuania	The Neth.	North-IRL	Poland	Portugal	Romania	Scotland	Serbia	Slovenia	Spain	Sweden	Switzerland	Ukraine
Informal sanctions																											
Diversion (non intervention, absolute discharge/withdrawal)	X	X		X	X	X	X	X	X	X	X	X	X	X	X	X	X	X	X	X	X	X	X	X	X	X	
Diversion with intervention	X[1]	X[1]	X	X[1]	X	X[2]	X	X	X	X	X	X	X	X	X	X	X	X	X	X	X	X	X	X	X	X	X
Diversionary measure																											X
Reprimand							X		X	X		X			X		X										
Suspending prosecution for probation period	X						X																				
Out of court settlement (victim-offender mediation, reparation)	X		X		X			X	X	X	X	X	X	X	X	X	X[3]		X	X	X[3]	X	X	X	X	X	
Community service	X		X							X	X	X	X		X	X					X	X		X		X	
Fines	X									X	X																
Special obligations/orders concerning everyday life, training courses			X						X	X	X	X	X	X		X		X				X					
Formal sanctions																											
Reprimand/Warning	X	X	X	X	X	X	X	X	X	X	X	X	X	X	X	X	X	X	X	X	X	X	X	X		X	X
Fines	X	X		X	X	X	X[4]	X	X	X	X	X	X	X	X	X	X	X	X	X		X	X			X	X
Victim-offender mediation, reparation						X	X	X	X	X	X	X	X	X	X	X	X	X	X	X	X	X	X	X	X		
Community service			X			X[6]	X[7]	X	X	X	X	X	X[5]	X	X	X	X	X	X	X	X		X	X	X	X	X
Special obligations/orders concerning everyday life, training courses						X[6]	X[8]	X[9]	X	X	X	X	X[5]			X		X	X	X	X		X	X	X	X	X
Attendance Centre			X				X					X	X				X		X					X			
Short time detention			X	X						X					X									X[11]			X
Supervision/Surveillance		X	X	X		X	X	X	X	X	X	X	X	X	X	X	X	X	X	X	X	X	X	X	X	X	X

(continued)

Table 11.1 (continued)

	Austria	Bulgaria	Croatia	Cyprus	Czech Rep	Denmark	Engl/Wal	Finland	France	Germany	Greece	Ireland	Kosovo	Latvia	Lithuania	The Neth.	North-IRL	Poland	Portugal	Romania	Scotland	Serbia	Slovenia	Spain	Sweden	Switzerland	Ukraine
Confiscation/disqualification from driving a vehicle	X															X		X	X					X			
Conviction without sentence										X															X		
Institutional educational measures			X	X	X	X			X		X	X[10]	X	X	X	X			X	X		X	X			X	X
Suspended/conditional imprisonment	X		X	X	X	X		X	X	X			X	X	X	X		X	X	X		X	X			X	X
Suspended/conditional imprisonment with supervision	X		X		X			X	X	X				X	X	X			X	X		X	X			X	X
Probation		X		X			X					X					X				X			X	X		
Imprisonment/detention	X	X	X	X	X	X	X	X	X	X	X	X	X	X	X	X	X	X	X	X	X	X	X	X	X	X	X

[1] Referral to social service
[2] Youth contract
[3] Youth/family conference
[4] Reparation order
[5] On the basis of supervision
[6] In case of suspended sanction
[7] Reparation order and community service order (offenders aged 16–17)
[8] Referral order, community service order, curfew order
[9] Juvenile punishment
[10] Probation order coupled with an obligation to reside in a certified hostel residence
[11] One to three weekends

resort (named the principle of "subsidiarity" in some countries, see e.g. §§ 5 and 17 of the Juvenile Justice Act in Germany). The second principle is the idea of "education over punishment" or of prioritizing the most promising educational sanctions in order to facilitate social re-integration. So the prevailing idea is to give the juvenile judge sufficient discretionary power to select the most appropriate sanction in the best interests of the juvenile. The new European Rules for Juveniles Subject to Sanctions or Measures from 5 November 2008 (Rec [2008]11) therefore state as one of the "Basic Principles" that "in order to adapt the implementation of sanctions and measures to the particular circumstances of each case the authorities responsible for the implementation shall have a sufficient degree of discretion without leading to serious inequality of treatment" (Rule No. 6).

As a general rule the applicable sanctions and measures follow a certain hierarchy. The least invasive sanctions are warnings or reprimands,[8] followed by a wide range of alternative sanctions that exert more or less influence on the life of the offender (see under New Alternatives below). In between we find the possibility to impose a fine on juvenile offenders which is theoretically possible in most European countries.[9] Supervision or surveillance orders can likewise be found in most European countries. In Austria, Germany and Sweden an offender can be convicted without receiving a concrete sentence. This can be seen as a special form of a warning. In the Netherlands, Poland, Portugal and Spain it is possible to confiscate a person's driver's license. In these cases the courts have to consider the possibility to unequal treatment, because there are special groups of juveniles or young adults who are more dependent on driving a car than others (due to work obligations, poor local infrastructure; See under New Alternative below).

Some European countries (Germany, Lithuania, Spain, and Ukraine) provide for the possibility of short-time detention in special disciplinary centres. The educational effect of detaining young people in a closed institution for a short period of time can be deemed questionable. German research results have shown extremely high recidivism rates among persons who experience short-time detention (70% within 4 years compared to less than 40% for educational community sanctions in the case of comparable offences, see Jehle et al. 2003). The research is not based on a comparison of real control groups, but it is evident that juveniles taking part in community sanctions such as social training courses or community service orders today are rather comparable to those who before the 1990s have been sentenced to short-term detention. The German sentencing practice insofar is a "natural experiment" by replacing short-term detention by community sanctions. The recidivism rates for short-term detention were always very high, whereas recidivism after community sanctions remained low, although more medium or higher risk offenders have been involved.

---

[8] Some countries do not provide for warnings or reprimands as a court decision, but still reprimands can be issued if the court or the public prosecutor decides to divert the case; see, for example, England/Wales, Germany or Lithuania, Table 11.1.

[9] Most countries rarely or almost never use this sanction for juvenile offenders. One exception is Finland; see below.

Many but not all European countries foresee the possibility of suspending a juvenile's prison sentence. In many cases this goes hand in hand with supervision by the probation service or a similar service with a social work approach. In Germany such supervision is obligatory. The Continental European model of suspended sentences implies the imposition of a youth prison sentence, the execution of which is not immediate. Should an offender fail to meet the conditions of his or her probation, the suspension is revoked and the juvenile serves the term of imprisonment set at the first trial. The Common Law countries provide for probation as a special sanction. This sanction is – as its name indicates – always connected with support from and control by the probation service. Contrary to the Continental European model, in Common Law countries no term of detention is fixed. Therefore, where an offender fails to comply with his or her probationary requirements the term of imprisonment is determined in a second sentencing trial.

No European country has managed to totally avoid the sentence of imprisonment or detention for juveniles.[10]

In general the sanction systems in juvenile justice follow the order that priority shall be given to the educational, most appropriate sanction. This regularly opens the possibility to combine several educational measures or sanctions. A second general principle that has been stressed particularly in the Council of Europe's Rec (2003) 20 is the principle of proportionality that also has to be adhered to when only educational or diversionary measures are applied (see Rule 7 cited above). We would propose the following levels of sanctioning, ordered from the least to the most intrusive.

1. Warnings, reprimands, conviction without sentence
2. Fines, community service, reparation orders, mediation
3. Social training courses and other more intensive educational sanctions
4. Mixed sentences, combination orders (which can be characterised as a more repressive way of dealing with juvenile offenders)
5. Probation
6. Suspended sentences with or without supervision by the probation service, electronic monitoring
7. Educational residential care, youth imprisonment and similar forms of deprivation of liberty

Many sanction systems provide educational measures (such as educational "directives", see Germany and Dünkel 2006) either as independent sanctions or as complementary elements of other sanctions such as, for instance, probation or suspended prison sentences. The aim of such educational directives is always to improve the educational impact on the one hand and to reduce the impact of risk factors in the juvenile's daily life on the other.

---

[10] Walsh in Dünkel et al. (2009) claims that imprisonment for juveniles in Ireland does not exist. Since March 2007, in Ireland a "child offender" (under 18 years of age) can not formally be sentenced to imprisonment. There is however an option for detention in a children's detention school (formerly reformatory schools) or St. Patrick's Institution which is likely to be comparable to youth imprisonment in other countries.

In the last 15 years the idea of education has taken on a more repressive connotation in some countries, the most prominent example being the British Labour policy calling for "tougher" and "more credible" community sanctions. The tendency towards more repressive community sanctions can be demonstrated by the new language that is now used compared to the 1960s and 1970s. The term "community treatment" was replaced by "community punishment" or "punishment in the community" in the 1980s and 1990s, as can be taken from the rhetoric of neo-liberal or "neo-correctionalist" (Cavadino and Dignan 2006) labour policies in England and Wales.

However, in Continental European countries such as Austria, Germany or Switzerland (and many East-European countries following their example) the classic ideal of education as support for the further development of a young person's personality and as enhancing pro-social orientations and social competences, still clearly dominates (see Dünkel et al. 2009).

New Alternatives: Inventions of the 1980s

The 1970s and 1980s were the era of developing new community sanctions. The starting point was the introduction of community service orders in 1972 in England and Wales which nowadays are amongst the most widespread community sanctions not only in the juvenile justice system.

In Germany a real "grass roots movement" of so-called new community sanctions emerged with four different measures that aimed to replace short-term detention: mediation, social training courses, community service and a special probationary directive (implying intensive care through the juvenile welfare services, see in detail Dünkel 2006). Intensive educational care is characteristic of these sanctions, although community service can also be administered as a more disciplinary sanction without intensive educational contents. This is supposedly an explanation for special age limits for the imposition of community sanctions.[11] Mediation, too, is a short-term intervention that can have educational effects, but it is not comparable to therapeutic interventions or programmes. Most European countries offer victim–offender mediation for juveniles as a court disposition. Furthermore, some countries provide such forms of mediation as a diversionary measure. Yet in some countries mediation is never or only seldom practiced because of a lack of organisational infrastructure at the local level.[12]

The so-called HALT projects in the Netherlands also deserve special attention. They provide a variety of alternative reactions, primarily as diversionary measures. This is an example of educationally meaningful measures often provided in the phase before any court sentence. Mediation (victim–offender reconciliation) is maybe the most prominent issue in this regard, and recently family group conferencing and other

---

[11] For example in Ireland and Northern Ireland community service can only be imposed on juveniles aged 16 or older.

[12] Reported for example in the reports on the Czech Republic, Poland and Kosovo; see Dünkel et al. 2009.

forms of restorative justice have been introduced in some countries (for example in Northern Ireland and Belgium, see O'Mahony and Campbell 2006 and O'Mahony in this volume). Family group conferences in Northern Ireland can also be based at the court level, although their primary field of application is the pre-court level.

As far as electronic monitoring has been introduced, we have serious doubts that this serves as an appropriate and proportional alternative to custody. These reservations are based on the fact that the measure is only oriented towards increased control. Wherever it is used for juveniles it should only be admitted as an additional control element for primarily educational sanctions and should never be used as an independent or stand-alone intervention. Furthermore, it must be strictly limited to cases where a custodial sanction would otherwise be inevitable (in order to prevent net-widening effects). It seems to us that electronic monitoring in the field of juvenile justice can not be a useful strategy except in very exceptional single cases. There are good reasons to rely more on dynamic factors in personal relationships with educational personnel than on technical devices.

Another new sanction is the temporary withdrawal of a driver's licence as an independent sanction, sometimes also discussed for more than only traffic-related offences such as drunk driving. However, here too we have serious reservations where the application of this sanction goes beyond only traffic-related offences. The future integration of juveniles is often more difficult when their possibilities of mobility are hampered. Therefore, educational efforts should be made to allow juveniles to participate in traffic in a responsible manner. Social traffic training courses seem to be the appropriate answer, rather than excluding juveniles from mobility – particularly when they live in rural areas.

Sanctioning Practice in Juvenile Justice Systems, Particularly of Youth Courts in Selected European Countries

Before presenting some first results of the above-mentioned AGIS project (see above, footnote 4), we have to present some comments that limit the informative value of our data:

The requested outline of the national reports contains two questions that deal with their sentencing practice. We asked the reporters to describe informal ways of dealing with juvenile delinquency and by this we wanted to know how often the possibility of diversion or other alternatives to prosecution for juvenile offenders are used in each country. In another separate chapter we then asked for data about juvenile court dispositions and their application in the different countries.

As can be seen from these questions in our outline, we refrained from stipulating how the reporters should present their data. For example, we did not ask for an imprisonment rate for young people per 100,000 of the relevant age group, for two reasons: First of all we are aware of the fact that – separate from the general problems that arise when working with statistical data about crime and reactions to crime in a large number of countries (see, for example, Cavadino and Dignan 2006, p. 4; Muncie and Goldson 2006, p. 2) – the collection of data about criminal behaviour and its sanctioning by juvenile justice and (more problematic) welfare authorities varies a lot in Europe. Sometimes an absence of reliable statistical records can be observed (see Muncie and Goldson 2006, p. 2), and even where statistical records do exist, practice of how crimes (and clear-ups) are recorded varies greatly (see Cavadino and Dignan 2006, p. 4). Thus, comparability can only be achieved through many interpretations.[13] This makes an international comparison of statistical data difficult enough. To complicate matters further, the different juvenile justice systems provide for a wide variety of possibilities for dealing with juvenile offenders. So for example the imprisonment rates for juvenile offenders in one country could be extremely low whereas simultaneously the rates of juveniles in closed residential facilities could be quite high. Concentrating on statistical data about imprisonment would ignore the great number of alternative placements to custodial sanctions in the juvenile justice systems. This is why imprisonment rates in the field of juvenile justice have to be interpreted extremely careful. Even if we try to compare other categories of interventions, the meaning of "educational measures" for example is not consistent between the countries. Some countries use the term "educational measures" to distinguish between custodial measures and other (= educational) measures. In some countries "educational measures" can also include closed residential care.

The age groups that are covered by the different juvenile justice systems all over Europe (see the table in the concluding chapter of Junger-Tas and Dünkel in this volume) additionally hinder comparability. While statistics in England deal with 10–17-year-old juveniles, the German juvenile justice sentencing statistics cover 14–20-year-old juveniles and young adults.

Our conclusion was to give the reporters in the AGIS project a rather wide scope of discretion in describing the national sentencing practice instead of strictly requiring them to adhere to a pre-determined form and structure of data presentation that many would have been unable to follow. Therefore, the result is not surprising: it is almost impossible to summarize the national data in one comparative table for all European countries. However, we can present some structural elements and tendencies within the specific countries, and we just pick out some examples that can be seen as being representative for different European regions. In many cases we have found interesting developments and changes in sentencing over the last 20 years.

Nevertheless, the ways in which the reporters have described the sentencing practice of their countries vary a lot. Therefore, we are not presenting a comprehensive sentencing comparison of all of Europe, but rather have focussed on the developments in some individual countries. We selected 6 countries that could be seen as somehow representative for different European regions: Germany for continental Europe, England and Wales for the Anglo-Saxon countries, Finland for Scandinavia, Lithuania and Slovenia for the Eastern European countries,

---

[13] The difficulties are shown by the fact that the European Sourcebook of Crime and Criminal Justice Statistics does not contain juvenile justice material (see Killias et al. 2003; Aebi et al. 2006) and even the SPACE project of the Council of Europe does not contain information about the sentencing practice in juvenile justice; see http://www.coe.int/T/E/Legal_affairs/Legal_co-operation/Prisons_and_alternatives/Statistics_SPACE_II/

one representing the Baltic states, the other being part of the former Yugoslavia, and Greece representing the Mediterranean region.

Germany

A good example for the general development in Europe towards increasingly relying on community sanctions is the German approach to juvenile justice policy and practice. With regard to the increased use of diversionary procedures, the proportion of "formal" sanctions imposed by the court has diminished to only 31 to 32% of all cases that might have entered the system at the juvenile court level. Interestingly, there were major changes in the juvenile court's sentencing practice in the 1980s and early 1990s (see Fig. 11.1). The proportion of sentences to short-term custody in a detention centre has dropped from 11% to only 6% (which amounts to a reduction of about 45%) in the West German federal states. Unconditional youth imprisonment (6 months up to 5 years, in exceptional cases up to 10 years) accounts for only 1.5% and suspended youth prison sentences account for 3.5% of all formal and informal sanctions against 14–21-year-old offenders. Since 1981 youth prison sentences were reduced from 8% to 5%, a 38% reduction. This is remarkable insofar as in the 1990s the proportion of youth prison sentences remained stable, although the number of violent offenders increased considerably. A drop in the share of community sanctions among all court disposals from 36% to 20% is attributable to an extended application of diversionary measures (see Dünkel in this volume).

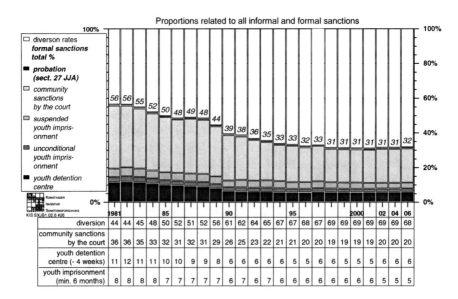

Fig. 11.1 Sanctioning practice in the juvenile justice of Germany, old federal states, 1981–2006

About 70% of sentences to youth imprisonment are suspended (2006: 69%, see Heinz 2008; combined with supervision by a probation officer). Ever since the mid-1970s almost 80% of all prison sentences of up to 1 year have been and still are suspended (2006: 78%). Even the longer prison sentences of more than 1 year up to 2 years are now suspended in 55% of the cases (2006), whereas in the mid-1970s this occurred only in exceptional cases (less than 20%). The extended practice of probation and suspended sentences (even for repeat offenders) has been a great success, since the revocation rates have dropped to only about 30%. The probation service has apparently improved its efficiency, but on the other hand the courts have also changed their practice by trying to avoid revoking a suspended sentence for as long as possible (see Dünkel 2003a, p. 96 ff.). Again it becomes clear that German juvenile court judges follow the internationally recognised principle of imposing youth imprisonment as a last resort ("*ultima ratio*") and for periods that are as short as possible (*minimum intervention approach*).

Overall, the average length of youth prison sentences has slightly increased. The structure of this development indicates that the proportion of prison sentences to up to 1 year has decreased, while terms lasting from 1–2 years have increased (see Table 11.2). However, this has been "compensated" by an increasing tendency towards suspending sentences (see above). The proportion of youth prison sentences to more than 5 years imprisonment remains stable and very low (2006: 0.5%), whereas the sentences from 2–5 years have increased. This is, however, not the result of more severe sentencing by juvenile judges but is rather due to the increasing conviction rate with regard to more serious crimes such as robbery and serious bodily injury (see Dünkel 2006 and Dünkel et al. 2009).

The practice of repeatedly suspending 1–2 year prison sentences already preceded the reform of 1990 to a great extent, with not less than 54% of such sentences being suspended in 1990 (the ratio in 1995 even went up to 60% and remained stable at about 55% in the following years, see Table 11.2). The extension of the applicability of alternatives to youth imprisonment to include young adults – who are more involved in crime than juveniles particularly concerning certain offences such as robbery – has contributed to the considerable decline of about 40% in the rate of juvenile- and young adults imprisonment between 1983 and 1990. Since 1990 the youth prisoners' rates, however, have risen because of an increase in the absolute number of violent offenders, but have been declining again recently. German sentencing policy therefore can be described as being very reasonable in that deprivation of liberty is only ordered as a very last resort.

England and Wales

England and Wales have often been labelled the prototype for harsher punishment in recent years. With regard to the informal ways of dealing with juvenile offenders, there have been interesting changes in the practice of how young people are cautioned. There had been a remarkable increase in the use of cautions from the 1970s up until

Table 11.2 Length and proportion of suspended youth prison sentences in Germany, 1975–2006, old federal states

Year	YI total (abs.)	Susp. YI (%)	6 m. – 1 J. (%)	6 m. – 1 y., susp. (% related to column 4)	1 – 2 y. (%)	1 – 2 y., susp. (% related to column 6)	2 – 3 y. (%)	3 – 5 y. (%)	5 – 10 y. (%)
1975	15,983	55.9	70.1	74.9	20.4	16.7	5.9		0.6
1980	17,982	62.2	71.0	79.4	20.1	28.6	4.5	2.1	0.7
1985	17,672	61.9	65.0	79.1	24.6	42.4	5.9	2.6	0.8
1990	12,103	64.3	62.2	79.2	28.0	53.7	6.4	2.4	0.6
1995	13,880	63.9	56.8	78.5	32.4	59.7	7.2	3.0	0.6
2000	17,753	62.1	54.8	78.5	33.8	56.4	7.9	2.9	0.5
2005	16,641	60.7	54.0	77.1	34.4	55.5	8.0	3.1	0.5
2006	16,886	60.5	53.7	77.6	34.0	55.3	8.4	3.3	0.5

m. months, *YI* youth imprisonment, *susp. YI* suspended youth imprisonment (probation), *y* year(s)

Source: Dünkel in Dünkel et al. 2009.

the early 1990s, whereas an enormous reduction followed in the following 10 years. Nowadays there are signs that indicate an end of the decline, as there have been slight increases in the cautioning rates for all age groups and across both genders since 2003 (see Dignan in Dünkel et al. 2009).

Taking a look at the development of formal sanctioning, Dignan has pointed out a remarkable reduction in the imposition of absolute discharges. Table 11.3 shows court dispositions for male offenders aged 15–17.[14] The proportion of discharges among all sentences dropped from 29% in 1992 to 11% in 2004. At the same time the imposition of fines has also declined. Parallel to these developments, the use of custodial sanctions increased from a share of 11% in 1992 to 17% in 1997, and dropped slightly again to 14% in 2004. The impact of the referral order[15] that was introduced in 2002 is by all means noticeable: in the year 2004 it accounted for 26% of all court dispositions for males aged 15–17.

These developments are indicative of a tightening of juvenile justice sentencing practice in England, even if the custody rates seem to have stabilised, albeit at quite a high level.[16] Referral orders demand more from the juveniles than a discharge, so we can say that England and Wales have substituted one rather lenient measure by a more invasive measure. To sum up, England and Wales follow a relatively invasive strategy of dealing with juvenile offenders, a strategy in which the role attributed to the idea of minimum intervention can be questioned. On the other hand, the notion of restricting custody to a measure of last resort seems to have been gaining importance again, although the level of custodial sanctions is still higher than in many other West-European countries.

Finland

The situation in Finland is rather different. Regarding informal sentencing, it is remarkable that diversion as it is used in Germany does not play an important role. For 15–17-year-old juvenile offenders non-prosecution occurs only in 5–6% of all cases dealt with by the prosecutor in that age group. While non-prosecution is

---

[14] The measures and sanctions vary a lot in England and Wales in the different age groups. The measures and sanctions in the age group 15–17 are considered the most comparable to other juvenile justice systems in Europe.

[15] The referral order sends the young offender to a Youth Offender Panel that consists of two community members and one representative of the Youth Offending Team. The panel holds a meeting which may include the offender, the offender's parents, a support for the offender and the victim and a victim supporter to discuss the crime and work on a solution. The panel (a) confronts the young offender with the impact of his crime in an attempt to prevent re-offending, (b) provides a forum for involved parties to discuss the circumstances leading up to the offence, (c) develops a plan of action (young offender contract) addressing reparation and the issues behind the offending behaviour; see http://www.restorativejustice.org/editions/2002/May2002/full_implementation_of_referral_ and O'Mahony and Doak in this volume.

[16] Compared to Germany, the proportion of 14% custodial sanctions in England implies a custody rate that is ten times higher; see Germany above.

Table 11.3 Court dispositions for young males aged 15–17, England and Wales, 1992–2004 in %

	1992	1993	1994	1995	1996	1997	1998	1999	2000	2001	2002	2003	2004
Referral order	–	–	–	–	–	–	–	–	–	–	17	25	26
Discharge	29	30	29	28	27	26	26	24	20	15	11	11	11
Fine	19	12	13	12	12	12	13	14	14	14	11	9	8
Supervision or probation order	17	20	21	22	22	21	21	20	17	17	16	16	15
Community service order	10	9	8	8	8	8	8	9	9	8	6	5	4
Attendance centre	10	12	11	11	10	10	9	10	8	6	4	3	4
Combination order	0	2	2	2	3	4	4	4	4	3	3	3	3
Curfew	–	–	–	0	0	0	0	0	1	2	3	4	6
Reparation order	–	–	–	–	–	–	–	–	4	7	4	3	3
Action plan	–	–	–	–	–	–	–	–	5	9	6	5	5
Custody	11	14	14	15	16	17	16	16	15	15	16	13	14
Other	4	2	2	2	2	2	2	3	3	4	3	3	1
Total	100	100	100	100	100	100	100	100	100	100	100	100	100
N (thous.)	28.8	26.2	28.6	30.1	32.5	33.6	35.0	35.0	33.9	34.3	33.7	31.4	31.8

Source: Dignan in Dünkel et al. 2009

therefore used in a fairly restrictive manner (as compared to many other jurisdictions), mediation (as a form of diversion, not as a formal sanction) has had a substantial role in the Finnish juvenile justice system since 1995. The mediation cases are not included in Table 11.4; therefore the diversion rate (withdrawals) is underestimated.

Regarding the Finnish court dispositions for juveniles, the low imprisonment rates in Finland are most remarkable. The imposition of prison sentences has declined over the years. In 1980 3.5% of all cases dealt with by the courts resulted in imprisonment, whereas it was only 0.8% in the year 2006. This implies that Finland is taking the principle of applying imprisonment as a last resort very seriously and is not influenced by any harshening tendencies. As a reason Lappi-Sepällä sees the reforms that he notices as "humane neo-classicism" (see Lappi-Sepällä in Dünkel et al. 2009). Law reforms in Finland stressed both legal safeguards against coercive care and the goal of less repressive measures in general. In sentencing, the principles of proportionality and predictability have become central values. The population seems to agree with these objectives and has not voiced any demands for harsher punishments, not even in cases of serious offending.

The alternative that is used in Finland is quite exceptional compared with practices in other European countries. *Fines* are the most common penalty for all age groups, accounting for 74% of court sentences issued against 15–17-year-old juveniles. This is very interesting because fines do not play a special role in the juvenile justice systems of the other countries in our project.[17] The second most relevant sanction in Finland is conditional imprisonment, accounting for over 17% of all interventions issued against 15–17-year-olds in 2005. This second place has been uncontested in Finland since the early 1990s, albeit having witnessed a slight decline since that time (see Table 11.4). Overall, one can conclude that Finland follows a strategy of minimum intervention, and that there have been no indications that practice has become or is becoming harsher or more severe.

Greece

In some aspects Greek sentencing practice is different from the countries that we have dealt with so far. Informal (diversionary) sanctions such as the absolute discharge, which has only been available since 2003, are only rarely applied.

With regard to formal sentencing, educational measures play a pivotal role, with approximately 75% of all cases resulting in the imposition of an educational measure (see Table 11.5 below). More specifically, the most common of these measures is the reprimand, accounting for more than 50% of all court dispositions. It is remarkable that imprisonment is the second most commonly ordered sentence in Greece. More than 20% of all dispositions are sentences to imprisonment. In certain cases, if an

---

[17] Fines cannot be issued against juveniles in Bulgaria, Croatia, Poland, Spain, Romania, Scotland and Serbia.

Table 11.4 Court dispositions for young offenders aged 15–17 in Finland, 1992–2005 in %

	1992	1993	1994	1995	1996	1997	1998	1999	2000	2001	2002	2003	2004	2005
Withdrawal	9	8.5	8.7	8.8	7.7	8	5.6	5.7	5.5	5.7	4.7	4.3	4.7	5.4
Fines	63.6	62.5	64.6	65.3	67	67.3	71	73.8	73.7	73.1	71.8	73.5	73.9	74.5
Community service	0	0.1	0.5	0.7	0.8	1.1	1.2	0.9	0.6	0.6	1.1	0.7	0.6	0.3
Juv. penalty[a]	0	0	0	0	0	0.9	1	1.5	1.9	0.8	0.6	0.8	0.7	1
Conditional imprisonment	22.9	24.8	23.4	23.1	22.8	20.9	18.5	16.3	17.2	18.6	20.2	19.6	18.8	17.3
Prison	4.5	4.1	2.9	2.1	1.7	1.8	2.7	1.9	1.2	1.3	1.6	1	1.4	1.5
Total	100	100	100	100	100	100	100	100	100	100	100	100	100	100
N	7,624	6,744	5,768	5,513	5,186	5,118	4,473	4,566	5,394	5,351	4,437	4,166	4,389	4,252

Source: Lappi-Seppälä in Dünkel et al. 2009

[a]"Juvenile punishment" is a 4–12-month-long community sanction comparable in severity to conditional imprisonment. It was introduced in the late 1990s on an experimental basis and was then rolled out nationwide by a law reform in 2005.

Table 11.5 Court dispositions for young offenders aged 13 to 17 in Greece, 1980–2003 in %

	1980	1985	1990	1995	2000	2003
Fines	0.5	0.3	1.5	0.2	0.2	0.5
Educational measures	81.1	88.7	75.3	84	75.7	75.3
Imprisonment[a] for up to 1 month	16.3	8.3	17.4	10.6	15	16.8
Imprisonment for 1–3 months	1	1.1	2.4	1	2.3	2.9
Imprisonment for 3–6 months	0.5	0.3	1.2	1	1.7	1.6
Imprisonment for 6–12 months	0.2	0.2	0.9	0.5	1.9	0.6
Imprisonment for 1–5 years	0.1	0.1	0.8	0.5	0.9	1
Secure prison[a] (5 up to 20 years)	0		0	0	–	–
Youth imprisonment (6 months up to 10, exceptionally 20 years)	0.2	1	0,5	2.1	2.1	1.2
Therapeutic measures	0.2	0.1	0	0	0.2	0
Total	100	100	100	100	100	100
N	122,759	108,003	109,184	91,960	58,708	73,157

[a]For juveniles who have reached the age of 18 during proceedings
Source: Pitsela in Dünkel et al. 2009

offender reaches the age of 18 during the proceedings, a mitigated adult sentence can be imposed. The judges seem to use this possibility quite often. However, around 70% of these cases result in a prison sentence of less than 1 month, and 90% of all sentences to prison are limited in length to less than 6 months. This means that short prison sentences are clearly predominant. What is more, they are executed only very rarely because they are often suspended (similar to probation). Fines are almost never issued against juveniles in Greece.

Greek sentencing data make no indication of an intensification or toughening-up of Greek practice. Greece does not seem to follow any strategies of non-intervention. Obviously the Greek system emphasises warning offenders through formal proceedings and sanctions that are in fact not very invasive on second glance (see *Pitsela* in Dünkel et al. 2009).

Slovenia

In Slovenia diversion plays a remarkable and predominant role in the juvenile justice system (see Filipčič in Dünkel et al. 2009). In 2002 for example, the state prosecutor dismissed almost two thirds of all cases. This practice of diverting large numbers of cases away from court is very similar to the situation in Germany.

With regard to formal sanctions by the juvenile court it can be shown that imprisonment is very rarely imposed (approximately 1% of all cases). However, commitment to a juvenile institution, as another form of deprivation of liberty, is applied more often. One can see though that over the last 25 years the number of juveniles sent to an educational institution has decreased considerably (in 1980, almost 14% of sentenced juveniles were sent to an educational institution, in 2002 it was only 4%, and in 2006 the proportion was at around 7%).

Community sanctions are much more important in the country. Imposing "instructions and prohibitions" increased very quickly after they were introduced in 1995. Supervision plays the most important role in Slovenian sentencing, accounting for more than 50% of all cases. After the adoption of the new Criminal Code in 1995 a steady decrease in the number of reprimands could be observed, which according to judges, were imposed as an emergency exit because of the lack of other adequate educational measures. This could be viewed as a tightening and intensification of sanctions if (as in the case of England and Wales) this replacement implies greater invasion and intrusion into the lives of juveniles. Altogether it should, however, be seen as the Slovenian strategy to monitor juvenile offenders in a rather mild way. Like in Germany, diversion strategies play an important role in Slovenia and overall the sentencing practice does not leave the impression of being overly harsh (Table 11.6).

Lithuania

The juvenile justice system in Lithuania provides for community sanctions as diversionary measures (see Table 11.7 below). These "educational measures" can only be imposed if the juvenile offender can be "released from his criminal responsibility." This possibility is only available for first time offenders. Furthermore, the Criminal Code also requires the reparation of damages, reduced criminal responsibility or other reasons for assuming that the offender will not re-offend in the future (see § 93 Criminal Code Lithuania).

The catalogue of formal sanctions provides two forms of "community sanctions": community service, and special obligations concerning for example the offender's whereabouts or a request for reparation. In the year 2007 34.8% of all juvenile offenders were formally sanctioned (see Table 11.7 for details). An "educational measure" was imposed (out of formal court proceedings) in 18.3% of the cases (they are covered in Table 11.8). 0.3% were found not guilty. The Lithuanian statistics do not allow any conclusions as to how the remaining cases (46.6%) were diverted from the court (see Sakalauskas in Dünkel et al. 2009).

Owing to a major amendment to the law in 2003, data on educational measures and court dispositions are only presented as of 2004 for reasons of comparability. It must, however, be emphasised that community sanctions had already prevailed over custodial disposals under the old law. In 2002, 61% of all sentences against 14–17-year-old juveniles were suspended prison sentences (probation) and only 31% were unconditional prison sentences (other non-custodial dispositions amounted to about 8%). Under the new law, suspended/conditional imprisonment remains the most important court disposition, followed by the newly introduced special obligations that can last between 3 months and 2 years and can include obligations/directives on a person's whereabouts or an obligation to restitute the damages caused by the offence.

Compared to West-European countries, and also to Slovenia, imprisonment is still used quite often for juveniles. Fines and community service (as a criminal

Table 11.6 Court dispositions for young offenders aged 14–17 in Slovenia, 1980–2005 in %

	1980	1985	1990	1995	1996	1997	1998	1999	2000	2001	2002	2003	2004	2005
Reprimand	36.4	48.6	58.3	58.1	53.4	42.8	35.2	33.6	29.5	29.3	29.8	30.1	23.9	20.3
Fines	–	–	–	0.2	1	1.5	1.9	1.8	0.8	0.9	1	0.7	0.8	0.6
Instructions and prohibitions	–	–	–	2.8	9.6	16.2	15.4	18.4	22.7	18.2	14.6	13.4	15.4	17.7
Supervision by a social assistance institution	39.5	33.1	28.8	29.3	29.8	33.5	39.5	40.4	40.8	47.3	49.9	48.4	53.3	52.8
Disciplinary centre	9.2	9.4	6.5	–	–	–	–	–	–	–	–	–	–	–
Commitment to a juvenile institution	13.8	7.9	6.1	8.2	5.6	5.8	7.9	5.1	4.6	3.5	4	6.7	4.7	6.8
Juvenile prison (6 months up to 10 years)	1.1	1	0.3	1.4	0.6	0.2	0.1	0.5	1.5	0.9	0.8	0.7	1.3	1.6
Total	100	100	100	100	100	100	100	100	100	100	100	100	100	100
N	856	1,098	997	499	500	617	636	706	591	571	728	568	615	498

Source: Filipcic in Dünkel et al. 2009.

Table 11.7 Court dispositions imposed on juveniles (14–17) in Lithuania, 2004–2007 in %

	2004	2005	2006	2007
Special obligations/directives[a]	–	23	26	30.1
Fines	6	8	5	3.8
Community service	6	2	2	0.7
Short time detention	7	10	4	4.3
Suspended short-time detention[b]	20	–	–	–
Exemption from punishment	2	1	0	0.6
Suspended/Conditional imprisonment	40	27	32	33
Imprisonment	19	29	27	27.6
Others	0	0,4	4	0
Total	100	100	100	100
N	1,690	1,421	1,285	1,195

[a]Since 13 July 2004
[b]Abolished 13 July 2004
Source: Sakalauskas in Dünkel et al. 2009

Table 11.8 Educational measures imposed on juveniles (14–17) in Lithuania, 2004–2007 in %

	2004	2005	2006	2007
Warning	16.6	14.3	15.7	18.2
Reparation	5.3	2.7	2.1	2.5
Community service	9.8	7.4	13.0	8.1
Supervision	14.4	6.1	5.8	4.4
Special obligations/directives concerning everyday life	53.5	67.8	63.1	66.0
Institutional educational measure	0.5	1.7	0.3	0.8
Total	100	100	100	100
N	984	693	986	795

Source: Sakalauskas in Dünkel et al. 2009

sanction) do not seem to play a major role in the Lithuanian juvenile justice system (for community service as an educational measure, see Table 11.8). Short-time detention is likewise not imposed very often.

The primary forms of educational measures are directives or obligations that influence a juvenile's everyday life. They can last from 30 days up to 12 months. For example, the court can impose a curfew requiring a juvenile to be at home at certain times, to attend a certain school, a vocational training course or other social training courses, drug and alcohol therapy or to be regularly involved in work. The court can also pronounce certain interdictions, for example, prohibiting a person from driving a motor vehicle or excluding a person from certain whereabouts.

Warnings/reprimands are second to obligations or directives. Community work is more often imposed as an educational measure than as a formal punishment, but with between 7 and 13% it is still only of secondary importance. The only measure involving deprivation of liberty, the so-called institutional educational measure, is applied only in very exceptional cases (regularly less than 1% of all educational measures; see Table 11.8).

In summary on can judge the Lithuanian sentencing practice as becoming less repressive and more educative, but still the use of community sanctions has not yet reached levels that are typical for West-European countries. Lithuania shares the difficulties of other former socialist countries in that the slow development of an infrastructure for the provision and delivery of community services and sanctions prevents any further reduction in the use of custodial sanctions. On the other hand, Lithuanian sentencing practice is definitely moving towards the educational goal as the "leitmotif" of its orientation.

Summary and Outlook

The present overview on developments of community sanctions in Europe and particularly in some selected countries reveals different strategies for dealing with juvenile offenders. Some countries prefer non-intervention (diversion, see also *Dünkel* in this volume), while others provide court-based community sanctions, but all take the international standard – which is often explicitly incorporated into national legislation – that deprivation of liberty must remain a reaction of last resort seriously. Nevertheless, practice varies considerably also in this regard. Juvenile imprisonment or custody in Germany and Finland account for less than 2% of all sanctions. This is in stark contrast to the by far more frequent use of imprisonment in England and Wales (about 15%) and in some East-European countries such as Lithuania (more than 30%). Therefore, extending the scope of community sanctions must be an issue of future sentencing policy reforms particularly in the latter-mentioned countries.

It should be noted in this context that in some countries custodial sanctions have been further limited by narrowing the scope of application for certain age groups that in principle are otherwise held criminally responsible. So in England and Wales detention in a youth prison such as a young offender institution is limited to those aged at least 15, whereas the age of criminal responsibility is 10. The same is true for Switzerland, which excludes prison sentences for under 15-year-old juveniles and also provides (primarily educational) residential care in the welfare system for older juveniles. Such legislative regulations, but also the general sentencing practice, contribute to an extensive use of community sanctions and measures particularly concerning the younger age groups within the different juvenile justice systems.

The priority given to community sanctions sometimes creates practical problems when budgetary restrictions limit the scope for more educational rather than repressive measures. The "triumphant" expansion of community service orders in some countries (which can be seen as a more retributive than educational measure) is also due to the limited or even reduced application of measures such as social training courses or other more "constructive", rehabilitative measures.

The Finnish preference for fines seems to be a model that should be investigated further. It is already becoming apparent that countries can be categorized according to common strategies that they share, such as for example Germany and Slovenia with respect to their diversion practice.

Evaluating the different forms of community sanctions prompts us to ask ourselves what qualifies one measure as being better than another. The question is whether or not we should think only in terms of recidivism rates or in less invasive measures: in terms of victim's rights to receive reparation (through reparation orders or victim–offender mediation which enables the victim to play also an active role in the "penal" process), or the possibilities to influence the life of the young offender (through supervision or special training courses). In the end, which community sanction can be seen as being the best one will depend on each single case. In this respect it has to be emphasized again that the "right" community sanction cannot just be based on the "needs" of the offender but must remain proportional to his or her guilt. Additionally, it should be mentioned that the persons who deliver community sanctions like probation officers, mediators or trainers (in social training courses) have an important role to play when it comes to the success of a measure, so they should receive the best available training.

The analysis of the sanctioning practice in six countries gives reason to question whether "penalties are becoming harsher and harsher" (Cavadino and Dignan 2006, p. 340) or if the "main trend in juvenile justice in a number of countries has been more repressive" (Junger-Tas 2006, p. 505). However, one may also observe that most East-European countries are not following this trend, but have instead shown tendencies to mitigating their formerly repressive systems. Our conclusion from only a few examples is that the trend towards harsher ("neo-liberal") juvenile justice policy cannot be universally verified all over Europe. Even if politicians in some countries call for tightening their juvenile laws (for example in England and Wales, France, the Netherlands, Spain or even in Germany to some extent) – and even if some laws are tightened, in most countries juvenile judges seem to be holding tight to their cautious way of dealing with juvenile offenders in practice. However, there is no doubt that practice has become harsher in some countries, particularly in England and Wales. Ironically, it is precisely this country that has provided the most sophisticated evaluation research demonstrating that community sanctions are more promising than custodial sanctions in terms of re-offending rates as well as under general cost-benefit considerations (see, for example, Goldblatt and Lewis 1998). Recently, research on restorative justice has shown positive effects concerning victim and offender satisfaction and reductions in recidivism (see Sherman and Strang 2007; Shapland et al. 2008; O'Mahony in this volume). With respect to the question whether restoration can work as an alternative in still punitive systems, see Cavadino and Dignan (2006, p. 210).

The criticism that community sanctions do not necessarily contribute to a reduction in custodial dispositions, but rather to a widening of the net of social control, has to be taken seriously. However, in Europe – with a few exceptions (see O'mahony and Doak in this volume) – there is no empirical evidence that such net-widening effects have in fact taken place.

In any case the search for constructive and effective community sanctions for all offenders, including recidivists and violent offenders (as proposed by the Council of Europe's Rec. (2003) 20 "New ways of dealing with juvenile delinquency …") remains an everlasting task for a rational juvenile policy.

Chapter 12
Custodial Establishments for Juveniles in Europe

Rob Allen

Studies of juvenile justice generally give a good deal of attention to how much use is made of detention both at the pretrial or remand stage and also as a punishment or treatment option. This is not surprising given the financial, social and ethical costs of incarceration. Rather less attention is usually given to the nature and practice of detention, the conditions in which juveniles are held, the types of regimes, staffing and treatment philosophy. This chapter attempts to describe some of the trends not in the number of young people locked up but in the way they are treated behind bars. After discussing the framework of international law, the chapter looks at the different types of establishments and the kinds of experience they provide for young people before looking at a number of key issues.

International Law

The Council of Europe's Council for Penological cooperation (PC-CP) since 2006 has been working on the European Rules for Juvenile Offenders Subject to Sanctions or Measures (ERJOSSM) that were adopted by the Committee of Ministers on 5 November 2008 (Rec. (2008) 11, see chapter 3 and Dünkel 2008a; 2008b). They provide important normative guidance building on the existing corpus of international law, rules and standards. These include the United Nations Convention on the Rights of the Child, and the United Nations Rules for the Protection of Juveniles Deprived of their Liberty (Havana Rules) as well as existing European standards such as the European Prison Rules (EPRs) and expectations set out by the Committee for the Prevention of Torture. Some of the detailed elements of these norms are discussed below, but it is worth emphasising three at the outset. First, children must only be locked up as a last resort and for the shortest possible time. Second, every child who is locked up must be separated from adults, unless it is in their best interests to do otherwise (UNCRC/EPRs). Third, the approach

R. Allen
International Centre for Prison Studies, King's College, London, UK

J. Junger-Tas and F. Dünkel (eds.), *Reforming Juvenile Justice*,
DOI: 10.1007/978-0-387-89295-5_12, © Springer Science + Business Media, LLC 2009

within establishments must be rehabilitative and educational rather than punitive. The Council of Europe's 2003 Recommendation on juvenile delinquency says preparation for release should begin on the first day based on a full risk and needs assessment and so do the ERJOSSM of 2008. Although seemingly uncontroversial, each of these principles can create considerable difficulties in practice.

Age Ranges

As discussed in chapter 4 and 13, the minimum age of criminal responsibility ranges widely in Europe from 8 to 18. The upper age limit of the juvenile juris-diction is generally 18,[1] but in most countries, juvenile custodial establishments will contain young people over 18 completing sentences imposed as or young adults (see the example of Germany). Owing to the flexibility of the law, minor detainees can remain under the protection of the juvenile justice system until 22–24, exceptionally (see Austria) 27 years of age (depending on the length of sanction). In some countries – notably Germany – courts can impose juvenile dispositions on young people up to 21. In these countries and others besides, juveniles can be held alongside young adults in youth prisons. In Finland all those who have committed their crime younger than 21 are regarded by the prison service as juveniles. The position in England and Wales is rather different; although young people under 21 are sentenced to Detention in a Young Offender Institution rather than prison, a discrete "secure estate" has been created for young people under 18, which provides much more in the way of education, training and regimes. On reaching their 18th birthday, minors are moved quickly on to the young adult estate, undoing much of the rehabilitative work that has been done.[2]

Types of Establishment

In most countries juveniles can find themselves locked up in a variety of establish-ments. The Council of Europe has developed a typology of six: Pretrial detention centres/departments, adult prisons (separate areas for juveniles), juvenile mental health institutions, welfare institutions, specialised juvenile prisons, and other. In this chapter a more basic categorisation will be used: specialised prisons, adult prisons and establishments under the social authorities.

---

[1]More and more countries follow the Recommendations of the Council of Europe of 2003 and 2008 to open the scope of application of juvenile justice jurisdiction to young adults and to apply sanctions of juvenile laws also on them, see Dünkel and Pruin 2009 and chapter 13.

[2]This was one of the rationale's used by Lord Chief Justice Woolf in releasing the two boys serving the sentence of Detention at Her Majesty's Pleasure following conviction for the murder of James Bulger.

Specialised Prisons

Probably the largest numbers are held in specialised prisons. In England and Wales for example of the 3,334 secure places for juveniles in July 2006, 2,825 were in specialised Young Offender Institutions, 235 in secure children's homes and 274 in secure training centres – specialised units run by the private sector. In Germany, there are 7,611 places in specialised juvenile prisons. France is in the process of creating six "établissements pénitentiaires pour mineurs" (EPM) which will provide a total of 360 places for 13–18-year-olds, almost half the total number of minors currently locked up. In Italy there are 17 Istituti Penali per Minorenni (young offenders' prisons) in addition to special remand centres designed to keep young people away from police stations.

The specialised prisons can be large establishments. Feltham Young Offender Institution in West London has 764 young prisoners, 240 of whom are juveniles and Hameln Juvenile Prison, the largest closed establishment for juveniles in Germany holds up to 727 young (male) adults aged from 14 to 24, on remand or serving sentences.

Adult Prisons

The European Prison Rules say that children under the age of 18 years should not be detained in a prison for adults, but in an establishment specially designed for the purpose. If children are nevertheless exceptionally held in such a prison there shall be special regulations that take account of their status and needs, and access to the social, psychological and educational services, religious care and recreational programmes or equivalents to them that are available to children in the community.

A number of countries continue to place children in adult jails. In England, although there is a dedicated secure estate for young people under 18, young people are sometimes placed in high-security prisons in the adult estate. In Scotland too, while in the Republic of Ireland a programme of building children detention schools is underway to enable children to be moved from Mountjoy prison. The former European Human Rights Commissioner was not impressed to find 637 young people under 18 in prison in France. In November 2005, many of them on remand were awaiting trial. While there are specialised units with trained staff, separation of remand from sentenced and juvenile from adult was not always possible. An experiment at Strasbourg and eight other prisons involves a team from the juvenile protection agency being permanently on duty in the prisons. As in many countries accommodating the small number of female juveniles presents a problem in France. In September 2005, Gil Robles found 11 minors held with 317 women at Fleury Merogis, which he described as "simply unacceptable".

Establishments Outside the Prison System

The best solution is undoubtedly provided through the provision of a variety of establishments outside the prison system. In the autonomous community of Catalonia in Spain, five types of custodial measure are provided by the General Directorate for Juvenile Justice – closed, semiopen, open, therapeutic custody and weekend residence in an education centre. The seven establishments are small institutions – L'Alzina in Palau de Plegamans, a closed institution for males, is the largest with a total capacity of 60. In the Netherlands there are two types of closed facilities: reception centres (opvanginrichtingen) and treatment centres (behandelinrichtingen) which specially cater for juveniles.

In many countries, closed facilities exist under the auspices of child welfare authorities. These are used for children too young to be held in prison (most usually those under the age of 15 but 13 in France and can sometimes be used as an alternative to prison. Secure Children's homes in England and Wales and secure accommodation in Scotland fall into this category as do two types of institutions in France. The 47 "centres éducatifs renforcés" (CER) deal with small groups of minor offenders with the aim of interrupting a delinquent lifestyle through a short educational placement of up to 6 months. More persistent offenders aged 13–16 can be placed in one of 11 "centres éducatifs fermés" set up following legislation in 2002. While the regime is educational and the security relaxed (in a centre visited by the author two of the residents attended the local lycee during the day), failure to comply with the regime during a 6-month placement can lead to detention.

In Scandinavia, specialist establishments outside prison have only recently been introduced following criticisms of the use of prison for young people under 18. In Sweden, since 1999, closed youth detention has been available for young people under the age of 18, organised by the National Board for Institutional Care (SiS). The punishment is for a fixed term – from 14 days to 4 years depending on the seriousness of the crime but the regime is focused on care and treatment.

In 2001 Denmark introduced a new juvenile sanction to the Criminal Code for young people with social adjustment problems who would previously have received an unconditional prison sentence of 30 days to 1 year. The sanction involves a stay in a secure institution between 2 months and 12 months, followed by a further period in an open facility before a period of supervision in the community. The sanction lasts 2 years in all – substantially longer than the prison sentence it replaced albeit under less restrictive and more therapeutic conditions.

What are the Characteristics of These Kinds of Custodial Establishments for Juveniles?

Obtaining a true picture of the characteristics of juvenile establishments is not straightforward. Some countries have an independent inspectorate which produces reports, other have active NGOs who take an interest in the well-being of young people in detention. The Committee for the Prevention of Torture (CPT), which visits all places where people have their liberty restricted, makes fairly regular inspections of juvenile establishments as does the European Commissioner for Human Rights. UN bodies, in particular the Committee on the Rights of the Child, take a particular interest in this field.

It seems clear that the conditions in establishments run by child welfare or specialised juvenile justice authorities are vastly superior to those run by the penitentiary authorities. In many cases child welfare establishments accommodate children at risk as well as those accused of or convicted for crimes. They are generally much smaller than prisons and have substantially greater staff to resident ratios. At Barby Home for young persons near Uppsala in Sweden, the CPT found a positive and personalised environment and a relaxed atmosphere with many residents speaking positively of the way they were treated by staff. Barby had 80 care workers, 7 social workers and 8 teachers looking after a total of 29 young people.

In Belgium, the CPT found good conditions at the closed centre of De Grubbe near Brussels. Each of the 50 residents have their own room (from 11–15 sq m in size); and the staff number 168 in total (particularly high number needed in order to meet the needs of both French and Flemish children accommodated there). Similarly, St Mary's Kenmure Secure Accommodation Service in Glasgow was found to be quite satisfactory, with a very relaxed atmosphere in the 36-bed children's detention facility and staff appeared dedicated. There was little visible indication of the closed nature of the facility. At Trinity House school in Ireland, 27 motivated staff were well equipped to work with children developing and providing individualised programmes. At L'Alcina in Catalonia, there are 12 square metres available per person in a single room and 6 sq m available per person in a double room. There are 58 educators working at the establishment.

These establishments are not without their problems. The Council on Application of Penal Sanctions and Child and Youth Protection is concerned about the situation in most closed youth facilities in the Netherlands. In December 2001 the Council expressed its concern that young people are locked in their rooms more than they should be, and a lack of staff, particularly teachers, which means the staff that are present are forced to concentrate on control rather than on education. This is not withstanding a staff complement of 120 for 79 children at the Jongeren opvangcentrum (JOC, Youth Reception Centre) in Amsterdam.

There has been much criticism in England and Wales about secure training centres run by private security companies. Although private not for profit child and youth care organisations are commonly involved (e.g. in Scotland, the Netherlands) and private security personnel play a small part in the one fully closed educational establishment in Catalonia, giving the private security industry the whole responsibility for a secure establishment is highly unusual in Europe.

The position in establishments that form part of the prison system is less reassuring, even in those which are designed or adapted especially for juveniles. Youth prisons in Germany are generally smaller than adult prisons, tend to have better levels and mixes of staffing, and like the juvenile young offender institutions in England provide better education, and vocational training opportunities

(Dünkel 2006). But the CPT did not find the physical conditions at Weimar/Ichterhausen satisfactory – small cells (two persons in 8.4 sq m), sparsely decorated, impersonal and austere with dirty bedding. Staffing levels were too low and there was concern about high levels of violence. Young people were entitled to visits for only an hour a month although more generous arrangements were made in practice. Dünkel's research has found that generally in Germany disciplinary measures are much more frequent in respect of young prisoners than adults although there are substantial variations which appear to relate to the individual attitudes of directors. The development of new prison laws in the Länder could introduce more consistency.

A scandal in November 2006 at the juvenile detention facility in Siegburg saw a 20-year-old prisoner hang himself following a prolonged period of torture by his three cell mates aged 17–20. Thirty young people under 18 have taken their lives in detention facilities in England and Wales since 1990, all but two in prison service establishments. Such tragedies of course focus attention on the inappropriateness of prisons for this age group but also on some particular questions such as the living accommodation. Given the risks of violence and bullying among teenage boys in particular, cell sharing let alone dormitory accommodation always carries risks. One of the key recommendations of the independent inquiry into the Siegburg tragedy set up by the North Rhine Westphalia Ministry of Justice was that juveniles should be accommodated in their own cell. This recommendation was followed by the youth prison legislation in 2007 in all 16 federal states in Germany by providing the statutory right to single accomodation in youth prisons (see Dünkel in Dünkel et al. 2009).

Yet perhaps the most difficult situation faces young people who are held in adult prisons awaiting trial. In France, the CPT found 25 juveniles in the Maison D' Arret in Loos – a jail with a capacity for 461 accommodating over 1,100 prisoners. The committee found the position of the juveniles "particularly worrying" with only four involved in training and ten taking part in a few hours a week maths, French or English classes. Policies are being developed to end the practice of holding juveniles in this way but it is likely to prove the better of two evils in countries which have very small numbers of young people under 18 in detention (see next section).

Key Issues

Separation

While the international rules are clear that juveniles should be held separately from adults, there is an exception where this is in the best interests of the child. The commentary to the EPRs makes it clear that this should be exceptional for example where there are few children in prison. The problem arises mainly in relation to pretrial detention, and indeed several European countries have entered reservations to Article 37 of the UNCRC (UK, Netherlands, Iceland, Switzerland).

Monaco countered criticism from the CPT by explaining that in the previous 16 years the number of children under 16 held in the maison d'arret was small and the periods of detention short – but nevertheless included one 13-year-old and two 14-year-olds. In Denmark the small number of 15–17 years in pretrial detention who cannot be placed in surrogate custody causes problems. Placements in a juvenile unit led to feelings of "isolation both in relation to other inmates and to their family and relatives. Owing to the distance to their home region it was often difficult for them to receive visits. This was felt not to be appropriate, because of the needs of young people to maintain as much contact with the family as possible. Those who cannot be held in alternative placements are currently placed in local prisons, subject to a careful assessment of the composition of the other inmates. To counter isolation within the prison, in exceptional circumstances, and only with consent from the Directorate of Prisons and Probation young people under 18 may be placed in day rooms with older inmates. In similar vein, Norway has no juvenile prisons, and because of the small number of persons concerned, keeping them separate from other adult inmates would result in their being virtually totally isolated. However, young inmates are followed up particularly closely by prison staff in order to prevent any harmful effects of their incarceration. The European Human Rights Commissioner was disappointed to find "still no separate section for juveniles in Oslo prison "but observed efforts to keep juveniles separate during the day time.

In Germany, the practice of holding juveniles and young adults together is widespread. The CPT considered this "can be beneficial to the young persons involved, but requires careful management to prevent the emergence of negative behaviours such as domination and exploitation, including violence". Elsewhere the CPT has been concerned about the practice of adult male prisoners being placed in cells for male juveniles, with the intention that they maintain control in those cells; female juveniles being accommodated together with adult women prisoners; and juvenile psychiatric patients sharing accommodation with chronically ill adult patients. After a visit to Austria, the committee's first recommendation was that juvenile prisoners should be accommodated separately from adult prisoners, and it has also been concerned in former Yugoslav countries – e.g. Bosnia where it considered "the current practice of placing juveniles together with older inmates in the admission unit in contrary is totally unsafe".

Clearly there may be circumstances where it is in the best interests of juveniles not to be separated from particular adults. It may also be possible to provide necessary safeguards through staff members to eliminate the risk of bullying. But as a rule, the international bodies believe this principle needs to be upheld. Article 28 of CPT rules says that "all minors deprived of their liberty must be kept in correctional homes especially built for persons of that life age, offering regime shaped according to their needs".

Mixing of Offenders with Other Children

Two related questions about juvenile institutions are their ability to keep untried juveniles separate from sentenced and the broader question of mixing children in criminal justice with other children who may be in secure conditions for their own protection.

It is not uncommon for remanded and sentenced juveniles to be mixed, although the European Human Rights Commissioner criticised the failure of the French government to consider separation in their plans for EPMs, arguing that different detention regimes are essential (Gil Robles, 2006b). A hard line stance on this does not appear either practicable or desirable, particularly when one considers the second question – whether children in conflict with the criminal law need to be held separately from other children who may be in secure care for reasons relating to their own protection.

In Denmark for instance, there are about 100 secure places in the child welfare system. Seventy percent of the juveniles are there as an alternative to pretrial prison and 10% are subject to the new Youth sanction. The remainder are children under the age of criminal responsibility and those who need to be in secure care for their own good. Each institution takes all categories of clients. A similar mixing takes place in England, Scotland and in the Netherlands. The argument for doing so is that children who cause problems do not differ much from children who have problems but the policy is sometimes contested. In Catalonia the seven juvenile centres are exclusively for offenders, with separate facilities for children in the care system who need residential placement.

Discipline, Control and Restraint

A third question relates to the types of disciplinary sanctions which may be imposed upon juveniles. International bodies have been concerned about the use of solitary confinement, a measure which can compromise the physical and/or mental integrity of children (CPT). The UN Committee on the Rights of the child required Denmark to review as a matter of priority the current practice of solitary confinement, limit the use of this measure to very exceptional cases, reduce the period for which it is allowed and seek its eventual abolition. Concerns about the practice have also been raised in Jersey, the Czech Republic and in England (Carlile 2006).

In a number of establishments they have visited, CPT delegations have been told that it was not uncommon for staff to administer the occasional "pedagogic slap" to juveniles who misbehaved. The Committee considers that, in the interests of the prevention of ill-treatment, all forms of physical chastisement must be both formally prohibited and avoided in practice, with juveniles dealt with only in accordance with prescribed disciplinary procedures. The Committee is not supportive of custodial staff who come into direct contact with juveniles openly carrying batons, because it is not conducive to fostering positive relations between staff and inmates. The committee would prefer custodial staff not to carry batons at all but in England the prison officers association is waging a campaign to be allowed to do so in juvenile Young offender institutions.

The UN Convention on the Rights of the Child takes a strong line arguing that "respect for the dignity of the child requires that all forms of violence in the treatment of children in conflict with the law must be prohibited and prevented". It goes on to emphasize that restraint or force should be used in detention in very limited circumstances – when the child poses an imminent threat of injury to himself or herself or others and only when all other means of control have been exhausted. It is not clear whether such an ultima ratio approach is applied in practice.

Links with Community and Preparation for Release

One of the most powerful criticisms of any custodial or institutional placement is that even if positive rehabilitative work can be achieved the lack of follow-up support on release can undermine it. Maintaining links with the family and community is particularly important so that a custodial sentence does not become an opportunity for a child's carers to slough off their responsibilities. The CPT attaches considerable importance to the maintenance of good contact with the outside world for all persons deprived of their liberty, with "the active promotion of such contacts ... especially beneficial for juveniles deprived of their liberty, many of whom may have behavioural problems related to emotional deprivation or a lack of social skills". Models of good practice here include the EPMs where weekly reports to parents are made outlining progress and challenges. The Folch I Torres Educational Centre outside Barcelona has no restrictions on family members visiting within normal working hours. Specific measures to prepare for release are made at the so-called "reso"-units in the Amsterdam JOC for the boys who are about to leave the JOC and return into society. There are possibilities that – with the approval of the youth judge or the public prosecutor – boys are allowed to go to school or to work outside the JOC, the so-called "night detention", plus programmes (so-called educational training programmes) to make the transition back to society easier.

The Siegburg inquiry recommended that North-Rhine Westphalia should implement more open sections in detention for juveniles, both to reduce the potential of interprisoner violence as well as help prepare young people for release.

Conclusions

There are many challenges facing the custodial establishments in Europe. As recently as 2004, visitors to Poland found children in small dormitory cells, with no personal items, wearing pyjamas and slippers throughout the day; no medical screening and no visits for a month. Reforms in such cases are easy to identify.

More difficult is the question of how next to organise juvenile detention. The rules suggest that prisons should ideally not be involved and certainly not adult prisons.

But the penitentiary authorities play a major role across the continent. Catalonia's separate juvenile justice directorate is not a common model. Eyes will be focussed on the French EPM experiment – a mixed model with 76 prison staff and 36 educators – the head of the centre is a prison governor and the deputy head a social worker. Is this the way forward for Europe?

One of the interesting recommendations in the Siegburg report was for better communication between detention centres. "The committee assert that a better communication between detention centres is useful to exchange experiences and to adopt different point of views". Although no doubt, the committee had Germany in mind, there is as much of a strong case for Europe as a whole.

In the view of the CPT, all juveniles deprived of their liberty, because they are accused or convicted of criminal offences, ought to be held in detention centres specifically designed for persons of this age, offering regimes tailored to their needs and staffed by persons trained in dealing with the young.

Moreover, the care of juveniles in custody requires special efforts to reduce the risks of long-term social maladjustment. This calls for a multidisciplinary approach, drawing upon the skills of a range of professionals (including teachers, trainers and psychologists), in order to respond to the individual needs of juveniles within a secure educative and sociotherapeutic environment, as it is also required by the European Rules for Juveniles Subject to Sanctions or Measures (see Rec. (2008) 11, Rule 15 and chapter 3 above).

Chapter 13
Reforming Juvenile Justice: European Perspectives

Josine Junger-Tas and Frieder Dünkel

Introduction

Many people, and even professionals in the field, tend to forget that most children in our part of the world grow up without any real problems, in good living conditions and with capable and loving parents. However, the media present us with quite another image of youth: they claim that many young people commit delinquent acts and that juvenile delinquency is for ever rising, constituting a severe threat to ordinary norm conforming citizens.

Now it is true that between 1960 and 1980 there was a steep rise in youth crime, followed by some limited increase till about the 1990s. The increase referred mainly to property crime and to vandalism, in short to "petty" crime, which was very annoying indeed but hardly serious. Among the causes of the change in the behaviour of many youngsters were the explosive economic boom in the 1960s related to rising prosperity, the development of self-service shops, the growing employment of mothers, the increase in mobility of young people (motors and scooters) and a decline of informal social control. These profound social and economic changes gave rise to an eruption in juvenile crime in many European countries and led to a new interest in delinquent youth, which was reflected by growing interventions of the police and the juvenile justice system.

The outcome of all this was – in most western countries – a continuous increase in police-recorded figures on both juvenile delinquency and young adult crime, which is going on to this very day. However, in addition to police figures there are two other measures of crime: victimization surveys and self-report studies. For example, systematic victimization surveys are held in The Netherlands since 1980. So two Dutch criminologists were able to examine crime trends in the country from 1980 to 2004 by comparing 25 years of victimization surveys to police statistics (Wittebrood and Nieuwbeerta 2006). Victimization surveys measure the prevalence

J. Junger-Tas (✉) and F. Dünkel
Willem Pompe Institute, University of Utrecht, Utrecht, The Netherlands;
Ernst-Moritz-Arndt-Universität Greifswald, Rechts- und Staatswissenschaftliche Fakultät, Greifswald, Germany

J. Junger-Tas and F. Dünkel (eds.), *Reforming Juvenile Justice*,
DOI: 10.1007/978-0-387-89295-5_13, © Springer Science + Business Media, LLC 2009

and frequency of victimizations. They inquire whether the victimizations have been reported to the police and whether, consequently, the police made the complainants sign a formal complaint form.

The outcomes are interesting because, contrary to the police-recorded rise in crime, the study showed considerable stability in crime victimizations. This was true with respect to violence, while property crime was even falling. The authors explained the discrepancy between the two data sources by pointing first to the increase of reporting violent incidents to the police from 20 to 25%. Similar increases in reporting behaviour are shown in Germany by Schwind et al. (2001, cited in Chap. 1), showing that a police-recorded increase of violent offending of 128% between 1975 and 1998 reflected a "real" rise in violence of only 24%.

The reason is that behaviour that was long considered as "a fact of life" is increasingly seen as unacceptable and tolerance for this kind of behaviour declined. The same tendency is clear with respect to juvenile delinquency where incidents such as a fight in the school playground may end in court before the juvenile judge. Second, the study showed that the police appeared increasingly prepared to make an official report of the offence: recording practice rose from 60 to 80%. The authors concluded that, although recorded police figures suggest substantial increases in crime over the 25 years, victimization trends show instead ongoing stability of crime incidents experienced by victims.

Similarly, systematic self-report surveys among youth populations also show great stability of delinquency since about the 1990s. Comparing new and old EU member states and using different data sources, Alex Stevens (Chap. 1) finds that juvenile property crime has fallen since 1990 and so has violent crime.

Summarizing the different factors that explain the discrepancy between police-recorded crime, and victimization or self-reported surveys, suggests the following:

- Increase of citizens reporting criminal incidents to the police
- Increase of police willingness to make an official recording of citizens complaints
- Increase in the probability of juveniles being caught
- Policy pressures on the police to give priority to arresting juvenile offenders
- Prosecution of young people for increasingly minor offences
- Abolition of the discretionary police power to drop charges in the case of petty offences

The accumulation of these actions and measures means that the police are extremely focussed on young people leading to an inflation of police-recorded youth crime. In reality the level of juvenile delinquency is pretty stable.

This does not mean that young people never commit any acts that we consider as antisocial or illegal: many do but in a recent study among 12–15-year-old children only 4 of a total of 15 delinquent acts had high prevalence: vandalism, shoplifting, group fights and carrying a weapon (mostly a knife) (Junger-Tas et al. 2008). However, the majority restricted this behaviour to one or two petty delinquent acts, such as destroying some property or stealing some object out of a shop. In fact we do not have to be overly concerned about these children: they will not develop into hardened criminals.

The children we have to worry about form only a tiny minority from the youth population: about 7–8% of the total population of delinquents (Junger-Tas et al. 2008). It is this minority which should end up in court but unfortunately many more are caught in the nets of the juvenile justice system.

This trend should also be seen in the light of the increase in (re)criminalization of petty offending and the rise of a "new punitiveness" (Goldson 2000; Pratt et al. 2005; see also Garland 2001a,b; Roberts and Hough 2002; Tonry 2004) in many European countries. Countries such as England, The Netherlands, France, Belgium, Ireland, and even Scotland have "moved away from the Welfare model of dealing with children and young people who offend to one which relies far more on punishment" (Solomon and Garside 2008). We have witnessed similar developments in several European countries that imply an intensification of juvenile justice policy and interventions through raising the maximum sentences for juvenile detention and by introducing other forms of secure accommodation. The juvenile justice reforms in the Netherlands in 1995 and in some aspects in France in 1996, 2002 and 2007 should be mentioned in this context, as should the reforms in England in 1994 and 1998 (for a summary, see Dünkel 2003a; Kilchling 2002; Cavadino and Dignan 2002, p. 284 ff.; 2006, p. 215 ff.; Junger-Tas and Decker 2006; Bailleau and Cartuyvels 2007). In other countries such as or the Scandinavian countries a juvenile crime policy oriented to welfare and a moderate justice approach is maintained (priority to diversion and "education instead of punishment", see Dünkel 2006). Many countries have implemented elements of "restorative justice" (reparation, mediation, family conferences, see e.g. Belgium and Northern Ireland, Dünkel et al. 2009 and chapter 10 in this volume).

The causes for the observed more repressive or "neo-liberal" approach in some countries are manifold. It is likely that the new "punitive" trend with penal law approaches of retribution and deterrence coming from the USA was not without considerable impact in some European countries, particularly in England and Wales. The "new punitiveness" does not stop in front of the doors of juvenile justice. However, juvenile justice is to a certain degree "immune" against neo-liberal tendencies, since the international human rights standards (see chapters 2 and 3) are preventing a total shift in juvenile justice policy. More repressive penal law orientations have gained importance in some countries that face particular problems with young migrants and/or members of ethnic minorities and problems with integrating young persons into the labour market, particularly with the growing number of young persons living in segregated and deteriorated city areas. They often have no real perspectives to escape "underclass" life; phenomena which "undermine society's stability and social cohesion and create mechanisms of social exclusion" (see Junger-Tas 2006, p. 522 ff., 524).

One recent issue within the debate on reforming the laws on juvenile welfare and justice is the notion of making the parents of young offenders criminally responsible. In England, the so-called *parenting order* can be imposed on parents who supervise their children insufficiently, making them criminally responsible for their children's criminal perpetrations by means of, for instance, a fine or an obligation to participate in parenting-support-courses (see chapter 5). France witnessed an intensification of parental liability in 2002, which implies that child benefits can be slashed should their child be accommodated in a secured institution. Furthermore, they can be issued a fine should they fail to appear before the youth court despite a court summons (see Kasten 2003, p. 387).

In England, the concept of responsibilisation has become a pivotal category of juvenile justice (see Graham 1998; critically: Cavadino and Dignan 2006; 2007). What is positive in this sense is that the promotion of responsibility is connected to the expansion of victim-offender-reconciliation, mediation and reparation. It is, however, more problematic in the light of the abolition of *doli incapax* for 10–14-year-olds which poses a considerable reduction of the age of criminal responsibility. The tendencies in English juvenile justice can be deemed as being symptomatic for neo-liberal orientations under the key-terms "responsibility, restitution (reparation), restorative justice" as well as (occasionally openly publicised) "retribution". The so-called "4 R's" have replaced the "4 D's" of the debates of the 1960s and 1970s (diversion, decriminalization, deinstitutionalization, due process) (see Dünkel 2003a; 2003b). The retributive character can be exemplified by the requirement for the imposition of community interventions to be "tough" and "credible". For example, "community treatment" of the 1960s was replaced by "community punishment" in the 1980s and 1990s. Cavadino and Dignan comprise these currents to the so-called "neo-correctional model" (see Cavadino and Dignan 2006, p. 210; see also Bailleau and Cartuyvels 2007). Moreover, in England and the Netherlands, for example, nuisance behaviour such as annoying or harassing passers-by may eventually lead to placement in an institution.[1] Also, in most of these countries more young people are locked up for long periods in institutions that are youth prisons rather than children's homes. If interventions and treatment are administered at all they are rarely tested on their effectiveness. Recidivism and reconvictions are extremely high, which does question the usefulness of institutionalization.

In the case of the continental European countries, there is nonetheless no evidence of a regression to the classical perceptions of the eighteenth and nineteenth centuries. There is an overall adherence to the prior principle of education or special prevention, even though justice elements have also been reinforced. Therefore, the area of conflict – if not paradox – between education and punishment remains evident. The reform laws that were passed in Austria in 1988 and 2001, in Germany in 1990, in the Netherlands in 1995, in Spain in 2000 and 2006, in Portugal in 2001, in France and Northern Ireland in 2002, as well as in Lithuania in 2000 (see Dünkel and Sakalauskas 2001), the Czech Republic in 2003 (see Válková 2006) or in Serbia in 2006 (see Škulić 2009) are suitable examples (see Dünkel 2003; Dünkel et al. 2009 for a summary). The reforms in Belgium (2007) and Northern Ireland (2002) are of particular interest, since these strengthened restorative elements in juvenile justice, including so-called family conferencing (see Christiaens and Dumortier 2009; O'Mahony and Campbell and chapter 10). It is true that countries in central and Eastern Europe tend to work in the welfare tradition, thereby following

---

[1] This refers to Anti-social Behaviour Orders, which is still an experiment in the Netherlands.

the Council of Europe's Recommendations and UN Rules as well as the example of Germany, a country still rooted firmly in the welfare approach. The same case can be made for the Scandinavian countries, although in Denmark and Sweden punitive tendencies are clearly apparent.

In the light of these trends in juvenile justice the authors of this book give with their contribution indications for other ways in meeting both the needs of the individual child as well as the needs of society to solve the problem of juvenile offending. In the final chapter we try to go a little further in proposing a number of concrete changes to juvenile justice practices: these are outlined in the following sections.

Young People's Rights in Juvenile Justice

One major weakness in the welfare approach is the position of extreme dependence of the child. On the basis of the principle of treatment, rehabilitation and protection, all "in the interest of the child" it was deemed unnecessary to give children the same procedural rights as adults. The system was very paternalistic: all actors in the system, in particular the juvenile judge, had great power in deciding the child's fate, while parents and children alike were powerless in their hands. This situation has been drastically changed with the introduction of the Justice model at the end of the 1980s. It was considered that when imposing more accountability for their offences on juveniles, they would be entitled to similar procedural rights as adults.

This has led to a number of UN Standard minimum rules on the *Administration of Juvenile justice* in 1985 and on *institutionalised children* in 1990, while the *European Prison rules* – adopted by the Committee of Ministers in 2006 – are not applying to minors. Therefore in 2008 the Council of Europe adopted the *European Rules for Juvenile Offenders subject to Sanctions and Measures* which are the most comprehensive human rights instrument for the imposition and execution of community sanctions and all forms of deprivation of liberty in Europe (see Dünkel 2008 and chapter 4).

One of the most important UN documents is the *Convention of the Rights of the Child*, adopted by the UN General Assembly in 1989 (see chapter 2), which in its articles 37 and 40 specifies the legal grounds of judicial intervention, the procedural rights which have to be observed and the conditions under which a child may be detained. One hundred and ninety-three states have signed the Convention,[2] which means it is binding law and judges have to comply with its rules. It is important to emphasize this aspect since judges may be slow to implement the CRC. For example, in the Netherlands it took quite some years before juvenile judges started to take the UN convention into account in their sentencing decisions.

In this section we wish to draw special attention to article 3 CRC, stating that "the best interest of the child" should be the primary consideration in all proceedings

---

[2] With the exception of the United States and Somalia.

concerning children. This means that in dealing with offending juveniles we should substitute the emphasis on retribution and repression by rehabilitation and restorative justice. An important recommendation by a UN independent expert (cited in chapter 2) refers to the establishment of independent monitoring bodies with the power to make unannounced visits to youth institutions and to investigate complaints about violence. In addition, the CRC committee recommends States to abolish the criminalisation of so-called status offences, such as running away from home, vagrancy or truancy, all rather problem behaviour than offences.

The European Recommendation on "New Ways of Dealing with Juvenile Delinquency and the Role of Juvenile Justice" of 2003 adds special attention towards victims of crime and to prevention. It emphasizes that resources should be particularly addressed to the most serious offenders and that community sanctions should also be developed for this group.

The "European Rules for Juvenile Offenders Subject to Sanctions and Measures of 2008" are extended to include the ages 18–21, an important renovation, which is in line with the 2003 Recommendation (see there Rule 11). It reflects the extended transition to adulthood in modern societies. The new Recommendation of 2008 (re) emphasizes that the most important objective of sanctions and measures should be education and social integration, independently of whether the child is deprived of his liberty or subject to community sanctions. Rule 4 states that the age of criminal responsibility should not be too low and in this respect is rather weak. But in the commentary it is clearly stated that the relevant age should be at least 14 or 15, which is the age limit fixed by most European countries (see Table 13.1). The rules establish the principle of individualized sanctions and measures, implying some discretionary power of implementing authorities. The rules oppose some countries' practice of using pretrial detention as some form of crisis intervention or to reduce public concern and fixes a maximum term of 6 months before the beginnings of the trial (see Rec. (2003) 20, Rule 16). Rule 20 of the Rec. (2008) 11 demands – as does the CRC – an independent monitoring body, not controlled by the government, which guarantees complaint procedures and effective supervision of the juvenile justice system by regular inspections (for further details see chapter 3).

The Age of Criminal Responsibility

It is no secret that countries differ in the age of criminal responsibility. If one considers these ages on a world scale the differences are striking, but if we look a little closer and limit ourselves to Europe the picture is somewhat less diverse: most countries have chosen for the ages 14–16, often leaving open the option of trying very serious offences at a younger age. However, there is no indication of a *harmonisation* of the age of criminal responsibility in Europe. The minimum age of criminal responsibility in Europe varies between 10 (England), 12 (Netherlands), 13 (France), 14 (Germany, Italy, Austria, Spain and numerous Central and Eastern European countries), 15 (the Scandinavian countries) and even 16 (for specific offences in

Table 13.1 Comparison of the age of criminal responsibility in Europe

Country	Minimum age educational measures of family/youth court (juvenile welfare law)	Age of criminal responsibility (juvenile criminal law)	Full criminal responsibility (adult criminal law can/must be applied; juvenile law or sanctions of the juvenile law can be applied)	Age range for youth detention/custody or similar forms of deprivation of liberty
Austria		14	18/21	14–27
Belgium		18	16ⁿ/18	Only welfare institutions
Belarus		14ᵇ/16	14/16	14–21
Bulgaria		14	18	14–21
Croatia		14/16ᶜ	18/21	14–21
Cyprus		14	16/18/21	14–21
Czech Republic		15	18/18 + (mit. sent.)	15–19
Denmarkᵈ		15	15/18/21	15–23
England/Wales		10/12/15ᶜ	18	10/15–21
Estonia		14	18	14–21
Finlandᵈ		15	15/18	15–21
France	10	13	18	13–18 + 6 m./23
Germany		14	18/21	14–24
Greece	8	13	18/21	13–21/25
Hungary		14	18	14–24
Ireland		10/12/16ᶜ	18	10/12/16–18/21
Italy		14	18/21	14–21
Latvia		14	18	14–21
Lithuania		14ᵇ/16	18/21	14–21
Macedonia		14ᵇ/16	14/16	14–21
Moldova		14ᵇ/16	14/16	14–21
Montenegro		14/16ᶜ	18/21	14–23
Netherlands		12	16/18/21	12–21
Northern Ireland		10	17/18/21	10–16/17–21
Norwayᵈ		15	18	15–21

(continued)

Table 13.1 (continued)

Country	Minimum age educational measures of family/youth court (juvenile welfare law)	Age of criminal responsibility (juvenile criminal law)	Full criminal responsibility (adult criminal law can/must be applied; juvenile law or sanctions of the juvenile law can be applied)	Age range for youth detention/custody or similar forms of deprivation of liberty
Poland	13		15/17/18	13–18/15–21
Portugal	12		16/21	12/16–21
Romania		14/16	18/(20)	16–21
Russia		14[b]/16	18/21	14–21
Scotland	8	16	16/21	16–21
Serbia		14/16[c]	18/21	14–23
Slovakia		14/15	18/21	14–18
Slovenia		14[b]/16	18/21	14–23
Spain		14	18	14–21
Sweden[d]		15	15/18/21	15–25
Switzerland	10	10	18[e]	10/15–22
Turkey	12	12	15/18	12–18/21
Ukraine		14[b]/16	18/21	14–21

[a] Only for road offences and exceptionally for very serious offences
[b] Only for serious offences
[c] Criminal majority concerning juvenile detention (youth imprisonment, etc.)
[d] Only mitigation of sentencing without separate juvenile justice legislation
[e] The Swiss penal Code provides as a special (educational) sanction the detention in an institution for young adults aged 18–25, where they can stay until the age of 30, see Art. 61 Swiss PC.
© Frieder Dünkel, University of Greifswald/Germany

Russia and other Eastern European countries). After the contemporary reforms in Central and Eastern Europe, the most common age of criminal responsibility is 14 (see Table 13.1).

In part, purely educational sanctions of the family and youth courts are applicable at an earlier age, as has most recently and explicitly been the case in France (from the age of 10 upwards) and Greece (from the age of 8). In Switzerland, the law only provides educational measures for 10- to 14-year-olds, whereas youth imprisonment is restricted to juveniles at the age of at least 15.

Further still, some countries employ a graduated scale of criminal responsibility, according to which only more serious and grave offences can be prosecuted from the age of 14, while the general minimum age of criminal responsibility lies at 16 (see Lithuania, Russia, Slovenia).

Whether these notable differences can in fact be correlated to variations in sentencing is not entirely clear. For within a system based exclusively on education, under certain circumstances the possibility of being accommodated in a home or in residential care (particularly in the form of closed or secure centres such as in England or France) as a "last-resort" can be just as intensive and of an equal (or even longer) duration as a sentence to juvenile imprisonment. Furthermore, the legal levels of criminal responsibility do not necessarily give any indication of whether the practice under juvenile justice or welfare is more or less punitive. Practice often differs considerably from the language used in the reform debates (see Doob and Tonry 2004, p. 16 ff.). Accordingly, legal intensifications are sometimes the *result* of changes in practice, and sometimes they contribute to changes in practice. Despite the dramatization of certain events by the mass media in some countries, there is for instance in Germany a remarkable degree of stability in juvenile justice practice (see Dünkel 2002; 2003b; 2006).

Chapter 4 draws attention to the fact that most countries have several age limits in juvenile justice, which are related to the age of prosecution. For example in countries which maintain some form of the *doli incapax* presumption, children are prosecuted some years later than the lower age of criminal responsibility, while in others prosecution will effectively take place at that specific age. In some jurisdictions there is a different age limit for status offences, while the Scandinavian countries – which have no juvenile justice system – have a special "intermediate" legislation for those aged 15–21, so as to avoid prosecution of this age group in the criminal court.

In view of the many variations in age limits of criminal responsibility, one wonders whether it would be possible to arrive at a satisfactory age limit which has reasonable validity on the basis of the present level of scientific knowledge and which would be acceptable to many states. In this respect we feel that chapter 3 gives us a number of valid arguments to try to propose such a general lower age limit of at least 14 years of age (see below).

The point of departure is the lack of maturity in decision-making capacities of adolescents – where adolescence is defined as the period between age 11/12–17/18 – compared with that of adults. Decision-making requires effective cognitive abilities, but these may be influenced by psychosocial factors such as susceptibility to peer influence, willingness to take risks, the lack of orientation to the future and impulsive reactions to emotional arousal (see chapter 3).

There now is neuroscientific evidence for continued maturation of the brain during, and even after adolescence. At the same time specific brain functions go together with behavioural and psychosocial shortcomings in adolescent's decision-making, suggesting a clear link. Moreover, these factors are developing and maturing during adolescence until about age 15–17. An empirical fact is that most young people aged 18–20 abandon delinquent behaviour when accepting adult responsibilities.

On the basis of the present scientific evidence a reasonable recommendation would be to determine the age of criminal responsibility at age 14 and the age of criminal majority at age 18–21.

Since the lower age is based on what we now know about the objective lack of capacities in decision-making under the age of 14, the age limit of criminal responsibility should be absolute and independent of the seriousness of the committed offence. For the upper age of 18–21 pleads the fact that it is in accordance with other civil age limits such as the right to vote, to get married, to drive a car or to join the army.

This is in agreement with the European Rules for Juvenile Offenders Subject to Sanctions or Measures (see chapter 3). According to the commentary on Rule 4 "… The majority of countries have fixed the minimum age between 14 and 15 years and this standard should be followed in Europe".

Rule 17 of the European rules is addressing the position of young adults aged 18–21, stating that "….in general they are in a transitional stage of life, which can justify their being dealt with by the juvenile justice agencies and juvenile courts" and pleads for mitigation of sentences and the application of educational sanctions and measures available for juveniles. The application of sanctions and measures of the juvenile laws to young adults reflects the extended transition to adulthood in modern societies and the fact that young adults can be better dealt with by the more constructive and educational sanctions of juvenile justice and welfare.

We fully endorse these rules and we hope that they will be adopted in all European states.

The Transfer of Minors to the Criminal Court

Most of us are familiar with the practice of transferring minors to the adult court of criminal justice in the United States. There has been an extreme increase in this practice since the 1980s, reflected in the gradual lowering of the juveniles' ages required to allow transfer as well as in the harshness and length of prison terms imposed on them (see chapter 4). However, since about 2000 there are signs of change. These are expressed in a decision of the Supreme Court that abolished capital punishment for minors under age 18 at the time of the offence. It is interesting to note that the decision was based on neuroscientific evidence that one cannot hold adolescents to adult standards of criminal responsibility (see chapter 3).

Change is also occurring in individual US states: two states rose the age of criminal responsibility from 16 to 18, Florida reduced the number of transfers by two thirds and several states abolished life sentences for juveniles and barred drug offences from transfer. These are hopeful signs and may signal a coming halt to equating juvenile justice with adult criminal justice.

However, there are also European systems which allow such transfers, often in the age group 16–18. Research on this problem between 1998 and 2004 done in two of them – the Netherlands and Belgium – is reported in chapter 5. Two outcomes deserve to be repeated here. The first is that transfer in both countries is very limited, referring to a small group of offenders and showing great stability over the years. The second is that transfer is not limited to serious violent offenders: the majority of committed offences in The Netherlands were property offences – thefts, followed by robberies, and in Belgium thefts, in some exceptional cases with aggravated circumstances. This is all the more serious in the light of the American follow-up studies on reconvictions of transferred juveniles as compared with similar offenders who remained in juvenile institutions (see Chapter 4). Transferred juveniles re-offended more quickly, more frequently and committed more serious and violent offences. Pinning down the differences between proceedings in the juvenile court and in adult court, research showed more opportunities for therapy, education and training in juvenile institutions, more sympathetic and better trained staff, and – last but not least – better perspectives of reintegration into society. Moreover, the long time company of older, serious offenders has a pernicious influence on developing adolescents.

Both what actual scientific knowledge has taught us about adolescent development and what we know about transfer proceedings lead us to one inescapable conclusion: the transfer of juveniles to adult criminal court should be abolished and all youth under the age of legal criminal majority should be judged in the juvenile justice system.

Parental Responsibility

Parents have always had some responsibility for their children's behaviour regulated by civil law. But this responsibility was in most cases limited to paying compensation in cases of damages caused by the child.

However, a number of countries want to do more and have taken legislative steps to punish parents according to penal law in cases where their children have committed offences or shown antisocial behaviour, such as throwing stones, harassing their neighbours, spraying graffiti or playing truant. Punishing parents have been introduced in England and Wales, Ireland, Scotland, Australia and the USA.[3]

The simplistic idea of punishing parents is based on the premise that juveniles offend because their parents fail to control them and that if you punish parents they

---

[3] A proposal for fining parents for the behaviour of their children had been put forward in The Netherlands but has not been pursued.

will understand that they have to change their behaviour and must better supervise their children.

In chapter 6, the author examines the relationship between parenting and youth offending and places question marks regarding the effectiveness of punishing parents to curb delinquency. It is true that parent malfunctioning has a great influence on the child's behaviour. However, parents do not operate in a vacuum and are themselves subject to the social and economic conditions in which they live. Unemployment, poverty, family conflict, family break-up, teen age parenthood, debts, alcohol- and drug abuse, psychosocial problems and psychiatric disorders are all implied in parent's failings to raise their children properly. In addition, most of these children live in deprived neighbourhoods where there is ample opportunity to offend. In a recent Dutch study we found that having unemployed parents was related to poor school achievement and to truancy, two variables predicting delinquency. Moreover, living in a deprived neighbourhood was directly related to offending (Junger-Tas et al. 2008).

If the state wants to punish such parents a prerequisite would be that the state had taken its duty towards its citizens and had provided all possible support and assistance to overcome the many problems parents are wrestling with. The argument can be made that in many cases the state fails in providing for adequate, prompt and sufficient assistance to problem families. Because of waiting lists, budget cuts, lack of collaboration between social agencies, lack of skilled staff, and insufficient mental health care, much support comes too late, is insufficient and ineffective.

We may conclude that punishing parents does not solve the many problems families of offending children suffer, and may even make things worse. If parents do not exercise more control on their children it is often by feelings of powerlessness rather than by indifference or ill will. Punishing parents for the behaviour of their children is a bad idea: it is counterproductive and should not be adopted in Juvenile justice legislation.

The Prevention of Juvenile Delinquency

Preventative measures instead of punishment should be addressed to parents and children. There is a broad consensus among criminologists, sociologists and developmental psychologists about the underlying risk factors of delinquency. These are found in the child, in the family and in the environment where the child is living. Important factors are, for example, an aggressive temperament, hyperactivity, family conflict, lack of parents' supervision, harsh and inconsistent discipline, poverty, deprived neighbourhood and a deviant peer group. Little attention has been given to the fact that crime is not the only outcome of such risk factors. Other adverse outcomes are poor health, frequent hospital admissions for illness, injuries and accidents, psychosocial and psychiatric problems, and unstable marriages. It should be kept in mind that none of these factors suffices to predict criminality. This illustrates the difficulty of predicting adequately later criminal behaviour, in particular if one defines criminality by criminal convictions for serious and chronic delinquency. An illustration is given in chapter 8, referring to Farrington and West's longitudinal study of 411 lower class London boys (Farrington and West 1990). Of all boys subject to poor parenting, having a criminal parent, coming from a large family, having a low IQ or living in a low-income family, only about one third became juvenile offenders. Moreover, although 70% of this group were defined as "very troublesome" at age 8–10, only 19% turned into repeated offenders and only 6% became so-called persistent offenders (Farrington 1987). The main problem being one of huge over-prediction, one should keep in mind that only a combination of multiple risk factors may lead to criminal behaviour. Moreover, we should not expect too much from prediction: children are malleable, "maturation" will occur, living circumstances may change; all these may result in behaviour change.

This does not mean that prevention of delinquency as well as of other adverse outcomes is not a worthwhile goal. The question is what should be the primary target of our efforts. Most of the prevention programs have been developed in the United States and are addressed to young children and/or their parents. Many of these have been conducted over a long period and were tested on their effectiveness. Unfortunately this is rare in Europe and it is one of the reasons we adopt so many American programmes. A disadvantage is that in most of these programmes the direct environment – the neighbourhood – where the child is living, plays no role. This might have to do with the fact that social support for poor families is less prominent in the USA than it is in Europe.

All the same, similar to prevailing trends in health policies, where prevention is since long a normal course of action, it is important to reflect on how to prevent delinquency rather than react after the fact. In this respect prevention programmes need to be addressed to parents, to their children and to the communities where they live.

First of all, local communities as well as the state have a special responsibility in preventing youth crime by developing policies to improve social housing, provide for sufficient social support services to assist multiple problem families, to guarantee quality schools, adequate vocational training options, and create employment possibilities for young people. In addition, local youth policies should include specialized health services for young people, create sports- and recreation opportunities, and deliver special assistance to young people in trouble.

Second, prevention programmes that target children should particularly be addressed to young children. Research has found that early interventions with young children have considerably more effects than later treatment of young delinquents (Tremblay and Craig 1995; Lösel and Beelmann 2005; 2006; Welsh and Farrington 2006; Beelmann and Raabe 2007; Krüger 2009).

In this respect great investments should be made in the education system by introducing early cognitive stimulation programmes to children aged 3–8 and by reducing learning disabilities. Moreover, social competence programmes in the school diminish aggression and behavioural problems in the classroom and improve learning. If young people have a successful school career, they will not develop a criminal career. In addition, they will have better jobs, higher incomes, will less rely on state benefits, have more stable marriages and better (mental) health.

Third, we propose a combined approach, adding prevention policies targeting families who present many risk factors. The justification for intervention may be found in the multitude of risk factors, which, if we do not do anything, will lead to marginalised and unhappy lives of their children at high costs to society. Thus at the same time prevention programmes are administered to young children, their parents should be approached with programmes that promote their caretaking skills and teach them what the community expects of them in terms of preparing their children to fulfill a useful role in society. Parents should be recruited as a matter of course and if there is no reaction, home visits should be made. In addition, the emphasis of parent training should not be placed on what they may have done wrong, but instead on information about how society is organised, how the school system is operating, what qualities children have to possess to be prepared for the labour market, and what parents may and should do to help them. Such parent training programmes should be repeated at the moment their children enter secondary education, preventing truancy and school drop-out. Since it is of great importance that parents attend these programmes, some modest financial incentive may be considered, for example, justified on the basis of parental investment in time and effort.

Should we exclude all compulsory programmes? We would not go as far as that. For example, in cases of child abuse and substance abuse or serious antisocial behaviour of the child, the court could exercise some pressure on parents to follow a programme such as Triple P, Functional Family Therapy, Child-Parent Interaction Programme, alongside other measures (see in detail Welsh and Farrington 2006; Beelmann and Raabe 2007). The Court could sentence the child to a (conditional) supervision order and propose Parent Training as an alternative to residential care, while following and supporting parents for some extended time.

Detention of Juvenile Offenders

In some European countries, juveniles are still locked up in adult prisons. Fortunately most countries have special institutions for juveniles, because young people held in prison have more discipline problems, are more often victim of violence and get less education or treatment because of staff shortage. Although youth institutions vary greatly in size and in form (closed, semiopen and open), they are always superior to prisons for a number of reasons. They are usually smaller in size, they have more staff and they are more oriented to education, treatment and care (see also chapter 6).

This being said conditions in youth establishments are not always good. Many of them, particularly in Central and Eastern European countries, still have dormitories or cell sharing which may lead to all forms of violence. Some institutions employ solitary confinement, physical punishment or collective punishment, handcuffing, and restraint by force as measures of discipline. These measures are used in particular where there is not enough well-trained staff. Many mix juveniles on remand with sentenced juveniles as well as with juveniles who are there for their own protection.

This is all the more damaging in the light of empirical findings that a (long) stay in an institution together with other delinquent or problematic juveniles is harmful for the development of adolescents (Dishion et al. 1999; Warr 2002; Gifford-Smith et al. 2005; Cho et al. 2005). Informal subcultures are formed and are controlled by the toughest delinquents, causing what is called "deviancy training". For example, Dutch research (Wartna et al. 2005) showed that 41% of juveniles, who had not had previous contacts with the juvenile justice system before being detained in a youth institution, were reconvicted after being released.

Parents are rarely involved in educative or treatment measures, which is absurd since most youth will return home after their stay in the institution. Finally, hardly anything is done to prepare the young people for their return to the community, nor is there any provision for sufficient aftercare, in order to bridge the difficult re-adaptation to ordinary life.

In addition, in many countries in Europe there is an increase of juveniles who are processed by the juvenile justice system and end up in detention either in pretrial detention or sentenced to custody. For example, in The Netherlands the number of places has increased fourfold between 1995 and 2006, while the number of sentences to custody increased by 82% (van der Heide and Eggen 2007). However, most juveniles are detained in pretrial detention, either as a form of punishment, to alleviate public unrest, or as a crisis intervention. A Dutch study in 2005 showed that 27% of detained juveniles had committed a property offence without violence and that 46% had only committed 1–2 offences before being sent to custody (Wartna et al. 2005). Moreover, recidivism after detention was sky-rocketing (Van der Heiden-Attema and Wartna 2000). Recidivism is highest after unconditional custody or internment: 84% of these juveniles are reconvicted in a period of 7 years with an average of six new contacts with the justice system. Similar results have been obtained in Germany (see Dünkel in Dünkel et al. 2009).

We can only conclude that locking up children to punish and discipline them and prevent them to offend again is vastly overrated. We are expecting too much of custody both in terms of general and special prevention and of rehabilitation. Indeed we have to reconsider seriously the function of detention in preventing crime. It is clear that detention has a punishment function, but it seems to us that this function can also be fulfilled in other ways. In this respect we do propose the following measures to be taken.

In addition to a specific youth psychiatric institution for mentally disturbed young offenders, we would need only a few small secure units for serious violent or persistent offenders. These should receive education, training and treatment either individually or in small groups. There is much to say for using a risk taxation instrument at intake, on the condition that its validity is empirically tested and that it is also measuring the problems and needs of the young person for care and treatment interventions.

The intramural period should be followed as soon as possible by extramural execution of the sanction. A good example of such execution is a European-funded programme called "Work wise". From the start of custody the juvenile is trained in a job according to market requirements, he is then placed outside the establishment for further training, and when released led to employment. Moreover, 6 months aftercare, housing and a social network are provided for by the institution.

Furthermore, parents should be allowed to visit regularly their child and should be involved as much as possible in all treatment measures taken, thus maximizing the home situation when the juvenile is released. In this respect it should be recalled that family bonds remain in tact throughout life and are rarely (completely) broken. Finally, knowing the risks of re-offending when the youth is returning to the community, a period of at least 6 months of aftercare is required, making sure the juvenile is adequately housed, is following training or is employed, and has a regular social network supporting him. These proposals are very much in line with the European Rules for Juveniles Subject to Sanctions or Measures of 2008, which should be used as guidelines for reforming institutions for the rehabilitation of young offenders deprived of their liberty (see also Dünkel 2008a; 2008b and chapter 3).

If some measure is required between custody and ambulatory alternatives one might impose electronic monitoring as long as this is accompanied by a clear rehabilitation trajectory implying training, employment or therapy, under strict supervision by a social worker.

However, in most cases community sanctions are possible and are to be preferred. These include fines, paying damages, all forms of reparation to the victim, diversion, restorative justice, community service; training programmes, such as social skills training, special vocational training, aggression reduction; programmes such as multi-systemic therapy, drugs- or alcohol therapy, psychosocial day treatment. These subjects are dealt with in the following sections.

Diversion

Diversion may be defined as an informal measure to avoid prosecution of the juvenile by the juvenile justice system. Diversion can be applied on the level of the police (Netherlands) or on the level of the prosecutor (Germany) in cases of petty crimes. There are two principal reasons for the application of diversion. The first is that the procedure relieves judicial authorities of the burden to have to formally process petty delinquency cases. The second reason is that formal juvenile justice intervention – with the possibility of a criminal record – may be more harmful to the young person than some unofficial measure. This is all the more so since these measures are addressed preferably to the victims of the offense and should have an educational character. Diversionary measures include fines, reparation to the victim by voluntary work or restitution, paying damages, offering apologies, or performing a limited number of hours of community service. Is diversion effective in terms of reducing recidivism? The evidence is mixed but tends to show that in the case of police diversion most young people do not come again in contact with the police after being diverted. However, on the basis of what we know about juvenile offending, they would probably not have come back even when nothing was done. Moreover, police diversion has had massive net-widening effects, drawing petty antisocial acts into police nets, followed by police intervention and registration. That is why we would plead for abolishing police diversion, (re)establishing a special juvenile police service and giving (back) to the police some degree of discretionary power to decide whether a case should be prosecuted or dismissed, eventually after some reprimand in presence of the parents.

Diversion by the prosecutor is different though, since the latter deals with cases submitted to him by the police. The prosecutor has the competence to dismiss cases after consideration of their seriousness. In this situation imposing some diversionary measures instead of referring the case to the juvenile judge is to be encouraged because it will save the young person a stigmatizing criminal record. There are indications that these measures are more effective in reducing recidivism than official prosecution in court (and eventual detention). However, more evaluation research is needed. From German and English research one can at least conclude that young offenders, diverted from formal court proceedings, do not re-offend more frequently than those formally sanctioned. Diversion has a warning function and impresses most juveniles sufficiently. And importantly, it is a cost-saving strategy of the juvenile justice system. Therefore there are good reasons for preferring prosecutorial diversion: given the temporary character of most juvenile delinquency, diversion is less stigmatizing and less harmful to young people and does not place as heavy a burden on their future as does a conviction or – worse – custody.

Restorative Justice

This is a quite different concept of justice than the traditional one of the system representing the state in recreating order by punishing the offender. Based on the notion that crime is in most cases a violation of people and relationships restorative justice reduces the role of the state and places the offender, victim – and eventually other interested family or friends – together, in order to set right the wrongs caused by the offender to the victim (see chapter 10), a process that should lead to forgiveness and reconciliation.

The idea of restorative justice is appealing to many and is endorsed by the European Union, the Council of Europe and the UN. But since its definition is rather vague, the practice shows great variation: in the extent to which it is integrated in existing juvenile justice structures; in its degree of legality or formality; in the agencies applying the programme (police or local organisations); and in the involvement of victims in the process.

Victim–offender mediation programmes are among the most popular and are adopted in the USA and Canada as well as in Europe. Usually victim and offender meet with a mediator facilitating the process to put right the harm caused.

A less attractive form – at least to these authors – are the Community Reparation Boards, used in the USA and in England and Wales as well as the English Youth Offender Panels, to which non-violent or first time offenders are referred by the court. These bodies then decide what is going to happen to the offender and which action should be taken. In the United Kingdom and in Northern Ireland police-led restorative cautioning programmes are rather similar to the Dutch police diversion, but all these schemes are characterized by low victim involvement, no evidence of the process being an alternative to prosecution, and by considerable net-widening. Moreover, in this model young people cannot have legal representation and the process may in some cases be too coercive.

The best known restorative model is family group conferencing, which Northern Ireland has integrated in its juvenile justice system. For reasons of "accountability, certainty and legitimacy" the model is based in statute. By doing that, the country has solved several problems related to the original model characterized by informality, variable approaches of a more or less coercive character, differential victim involvement and a weak legal position of the offender caused by the lack of legal representation.

Diversionary conferences are ordered by the prosecutor in cases where offenders should normally be referred to the juvenile judge but where the offender had admitted guilt and has consented to the process. The conference coordinator must provide a plan on how to deal with the offender. If the plan is successfully completed the case is dismissed and the juvenile will have no criminal conviction. Conferences can also be ordered by the court. In fact all court cases must be referred to a conference, except a small group of very serious cases. The conference designs an action plan taking into account the offense, the needs of the victim and the needs of the young person, which must be completed in 1 year. According to one study in 2007, victims were involved in 69% of conferences: 40% were personal victims (most of violence), 60% were victim representatives (mainly of theft). Importantly, victims were not motivated by a desire to seek vengeance and showed no signs of hostility towards the offender. Most cases ended with an apology and some form of reparation or work done for the victim. Although offenders were motivated by their desire to avoid court appearance and felt nervous at the prospect of meeting their victim, they accepted their responsibility, sought forgiveness and were able to put the offense behind them. Most of the action plans contained elements to help offender and victim and 73% had no specific punishment element. In fact victims preferred the conference process instead of going to court: the conference provided for both parties a meaningful event and appeared to be a way of moving forward.

The authors conclude by stating that conferencing in Northern Ireland has been shown to be a successful way to deliver justice that holds the offender accountable for his acts while giving victims a voice in the process, producing high levels of satisfaction for participants.

Conclusions

In this chapter we have taken clear positions with respect to juvenile justice reform, based on the present level of research evidence. Summarizing the outcomes presents the following picture.

- Full respect of young people's rights in juvenile justice according to the UN Convention of the Rights of the Child and the various Recommendations of the Council of Europe.
- Fixing the age of criminal responsibility at 14–15 and the age of criminal majority at 18–21 – in view of present knowledge on brain development, including the option for young adults to be judged according to juvenile justice legislation.
- Abolition of the transfer of juveniles under age 18 to adult courts, in view of the harmful effects of harsher sentences and particularly of prison.
- No punishment for parents for delinquent acts of their children. Instead, parent collaboration should be sought with all measures addressed to their children.
- Considerable investments should be made by authorities in prevention: evidence-based programmes should be addressed to young children, schools, parents and communities.
- Custody should be restricted to violent offenders, who should be detained in a few small secure (psychiatric or social therapeutic) units. Parents should be involved in evidence-based treatment, and a period of aftercare (6–12 months) should be compulsory.
- Extra-mural execution should be imposed as a matter of course in the form of community sanctions, training and employment.
- Diversion at the level of the prosecutor should be encouraged, while police diversion should be abolished.
- Restorative justice in statute and integrated in the juvenile justice system offers an interesting perspective, on the condition that the victim is involved and the rights of the offender safeguarded.

However, there are a number of conditions that have to be fulfilled if reform is to be realized.

First, investments are necessary in juvenile justice establishments: more personnel, better working conditions, more higher trained collaborators. This should reflect growing appreciation for those who work with difficult children.

Second, the system would need extra resources in training adequate staff for the many different functions: for applying evidence-based programmes in prevention, within establishments, and in community programmes, for managing and implementing reform, such as the restorative justice model. Moreover, training facilities should have a permanent character in view of personnel mutations.

Third, special training should be given to probation workers, who have to administer programmes, control and guide young people in the community, and a role of great responsibility. This is all the more important since popular support and public opinion depends on the success of these interventions.

Fourth, juvenile justice research in the workings of the system, as well as in evaluation research of innovative programmes, remains all important in order to go on improving the system.

Bibliography

Administration for Children, Youth and Families. (1983): *The Effects of the Head Start Program on Children's Cognitive Development. Preliminary Report.* Washington, DC: U.S. Department of Health and Human Services.

Advisory Commission on Criminal Justice Standards and Goals. (1973) (Ed.): *Task Force on Corrections.* Washington, DC.

Aebi, M., et al. (2006): *European Sourcebook of Crime and Criminal Justice Statistics – 2006.* 3rd ed., Den Haag: WODC.

Albrecht, H.J. (2004): Youth Justice in Germany, in Tonry, M. & Doob, A.N. (eds.) *Youth Crime and Youth Justice,* Chicago: University of Chicago Press, 443–493.

Alexander, P. W. (1948): What's this about punishing parents? *Federal Probation* 12, 23–29.

Andrews, D. A., Bonta, J., Hoge, R. D. (1990a): Classification for effective rehabilitation: rediscovering psychology. *Criminal Justice and Behavior* 17, 19–52.

Andrews, D. A., et al. (1990b): Does correctional treatment work? A clinically relevant and psychologically informed meta-analysis. *Criminology* 28, 369–404.

Anneveldt Committee, (1982): *Sanctierecht voor jeugdigen, Rapport van de Commissie voor de herziening van het kinderstrafrecht en het kinderstrafprocesrecht,* 's-Gravenhage: Staatsuitgeverij.

Applebome, P. (1996): Parents face consequences as children's misdeeds rise. *The New York Times,* April 10.

Arthur, R. (2002): Tackling youth crime: supporting families in crisis. *Child and Family Law Quarterly* 14, 401–426.

Arthur, R. (2005): Punishing parents for the crimes of their children. *Howard Journal of Criminal Justice* 44, 233–253.

Arthur, R. (2007a): *Family Life and Youth Offending: Home Is Where the Hurt Is.* London: Routledge.

Arthur, R. (2007b): Youth crime prevention – the role of children's services. In: Davies, Z., McMahon, W. (Eds.): *Debating Youth Justice: From Punishment to Problem Solving?* London: Centre for Crime and Justice Studies, King's College.

Ashford, M., Chard, A. (2000): *Defending Young People in the Criminal Justice System.* 2nd ed., London: Legal Action Group.

Ashworth, A. (1992): *What Victims of Crime Deserve.* Paper presented to the Fulbright Commission on Penal Theory and Penal Practice, September 1992, University of Stirling, Stirling.

Audit Commission. (1999): *Children in Mind: Child and Adolescent Mental Health Services.* London: Audit Commission.

Austin, J., Krisberg, B. (1981): Wider, stronger and different nets: the dialectics of criminal justice reform. *Journal of Research in Crime and Delinquency* 18, 165–196.

Austin, J., Krisberg, B. (1982): The unmet promise of alternatives to incarceration. *Crime and Delinquency* 28, 374–409.

Bailleau, F., Cartuyvels, Y. (2007) (Eds.): *La Justice Pénale des Mineurs en Europe – Entre modèle Welfare et infléxions néo-libérales.* Paris: L'Harmattan.

Bakker, I., Bakker, K., van Dijke, A., Terpstra, L. (1997): *O + O = O² – Naar een samenhangend beleid en aanbod van Opvoedings-ondersteuning en Ontwikkelingsstimulering voor kinderen en ouders in risicosituaties.* Utrecht: NIZW.

Ball, C., Connolly, J. (2000): Educationally disaffected young offenders - youth court and agency response to truancy and school exclusion. *British Journal of Criminology* 40, 594–616.

Ball, C., McCormac, K., Stone, N. (2001): *Young Offenders: Law, Policy and Practice.* 2nd ed., London: Sweet and Maxwell.

Banay, R. S. (1947): Homicide among children. *Federal Probation* 11, 11–20.

Bannenberg, B., Rössner, D. (2003): New developments in restorative justice to handle family violence. In: Weitekamp, E., Kerner, H. (Eds.): *Restorative Justice in Context: International Practice and Directions.* Cullompton: Willan Publishing.

Barclay, G., Tavares, C. (1999): *Digest 4: Information on the Criminal Justice System in England and Wales.* London: Research, Development & Statistics Directorate.

Barclay, G., Taares, C., Siddique, A. (2001): *International Comparisons of Criminal Justice Statistics 1999.* London: Research, Development & Statistics Directorate.

Bareinske, C. (2004): *Sanktion und Legalbewährung im Jugendstrafverfahren in Baden-Württemberg.* Freiburg i. Br.: Max-Planck-Institut für ausländisches und internationales Strafrecht.

Barnum, R. (1987): Biomedical problems in juvenile delinquency: issues in diagnosis and treatment. In: Wilson, J. Q., Loury, G. C. (Eds.): *From Children to Citizens: Families, Schools and Delinquency Prevention.* New York: Springer, pp. 51–87.

Bartol, C. R., Bartol, A. M. (1998): *Delinquency and Justice: A Psychological Approach.* Englewood Cliffs, NJ:Prentice Hall.

Bazemore, G., Umbreit, M. (2004): *Balanced and Restorative Justice.* Washington: Office for Juvenile Justice and Delinquency Prevention.

Beelmann, A., Raabe, T. (2007): *Dissoziales Verhalten von Kindern und Jugendlichen.* Göttingen et al.: Hogrefe.

Belsky, J., Melhuish, E., Barnes, J., Leyland, H., Romaniuk, H. (2006): Effects of surestart local programmes on children and families: early findings from a quasi-experimental, cross sections study. *British Medical Journal* 332, 1476–1748.

Bennett, T. (2000): *Drugs and Crime: The Results of the Second Developmental Stage of the NEW-ADAM Programme.* London: Home Office.

Bishop, D. M., Decker, S. H. (2006): Punishment and control: Juvenile Justice Reform in the USA, in: J. Junger-Tas & S. H. Decker (Eds.) *International Handbook of Juvenile Justice* (pp. 3–35) Dordrecht: Springer.

Bishop, D. M., Frazier, C. E. (2000): The consequences of transfer. In: Fagan, J., Zimring, F. (Eds.): *The Changing Borders of Juvenile Justice: Transfer of Adolescents to the Criminal Court.* Chicago: University of Chicago Press, pp. 227–276.

Bishop, D. M., Frazier, C. E., Lanza-Kaduce, L., Winner, L. (1996): The transfer of juveniles to criminal court: does it make a difference? *Crime and Delinquency* 42, 171–191.

Bol, M. W., Terlouw, G. J., Blees, L. W., Verwers, C. (1998): Jong en gewelddadig; ontwikkeling en achtergronden vande geweldscriminaliteit onder jeugdigen. *Onderzoek en beleid* 174.

Bottoms, A. E., Dignan, J. (2004): Youth justice in Great Britain. In: Tonry, M., Doob, A. N. (Eds.): *Youth Crime and Youth Justice: Comparative and Cross-national Perspectives. Crime and Justice: A Review of Research,* Vol. 31. Chicago: University of Chicago Press, pp. 21–183.

Braithwaite, J. (1989): *Crime, Shame and Reintegration.* Cambridge: Cambridge University Press.

Braithwaite, J. (2002): *Restorative Justice and Responsive Regulation.* New York: Oxford University Press.

Braithwaite, J., Mugford, S. (1994): Conditions of successful reintegration ceremonies: dealing with juvenile offenders. *British Journal of Criminology* 34, 139.

Breckenridge, S. P., Abbott, E. (1912): *The Delinquent Child and The Home*. New York: Charities Publication Committee.

Brownlee, S. (1999): Inside the teen brain. *U.S. News and World Report*, August 9, 44–48.

Bruckmüller, K. (2006): Austria: a protection model. In: Junger-Tas, J., Decker, S. H. (Eds.): *International Handbook of Juvenile Justice*. Berlin, New York: Springer, pp. 263–294.

Bruckmüller, K., Pilgram, A., Stummvoll, G. (2009): Austria. In: Dünkel, F., Grzywa, J., Pruin, I. (Eds.): *Juvenile Justice Systems in Europe – Current Situation, Reform Developments and Good Practices*. Mönchengladbach: Forum Verlag Godesberg (in preparation).

Bruins, J. (1999): De Stopreactie voor kinderen jonger dan twaalf jaar, *Proces* 7/8, 110–113.

Bulten, E., van Limbeek, J., Wouters, L., Geerlings, P., van Tilburg, W. (1992): *Psychische stoornissen in Detentie*. Vught: Brakkenstein.

Bundesministerium der Justiz. (1989) (Ed.): *Jugendstrafrechtsreform durch die Praxis*. Bonn: Bundesministerium der Justiz.

Bureau of Justice Statistics. (1997): *Correctional Populations in the United States, 1995*. Washington, DC: United States Department of Justice.

Buruma, Y. (2004): Doubts on the upsurge of the victim's role in criminal law. In: Kaptein, H., Malsch, M. (Eds.): *Crime, Victims, and Justice. Essays on Principles and Practice*. Aldershot: Ashgate.

Burman, M., Bradshaw, P., Hutton , N., McNeill, F., Munro, M. (2006): The End of an Era? Youth Justice in Scotland, in: : J. Junger-Tas & S.H. Decker (Eds.) *International Handbook of Juvenile Justice* (pp. 439–471) Dordrecht: Springer.

Campbell, C., Devlin, R., O'Mahony, D., Doak, J., Jackson, J., Corrigan, T., McEvoy, K. (2006): *Evaluation of the Northern Ireland Youth Conference Service NIO Research and Statistics Series: Report No. 12*. Belfast: Northern Ireland Office.

Carlile (2006): Independent inquiry by Lord Carlile of Berriew QC into physical restraint, solitary confinement and forcible strip searching of children in prisons, secure training centres and local authority secure children's homes.

Casto, G., White, K. (1984): The efficacy of early intervention programs with environmentally at-risk infants. *Journal of Children in Contemporary Society* 17, 37–50.

Catalano, R. F., Hawkins, J. D. (1996): The social development model: a theory of antisocial behavior. In: Hawkins, J. D. (Ed.): *Delinquency and Crime – Current Theories*. Cambridge: Cambridge University Press, pp. 149–198.

Cauffman, E., Steinberg, L. (2000): (Im)maturity of judgment in adolescence: Why adolescents may be less culpable than adults, *Behavioral Sciences and the Law* 18, 1–21.

Cauffman, E., Steinberg, L. (2000a): Researching adolescents' judgment and culpability. In: Grisso, T., Schwartz, R. G. (Eds.): *Youth on Trial: A Developmental Perspective on Juvenile Justice*. Chicago: University of Chicago Press, pp. 325–343.

Cauffman, E., Steinberg, L. (2000b): (Im)maturity of judgment in adolescence: why adolescents may be less culpable than adults. *Behavioral Sciences and the Law* 18, 741–760.

Cavadino, M., Dignan, J. (2002): *Penal Policy and Political Economy*. Thousand Oaks: Sage.

Cavadino, M., Dignan, J. (2006): *Penal Systems. A Comparative Approach*. Thousand Oaks: Sage.

Cavadino, M., Dignan, J. (2007): *The Penal System: An Introduction*. 4th ed., Thousand Oaks: Sage.

Cedar, B., Levant, R. F. (1990): A meta-analysis of the parent effectiveness training. *American Journal of Family Therapy* 18, 373–384.

Centers for Disease Control and Prevention, U.S. Department of Health and Human Services. (2007): *Effects on Violence of Laws and Policies Facilitating the Transfer of Youth from the Juvenile to the Adult Justice System*. Morbidity and Mortality Weekly Report, Vol. 56, no. RR-9. Atlanta: Centers for Disease Control and Prevention.

Cernkovich, S. A., Giordano, P. C. (1987): Family relationships and delinquency. *Criminology* 25, 295–321.

Chief Secretary to the Treasury. (2003): *Every Child Matters*. London: HMSO.

Cho, H., Hallfors, D. D., Sanchez, V. (2005): Evaluation of a high-school peer group intervention for at-risk youth. *Journal of Abnormal Psychology* 33, 363–382.

Christiaens, J., Dumortier, E. (2009): Belgium. In: Dünkel, F., Grzywa, J., Pruin, I. (Eds.): *Juvenile Justice Systems in Europe – Current Situation, Reform Developments and Good Practices*. Mönchengladbach: Forum Verlag Godesberg (in preparation).

Claassen, R. (1996): *Restorative Justice: Primary Focus on People Not Procedures*. Fresno: Fresno Pacific University. Available at http://peace.fresno.edu/docs/rjprinc2.html.

Cleaver, H., Unell, I., Aldgate, J. (1999): *Children's Needs - Parenting Capacity. The Impact of Parental Mental Illness, Problem Alcohol and Drug Use, and Domestic Violence on Children's Development*. London: The Stationery Office.

Collinson, M. (1994): Drug offenders and criminal justice: careers, compulsion, commitment and penalty. *Crime, Law and Social Change* 21, 49–71.

Commission on Families and Wellbeing of Children. (2005): *Families and the State: Two-Way Support and Responsibilities. An Inquiry into the Relationship Between the State and the Family in the Upbringing of Children*. London: Policy Press.

Cooper, P. (2002): *Delivering Quality Children's Services. Inspection of Children's Services*. London: Department of Health.

Cornish, D. B., Clarke, R. V. G. (1975): *Residential Treatment and Its Effects on Delinquency*, no. 76. London: Home Office Research and Planning Unit.

Council of Europe. (1999): *European Sourcebook of Crime and Criminal Justice Statistics*. Strasbourg: Council of Europe.

Council of Europe. (2003): *European Sourcebook of Crime and Criminal Justice Statistics*. 2nd ed., The Hague: Ministry of Justice, WODC.

Council of Europe. (2006): *European Sourcebook of Crime and Criminal Justice Statistics*. The Hague: Ministry of Justice, WODC.

Craig, G., Adamson, S., Ali, N., Ali, S., Atkins, L., Dadze-Arthur, A., Elliot, C., McNamee, S., Murtuja, B. (2007): *Sure Start and Black and Minority Ethnic Populations*. London: DFES.

Crasmöller, B. (1996): *Wirkungen strafrechtlicher Sozialkontrolle jugendlicher Kriminalität*. Pfaffenweiler: Centaurus Verlag.

Crawford, A., Newburn, T. (2002): Recent developments in restorative justice for young people in England and Wales: community participation and representation. *British Journal of Criminology* 42, 476–495.

Criminal Justice Review Group. (2000): *Review of the Criminal Justice System*. Belfast: HMSO.

Crofts, T. (2002): *The criminal responsibility of children and young persons. A comparison of English and German law*, Burlington: Ashgate.

Cullen, R. (2004): The referral order: the main issues arising from its evaluation and the Youth Justice Board's efforts to address them. *Childright* 204, 8–9.

Cummings, P., Theis, M. K., Mueller, B. A., Rivera, F. P. (1994): Infant injury death in Washington state, 1981 through 1990. *Archives of Pediatrics and Adolescent Medicine* 148, 1041–1054.

Dahl, R. E. (2004): Adolescent brain development: a period of vulnerabilities and opportunities. *Annals of the New York Academy of Sciences* 1021, 1–22.

Davis, G. (1992): *Making Amends: Mediation and Reparation in Criminal Justice*. London: Routledge.

Department of Health. (1991): *The Children Act 1989 Guidance and Regulations Volume 2. Family Support, Day Care and Educational Provision for Young Children*. London: HMSO.

De Regt, A. (1984): *Arbeidersgezinnen en Beschavingsarbeid; Ontwikkelingen in Nederland 1870–1940*. Meppel: Boom.

Dignan, J. (2005): *Understanding Victims and Restorative Justice*. Maidenhead: Open University Press.

Dignan, J. (2009): England. In: Dünkel, F., Grzywa, J., Pruin, I. (Eds.): *Juvenile Justice Systems in Europe – Current Situation, Reform Developments and Good Practices*. Mönchengladbach: Forum Verlag Godesberg (in preparation).

Dignan, J., Lowey, K. (2000): *Restorative Justice Options for Northern Ireland: A Comparative Review*. Belfast: HMSO.

DiIulio, J. (1995): The coming of the super-predators. *The Weekly Standard*, November 19, 23–29.

Dishion, T. J., Dodge, K. A. (2005): Peer contagion in interventions for children and adolescents: moving towards an understanding of the ecology and dynamics of change. *Journal of Abnormal Child Psychology* 33, 395–400.

Dishion, T. J., McCord, J., Poulin, F. (1999): When interventions harm – peer groups and problem behavior. *American Psychologist* 54, 755–764.

Doak, J., O'Mahony, D. (2007): The vengeful victim? Assessing the attitudes of victims participating in restorative youth conferencing. *International Review of Victimology* 13, 157.

Doob, A. N., Tonry, M. (2004): Varieties of youth justice. In: Tonry, M., Doob, A. N. (Eds.): *Youth Crime and Justice*, Crime and Justice, Vol. 31. Chicago: University of Chicago Press, pp. 1–20.

Dooley, M. (1995): *Reparative Probation Program*. Waterbury: Department of Corrections.

Doreleijers, T. A. H. (1995): *Diagnostiek tussen Jeugdstrafrecht en Hulpverlening*. Arnhem: Gouda Quint.

Dreher, G., Feltes, T. (1997) (Eds.): *Das Modell New York: Kriminalprävention durch 'Zero Tolerance'?* Holzkirchen: Felix Verlag.

DSP Research Group. (2004): *Final Report 4 CtC Pilot Sites*. Amsterdam: DSP.

Dünkel, F. (1990): *Freiheitsentzug für junge Rechtsbrecher. Situation und Reform von Jugendstrafe, Jugendstrafvollzug, Jugendarrest und Untersuchungshaft in der Bundesrepublik Deutschland und im internationalen Vergleich*, Bonn: Forum Verlag Godesberg.

Dünkel, F. (2002): Le Droit Pénal des Mineurs en Allemagne: entre un Système de Protection et de Justice. *Déviance et Société* 26, 297–313.

Dünkel, F. (2003a): Entwicklungen der Jugendkriminalität und des Jugendstrafrechts in Europa – ein Vergleich. In: Riklin, F. (Ed.): *Jugendliche, die uns Angst machen. Was bringt das Jugendstrafrecht?* Luzern: Caritas-Verlag, pp. 50–124.

Dünkel, F. (2003b): Youth violence and juvenile justice in Germany. In: Dünkel, F., Drenkhahn, K. (Eds.): *Youth Violence: New Patterns and Local Responses – Experiences in East and West*. Mönchengladbach: Forum Verlag Bad Godesberg, pp. 96–142.

Dünkel, F. (2006): Juvenile justice in Germany: between welfare and justice. In: Junger-Tas, J., Decker, S. H. (Eds.): *International Handbook of Juvenile Justice*. Berlin, New York: Springer, pp. 225–262.

Dünkel, F. (2008a): Jugendstrafrecht im europäischen Vergleich im Licht aktueller Empfehlungen des Europarats. *Neue Kriminalpolitik* 20, 102–114.

Dünkel, F. (2008b): Die Europäische Empfehlung für inhaftierte und ambulant sanktionierte jugendliche Straftäter ("European Rules for Juvenile Offenders Subject to Sanctions and Measures", ERJOSSM) und ihre Bedeutung für die deutsche Gesetzgebung. *Recht der Jugend und des Bildungswesens* 57, 376–404.

Dünkel, F., Baechtold, A., van Zyl Smit, D. (2007): Europäische Mindeststandards und Empfehlungen als Orientierungspunkte für die Gesetzgebung und Praxis – dargestellt am Beispiel der Empfehlungen für inhaftierte Jugendliche und Jugendliche in ambulanten Maßnahmen (die "Greifswald Rules"). In: Goerdeler, J., Walkenhorst, P. (Eds.): *Jugendstrafvollzug in Deutschland. Neue Gesetze, neue Strukturen, neue Praxis?* Mönchengladbach: Forum Verlag Godesberg 2007, 114–140.

Dünkel, F., Grzywa, J., Pruin, I. (2009) (Eds.): *Juvenile Justice Systems in Europe – Current Situation, Reform Developments and Good Practices*. Mönchengladbach: Forum Verlag Godesberg (in preparation).

Dünkel, F., Pruin, I. (2009): Young adult offenders in the criminal justice systems of European countries. In: Lösel, F., Bottoms, A., Farrington, D. (Eds.): *Lost in Transition? Young adult offenders in the criminal justice system*. Devon: Willan Publishing (in print).

Dünkel, F., Sakalauskas, G. (2001): Jugendstrafrecht und Jugendstrafrechtsreform in Litauen. *DVJJ-Journal* 12, 72–80.

Dünkel, F., van Kalmthout, A., Schüler-Springorum, H. (1997) (Eds.): *Entwicklungstendenzen und Reformstrategien im Jugendstrafrecht im europäischen Vergleich*. Mönchengladbach: Forum Verlag Godesberg.

Dünkel, F., Scheel, J., Schäpler, P. (2003): Jugendkriminalität und die Sanktionspraxis im Jugendstrafrecht in Mecklenburg-Vorpommern. *Zeitschrift für Jugendkriminalrecht und Jugendhilfe* 14, 119–132.

Durlak, J. A., Fuhrman, T., Lampman, C. (1991): *Effectiveness of Cognitive Behavior Therapy for Maladapting Children: A Meta-Analysis.* Chicago: Loyola University.

Duzinski, G. A. (1987): *The Educational Utility of Cognitive Behavior Modification Strategies with Children.* Dissertation Abstracts International 48: 339A. Chicago: University of Illinois.

Edgar, N., Newell, T. (2006): Restorative Justice in Prisons: A Guide to Making it Happen. (Winchester, Waterside Press).

Eisner, M. (2002): Crime, problem drinking, and drug use: patterns of problem behavior in cross-national perspective. *The Annals of the American Academy of Political and Social Science* 580, 201–225.

Eisner, M. (2003): *Jahrbuch'03 für Rechts- und Kriminalsoziologie.* Baden-Baden: Nomos Verlagsgesellschaft.

Erez, E., Tontodonato, P. (1992): Victim Participation in Sentencing and Satisfaction with Justice. *Justice Quarterly* 9:394–415.

Eron, L. D. (1990): Understanding aggression. *Bulletin of the International Society for Research on Aggression* 12, 5–9.

Estrada, F. (1999): Juvenile crime trends in post-war Europe. *European Journal on Criminal Policy and Research* 7, 23–42.

Estrada, F. (2001): Juvenile violence as a social problem: trends, media attention and societal response. *British Journal of Sociology* 41, 639–655.

Estrada, F. (2004): The transformation of the politics of crime in high crime societies. *European Journal of Criminology* 1, 419–443.

Fagan, J. (1996): The comparative advantage of juvenile versus criminal court sanctions on recidivism among adolescent felony offenders. *Law and Policy* 18, 77–119.

Fagan, J. (2005): Adolescents, maturity, and the law: why science and development matter in juvenile justice. *American Prospective Online (Special Report: Juvenile Justice)* August 15. Available at http://www.prospect.org.

Fagan, J., Forst, B. (1996): Risks, fixers, and zeal: implementing experimental treatments for violent juvenile offenders. *The Prison Journal* 76, 22–59.

Fagan, J., Wilkinson, D. L. (1998): Guns, youth violence, and social identity in inner cities. In: Tonry, M., Moore, M. (Eds.): *Youth Violence – Crime and Justice: A Review of Research*, Vol. 24. Chicago: University of Chicago Press, pp. 105–188.

Fagan, J., Kupchik, A., Liberman, A. (2007): *Be Careful What You Wish For: Legal Sanctions and Public Safety Among Adolescent Felony Offenders in Juvenile and Criminal Court.* Law Research Paper No. 03-61. New York: Columbia Law School Pub. Available at http://ssrn.com/abstract=491202.

Farrington, D. P. (1986a): *The Origins of Crime: The Cambridge Study in Delinquent Development.* Research Bulletin No. 27, 29–32. London: Home Office Research and Planning Unit.

Farrington, D. P. (1986b): Stepping stones to adult criminal careers. In: Olweus, D., Block, J., Yarvow, M. K. (Eds.): *Development of Antisocial and Prosocial Behavior.* New York: Academic.

Farrington, D. P. (1987): Early precursors of frequent offending. In: Wilson, J. Q., Loury, G. C. (Eds.): *From Children to Citizens.* New York: Springer.

Farrington, D. P. (1988): Long-term prediction of offending and other life outcomes. In: Wegener, H., Lösel, F., Haisch, J. (Eds.): *Criminal Behavior and the Justice System: Psychological Perspectives.* New York: Springer.

Farrington, D. P. (1994): Early developmental prevention of juvenile delinquency. *Criminal Behaviour and Mental Health* 4, 29.

Farrington, D. P. (1995): Illness, injuries and crime. *Criminal Behavior and Mental Health* 5, 261–279.

Farrington, D. P. (1996): *Understanding and Preventing Youth Crime.* York: Joseph Rowntree Foundation.

Farrington, D. P., West, D. (1990): The Cambridge study in delinquent development: a long-term follow-up of 411 males. In: Kaiser, G., Kerner, H. J. (Eds.): *Criminality: Personality, Behaviour, Life-History*. Berlin: Springer.

Farrington, D. P., Loeber, R., van Kammen, W. (1996): Long-term criminal outcomes of hyperactivity-impulsivity-attention deficit and conduct disorder in childhood. In: Robins, L., Holloway, I. (Eds.): *Health Status of Young Offenders – A Survey of Young Offenders Appearing Before the Juvenile Courts*. Paper presented to the International Congress of Law and Psychology, Sienna, Italy.

Felson, M. (1994): *Crime and Everyday Life – Insights and Implications for Society*. Thousand Oaks: Pine Forge Press.

Fergusson, D. M., Lynskey, M. T. (1996): Adolescent resiliency to family adversity. *Journal of Child Psychology and Psychiatry* 36, 597–615.

Field, S. (2007): Practice cultures and the 'new' youth justice in (England and) Wales. *British Journal of Criminology* 47, 311–330.

Filipcic, K. (2006): Welfare Versus Neo-Liberalism: Juvenile Justice in Slovenia, in: : J. Junger-Tas & S.H. Decker (Eds.) *International Handbook of Juvenile Justice* (pp. 397–413) Dordrecht: Springer.

Fionda, J. (2005): *Devils and Angels. Youth Policy and Crime*, Oxford: Hart.

Flavell, J. (1993): *Cognitive development* (3rd edition) Englewood Cliffs, MH: Prentice Hall.

Flood-Page, C., Campbell, S., Harrington, V., Miller, J. (2000): *Youth Crime: Findings from the 1998/99 Youth Lifestyles Survey*. London: Home Office.

Forst, M., Fagan, J., Vivona, T. S. (1989): Youth in prisons and training schools: perceptions and consequences of the treatment-custody dichotomy. *Juvenile and Family Court Journal* 39, 1–14.

Freer, A. B. (1964): Parental liability for torts of children. *Kentucky Law Journal* 53, 254.

Frensch, K., Cameron, G. (2002): Treatment of choice or a last resort? A review of residential mental health placements for children and youth. *Child and Youth Care Forum* 31, 307.

Furby, L., Beyth-Marom, R. (1992): *Risk-Taking in Adolescence: A Decision-Making Perspective*. Washington, DC: Carnegie Council on Adolescent Development.

Gardner, M., Steinberg, L. (2005): Peer influence on risk taking, risk preference, and risky decision making in adolescence and adulthood: an experimental study. *Developmental Psychology* 41, 625–635.

Garland, D. (2001a): *The Culture of Control. Crime and Social Order in Contemporary Society*. Chicago: The University of Chicago Press.

Garland, D. (2001b) (Ed.): *Mass Imprisonment. Social Causes and Consequences*. London: Sage.

Ghate, D., Ramella, M. (2002): *Positive Parenting. The National Evaluation of the Youth Justice Board's Parenting Programme*. London: Youth Justice Board.

Gibbons, D. C., Blake, G. F. (1976): Evaluating the impact of juvenile diversion programmes. *Crime and Delinquency* 22, 411–420.

Giedd, J. et al. (1999): Brain development during childhood and adolescence: a longitudinal MRI study. *Nature Neuroscience* 2, 861–863.

Gifford-Smith, M., Dodge, K. A., Dishion, T. J., McCord, J. (2005): Peer influence in children and adolescents: crossing the bridge from developmental to intervention science. *Journal of Abnormal Psychology* 33, 255–265.

Gil Robles (2006 b): Follow up report on Norway (2001–2005) Assessment of the progress made in implementing the recommendations of the Council of Europe Commissioner for Human Rights.

Glass, N. (2005): Surely some mistake. *The Guardian*, January 5.

Glass, N. (2006): Sure start: where did it come from; where is it going? *Journal of Children's Services* 1, 51–57.

Glueck, S., Glueck, E. (1950): *Unraveling Juvenile Delinquency*. Cambridge: Harvard University Press.

Goiset, D. (2000): Dessaisissement. Une mesure exceptionnelle ? *Journal du Droit des Jeunes* 199, 14–23.

Goldberg, E. (2001): *The Executive Brain: Frontal Lobes and the Civilized Mind*. New York: Oxford University Press.

Goldblatt, P., Lewis, C. (1998) (Eds.): *Reducing Offending: An Assessment of Research Evidence on Ways of Dealing with Offending Behaviour*. London: Home Office.

Goldson, B. (2000) (Ed.): *The New Youth Justice*. Lyme Regis: Russell House.

Goldson, B., Jamieson, J. (2002): Youth crime, the 'parenting deficit' and state intervention: a contextual critique. *Youth Justice* 2, 2.

Gottfredson, M. R., Hirschi, T. (1990): *A General Theory of Crime*. Stanford: Stanford University Press.

Goulden, C., Sondhi, A. (2001): *At the Margins: Drug Use by Vulnerable Young People in the 1998/99 Youth Lifestyle Survey*. London: Home Office.

Graham, P. (1986): Behavioural and intellectual development in childhood epidemiology. *British Medical Bulletin* 42, 155–162.

Graham, J. (1998): Aktuelle Entwicklungen in der Jugendjustiz in England und Wales. *DVJJ-Journal* 9, 317–321.

Graham, J., Bowling, B. (1995): *Young People and Crime*. London: Home Office.

Gravesteijn, C. (2003): *Effecten van Levensvaardigheden. Een sociaal-emotioneel vaardigheidsprogramma voor adolescenten*. Rotterdam: GGD.

Griffin, P. (2003): *Trying and Sentencing Juveniles as Adults: An Analysis of State Transfer and Blended Sentencing Laws*. Pittsburgh: National Center for Juvenile Justice.

Grisso, T. (2000): 'What we know about youth's capacities as trial defendants' in Grisso, Th. & Schwartz, R.G. (eds.) *Youth on Trial. Developmental Perspectives on Juvenile Justice*. Chicago: University of Chicago Press.

Grisso, T., Steinberg, L., Woolard, J., Cauffman, E., Scott, E., Graham, S., Lexcen, F., Reppucci, N., Schwartz, R. (2003): Juveniles' competence to stand trial: A comparison of adolescents' and adults' capacities as trial defendants, *Law and Human Behavior* 27, 333–363.

Gruszczyñska, B., Gruszczyñski, M. (2005): Crime in enlarged Europe: comparison of crime rates and victimization risks. *Transition Studies Review* 12, 337–345.

Guerra, N. G., Huesmann, L. R., Tolan, P. H., van Acker, R., Eron, L. D. (1995): Stressful events and individual beliefs as correlates of economic disadvantage and aggression among urban children. *Journal of Consulting and Clinical Psychology* 63, 518–528.

Gur, R. C. (2002): Declaration of Ruben C. Gur, Ph. D. In: Hart, J. G. (Counsel): *Patterson v. Texas*. Petition for Writ of Certiorari to U.S. Supreme Court. Available at http://www.abanet.org/crimjust/juvjus/patterson.html.

Haines, K., O'Mahony, D. (2006): Restorative approaches, young people and youth justice. In: Goldson, B., Muncie, J. (Eds.): *Youth Crime and Justice*. London: Sage.

Hammersley, R., Marsland, L., Reid, M. (2003): *Substance Use by Young Offenders: The Impact of the Normalisation of Drug Use in The Early Years of The 21st Century*. London: Home Office.

Harper, G., Chitty, C. (2005): *The Impact of Corrections on Re-offending: A Review of 'What Works'*. London: Home Office (Home Office Research Study 291).

Harris, T. L. (1914): Ben B. Lindsey. In: Webb, M. G., Webb, E. L. (Eds.): *Famous Living Americans*. Greencastle: Charles Webb and Company, pp. 300–312.

Harris, L. J. (2006): An empirical study of parental responsibility laws: sending messages, but what kind and to whom? *Utah Law Review* 5, 5–34.

Hassemer, W. (1998): "Zero Tolerance" – Ein neues Strafkonzept? In: Albrecht, H.-J., et al. (Eds.): *Internationale Perspektiven in Kriminologie und Strafrecht. Festschrift für Günther Kaiser*. Berlin: Duncker & Humblot, pp. 793–814.

Hawkins, J. D., et al. (1992a): *Communities that Care*. San Francisco: Jossey-Bass Publishers.

Hawkins, J. D. et al. (1992b): The Seattle social development project: effects of the first four years on protective factors and problem behaviors. In: McCord, J., Tremblay, R. E. (Eds.): *Preventing Antisocial Behavior: Intervention from Birth Through Adolescence*. New York: Guilford.

Hawkins, J. D., Catalano, R. F., Brewer, D. D. (1995): Effective strategies from conception to age 6. In: Howell, J. C., Krisberg, B., Hawkins, J. D., Wilson, J. (Eds.): *Serious, Violent and Chronic Juvenile Offenders: A Sourcebook.* London: Sage.

Healthcare Commission, HM Inspectorate of Probation. (2006): *Lets Talk About It: A Review of Healthcare in the Community for Young People Who Offend.* London: Commission for Health Care Audit and Inspection.

Heinz, W. (2005): Zahlt sich Milde aus? Diversion und ihre Bedeutung für die Sanktionspraxis. Teil 1 und 2. *Zeitschrift für Jugendkriminalrecht und Jugendhilfe* 16, 166–178, 302–312.

Heinz, W. (2006): Rückfallverhütung mit strafrechtlichen Mitteln. Diversion – eine wirksame Alternative zu "klassischen" Sanktionen. *Soziale Probleme* 17, 174–192.

Heinz, W. (2008): *Das strafrechtliche Sanktionensystem und die Sanktionierungspraxis in Deutschland 1882–2006.* Available at www.uni-konstanz.de/rtf/kis/Sanktionierungspraxis-in-Deutschland-Stand-2006.pdf. Version 1/2008.

Heinz, W., Storz, R. (1994) (Eds.): Diversion im Jugendstrafverfahren der Bundesrepublik Deutschland. 3rd ed., Bonn: Forum Verlag Godesberg.

Henricson, C. (2001): *National Mapping of Family Services in England and Wales.* London: National Family Parenting Institute.

Hill, R. (2002): Restorative justice and the absent victim: new data from the Thames Valley. *International Review of Victimology* 9, 273.

Hirschi, T. (1969): *Causes of Delinquency.* Berkeley: University of California Press.

Hirschi, T. (1994): Family. In: Hirschi, T., Gottfredson, M. R. (Eds.): *The Generality of Deviance.* New Brunswick: Transaction Publishers.

HM Government. (2006): *Reaching Out: An Action Plan on Social Exclusion.* London: Cabinet Office.

HM Treasury. (2004): *Child Poverty Review.* Norwich: HMSO.

HM Treasury, Department for Education and Skills. (2007): *Aiming High for Children: Supporting Families.* London: The Stationery Office.

Hollingsworth, K. (2007): Responsibility and rights: children and their parents in the youth justice system. *International Journal of Law, Policy and The Family* 21, 190–219.

Home Office. (1997): *No More Excuses: A New Approach to Tackling Youth Crime in England and Wales.* Cmnd 3809. London: Home Office.

Home Office. (1998): *Supporting Families: A Consultation Document.* London: Home Office.

Home Office. (2002): *The Referral Order and Youth Offender Panels: Guidance for Courts, Youth Offending Teams and Youth Offender Panels.* London: Home Office.

Howard, J., Zibert, E. (1990): Curious, bored and wanting to feel good: the drug use of detained young offenders. *Drug and Alcohol Review* 9, 225–231.

Howell, J. C. (2003): *Preventing and Reducing Juvenile Delinquency.* Thousand Oaks: Sage.

Hoyle, C., Young, R., Hill, R. (2002): *Proceed with Caution: An Evaluation of the Thames Valley Police Initiative in Restorative Cautioning.* York: Rowntree.

Huesmann, L. R., Eron, L. D., Lefkowitz, M. M., Walder, L. O. (1984): Stability of aggression over time and generations. *Developmental Psychology* 20, 1120–1134.

Huizinga, D., Loeber, R., Thornberry, T. (1994): *Urban Delinquency and Substance Abuse.* Washington, DC: Office of Juvenile and Delinquency Prevention, U.S. Department of Justice.

Human Rights Watch, Amnesty International. (2005): *The Rest of Their Lives: Life Without Parole for Child Offenders in the United States.* New York: Amnesty International. Available at http://hrw.org/reports/2005/us1005/.

Ince, D., Beumer, M., Jonkman, H., Vergeer, M. (2004): *Veelbelovend en effectief, overzicht van preventieprojecten en – programma's in de domeinen gezin, school, kinderen en jongeren, wijk.* Utrecht: NIZW.

Inciardi, J., Pottieger, A. (1991): Kids, crack and crime. *Journal of Drug Issues* 21, 257–270.

Ironside, P. (2002): Rwandan Gacaca: seeking alternative means to justice, peace, and reconciliation. *New York International Law Review* 15, 31.

James, O. (1995): *Juvenile Violence in a Winner–Loser Culture*. London: Free Association Books.

Jehle, J.-M., Wade, M. (2006): *Coping with Overloaded Criminal Justice Systems. The Rise of Prosecutorial Power Across Europe*. Berlin, Heidelberg, New York: Springer.

Jehle, J.-M., Heinz, W., Sutterer, P. (2003): *Legalbewährung nach strafrechtlichen Sanktionen*. Berlin: Bundesministerium der Justiz (see also http://www.bmj.bund.de).

Jensen, E. J., Jepsen, J. (2006) (Eds.): Juvenile Law Violators, Human Rights and the Development of New Juvenile Justice Systems. Oxford: Oxford University Press.

Jesionek, U. (2001): *Das Österreichische Jugendgerichtsgesetz*, Wien: MANZ'sche.

Jesionek, U. (2001): *Das österreichische Jugendgerichtsgesetz*. 3rd ed., Wien: Juridica Verlag.

Johnson, R. E. (1986): Family structure and delinquency: general patterns and gender differences. *Criminology* 24, 65–84.

Johnson, D. L. (1990): The Houston Parent–child Development Center Project: dissemination of a viable program for enhancing at-risk families. In: Lorion, R. P. (Ed.): *Protecting the Children: Strategies for Optimizing Emotional and Behavioral Development*. London: Haworth Press.

Junger, M. (1990): *Delinquency and Ethnicity: An Investigation on Social Factors Relating to Delinquency Among Moroccan, Turkish, Surinamese and Dutch Boys*. Boston: Kluwer Law and Taxation.

Junger, M., Steehouwer, L. C. (1990): *Verkeersongevallen bij kinderen uit Etnische Minderheden*. Den Haag: Ministerie van Justitie, WODC.

Junger, M., Terlouw, G. J., van der Heijden, P. G. M. (1995): Crime, accidents and social control. *Criminal Behavior and Mental Health* 5, 386–410.

Junger-Tas, J. (1996): Youth and violence in Europe. *Studies on Crime and Crime Prevention* 5, 31–58.

Junger-Tas, J. (2006): Trends in international juvenile justice: what conclusions can be drawn? In: Junger-Tas, J., Decker, S. H. (Eds.): *International Handbook of Juvenile Justice*. Berlin, New York: Springer, pp. 505–532.

Junger-Tas, J., Decker, S. H. (2006) (Eds.): *International Handbook of Juvenile Justice*. Berlin, New York: Springer.

Junger-Tas, J., Haen Marshall, I., Ribeaud, D. (2003a): *Delinquency in an International Perspective – The International Self-report Delinquency Study*. Monsey/Den Haag: Criminal Justice Press/Kugler Publications.

Junger-Tas, J., Cruyff, M. J. L. F., van de Looij-Jansen, P. M., Reelick, F. (2003b): *Etnische minderheden en het Belang van Binding: een onderzoek naar antisociaal gedrag van jongeren*. Den Haag: Koninklijke Vermande.

Junger-Tas, J., Steketee, M., Moll, M. (2008): *Achtergronden van jeugddelinquentie en middelengebruik*. Utrecht: Vervey-Jonker-Institute.

Kadzin, A. E. et al. (1992): Cognitive problem-solving skills training and parent management training in the treatment of antisocial behavior in children. *Journal of Consulting and Clinical Psychology* 60, 733–747.

Kasten, A. (2003): Das französische Jugendstrafrecht. Die Auswirkungen der französischen Strafrechtsreform vom 9. September 2002 auf das französische Jugendstrafrecht. *Zeitschrift für Jugendkriminalrecht und Jugendhilfe* 1, 382–388.

Keating, D. (1990): Adolescent thinking, in: S.S. Feldman and G.R. Elliott (eds.) *At the threshold: The developing adolescent*, Cambridge, MA: Harvard University Press, 54–-89.

Kellam, S. G., Ling, X., Merisca, R., Brown, C. H., Ialongo, N. (1998): The effect of the level of aggression in the first grade classroom on the course and malleability of aggressive behavior into middle school. *Development and Psychopathology* 10, 165–185.

Kempf-Leonard, K., Peterson, E. (2002): Expanding realms of the new penology: the advent of actuarial justice for juveniles. In: Muncie, J., Hughes, G., McLaughlin, E. (Eds.): *Youth Justice: Critical Readings*. London: Sage, pp. 431–451.

Kerner, H.-J. (1983) (Ed.): *Diversion statt Strafe? Probleme und Gefahren einer neuen Strategie strafrechtlicher Sozialkontrolle*. Heidelberg: Kriminalistik Verlag.

Kilchling, M. (2002): Vergleichende Perspektiven. In: Albrecht, H.-J., Kilchling, M. (Eds.): *Jugendstrafrecht in Europa*. Freiburg i. Br.: Max-Planck-Institut für ausländisches und internationales Strafrecht, pp. 475–532.

Killias, M., et al. (2003): *European Sourcebook of Crime and Criminal Justice Statistics – 2003.* 2nd ed., Den Haag: WODC.

Kolvin, I., Miller, F. J. W., Scott, D. M., Gatzanis, S. R. M., Fleeting, M. (1990): *Continuities of Deprivation? The Newcastle 1000 Family Study*. Avebury: Aldershot.

Kook, H. (1996): *Effectevaluatie van Overstap. Een interventieprogramma voor leesbevordering*. Amsterdam: Universiteit van Amsterdam, Inst. Voor Taalonderzoek en Taalonderwijs voor anderstaligen.

Krisberg, B., Marchionna, S. (2007): Attitudes of US voters toward youth crime and the justice system. Oakland: National Council on Crime and Delinquency. Available at http://www.nccd-crc.org/nccd/n_pubs_main.html.

Kroese, G. J., Staring, R. H. J. M. (1993): *Prestige, Professie en Wanhoop: een onderzoek onder gedetineerde overvallers*. Arnhem: Gouda Quint/WODC.

Krüger, M. (2009): Frühprävention dissozialen Verhaltens. Entwicklungen in der Kinder- und Jugendhilfe. Mönchengladbach: ForumVerlag Godesberg.

Kyvsgard, B. (2004): Youth justice in Denmark. In: Tonry, M., Doob, A. N. (Eds.): *Youth Crime and Youth Justice: Comparative and Cross-national Perspectives. Crime and Justice: A Review of Research*, Vol. 31. Chicago: University of Chicago Press, pp. 349–390.

Lamon, P. (2002): Crime trends in thirteen industrialized countries. In: Nieuwbeerta, P. (Ed.): *Crime victimization in comparative perspective: results from the International Crime Victims Survey, 1989–2000*. Den Haag: Boom Juridische uitgevers.

Lanza-Kaduce, L., Frazier, C. E., Lane, J., Bishop, D. M. (2002): *Juvenile Transfer to Criminal Court Study: Final Report*. Tallahassee: Florida Department of Juvenile Justice.

Lanza-Kaduce, L., Lane, J., Bishop, D. M., Frazier, C. E. (2005): Juvenile offenders and adult felony recidivism: the impact of transfer. *Journal of Crime and Justice* 28, 59–78.

Laub, J. H., Sampson, R. J. (1988): Unraveling families and delinquency: a reanalysis of the Gluecks' data. *Criminology* 26, 19–46.

Laub, J. H., Sampson, R. J. (2003): *Shared Beginnings, Divergent Lives – Delinquent Boys to Age 70*. Cambridge: Harvard University Press.

Leblanc, M. (1997): Identification of potential juvenile offenders. *European Journal on Criminal Policy and Research* 5, 9–33.

Lee, M. (1998): *Youth, Crime and Police Work*. London: Macmillan.

Lesemann, P., Fahrenfort, M., Oud, W., Schoufour, J., Betrand, R., Klaver, A. (1998): *Experimenten Opvoedingsondersteuning*. Amsterdam: SCO Kohnstamm Instituut.

Lesemann, P., Veen, A., Triesscheijn, B., Otter, M. (1999): *Evaluatie van Kaleidoscoop en Piramide – Verslag van de tussentijdse resultaten*. Amsterdam: SCO Kohnstamm Instituut.

Leung, C., Sanders, M. R., Ip, F., Lau, J. (2006): Implementation of triple p-positive parenting program in Hong Kong: predictors of programme completion ad clinical outcomes. *Journal of Children's Services* 1, 4–17.

Library Information Specialists. (1995): *Offenders Under 18 in State Adult Correctional Systems: A National Picture. Special Issues in Correction*. Longmont: National Institute of Corrections.

Lipsey, M. W. (1992): Juvenile delinquency treatment: a meta-analytic inquiry into the variability of effects. In: Cook, T. D., Cooper, H., Cordray, D. S., Hartmann, H., Hedges, L. V., Light, R. J., Louis, T. A., Mosteller, F. (Eds.): *Meta-Analysis for Explanation*. New York: Russell Sage Foundation.

Lipsey, M. W. (1999): Can rehabilitative programs reduce the recidivism of juvenile offenders? An inquiry into the effectiveness of practical programs. *Virginia Journal of Social Policy and the Law* 6, 611–641.

Lipsey, M. W., Wilson, D. B. (1993): The efficacy of psychological, educational and behavioural treatment: confirmation from meta-analysis. *American Psychologist* 48, 1181–1209.

Lipsey, M. W., Wilson, D. B. (1998): Effective intervention for serious juvenile offenders: a synthesis of research. In: Loeber, R., Farrington, D. P. (Eds.): *Serious and Violent Juvenile Offenders: Risk Factors and Successful Interventions*. Thousand Oaks: Sage, pp. 313–345.

Lipton, D., Martinson, R., Wilks, J. (1975): *The Effectiveness of Correctional Intervention: A Survey of Treatment Evaluation Studies*. New York: Praeger.

Lloyd, C. (1998): Risk factors for problem drug abuse: identifying vulnerable groups. *Drugs Education Prevention and Policy* 5, 217–232.

Loeber, R. (1987): What policy makers and practitioners can learn from family studies of juvenile conduct problems and delinquency. In: Wilson, J. Q., Loury, G. C. (Eds.): *From Children to Citizens*. New York: Springer. pp. 87–112.

Loeber, R. (1991): Antisocial behavior: more enduring than changeable? *American Academy of Child and Adolescent Psychiatry* 30, 393–397.

Loeber, R., Stouthamer-Loeber, M. (1986a): The prediction of delinquency. In: Quay, H. C. (Ed.): *Handbook of Juvenile Delinquency*. New York: Wiley.

Loeber, R., Stouthamer-Loeber, M. (1986b): Family factors as correlates and predictors of juvenile conduct problems and delinquency. *Crime and Justice: An Annual Review of Research* 7, 29–151.

Loeber, R., Farrington, D. P., Stouthamer-Loeber, M., van Kammen, W. B. (1998): *Antisocial Behavior and Mental Health Problems*. Mahwah: Lawrence Erlbaum Associates.

Lösel, F. (1995): L'évaluation des interventions psycho-sociales en prison et en d'autres contextes pénaux. In: Conseil de l'Europe (Ed.): *Les Interventions psychosociales dans le système de Justice pénale. Rapport du Conseil de l'Europe – 20e Conférence de Recherches Criminologiques*. Strasbourg: Council of Europe.

Lösel, F., Beelmamm, A. (2005): Social problem-solving programs for preventing antisocial behaviour in children and youth. In: McMorran, M., McGuire, J. (Eds.): *Social problem solving and offending: Evidence, evaluation and evolution*. New York, NY: Wiley, 127–143.

Lösel, F., Beelmann, A. (2006): Child skills training. In: Welsh, B. C., Farrington, D. P. (Eds.): *Preventing crime: What works for children, offenders, victims, and places*. Dortrecht: Wadswort Publishing, 33–54.

Lytton, H. (1990): Child and parent effects in boys' conduct disorder: a reinterpretation. *Developmental Psychology* 26, 683–697.

Mack, J. W. (1909): The juvenile court. *Harvard Law Review* 23, 104–122.

MacKenzie, D. L. (1991): The parole performance of offenders released from shock incarceration (boot camp prison): a survival time analysis. *Journal of Quantitative Criminology* 7, 213–236.

MacKenzie, D. L., Souryal, C. (1992): *Inmate Attitude Change During Incarceration: A Comparison of Boot Camp and Traditional Prison*. Paper for the Annual Meeting of the American Society of Criminology, November, New Orleans.

Maher, G. (2005): Age and Criminal Responsibility, *Ohio State Journal of Criminal Law* 2, 493–512.

Marshall, T. F. (1999): *Restorative Justice: An Overview*. London: HMSO.

Matthews, R., Pitts, J. (2000): Rehabilitation, recidivism and realism: evaluating violence reduction programmes in prison. In: Jupp, V., Davies, P., Francis P. (Eds.): *Doing Criminological Research*. London: Sage.

Maxwell, G., Morris, A. (1993): *Family, Victims and Culture: Youth Justice in New Zealand*. Wellington: Social Policy Agency and Institute of Criminology, Victoria University of Wellington.

Maxwell, G., Morris, A. (2002): Restorative Justice and Reconviction. *Contemporary Justice Review* 5, 133–146.

McCold, P. (1996): Restorative justice and the role of community. In: Galaway, B., Hudson, J. (Eds.): *Restorative Justice: International Perspectives*. Amsterdam: Kugler, pp. 85–101.

McCold, P. (1998): Restorative justice: variations on a theme. In: Walgrave, L. (Ed.): *Restorative Justice for Juveniles. Potentialities, Risks and Problems for Research*. Leuven: Leuven University Press.

McCold, P. (2000): Towards a holistic vision of restorative juvenile justice: a reply to the maximalist model. *Contemporary Justice Review* 3, 357.

McCold, P., Watchel, B. (1998): Community is not a place: a new look at community justice initiatives. *Contemporary Justice Review* 1, 71.

McEvoy, K., Mika, H. (2002): Restorative justice and the critique of informalism in Northern Ireland. *British Journal of Criminology* 42, 534.

Mestitz, A., Ghetti, S (2004): *What do prosecutors and judges think about victim-offender mediation with juvenile offenders?* Paper presented at the Third Conference of the European Forum for Victim-Offender Mediation and Restorative Justice, "Restorative Justice in Europe: Where are we heading?", Budapest, Hungary, 14–16 October.

Miers, D. (2001): *An International Review of Restorative Justice.* Crime Reduction Series, Paper 10. London: Home Office.

Morash, M., Rucker, L. (1989): An exploratory study of the connection of mother's age at childbearing to the children's delinquency in four data sets. *Crime and Delinquency* 35, 45–93.

Morris, A., Giller, H. (1977): The Juvenile Court: The Client's Perspective, in *Criminal Law Review*, 198–205.

Morris, A., Maxwell, G. (1998): Restorative justice in New Zealand: family group conferences as a case study. *Western Criminology Review* 1, 1–29.

Moxon, D. (1998): The role of sentencing policy. In: Goldblatt, P., Lewis, C. (Eds.): Reducing Offending: *An Assessment of Research Evidence on Ways of Dealing with Offending Behaviour.* London: Home Office Research Study 187, pp. 85–100.

Mullan, S., O'Mahony, D. (2002): *A Review of Recent Youth Justice Reforms in England and Wales.* Research and Statistical Series Report, No. 8. Belfast: Northern Ireland Office.

Mulvey, E. P., Peeples, F. L. (1996): Are disturbed and normal adolescents equally competent to make decisions about mental health treatments? *Law and Human Behavior* 20, 273–286.

Muncie, J., Goldson, B. (2006): *Comparative Youth Justice.* London: Sage.

Myers, D. L. (2001): *Excluding Violent Youths from Juvenile Court: The Effectiveness of Legislative Waiver.* New York: LFB Publishing.

Nagin, D. S., Piquero, A. R., Scott, E. S., Steinberg, L. (2006): Public preference for rehabilitation versus incarceration of juvenile offenders: evidence from a contingent valuation study. *Criminology and Public Policy* 5, 627–652.

National Evaluation of the Children's Fund. (2004): *Prevention and Early Intervention in the Social Inclusion of Children and Young People.* Nottingham: DFES.

National Evaluation of Sure Start. (2005): *Variation in Sure Start Local Programmes Effectiveness: Early Preliminary Findings.* Nottingham: DFES.

Nejelski, P. (1976): Diversion: the promise and the danger. *Crime and Delinquency* 22, 393–410.

Newburn, T. (1999): Drug prevention and youth justice: issues of philosophy, politics and practice. *British Journal of Criminology* 39, 609–624.

Newburn, T., Crawford, A., Earle, R., Goldie, S., Hale, C., Masters, G., Netten, A., Saunders, R., Sharpe, K., Uglow, S. (2001): *The Introduction of Referral Orders into the Youth Justice System.* London: HMSO.

Newburn, T., Crawford, A., Earle, R., Goldie, S., Hale, C., Masters, G., Netten, A., Saunders, R., Sharpe, K., Uglow, S. (2002): *The Introduction of Referral Orders into the Youth Justice System.* London: Home Office Research Study 242.

Nothhafft, S. (2003): Conflict resolution and peer mediation: a pilot programme in Munich secondary schools. In: Weitekamp, E., Kerner, H.-J. (Eds.): *Restorative Justice in Context: International Practice and Directions.* Cullompton: Willan Publishing.

Nuytiens, A., Christiaens, J., Eliaerts, C. (2005): *Ernstige jeugddelinquenten gestraft? Praktijk van de uithandengeving.* Gent: Academia Press.

Nuytiens, A., Christiaens, J., Eliaerts, C., Brolet, C. (2006): Trajecten van uithanden gegeven jongeren in het strafrecht. Ernstige jeugddelinquenten testraft - deel 2. Gent: Academia Press.

Nuytiens, A. (2006): De uithandengeving (art. 38 Wjb): toepassing door de jeugdrechtbank. *Panopticon* 1, 77–80.

Nye, I. (1958): *Family Relationships and Delinquent Behaviour.* New York: Wiley.

Office for National Statistics. (2000): *Mental Health of Children and Adolescents in Great Britain.* London: The Stationery Office.

Ofsted. (2007): *Narrowing the Gap: The Inspection of Children's Services.* London: Ofsted.

Olds, D. L., Henderson, C. C. R., Chamberlin, R., Tatelbaum, R. (1986): Preventing child abuse and neglect: a randomized trial of nurse home visitation. *Pediatrics* 78, 65–78.

Olds, D. L., Henderson, C. C. R., Tatelbaum, R., Chamberlin, R. (1988): Improving the life course development of socially disadvantaged mothers: a randomized trial of nurse home visitation. *American Journal of Public Health* 78, 1436–1445.

Olweus, D. (1979): Stability of aggressive reaction patterns in males: a review. *Psychological Bulletin* 86, 852–875.

O'Mahony, D., Doak, J. (2004): Restorative justice: is more better? *Howard Journal* 43, 484.

O'Mahony, D., Campbell, C. (2006): Mainstreaming restorative justice for young offenders through youth conferencing – the experience of Northern Ireland. In: Junger-Tas, J., Decker, S. (Eds.): *International Handbook of Juvenile Justice.* Amsterdam: Springer, pp. 93–115.

O'Mahony, D., Chapman, T., Doak, J. (2002): *Restorative Cautioning: A Study of Police Based Restorative Cautioning Pilots in Northern Ireland.* Northern Ireland Office Research and Statistics Series: Report No. 4. Belfast: Northern Ireland Office.

Oppenheim, N. (1898): *The Development of the Child.* New York: MacMillan.

Osborn, S. G. (1980): Moving home, leaving London and delinquent trends. *British Journal of Criminology* 20, 54–61.

Palmer, T. B. (1991): The effectiveness of intervention: recent trends and current issues. *Crime and Delinquency* 37, 330–346.

Parent, D. G., Lieter, V., Kennedy, S., Livens, L., Wentworth, D., Wilcox, S. (1994): *Conditions of Confinement: Juvenile Detention and Corrections Facilities.* Washington, DC: National Institute of Justice, Office of Juvenile Justice and Delinquency Prevention.

Patterson, G. R. (1994): Some alternatives to seven myths about treating families of antisocial children. In: Henricson, C. (Ed.): *Crime and the Family.* Proceedings of an International Conference, London, February 1994. London: Family Policy Studies Centre, no. 20, pp. 26–50.

Patterson, G. R., Chamberlain, P., Reid, J. B. (1982): A comparative evaluation of a parent training programme. *Behaviour Therapy* 13, 638–650.

Patterson, G. R., Reid, J. B., Dishion, T. J. (1992): *Antisocial Boys.* Eugene: Casalia.

Pfeiffer, C. (1998): Juvenile crime and violence in Europe. *Crime and Justice* 23, 255–328.

Piquero, A. R., Farrington, D. P., Blumstein, A. (2007): *Key Issues in Criminal Career Research: New Analyses of The Cambridge Study in Delinquent Development.* Cambridge: Cambridge University Press.

Podkopacz, M. R., Feld, B. C. (1996): The end of the line: an empirical study of judicial waiver. *Journal of Criminal Law and Criminology* 86, 449–492.

Pratt, J., et al. (2005) (Eds.): *The New Punitiveness. Trends, Theories, Perspectives.* Cullompton: Willan Publishing.

Prein, G., Schumann, K. F. (2003): Dauerhafte Delinquenz und die Kumulation von Nachteilen. In: Schumann, K. F. (Ed.): *Delinquenz im Lebensverlauf. Bremer Längsschnittstudie zum Übergang von der Schule in den Beruf bei ehemaligen Hauptschülern,* Vols. 1 and 2. München: Juventa, pp. 181–208.

President's Commission on Law Enforcement and Administration of Justice. (1967) (Ed.): *Task Force Report. Juvenile Delinquency and Youth Crime.* Washington, DC: U.S. Government Printing Office.

Pruin, I. R. (2007): *Die Heranwachsendenregelung im deutschen Strafrecht. Jugendkriminologische, entwicklungspsychologische, jugendsoziologische und rechtsvergleichende Aspekte.* Mönchengladbach: Forum Verlag Godesberg.

Quispel, T.J.W. (2000) STOP, een HALTe te ver?, *Delikt en Delinkwent,* 67.

Quinn, K., Epstein, M. H. (1998): Characteristics of children, youth and families served by local interagency systems of care. In: Epstein, M. H., Kutash, K., Duchnowski, A. (Eds.): *Outcomes for Children and Youth with Emotional and Behavioural Disorders and Their Families*. Austin: Pro-Ed.

Raiser, T. (2007): Grundlagen der Rechtssoziologie: Das lebende Recht. 4th ed., Stuttgart: Mohr Siebeck.

Rankin, J. H. (1983): The family context of delinquency. *Social Problems* 30, 466–479.

Rehberg, J. (2001): Strafrecht II. Strafen und Massnahmen, Jugendstrafrecht, Zürich: Schulthess.

Reiss, A. J., Roth, J. A. (1993) (Eds.): Panel on the understanding and control of violent behavior. *Understanding and Preventing Violence*. Washington, DC: National Academy Press.

Renucci, J.F. (1998): *Le droit pénal des mineurs*, Paris: PUF.

Revill, J. (2006): NHS failing children on mental health. *The Observer*, July 23.

Riley, D., Shaw, M. (1985): *Parental Supervision and Juvenile Delinquency*, no. 83. London: Home Office Research and Planning Unit.

Rivera, F. P. (1995): Crime, violence and injuries in children and adolescents: common risk factors? *Criminal Behavior and Mental Health* 5, 367–386.

Robert, L., Peters, T. (2003): How restorative justice is able to transcend the prison walls: a discussion of the project 'restorative detention'. In: Weitekamp, E., Kerner, H.-J. (Eds.): *Restorative Justice in Context: International Practice and Directions*. Cullompton: Willan Publishing.

Roberts, J., Hough, M. (2002) (Eds.): *Changing Attitudes to Punishment. Public Opinion, Crime and Justice*. Cullompton: Willan Publishing.

Rutenfrans, C. J. C., Terlouw, G. J. (1994): *Delinquentie, sociale controle en 'Life events'*. Arnhem: Gouda Quint/WODC.

Rutherford, A. (2000): An Elephant on the Doorstep: Criminal Policy without Crime in New Labour's, in: P. Green & A. Rutherford (eds.) *Criminal Policy in Transition*, Oxford: Hart.

Rutter, M. (1979): Protective factors in children's responses to stress and disadvantage. In: Kent, M. W., Rolf, J. E. (Eds.): *Primary Prevention of Psychopathology*, Vol. 3. Hannover, NH: University Press of New England, pp. 49–74.

Rutter, M. (1980): *Changing Youth in a Changing Society*. Cambridge: Harvard University Press.

Rutter, M. (1990) (Ed.): *Straight and Devious Pathways from Childhood to Adulthood*. Cambridge: Cambridge University Press.

Rutter, M., Giller, H. (1983): *Juvenile Delinquency – Trends and Perspectives*. Harmondsworth: Penguin Books.

Rutter, M., Smith, D. J. (1995) (Eds.): *Psychosocial Disorders in Young People: Time, Trends and Their Causes*. London: Wiley.

Rutter, M., Giller, H., Hagell, A. (1998): *Antisocial Behaviour by Young People*. New York: Cambridge University Press.

Ryerson, E. (1978): *The Best Laid Plans: America's Juvenile Court Experiment*. New York: Hill and Wang.

Sampson, R. J., Laub, J. H. (1993): *Crime in the Making – Pathways and Turning Points Through Life*. Cambridge: Harvard University Press.

Sanders, A., Hoyle, C., Morgan, R., Cape, E. (2001): "Victim Impact Statements: Don't Work, Can't Work." *Criminal Law Review*, pp. 447–458.

Scarr, S. (1969): Social introversion–extraversion as a heritable response. *Child Development* 40, 823–832.

Schumann, K. F. (2003a) (Ed.): *Delinquenz im Lebensverlauf. Bremer Längsschnittstudie zum Übergang von der Schule in den Beruf bei ehemaligen Hauptschülern*, Vols. 1 and 2. München: Juventa.

Schumann, K. F. (2003b): Delinquenz im Lebenslauf – Ergebnisbilanz und Perspektiven. In: Schumann, K. F. (Ed.): *Delinquenz im Lebensverlauf. Bremer Längsschnittstudie zum Übergang von der Schule in den Beruf bei ehemaligen Hauptschülern*, Vols. 1 and 2. München: Juventa, pp. 209–222.

Schumann, K. F., Voß, M., Papendorf, K. (1986): Über die Entbehrlichkeit des Jugendstrafvollzugs. In: Ortner, H. (Ed.): *Freiheit statt Strafe. Plädoyers für die Abschaffung der Gefängnisse – Anstöße machbarer Alternativen*. 2nd ed., Tübingen: AS-Verlag, pp. 50–84.

Schweinhart, L. J. (1987): Can preschool programs help prevent delinquency? In: Wilson, J. Q., Loury, G. C. (Eds.): *From Children to Citizens*, Vol. III. New York: Springer, pp. 135–154.

Schweinhart, L. J. et al. (1993): *Significant Benefits: The High/Scope Perry Preschool Study Through Age 27*. Ypsilanti: The High/Scope Press.

Schweinhart, L. J., Montie, J., Xiang, Z., Barnett, W. S., Belfield, C. R., Nores, M. (2005): *The High/Scope Perry Preschool Study Through Age 40*. Ypsilanti: The High/Scope Press.

Schwind, H. D., et al. (2001): *Kriminalitätsphänomene im Langzeitvergleich am Beispiel einer deutschen Großstadt. Bochum 1975–1986–1998*. Neuwied: Hermann Luchterhand Verlag.

Scott, E., Reppucci, N., Woolard, J. (1995): Evaluating adolescent decision-making in legal contexts, *Law and Human Behavior* 19, 221–244.

Scott, E., Grisso, T. (1997): The evolution of adolescence: A developmental perspective on juvenile justice reform, *Journal of Criminal Law and Criminology* 88, 137–189.

Scott, E. S., Steinberg, L. (2003): Blaming youth. *Texas Law Review* 81, 799–840.

Scott, S., O'Connor, T., Futh, A. (2006): *What Makes Parenting Programmes Work in Disadvantaged Areas*. York: Joseph Rowntree Foundation.

Scottish Executive. (2004): National pilot planned for parenting orders. *Scottish Executive News Release*, December 13.

Scottish Law Commission (2001) Age of Criminal Responsibility, Discussion Paper 115, available at http://www.scotlawcom.gov.uk/downloads/dp115_criminal_response.pdf

Sechrest, L. B., White, S. O., Brown, E. D. (1979) (Eds.): *The Rehabilitation of Criminal Offenders*. Washington, DC: National Academy of Sciences.

Secretary of State for Education and Skills. (2005): *Youth Matters*. Cm6629. London: HMSO.

Sedlak, A. J. (1991): *National Incidence and Prevalence of Child Abuse and Neglect*. Washington, DC: U.S. Department of Health and Human Services.

Seymour, M. (2006) Transition and Reform: Juvenile Justice in the Republic of Ireland, in: J. Junger-Tas & S.H. Decker (Eds.) *International Handbook of Juvenile Justice* (pp.117-143) Dordrecht: Springer.

Shapland, J., Atkinson, A., Colledge, E., Dignan, J., Howes, M., Johnstone, J., Pennant, R., Robinson, G., Sorsby, A. (2004): *Implementing Restorative Justice Schemes – A Report on the First Year*. London: Home Office Online Report 32/04.

Shapland, J., Atkinson, A., Atkinson, H., Chapman, B., Colledge, E., Dignan, J., Howes, M., Johnstone, J., Robinson, G., Sorsby, A. (2006): *Restorative Justice in Practice – Findings from the Second Phase of the Evaluation of Three Schemes*. London: Home Office Research Findings No. 274.

Shapland, J., et al. (2008): *Does Restorative Justice Affect Reconviction? The Fourth Report from The Evaluation of Three Schemes*. London: Ministry of Justice (Research Series 10/08).

Sherman, L., et al. (2006): *Evidence-Based Crime Prevention*. London: Routledge.

Sherman, L. W., Strang, H. (2007): *Restorative Justice: The Evidence*. London: Smith Institute. Available at http://www.smith-institute.org.uk/pdfs/RJ_full_report.pdf.

Siegler, R. (1991): *Children's thinking* (2nd edition) Englewood Cliffs, NJ: Prentice Hall.

Skelton, A. (2002): Restorative justice as a framework for juvenile justice reform. *British Journal of Criminology* 42, 496.

Skogan, W. G., Hartnett, S. M. (1997): *Community Policing, Chicago Style*. Oxford: Oxford University Press.

Škuli , M. (2009): Serbia. In: Dünkel, F., Grzywa, J., Pruin, I. (Eds.): *Juvenile Justice Systems in Europe – Current Situation, Reform Developments and Good Practices*. Mönchengladbach: Forum Verlag Godesberg (in preparation).

Slavin, R. E., Madden, N. A., Karweit, N. L., Livermin, B. J., Dolan, L. (1990): Success for all: first-year outcomes of a comprehensive plan for reforming urban education. *American Educational Research Journal* 27, 255–278.

Slavin, R. E., Madden, N. A., Dolan, L. J., Wasik, B. A., Ross, S. M., Smith, L. J. (1993): 'Whenever and wherever we choose' – the replication of 'Success for All'. *Phi Delta Kappan* 75, 639–647.

Smith, L. (1995): Can we really legislate good parenting. *LA Times*, January 18.

Smith, C. A., Stern, S. B. (1997): Delinquency and antisocial behaviour. A review of family processes and intervention research. *Social Services Review* 71, 382–420.

Social Services Inspectorate. (2005): *Safeguarding Children. The Second Joint Chief Inspectors' Report on Arrangements to Safeguard Children*. London: Department of Health.

Solomon, E., Garside, R. (2008): *Ten Years of Labour's Youth Justice Reforms: An Independent Audit*. London: Centre for Crime and Justice Studies, King's College.

Sowell, E. R. et al. (2001): Mapping continued brain growth and gray matter density reduction in dorsal frontal cortex: inverse relationships during postadolescent brain maturation. *Journal of Neuroscience* 21, 8819–8829.

Sowell, E. R. et al. (2002): Development of cortical and subcortical brain structures in childhood and adolescence. *Developmental Medicine and Child Neurology* 44, 4–16.

Spinellis, C. D., Tsitsoura, A. (2006): The emerging juvenile justice in Greece. In: Junger-Tas, J., Decker, S. H. (Eds.): *International Handbook of Juvenile Justice*. Berlin, New York: Springer, pp. 309–324.

Spittler, G. (1970): *Norm und Sanktion*. 2nd ed., Olten: Walter.

Statham, J., Dillon, J., Moss, P. (2001): *Placed and Paid For: Supporting Families Through Sponsored Day Care*. London: The Stationery Office.

Stattin, H., Romelsjö, A. (1995): Adult mortality in the light of criminality, substance abuse and behavioral and family risk factors in adolescence. *Criminal Behavior and Mental Health* 5, 279–312.

Steinberg, L., Cauffman, E. (2000): A developmental perspective on jurisdictional boundary. In: Fagan, J., Zimring, F. E. (Eds.): *The Changing Borders of Juvenile Justice*. Chicago: University of Chicago Press, pp. 379–406.

Steinberg, L., Cauffman, E. (1996): Maturity of judgment in adolescence: Psychosocial factors in adolescent decision-making, *Law and Human Behavior*, 20, 249–272.

Steinberg, L. (2002): *Adolescence* (6th edition) New York: McGraw Hill.

Steinberg, L., Scott, E. (2003): Less guilty by reason of adolescence: Developmental immaturity, diminished responsibility, and the juvenile death penalty, *American Psychologist* 59, 1009–1018.

Steketee, M., Mak, J., Huygen, A. (2006): *Opgroeien in Veilige Wijken – Communities that Care als instrument voor lokaal preventief Jeugdbeleid*. Utrecht: Verwey-Jonker Instituut.

Stoorgard, A. (2004): Juvenile justice in Scandinavia. *Journal of Scandinavian Studies in Criminology and Crime Prevention* 5, 188–204.

Storz, R. (1994): Jugendstrafrechtliche Reaktionen und Legalbewährung. In: Heinz, W., Storz, R. (Eds.): *Diversion im Jugendstrafverfahren der Bundesrepublik Deutschland*. 3rd ed., Bonn: Forum Verlag Godesberg, pp. 131–222.

Straus, M. A., Gelles, R. J., Steinmetz, S. K. (1980): *Behind Closed Doors: Violence in the American Family*. Garden City: Doubleday.

Stump, B. (2003): *'Adult time for adult crime'. Jugendliche zwischen Jugend- und Erwachsenenstrafrecht*, Mönchengladbach: Forum Verlag Godesberg.

Tanenhaus, D. S. (2004): *Juvenile Justice in the Making*. New York: Oxford University Press.

Tonry, M. (2004): *Punishment and Politics*. Cullompton: Willan Publishing.

Tonry, M., Doob, A.N. (Eds.) (2004): *Youth Crime and Youth Justice. Comparative and Cross-National Perspectives*, Chicago: University of Chicago Press.

Torbet, P., Gable, R., Hurst, IV, H., Montgomery, I., Szymanski, L., Thomas, D. (1996): *State Responses to Serious and Violent Juvenile Crime*. Pittsburgh: National Center for Juvenile Justice.

Tracy, P. E., Wolfgang, M. E., Figlio, R. M. (1990): *Delinquency Careers in two Birth Cohorts*. New York: Plenum.

Travis, T. (1908): *The Young Malefactor: A Study in Juvenile Delinquency Its Causes and Treatment*. New York: Thomas Y. Crowell and Company.

Tremblay, R. E. et al. (1992): Parent and child training to prevent early onset of delinquency: the Montreal longitudinal-experimental study. In: McCord, J., Tremblay, R. E. (Eds.): *Preventing Antisocial Behavior: Interventions from Birth Through Adolescence*. New York: Guilford.

Tremblay, R. E., Craig, W. M. (1995): Developmental crime prevention. In: Tonry, M., Farrington, D. P. (Eds.): *Building a Safer Society: Strategic Approaches to Crime Prevention. Crime and Justice: A Review of Research*, Vol. 19. Chicago: The University of Chicago Press, pp. 151–237.

Tonry, M. & Doob, A.N. (Eds.) (2004) *Youth Crime and Youth Justice. Comparative and Cross-National Perspectives*, Chicago: University of Chicago Press.

Tuthill, R. S. (1904): History of the children's court in Chicago. In: Barrows, S. J. (Ed.): *Children's Courts in the United States: Their Origin, Development, and Results*. New York: The International Prison Commission.

Umbreit, M., Coates, R., Bradshaw, W. (2003): Victims of severe violence in dialogue with the offender: key principles, practices, outcomes and implications. In: Weitekamp, E., Kerner, H. J. (Eds.): *Restorative Justice in Context: International Practice and Directions*. Cullompton: Willan Publishing.

United States Children's Bureau. (1923): *Juvenile-Court Standards: Report of the Committee Appointed by the Children's Bureau, August, 1921, to Formulate Juvenile-Court Standards, Adopted by a Conference Held Under the Auspices of the Children's Bureau and the National Probation Association, Washington, DC, May 18, 1923*. Publication no. 121. Washington, DC: U.S. Government Printing Office.

Válková, H. (2006): Restorative approaches and alternative methods: juvenile justice reform in the Czech Republic. In: Junger-Tas, J., Decker, S. H. (Eds.): *International Handbook of Juvenile Justice*. Dordrecht: Springer, pp. 377–395.

Válková, H., Hulmáková, J. (2009): Czech Republic. In: Dünkel, F., Grzywa, J., Pruin, I. (Eds.): *Juvenile Justice Systems in Europe – Current Situation, Reform Developments and Good Practices*. Mönchengladbach: Forum Verlag Godesberg (in preparation).

Van der Heide, W., Eggen, A. T. J. (2007) (Eds.): *Criminaliteit en Rechtshandhaving*. Den Haag: CBS/WODC, p. 479.

Van der Heiden-Attema, N., Wartna, B. S. J. (2000): *Recidive na een verblijf in een JBI*. Den Haag: Ministerie van Justitie, WODC.

Van der Laan, P. H. (2006): Just desert and welfare: juvenile justice in the Netherlands. In: Junger-Tas, J., Decker, S. H. (Eds.): *International Handbook of Juvenile Justice*. Dordrecht: Springer, pp. 145–173.

Van Dijk, C., Dumortier, E., Eliaerts, C. (2006): Survival of the protection model? Competing goals in Belgian juvenile justice. In: Junger-Tas, J., Decker, S. H. (Eds.): *International Handbook of Juvenile Justice*. Berlin, New York: Springer, pp. 187–223.

Van Dijk, J., Manchin, R., van Kesteren, J., Nevala, S., Hideg, G. (2005): *EUICS Report: The Burden of Crime in the EU*. Brussels: Gallup Europe.

Van Kalmthout, A. M., Bahtiyar, Z. (2009): The Netherlands. In: Dünkel, F., Grzywa, J., Pruin, I. (Eds.): *Juvenile Justice Systems in Europe – Current Situation, Reform Developments and Good Practices*. Mönchengladbach: Forum Verlag Godesberg (in preparation).

Van Kesteren, J. N., Mayhew, P., Nieuwbeerta, P. (2000): *Criminal Victimisation in Seventeen Industrialised Countries: Key-findings from the 2000 International Crime Victims Survey*. The Hague: Ministry of Justice, WODC.

Van Lier, P. A. C. (2002): *Preventing Disruptive Behavior in Early Elementary Schoolchildren*. Rotterdam: Erasmus University.

Van Ness, D. W., Strong, K. (1997): *Restoring Justice*. Cincinnati: Anderson Publishing Co.

Van Tuijl, C. (2002): *Effecten van Opstap Opnieuw bij follow-up: effecten van Opstap Opnieuw bij Turkse en Marokkaanse leerlingen op middellange termijn*. Alkmaar: Extern Print.

Vennard, J., Hedderman, C. (1998): Effective interventions with offenders. In: Goldblatt, P., Lewis, C. (Eds.): *Reducing Offending: An Assessment of Research Evidence on Ways of Dealing with Offending Behaviour*. London: Home Office Research Study 187, pp. 101–119.

Vanneste, C. (2001): Une recherché sur les decisions prises par les magistrates du parquet et les juges de la jeunesse, *Journal du Droit des Jeunes* 207, 5–12.

Wacquant, L. (1999): *Les Prisons de la Misère*. Paris: Editions Raison d'Agir.

Warr, M. (2002): *Companions in Crime: The Social Aspects of Criminal Conduct*. Cambridge: Cambridge University Press.

Wartna, B. S. J., el Harbachi, S., van der Laan, A. M. (2005): *Jong vast – een cijfermatig overzicht van de strafrechtelijke recidive van ex-pupillen van justitiële jeugdinrichtingen*. Den Haag: WODC/Boom.

Weisstub, D. (1986): Victims of crime in the criminal justice system. In: Fattah, E. (Ed.): *From Crime Policy to Victim Policy*. London: Macmillan.

Weijers, I. (2004): Requirements for Communication in the Courtroom: A Comparative Perspective on the Youth Court in England/Wales and The Netherlands, Youth Justice. *The Journal of the National Association for Youth Justice* 4, 22–31.

Weijers, I. (2006): *Jeugdige dader, volwassen straf?* Deventer: Kluwer.

Weithorn, L., Campbell, S. (1982): The competency of children and adolescents to make informed treatment decisions. *Child Development* 53, 1589–1598.

Wells, L. E., Rankin, J. H. (1988): Direct parental controls and delinquency. *Criminology* 26, 263–285.

Wells, L. E., Rankin, J. H. (1991): Families and delinquency: a meta-analysis of the impact of broken homes. *Social Problems* 38, 71–93.

Wells, K., Whittington, D. (1993): Characteristics of youths referred to residential treatment: Implications for program design. *Children and Youth Services Review* 15, 195–271.

Welsh, B. C., Farrington, D. P. (Eds.): *Preventing crime: What works for children, offenders, victims, and places*. Dortrecht: Wadswort Publishing.

West, D. J. (1969): *Present Conduct and Future Delinquency. First Report of the Cambridge Study in Delinquent Development*. London: Heinemann.

West, D. J. (1973): *Who Becomes Delinquent? Second Report of the Cambridge Study in Delinquent Development*. London: Heinemann.

West, D. J. (1982): *Delinquency: Its Roots, Careers and Prospects*. London: Heinemann.

West, D. J., Farrington, D. P. (1977): *The Delinquent Way of Life. Third Report of the Cambridge Study in Delinquent Development*. London: Heinemann.

Westfelt, L., Estrada, F. (2005): International crime trends: sources of comparative crime data and post-war trends in Western Europe. In: Sheptycki, J., Wardak, A. (Eds.): *Transnational and Comparative Criminology*. Abingdon: Glasshouse Press, pp. 19–48.

White, J. L., Moffit, T. E., Earls, F., Robins, L., Silva, P. A. (1990): How early can we tell? Predictors of childhood conduct disorder and adolescent delinquency. *Criminology* 28, 507–533.

Whyte, B. (2001): Reviewing Youth Crime in Scotland: Beyond Childrens Hearings, *Juvenile Justice Worldwide Winter* 2000/2001, 17–19.

Widom, C. S. (1989): The cycle of violence. *Science* 244, 160–166.

Wikström, P. O. (1998): Communities and crime. In: Tonry, M. (Ed.): *The Handbook of Crime and Punishment*. New York: Oxford University Press, pp. 269–302.

Wikström, P. O. H., Butterworth, D. A. (2006): *Adolescent Crime – Individual Differences and Lifestyles*. Cullompton: Willan Publishing.

Wikström, P. O. H., Sampson, R. J. (2006): *The Explanation of Crime: Context, Mechanisms and Development*. Cambridge: Cambridge University Press.

Wilkinson, K. (1980): The broken home and delinquent behavior: an alternative interpretation of contradictory findings. In: Hirschi, T., Gottfredson, M. (Eds.): *Understanding Crime: Current Theory and Research*. Beverly Hills: Sage.

Winner, L., Lanza-Kaduce, L., Bishop, D. M., Frazier, C. E. (1997): The transfer of juveniles to criminal court: reexamining recidivism over the long term. *Crime and Delinquency* 43, 548–563.

Wittebrood, K., Nieuwbeerta, P. (2006): Een kwart eeuw stijging in geregistreerde criminaliteit: vooral meer registratie, nauwelijks meer criminaliteit. *Tijdschrift voor Criminologie* 48, 227–243.

Wolfgang, M. E., Figlio, R. M., Sellin, T. (1972): *Delinquency in a Birth Cohort*. Chicago: University of Chicago Press.

Wolfgram, P. (1999): KEA schooljaar 1998–1999 – de resultaten op een rijtje. Rotterdam: Centrum Educatieve Dienstverlening.

Wright, M. (1997): *Victim/Offender Mediation in The United Kingdom: Legal Background and Practice.* Paper presented at Seminar on Mediation Between Juvenile Offenders and Their Victims, October 22–24, Popowo, Poland.

Wright, W. F., Dixon, M. C. (1977): Community treatment of juvenile delinquency: a review of evaluation studies. *Journal of Research in Crime and Delinquency* 19, 35–67.

Yoshikawa, H. (1994): Prevention as cumulative protection: effects of early family support and education on chronic delinquency and its risks. *Psychological Bulletin* 115, 28–54.

Young, R., Goold, B. (1999): Restorative police cautioning in Aylesbury: from degrading to reintegrative shaming ceremonies? *Criminal Law Review* 126–138.

Youth Justice Board. (2002): *A Summary of Research into the Issues Raised in 'The Introduction of Referral Orders in the Youth Justice System'.* London: Youth Justice Board.

Zehr, H. (2005): *Changing Lenses: A New Focus for Crime and Justice.* 3rd ed., Waterloo: Herald Press.

Zehr, H., Mika, H. (2003): Fundamental concepts of restorative justice. In: Mclaughlin, E., Furgusson, R., Hughes, G., Westmarland, L. (Eds.): *Restorative Justice Critical Issues.* Milton Keynes: Open University Press.

Zermatten, J. (2004): The Swiss Federal Statute on Juvenile Criminal Law, paper conference ESC 2004, Amsterdam.

Zimring, F. E. (2000): The common thread: diversion in juvenile justice. *California Law Review* 88, 2477–2495.

Zimring, F. E. (2005): *American Juvenile Justice.* New York: Oxford University Press.

Index

Printed in the United States
149457LV00001B/33/P

9 780387 892948